Perspectives, Trends, and Applications in Corporate Finance and Accounting

Constantin Zopounidis
Technical University of Crete, Greece

Apostolos G. Christopoulos
National and Kapodistrian University of Athens, Greece

Petros Kalantonis
Technological Education Institute (TEI) of Piraeus, Greece

A volume in the Advances in Finance, Accounting, and Economics (AFAE) Book Series

IGI Global
DISSEMINATOR OF KNOWLEDGE

Published in the United States of America by
IGI Global
Business Science Reference (an imprint of IGI Global)
701 E. Chocolate Avenue
Hershey PA, USA 17033
Tel: 717-533-8845
Fax: 717-533-8661
E-mail: cust@igi-global.com
Web site: http://www.igi-global.com

Library of Congress Cataloging-in-Publication Data

Names: Zopounidis, Constantin, editor. | Christopoulos, Apostolos G., 1965- editor. | Kalantonis, Petros, 1970- editor.
Title: Perspectives, trends, and applications in corporate finance and accounting / Constantin Zopounidis, Apostolos G. Christopoulos, and Petros Kalantonis, editors.
Description: Hershey, PA : Business Science Reference, [2018]
Identifiers: LCCN 2018000586| ISBN 9781522561149 (hardcover) | ISBN 9781522561156 (ebook)
Subjects: LCSH: Corporations--Finance. | Corporations--Accounting. | Stocks--Prices. | Derivative securities--Accounting. | Accounting--Standards.
Classification: LCC HG4026 .P457 2018 | DDC 332/.041--dc23 LC record available at https://lccn.loc.gov/2018000586

This book is published in the IGI Global book series Advances in Finance, Accounting, and Economics (AFAE) (ISSN: 2327-5677; eISSN: 2327-5685)

British Cataloguing in Publication Data
A Cataloguing in Publication record for this book is available from the British Library.

Advances in Finance, Accounting, and Economics (AFAE) Book Series

ISSN:2327-5677
EISSN:2327-5685

Editor-in-Chief: Ahmed Driouchi, Al Akhawayn University, Morocco

MISSION

In our changing economic and business environment, it is important to consider the financial changes occurring internationally as well as within individual organizations and business environments. Understanding these changes as well as the factors that influence them is crucial in preparing for our financial future and ensuring economic sustainability and growth.

The **Advances in Finance, Accounting, and Economics (AFAE)** book series aims to publish comprehensive and informative titles in all areas of economics and economic theory, finance, and accounting to assist in advancing the available knowledge and providing for further research development in these dynamic fields.

COVERAGE

- Investments and Derivatives
- International Trade
- Bankruptcy
- Accounting Standards
- Ethics in Accounting and Finance
- Evidence-Based Studies
- Economic Policy
- Internet Banking
- Borrowing and Lending
- Stock Market

IGI Global is currently accepting manuscripts for publication within this series. To submit a proposal for a volume in this series, please contact our Acquisition Editors at Acquisitions@igi-global.com or visit: http://www.igi-global.com/publish/.

The Advances in Finance, Accounting, and Economics (AFAE) Book Series (ISSN 2327-5677) is published by IGI Global, 701 E. Chocolate Avenue, Hershey, PA 17033-1240, USA, www.igi-global.com. This series is composed of titles available for purchase individually; each title is edited to be contextually exclusive from any other title within the series. For pricing and ordering information please visit http://www.igi-global.com/book-series/advances-finance-accounting-economics/73685. Postmaster: Send all address changes to above address.

Titles in this Series

For a list of additional titles in this series, please visit:
https://www.igi-global.com/book-series/advances-finance-accounting-economics/73685

Fractal Approaches for Modeling Financial Assets and Predicting Crises
Inna Nekrasova (Southern Federal University, Russia) Oxana Karnaukhova (Southern Federal University, Russia) and Bryan Christiansen (PryMarke, LLC, USA)
Business Science Reference • ©2018 • 300pp • H/C (ISBN: 9781522537670) • US $215.00

Regulation and Structure in Economic Virtualization Emerging Research and Opportunities
Denis Ushakov (Suan Sunandha Rajabhat University, Thailand)
Business Science Reference • ©2018 • 238pp • H/C (ISBN: 9781522549666) • US $145.00

Accountancy and the Changing Landscape of Integrated Reporting
Ioana Dragu (Babes-Bolyai University, Romania)
Business Science Reference • ©2018 • 303pp • H/C (ISBN: 9781522536222) • US $195.00

Foreign Direct Investments (FDIs) and Opportunities for Developing Economies in the ...
Venkataramanaiah Malepati (University of Gondar, Ethiopia) and C. Mangala Gowri (University of Gondar, Ethiopia)
Business Science Reference • ©2018 • 315pp • H/C (ISBN: 9781522530268) • US $215.00

Economic Growth in Latin America and the Impact of the Global Financial Crisis
Mauricio Garita (Universidad del Valle de Guatemala, Guatemala) and Celso Fernando Cerezo Bregni (Universidad del Valle de Guatemala, Guatemala)
Business Science Reference • ©2018 • 240pp • H/C (ISBN: 9781522549819) • US $180.00

Uncertainties and Risk Assessment in Trade Relations
Marianne Ojo (George Mason University, USA)
Business Science Reference • ©2018 • 385pp • H/C (ISBN: 9781522541318) • US $225.00

Economic Reforms for Global Competitiveness
Denis Ushakov (International College Suan Sunandha Rajabhat University, Thailand & Russian Academy of National Economy and Public Administration–South, Russia)
Business Science Reference • ©2018 • 363pp • H/C (ISBN: 9781522538561) • US $235.00

For an entire list of titles in this series, please visit:
https://www.igi-global.com/book-series/advances-finance-accounting-economics/73685

IGI Global
DISSEMINATOR OF KNOWLEDGE

701 East Chocolate Avenue, Hershey, PA 17033, USA
Tel: 717-533-8845 x100 • Fax: 717-533-8661
E-Mail: cust@igi-global.com • www.igi-global.com

Table of Contents

Detailed Table of Contents

The goal of this chapter is to assess the influence of specific corporate and market features on Greek firms' profitability and the determination of the optimal debt ratio before and during the Greek crisis. The empirical results exhibit an average profitability of 6.97%, which varies significantly both between firms and during the time period examined. Another finding of this study is the verification of the theoretical relationship between the independent variables and Greek firms' profitability between 2005 and 2016. Related to the determination of the optimal debt ratio of Greek firms, the authors found that during the first sub-period examined (before the Greek economic crisis – 2005-2009), the results extracted are not consistent with the MM theory in contrary to the second sub-period (the period of the deep recession 2010-2016). During this period, the optimal debt ratio is estimated to be 40.9% and the turning point decreased considerably compared to the whole period sample (52.6%) 2005-2016.

panel results and Eurozone panel results fail to support the bank credit-led growth hypothesis. These results are inconsistent with other studies, which however employ only full regional panels.

Constantine Cantzos, Piraeus University of Applied Sciences, Greece
Petros Kalantonis, Piraeus University of Applied Sciences, Greece
Aristidis Papagrigoriou, Piraeus University of Applied Sciences, Greece
Stefanos Theotokas, Piraeus University of Applied Sciences, Greece

This chapter examines the relationship between stock returns of companies listed in the FTSE-20 on the Athens Exchange and behavioral indicators. The research is based on the behavioral APT model, which examines stock returns' risk factors through the involvement of macroeconomic variables and behavioral indicators. The data is the closing price of 17 shares listed in the FTSE-20 index, a number of macroeconomic variables, and a series of behavioral indicators for the period of January 2001-December 2014. Regressions were conducted with dependent variable stock returns of a portfolio invested equally in these 17 stocks. In addition, the research tests the existence of long-run and short-run equilibrium and causality. The change in the industrial production index along with the risk premium have a positive and significant impact on the portfolio returns. Johansen's test showed that there is a long-run equilibrium between stock returns, macroeconomic variables, and behavioral indicators. The VECM and VAR models showed that there is not long and short-run causality, not even Granger causality. No similar research has been conducted in Greece, thus it fills a literature gap.

Antonis Pavlou, Technical University of Crete, Greece
Michalis Doumpos, Technical University of Crete, Greece
Constantin Zopounidis, Technical University of Crete, Greece & Audencia Business School, France

The optimization of investment portfolios is a topic of major importance in financial decision making, and many relevant models can be found in the literature. These models extend the traditional mean-variance framework using a variety of other risk-return measures. Existing comparative studies have adopted a rather restrictive approach, focusing solely on the minimum risk portfolio without considering the whole set of efficient portfolios, which are also relevant for investors. This chapter

progress. That is why annual reports include both quantitative and qualitative data; the former could take the form of figures, tables, and ratios, whereas the latter are expressed as management views on present situation, future prospects, risks, and proposed strategy. Our study investigates the disclosure policy that companies follow in their published statements focusing on the determinant factors of quality Management Commentary Reports.

Preface

It is generally accepted that Corporate Finance and Accounting have been significantly developed, mainly, since the second half of the previous century. In thousands of research papers, topics such as earnings management, IFRS and Accounting Standards, financial reporting, failure prediction, capital structure, investments, portfolio management, behavioral finance, pricing models, banking etc. have been investigated. The criticism of the accepted theories and methods and the proposal of alternative or new theories determine the development of knowledge and the evolution of every science. Although Accounting and Corporate Finance have been significantly enriched, theories and practices of these topics have been also revised or replaced in the recent or prior decades.

However, almost ten years after the housing bubble of 2008 in the U.S. which led through contagion to a global financial crisis, affecting negatively even the Eurozone Financial Markets, and especially those of the weaker economies, the global economic environment is still under uncertainty. The bankruptcy of Lehman Brothers, the sovereign debt crisis in the EU and the economic and social turmoil in several countries has significant effects on the financial markets and the financial systems worldwide.

Initially the Central Bank of the US and soon after the ECB took conventional and unconventional measures to secure their financial systems and to boost the real economy. Especially in the EU, since the beginning of 2017 the single European banking system has been established. At the same time the BIS is preparing the new framework of Basel IV to strengthen the banking system which faces serious challenges especially in terms of capital requirements.

Further to the actions of the Authorities, corporate strategies are also in the forefront of the private firms which implement restructuring plans mainly towards their capital structure and operational costs.

Additionally, major economic and social facts, which affect the financial markets, provide a novel field for empirical studies. In a globalized financial system, regional or national financial crisis may affect the corporate strategies and corporate performance of all countries around the world.

In this research book the selected papers focus on the consequences of the recent and prior financial crises. Specifically, the impact of crisis which became evident on the firms' performance, the stock markets and the banking systems and consequently led to public deficits is examined in the first part of this book. In the following section the relation between stock market and macroeconomics factors is explored, while other topics include earnings management, portfolio and pricing models as well as the reporting of accounting information and accounting standards.

In more detail, Katsampoxakis, I., Basdekis, C. and Anathreptakis, K. assess the influence of specific corporate and market features on the Greek firms' profitability and investigate the optimal debt ratio before and during the crisis based on the theory of Modigliani- Miller. Christopoulos, A., Demiroglou, N., and Dokas, I., explore the relation between capital markets' performance and macroeconomic variables. They find evidence that crisis affected households and business which reduced their planning horizon with respect to consumption and investment respectively. They also showed that the causality relationship between the stock indices OMX and IBEX of Denmark and Spain respectively and the key of economic variables are more interactive. Giannopoulos, N., and Hyz, A. focus on capital controls of the Greek banking sector and they analyze the evolution of the use of electronic payments in Greece during the capital controls and examine the prospects generated for the Greek banking system and the national economy from their use. They propose that the Greek society, driven by the shock of capital controls, has completely redefined its attitude towards electronic means of payments, overtaking taboos and phobias of the past turned into a significant increase of the use of internet banking.

Chytis, E., Filos, I. and Gkouma, O. examine the information content of tax losses and the increased deficits in Greece before and during the financial crisis. They investigate the importance of Deferred Tax Assets by sector and index for the period before and after the financial crisis (2005-2012) and they find that supervisory authorities have a great impact on evaluation when they face Deferred Tax Assets from Tax Loss Carryforwards. They find that the role of external audit is significant, as it is required to receive an audit opinions based on the "going concern" basis.

The starting point for the research of Koy, A. was the fact that after the Asian Financial Crises, Asian economies needed to change their exchange rate policies. In her study Koy, A. brings insight on how the international portfolio flows to Asian Stock markets are affected from the shocks on EUR/USD parity. The results of this study indicate that the shocks on EUR/USD parity have positive effects on the examined countries' portfolio flows except Malaysia.

Viewing the research studies which are not related with the consequences of the recent and prior economic crises we find two papers which investigate the interactions between macroeconomic factors and stock markets. Specifically, Georgantopoulos, A., Filos, I., and Poutos, E. examine the impact of banks and stock markets on economic growth for the twenty-eight EU member states. According to their finding the stock market led growth hypothesis is supported only in the case of the full sample panel. Cantzos, C., Kalantonis, P., Papagrigoriou, A., and Theotokas, S. are based on the behavioral APT - model, to examine the relationship between stock returns of listed firms in FTS E-20 indicator of the Athens Exchange and specific behavioral indicators. They find that the change in the industrial production index along with the risk premium, have significant positive impact on the portfolio returns. They also apply the Johansen's test to show that there is long run equilibrium between stock returns, macroeconomic variables and behavioral indicators.

The out of sample robustness of efficient portfolios derived by popular optimization models is explored by Pavlou, A., Doumpos, M. and Zopounidis, C. They examine the S&P 500 stockd, over the period 2005-2016 by using novel performance indicators representing the deviations between historical efficient frontiers, actual out of sample efficient frontiers and realized and of sample portfolio frontiers. Pricing models and simulation approaches take place in the following paper by Dede, G., Hatzithanasis, G., Kamolakis, T. and Michalakelis, C., focusing on the analysis of the Claud Broker Business Model and specifically on the broker's vital role and the benefits that arise from the implementation of its services.

The following three research papers focus on the financial reporting quality. It is commonly known that Earnings Management is a factor which has significant impact on the reporting quality of firms. In their study, Aybars, A. and Alaunal. L., evaluate the role of institutional investors on earnings management, analyzing data of Turkish listed firms. Their findings indicate that there is a significant and negative relation between institutional ownership level and managerial discretion exercised in opportunistic management of accruals. They also confirmed the substantial role of institutional investors in monitoring and disciplining corporate managers.

In addition, Garefalakis, A., Dimitras, A. and Ballas., P. investigate the determinant factors of the quality management commentary reports. More specifically, they explore the type and load of information disclosed in Management Discussion and Analysis, Management Commentary report or Operating and Financial Review reports and they make comparisons between contexts where it is compulsory to issue such statements and contexts that it is voluntary to do so. A key finding of their study was that entities operating in larger capital markets may disclose more information compared to entities which operate in small countries.

Last but not least Ballas, A., Sykianakis, N. Tzovasand, C. and Vasilakopoulos, C., explore the Greek Firms compliance with IFRS mandatory disclosure requirements. They implement two methods of compliance, to measure and compare their results. However, no significant results have been produced from the implementation of the dichotomous method and the partial compliance method.

The IJCFA has contributed to these fields by publishing already eight semi-annual issues with very interesting papers on issues like contagion, corporate governance, banking evaluation, differed taxes, derivatives markets etc.

With this book it is aimed to contribute further to the recent trends by publishing papers of past issues, enhanced by their authors to cover current developments, but also selected new papers which deal with problems and propose solutions that will contribute to policy makers in order to overpass the present difficulties as soon as possible.

The 12 high-quality selected papers of this issue are addressed mainly to policy makers for the economy and the markets, investors, lenders and borrowers and governments and it is our believe that this edition will contribute to the dissemination of knowledge in Accounting and Corporate Finance research and will add to the evolution of the research activity in corporate Finance and Accounting.

As the scope of this book remains to publish high-quality papers and to encourage debate on the merits of various approaches to qualitative research all the papers of this issue have been peer reviewed by three anonymous reviewers, who we want to thank for their support to this edition.

Apostolos G. Christopoulos
National and Kapodistrian University of Athens, Greece

Petros Kalantonis
Piraeus University of Applied Sciences, Greece

Constantin Zopounidis
Technical University of Crete, Greece

Chapter 1
How the Greek Crisis Determined Firm Profitability and Optimal Debt Ratio

Ioannis Katsampoxakis
University of Athens, Greece

Haralampos Basdekis
Ministry of Finance, Greece & University of Athens, Greece

Konstantinos Anathreptakis
Alpha Bank, Greece

ABSTRACT

The goal of this chapter is to assess the influence of specific corporate and market features on Greek firms' profitability and the determination of the optimal debt ratio before and during the Greek crisis. The empirical results exhibit an average profitability of 6.97%, which varies significantly both between firms and during the time period examined. Another finding of this study is the verification of the theoretical relationship between the independent variables and Greek firms' profitability between 2005 and 2016. Related to the determination of the optimal debt ratio of Greek firms, the authors found that during the first sub-period examined (before the Greek economic crisis – 2005-2009), the results extracted are not consistent with the MM theory in contrary to the second sub-period (the period of the deep recession 2010-2016). During this period, the optimal debt ratio is estimated to be 40.9% and the turning point decreased considerably compared to the whole period sample (52.6%) 2005-2016.

DOI: 10.4018/978-1-5225-6114-9.ch001

1. INTRODUCTION

The estimation of the factors that affect the future course of firms' profits contributes to the acquisition of important information for the optimal financial management and profit maximization. Managers should follow an active policy in order to manage and offset potential risks. Therefore, the knowledge of the determinant factors' impact on firms' profitability will contribute to a better financial management and reduction of potential risk.

There are many important factors that affect firms' profitability, and they usually vary depending on the country and time period. The main factors significantly affecting the future profitability of firms are firms' size, financial leverage, accruals and volatility of profitability. Moreover, there are numerous macroeconomic factors that can affect the outlook of firms' profits.

Our research is twofold. On one side, it focuses on how the above factors affect Greek firms' profitability and on the other side it determines the optimal level of firms' leverage to achieve high profitability. Before starting to analyze the way and extent that, firm and market characteristics influence firm's profitability, it is very important to note that the situation of the Greek economy affects Greek firms' profitability in a serious and deterministic way. More specifically, Greece's economy after 2009 has shrunk and its GDP has decreased by approximately 25%. This chronic shrinking of Greek GDP and the recession of the Greek economy have led to the increase of the Greek government's borrowing cost, which, in turn, has affected the banking sector, loan provisions and the borrowing costs of Greek firms.

Prior empirical studies have examined the impact of such determinant factors on firms' profitability. The results of these studies either agree or contradict with financial theory or fail to confirm the expected impact on net income. Nevertheless, in the frame of this study, the empirical findings of the relationship between the variables used and firms' profitability show that the maximization of firms' profitability is closely connected with better financial management and the favorable distribution of available resources.

Introducing to the second goal of the present study, it is necessary to clarify, that capital structure is a vital issue not only to companies that try to maximize their market value, but it acquires special sense and substance during economic recession. The theory that forms the ground behind capital structure is that of Modigliani – Miller (MM). According to MM (1958 & 1963), the value of the firm increases with debt financing, due to the advantage that the debt serves to shield earnings from taxes which decreases the average cost of capital. But, in none case, that means that all firms have to be totally levered, as the existence of cost of financial distress directly affects the advantages of tax deduction and therefore firm's value and increases the level of bankruptcy risk. So there is an upper level of debt, firms can bear in order to maximize their value. Consequently, the optimal leverage level, meaning the proportion of debt and equity which is better to use in order to avoid default risk and to achieve high profitability is the central idea of the present paper, which focuses on the case of Greek listed companies for the period before and during the economic crisis.

The article is developed as follows: Section 2 presents a brief literature review, section 3 presents the theoretical background of the variables affecting firms' profitability, section 4 describes the data and variables used, while section 5 and section 6 present the methodology and the empirical results, respectively. Finally, at the end of the paper, important conclusions are discussed.

2. LITERATURE REVIEW

The study of the course of profitability consists a scientific timeless phenomenon and is very important for the strategy companies will follow in the long-run. Recent literature examines firm's profitability as independent variable, using for its computation financial indicators as net operating profitability (NOP) (Raheman et al., 2010), (Dong and Su, 2010), return on total assets (ROTA) (Deloof, 2003), (Padachi, 2006), return on invested capital (ROIC), return on assets (ROA) (Narware, 2010).

In the frame of examining profitability at the microeconomic level (Burja 2011), there are used also indicators such as current ratio, liquid ratio, receivables turnover ratio and working capital to total asset (Singh and Pandey, 2008). Other studies consider performance assessment expressed by earnings before interests and taxes (EBIT) and the associated risk resulted from the influence of using a certain financing structure (Akintoye, 2008) or expressing it though economic value added (EVA), return on equity (ROE), operating profit margin (OPM), earnings per share (Rayan, 2008).

The study of the literature concerning the factors that affect firms' profitability, such as firms' size and financial leverage, leads to equivocal results. Christopoulos et al. (2013) provided the liquidity status of firms as a significant factor that affects firms' profitability and viability.

Goddard et al. (2005) found that the firms indicate a negative relationship between firm size, gearing ratio and profitability, while the impact of market share and liquidity on profitability seems to be positive. Abor (2005) distinguished the effects of short-term and long-term leverage on firms' profitability. More specifically, he revealed a significantly positive relationship between short-term financial leverage and firms' profitability. However, this impact becomes negative when examining the influence of long-term financial leverage on firms' profitability, and the ratio of total debt to total assets indicates a strong negative impact on Return on Equity (ROE).

Eriotis et al. (2007) mentioned that there is a negative relationship between the debt ratio of the firms listed in Athens Stock Exchange (ASE) and their growth, while firms' size is positively related with their debt-to-asset ratios. They also found that there is a differentiation in the capital structure among firms with a debt ratio greater than 50 percent and those with a debt ratio less than 50 percent. These findings are confirmed by the research of Daskalakis and Psillaki (2008). According to their analysis, firm size is positively related to financial leverage.

Li and Hwang (2011) concluded in the case of firms with low earnings that an increase in financial leverage has a negative impact on earnings. However, they revealed that there is a positive correlation between financial leverage and corporate profits for the most profitable firms.

Liargovas and Skandalis (2010) results showed that leverage, centrality of the location, firm size, export activity, liquidity and management competence have a significant impact on firm competitiveness measured by three variables including return on assets, return on equity or return on sales. Pervan and Visic (2012) showed that firm size and asset turnover have a weak positive influence on firm profitability, while debt ratio has a negative effect on profitability.

According to Srinivasan et al. (2011) financial leverage seems to have a significant positive impact on firms' profitability, but the extent of its influence on ROE is limited in recession periods. Finally, firm size exhibits a statistically significant negative impact on profitability.

Salman and Yazdanfar (2012) found that growth of sales and total factor productivity have a significant positive effect on firm's profitability, while the firm's size is being proved to have a significant negative effect on firm's profitability. They also concluded that the profitability of SMEs firms plays a dominant role on firms' evolution and regional development.

Giovanis and Ozdamar (2014) results indicated that firm size and debt have positive effects on profitability but only up to a certain point after which the relationship becomes negative. The assets-to-sales, vice versa, seems to follow a different direction, meaning to have a negative impact on profitability at the beginning, but, after some point, the relationship becomes positive. Tailab (2014) study's results concluded that debt ratio, higher levels of inventory, and firm's growth are negatively related to profitability, while liquidity and size have a positive impact on profitability. Katsampoxakis et al. (2015) found that firm's size, earnings smoothness and 10-year government bond affect profitability in a negative way, while firm's leverage seems to have positive influence on firm's value. Nevertheless, the impact of the independent variables on ROE does not remain constant over time, as their coefficients vary, mainly due to the impact of the global financial crisis and the sovereign crisis in Greece.

Farah and Supartica (2016) examined factors affecting profitability such as firm size, firm age, growth, lagged profitability, productivity, and industry affiliation of SMEs firm listed in Indonesia Stock Exchange. They concluded that firm size, growth, lagged profitability have a negative effect on profitability, while productivity and industry affiliation have a positive impact on profitability. On the contrary, firm's age does not seem to affect firm's profitability in some way.

As is clear from the preceding theoretical analysis, there is no consensus on the impact of firm specific factors on its profitability. Therefore, the present study will attempt to provide with more evidence the contradictory results revealed by previous studies conducted.

3. THEORETICAL BACKGROUND

This part of the paper presents the theoretical background of corporate profitability and the variables affecting it based on financial theory and earlier empirical studies.

Profitability

Firms aim to achieve the optimum utilization of productivity factors in order to maximize profit. Therefore, firms' management – taking into account several restrictions – moves towards the achievement of maximum profits (EBIT or NOPAT). This profitability can be considered as a proxy of Return on Equity. ROE is calculated as a percentage of net profit to total firm equity. ROE measures the firm's ability to generate earnings compared to the capital invested. In addition, ROE is used in many studies in order to investigate firms' profitability as a criterion for comparison between companies in different sectors and an overtime comparison of corporate profit performance. Other important proxies used to determine profitability is Return on Assets and Gross Operating Income.

According to Gitman and Zutter (2012), profitability is the ratio to measure the performance of the company. It gives a clear picture of a company's financial reporting and shows a company's ability to generate earnings for a certain period, improving their sales, assets and increasing capital stock. The deep understanding of profitability consists the key factor that helps managers in developing an effective profitability strategy for their company, as it provides feedback for the management decision for the long-term success of the company. Furthermore, Yazdanfar (2013) emphasizes that profitability is the most important precondition for long-term firm survival and success.

Size

Firm size is a factor that can affect profitability. In fact, large companies have easier access to international markets, thus reducing the borrowing cost. Moreover, the strong bargaining power over their suppliers has led them to achieve more favorable terms in their deals. They also have low probability of default of their future liabilities, while the possibility of manipulation of financial results through internal information is considered limited. Therefore, it is expected that the market behavior of large companies is more rational and objective. This, in turn, may lead to a positive relationship between profitability and firm size. This conclusion is found in previous studies by Deloof (2003), Lazaridis and Trifonidis (2006), Padachi (2006), Stierwald (2009), Dong and Su (2010), Mathuva (2010), Gurbuz et al. (2010), Vijayakumar (2011), Ayele (2012), Dogan (2013) and Akben-Selcul (2016). However, there are studies that support that there is no statistically significant relationship between profitability and firm size (Eljelly 2004, Gill et al. 2010, Charitou et al. 2010). On the contrary, Ramasamy (2005), Goddard et al. (2005) and Salman and Yazdanfar (2012) found that firm size is negatively related to profitability. Dhawan (2001) found that companies with a smaller size will result in higher profits but they cannot be able to compete larger companies.

In order to determine the size of a company, various proxies, such as the logarithm of sales and the number of employees, have been used. For the purposes of our paper, the logarithm of total assets is used.

Financial Leverage

Financial leverage can be considered an important factor influencing profitability. It contributes to the increase in returns volatility regardless of the way it is measured, even through the use of net income, ROE or earnings per share. According to Modigliani & Miller, loan provisions positively affect firms' value unless they are highly levered, as highly levered companies can be considered those exhibiting a financial leverage ratio higher than the average.

Therefore, we expect that the debt-to-total-assets ratio will have a positive effect on ROE, under the condition that the company is not over indebted. In the case of highly levered companies, a negative relationship between the financial leverage ratio and ROE is expected. This result is consistent with Tailab's (2014), Goddard et al. (2005) and Akben-Selcul (2016) studies. According to Dogan (2013), the impact of leverage and capital intensity on financing was found to be negative. According to Akbar et al. (2013), the crisis adversely affects the firms' leverage ratio and found to have significant and negative effect on the short-term financing channels, which makes private firms to hold cash and issued equity for hedging the negative effect of contradiction. This conclusion is coherent with that of Vermeulen, 2002; Benito and Hernando, 2007; Martinez-Carrascal and Herrando, 2008; Pal and Ferrando, 2010; Kalemli - Ozcan et al., 2015a; Barbiero et al., 2016.

The above background indicates contradictory results. Mc Connell and Servaes (1995) found that companies with high growth prospects show a positive correlation between financial leverage ratios and firm value, while companies with limited growth prospects indicate a negative correlation between financial leverage ratios and firm value. In contrast, recent studies have concluded that there is a negative relationship between the financial leverage of a company and its profitability (Jandik and Makhija 2005, Gill et al. 2010, Mathuva 2010, Charitou et al. 2010, Hayajneh and Yassine 2011). Qiu and La (2010) found that although levered firms are generally more profitable than unlevered firms, profitability decreases the debt ratio of levered firms. Concerning the level of firms' optimal leverage, Kim et al. (2005) assumed that factors such as uniqueness, industrial sector, and trend may cause companies to deviate from their optimal leverage, while Zeitun et al. (2017) showed that the adjustment speed toward optimal leverage is on average slower after the crisis, and assumed that it was due to the lack of debt financing supply. Gebauer et al (2017), derived thresholds beyond which leverage has a negative and significant impact on investment in five peripheral countries for the period 2005-2014. According to their findings, an overleveraged firm with a debt-to-asset ratio of 90 percent has, ceteris paribus, 0.7 percentage point of forgone investment per year compared with a firm with a debt-to-asset ratio of 80 percent. Moreover, after 2008, a firm with a debt-to-asset ratio of 30 percent had additional annual investment of 1.4 percentage points compared with a firm with a debt ratio of 60 percent, and 2.4 percentage points compared with a firm with a debt ratio of 80 percent. This negative investment impact of high debt is observed for micro, small and medium-sized firms, but not for large firms. Arcand et al (2015) applied a nonlinear model to examine the impact of leverage on economy and they found that economies may reach a point of too much finance. Beck et al (2012) extracted the conclusion that the relationship between household debt and growth is more elusive. Checherita and Rother (2010) examined the average relationship between the government debt-to-GDP ratio and the per-capita GDP growth rate for 12 euro area countries for a time period of four decades starting in 1970. According to their results, the debt-to-GDP turning point is roughly between 90% and 100%, meaning that for the case of European countries examined a public debt-to-GDP ratio above that threshold will affect economic growth in a negative way. However, confidence intervals for the debt turning point suggest that the negative growth effect of high debt may start already from levels of around 70-80% of GDP and that has to enforce governments to implement policies in order to avoid such a detrimental situation.

Accruals

Accruals are defined as the accounting-accrued net profits of firms. Accruals are computed as the difference between net profits minus cash flows from firms' operational activities. According to Dechow (1994) and Dechow et al. (1998), accruals compose a measure of performance and have better predictive ability than cash flows from operational activities and net profits separately.

Companies with high positive accruals will have high non-cash earnings, which will appear in financial statements as increased sales that have not yet been received. On the contrary, companies register negative non-cash earnings when payments of goods and services are made in advance and recognized as revenue, when they have yet to take place, or when there are high non-cash expenses (e.g., depreciation).

Historically, investors have considered that companies with high positive accruals over time indicate high chances of poor quality profitability, and vice versa (Richardson et al. - 2001). Sloan (1996) confirmed the above findings, noting accruals as a leading indicator. This implies a negative relationship between accruals and future firm profitability.

Dechow and Dichev (2002) argued that the quality of accruals reflects the realization of cash flows either in advance for the current period or in a subsequent period after their realization. Factors such as earnings volatility and the volatility of cash flows from operational activities have the greatest impact on accruals' quality.

Earnings Smoothness

Firms' earnings smoothness is measured by the ratio of the standard deviation of net income to the standard deviation of cash flows from operational activities. In general, investors tend to declare high investment interest to companies that exhibit temporal earnings smoothness, as they very positively assess companies' likelihood of generating earnings and keeping them for a long time (Barnea et al. 1975, Chaney and Lewis 1995). Thereafter, companies with a low volatility ratio of net earnings to operational activities indicate a positive impact on firm profitability, as they are characterized by reduced business risk, and vice versa (Beidleman 1973).

Other empirical studies combine earnings smoothness with the cost of capital. Trueman and Titman (1988) and McInnis (2010) argued that companies that exhibit normality in their profitability will have a lower cost of capital.

There are also contradictory views on the effect of earnings smoothness on firms' net profits. Leuz et al. (2003) argued that the earnings smoothness index is used by insiders in order to reap private benefits. Bhattacharya et al. (2003) argued that earnings smoothness leads to greater opacity of profitability, while Myers et al. (2007) concluded that companies use the earnings smoothness index as a management tool for profits in order to technically keep increasing the index of earnings per share for an extended period.

Real GDP Growth Rate

The real Gross Domestic Product (GDP) growth rate in Greece reflects the overall economic activity of the country. In periods in which GDP exhibits a strong positive growth rate, both domestic demand and firms' sales will increase considerably. In contrast, in periods of economic slowdown and recession, business activity is expected to reduce, as total demand will be limited. Previous studies have used the real GDP growth rate as an explanatory variable for firms' profitability. Studies by Teruel and Solano (2007), Nazir and Afza (2009) and Karaduman et al. (2010) found that increased economic activity has a positive impact on corporate profitability.

Greek Government Borrowing Cost

The Greek 10-year government bond yield is considered a benchmark for the borrowing cost of companies and for the weighted average cost of capital. In periods when the borrowing cost is low, companies' access to global capital markets is easy, and the interest rate is quite attractive. In such periods, the weighted average cost of capital is low, and firms' value is high. A low 10-year Greek bond yield implies that companies may have strong profitability, and vice versa. Therefore, a negative correlation between the Greek government borrowing cost and corporate profitability is expected. Alesina et al. (1992) report a small positive effect of higher public debt on the spread between private and public rates of return in twelve OECD countries. By contrast, Krishnamurthy and Vissing-Jorgensen (2010) found that the spread between corporate versus U.S. Treasury bonds declines with a higher level of U.S. federal government debt. Arteta and Hale (2008), found that these crises are systematically accompanied by a decline in foreign credit to domestic private firms, while Celasun and Agsa (2009) Agsa and Celasun (2012), documented that the corporate sector faces higher borrowing costs when the external debt of the public sector is higher. Sovereign defaults have been shown to curtail the private sector's access to foreign finance (Arteta and Hale, 2008, Kolscheen and O'Connel, 2008); lower international trade (Rose, 2005), and hurt the private sector through reduced domestic private credit and the increased incidence of banking crises (Borensztein et al. 2007, Martinez and Sandleris, 2008).

4. HYPOTHESES, DATA, AND VARIABLES

Hypotheses

The estimation of the factors influencing the prospects of corporate profits contributes to the receipt of important information related to the optimal financial structure which may lead to profit maximization. There are many important factors that affect firms' profitability, leading to different results and conclusions according to the country and time period.

More specifically, for the case of Greek firms, the last years this can be dealt as an important sustainability bet, taking into consideration that Greece's economy after 2009 has shrunk and its GDP has decreased dramatically, leading to a durable raise of the Greek government's borrowing cost.

There are numerous prior researches which examined the impact of such determinant factors on firms' profitability. The results of these studies either agree or contradict with financial theory or fail to confirm the expected impact on earnings. Nevertheless, in the frame of this study, the empirical findings of the relationship between the micro and macro variables used and firms' profitability show that the maximization of firms' profitability is closely connected with better financial management, which is being linked not only with the way variables affect firms' profitability, but also with the capital structure applied and the level of debt.

More specifically we examine the following hypotheses:

1. Does the selected micro and macro variables affect firm's profitability as suggested by the financial theory?
2. Is the relationship between leverage ratio and firm profitability nonlinear and what is the estimated turning point of debt ratio?
3. Does the economic crisis in Greece affect the above hypothesis results?

Sample

For the purposes of the empirical part of this paper, we included 51 non – financial companies (see Table 1) listed on the Athens Stock Exchange (ASE – General Index) for the period starting from 2005 to 2016. We excluded from our analysis financial corporations (banks, insurance companies, etc), as the structure of their balance sheet differs to a great extent from those of non-financial corporations. The starting date of our analysis is 2005, as this was the first year of IFRS implementation by Greek listed companies. The financial data of companies used in the sample are being extracted by Bloomberg database.

Table 1. Companies sample

N	Name	N	Name
1	Coca-Cola HBC AG	27	Intracom Holdings SA
2	Mytilineos Holdings SA	28	Thrace Plastics Co SA
3	Motor Oil Hellas Corinth Refineries SA	29	Athens Medical Center SA
4	Hellenic Telecommunications Organization	30	Kri-Kri Milk Industry SA
5	OPAP SA	31	Halcor SA
6	FF Group	32	Thessaloniki Water Supply & Sewage Co SA
7	JUMBO SA	33	Eltech Anemos SA
8	Titan Cement Co SA	34	Technical Olympic SA
9	Hellenic Petroleum SA	35	Diagnostic & Therapeutic Center of Athens
10	GEK Terna Holding Real Estate Construction	36	Quest Holdings SA
11	LAMDA Development SA	37	MLS Innovation Inc
12	Athens Water Supply & Sewage Co SA	38	J&P-Avax SA
13	Public Power Corporation SA	39	Korres Natural Products
14	Aegean Airlines SA	40	Plaisio Computers SA
15	Fourlis Holdings SA	41	Nireus Aquaculture SA
16	Viohalco SA	42	Flexopack SA
17	Ellaktor SA	43	Karatzis SA
18	Sarantis SA	44	Elastron S.A.
19	Terna Energy SA	45	Iktinos Hellas SA
20	Intralot SA	46	Loulis Mills SA
21	Piraeus Port Authority SA	47	Elton Chemicals
22	Plastika Kritis SA	48	Petros Petropoulos AE
23	Autohellas SA	49	I Kloukinas-I Lappas SA
24	Lampsa Hotel Co	50	AS Co AE
25	Iaso SA	51	Intracom SA Technical & Steel Construction
26	Thessaloniki Port Authority SA		

Variables

ROE is the proxy variable used for firms' profitability, and is defined as the ratio of net profit to total equity. The above-mentioned factor is used as the dependent variable in our model. The independent variables which complete our model are the following:

- **Debt Ratio:** The debt ratio is defined as the ratio of firms' total liabilities to total assets, and it shows the degree of firms' financial leverage compared to total assets.
- **Logarithm of Total Assets:** The natural logarithm of total assets is used as proxy variable for firms' size.
- **GDP:** For the purposes of this paper, the annual percentage change in real GDP is used. This variable is very important to capture the overall economic activity of Greek economy.
- **10-Year Greek Government Bond Yield:** The 10-Year Greek government bond yield is used as a proxy variable of Greek borrowing cost. It is worth noting that it consists a robust benchmark for the determination of weighted average cost of capital. This variable is used with one-year time lag, as it considered as a leading factor.
- **Accruals:** Accruals are defined as the difference between net income and net cash flows from operational activities. This variable is used as an indication of earnings' quality and depicts profits' outlook. The above variable is used with one-year time lag, as it is considered as a leading indicator.
- **Earnings Smoothness:** This variable is defined as the ratio of the standard deviation of net income to the standard deviation of net cash flows from operational activities and denotes earnings' volatility. It is also used with one-year time lag, as it is considered as a leading indicator.

5. METHODOLOGY

This paper pursuit is twofold. On the one hand, it examines the impact of debt ratio as well as specific micro and macro variables on firm's profitability. On the other hand, it determines the optimal debt ratio taking into account the existence of non - linearity. In order to capture the factors influencing firms' profitability, the paper is based on a previous study of Katsampoxakis et al. (2015). Moreover, for the estimation for the estimation of the progress of the non-linear relationship between debt ratio and ROE, a quadratic equation was introduced which is based on the study of Checherita and Rother (2010). The regression equation estimation is as follows:

$$ROE_{i,t} = a_0 + a_1 * Earnings\ Smoothness_{i,t-1} + a_2 * Accruals_{i,t-1} + a_3 * Ln\ Total\ Assets_{i,t} + a_4 * Debt\ Ratio_{i,t} + a_5 * Debt\ Ratio^2_{i,t} + \gamma_1 * GDP Growth_t + \gamma_2 * 10Y\ Yield_{t-1} + \mu_i + u_{i,t} \quad (1)$$

where,

$ROE_{i,t}$, is the return on equity of firm i at time t (i = 1, …,51, t = 2005, …, 2016).

$Earnings\ Smoothness_{i,t-1}$, is the ratio of the volatility of net profit to cash flows from operational activities with one time lag (i = 1, …,51, t = 2005, …, 2016).

$Accruals_{i,t-1}$, is the difference between the net profit and cash flows from operational activities with one time lag (i = 1, …,51, t = 2005, …, 2016).

$Ln\ Total\ Assets_{i,t}$, is the firm's size, approached by the natural logarithm of total assets (i = 1, …,51, t = 2005, …, 2016).

$Debt\ Ratio_{i,t}$ is the firm i debt ratio at time t (i = 1, …,51, t = 2005, …, 2016).

$Debt\ Ratio_{i,t}^2$ is the firm's i squared debt ratio at time t (i = 1, …,51, t = 2005, …, 2016).

$GDP\ Growth_t$ is the annual percentage Greek GDP (i = 1, …,51, t = 2005, …, 2016).

$10Y\ Yield_{t-1}$, is the 10-year Greek government bond yield with one time lag (i = 1, …,51, t = 2005, …, 2016).

μ_i is company's fixed effects (i = 1, …,51).
$u_{i,t}$ is the stochastic term error (i = 1, …,51, t = 2005, …, 2016).

Accruals, earnings smoothness and 10-year Greek government bond yield are used in the above model with one-year time lag, as it is expected to have an impact on firms' profitability outlook. Moreover, the debt ratio was included in the model both in levels and squared terms in order to take into account the non-linear impact of debt on firm's value and earnings. Furthermore, the above adjustment is of determinant importance for the estimation of the turning point, beyond which bound, the debt ratio imposes a negative impact on firms' earnings according to MM theory.

Trying to be consistent with the fundamental theory related to the expectations of the factors' attitude used in our model, it is considered that the coefficients a_2 (accruals), a_3 (ln Total Assets) and γ_1 (GDP Growth) take positive values, while the coefficients a_1 (Earnings Smoothness) and γ_2 (10 Year Yield) is expected to take negative values.

As far as debt ratio coefficients is concerned, it is expected a_4 (levels of Debt Ratio) to be positive while a_5 (squared Debt Ratio) has to take negative values, in order to verify the theory, that debt ratio has positive impact on firms' profitability till the point debt ratio approaches to the optimal level. Beyond optimal debt ratio threshold, the impact on firms' earnings is expected to be negative. In order to calculate the optimal debt ratio, it is needed to set the first partial derivative of the equation (1) to debt ratio to be equal to zero and afterwards to solve for debt ratio so to find the critical point. Thus, the turning point is being estimated by computing the ratio $\left(\frac{a_4}{-2 * a_5}\right)$. Furthermore, the second partial derivative of equation (1) to debt ratio has to be negative in order to be consistent with the financial theory ($a_5 < 0$). In case the second derivative of the equation is negative, then the dependent variable (ROE) will enjoy a local maximum at the critical point (optimal debt ratio). Since the relationship between debt ratio and ROE is non-linear (the ratio of estimated coefficients debt ratio/[-2* squared debt ratio]), the normal distribution at 95% confidence interval estimated for each coefficient cannot be used to compute the confidence interval for the turning point. In order to sort the above problem out, we used the delta method computed using analytic derivatives to estimate the standard error of the ratio $\frac{a_4}{-2 * a_5}$.

The econometric model was estimated using panel data for the total of 51 companies of the sample. The panel data model is considered a typical micro-panel data, as there are more cross sections observations than the number of years included in the sample. The econometric results of the panel regression using ordinary least squares (OLS) method in the above equation are unbiased and consistent, but there are not efficient. We applied different estimation methods in order to get more robust standard errors, following all the appropriate diagnostic tests to deal with heteroscedasticity and potential correlation between periods. The coefficients and standard errors of the explanatory variables after the appropriate adjustments are assumed to be efficient and consistent with the panel feasible GLS method.

Given that feasible GLS ignores the fact that the companies of our sample belong to different sectors and have different size, we specified fixed effects on cross-sections in order to take into account the heterogeneity of companies. We have to point out that we did not use time fixed effects as we have included in the model the variables 10-year Greek government bond yield and GDP growth as they are equivalent for all firms, each specific time.

A far as the research hypotheses is concerned, we have to denote that the first hypothesis will be validated through simple t and F tests of the coefficients for all independent variables for all period sample. For the second hypothesis, we first test if the coefficients a_4 and a_5 are statistical significant and then we verify whether

a_4 coefficient (Debt ratio) is positive and a_5 coefficient (squared Debt ratio) takes negative values, so to confirm the theoretical approach. In case the above conditions are fulfilled, we then calculate the turning point at the 95% confidence interval.

Moreover, for the purposes of the present paper we examined the model's coefficients stability and the way Greek economic crisis affects model's results. In order to be able to get a clear picture, we first estimated the model for the whole period (2005 – 2016) and then we split the sample out to two sub - periods. As far as the third hypothesis is concerned, we applied the aforementioned tests for the two split samples. The first sub - period relates the period before the beginning of the Greek economic crisis (2005-09), while the second sub - period is identified with the period of Greek economic crisis (2010-16). We applied all the above methodology and diagnostic tests for both the two sub - periods examined.

6. EMPIRICAL RESULTS

Descriptive Statistics

In Table 2, are being presented the descriptive statistics of the variables used in the model; meaning the mean, the standard deviation, the minimum and maximum value, the range of values, the coefficient of asymmetry, kurtosis and Jarque-Bera statistic. The average ROE is 6.97%, fluctuating between 304.43% (the highest price – Aegean 2006) and -182.32% (the lowest price – Quest GA 2013). The standard deviation (24.34%) and the range of values of ROE indicate excessive high volatility of the data. The average natural logarithm of total assets in the sample is 6.09. The highest value is observed for PPC (2014) while the smallest one for MLS (2005). The average leverage ratio stands at 54.10%. This means that companies exhibiting a higher ratio of total liabilities to total assets than the average are characterized by high leverage, in contrast to firms with low leverage ratios. The most levered companies of the sample are Aegean Airlines in 2005 (98%), J&P-Avax in 2016 (91%) and Halcor SA in 2013 (91%). The least levered companies are Thessaloniki Port Authority in 2013 (9%), MLS in 2005 (11%) and Thessaloniki Water Supply & Sewage Co in 2016 (20%). The average value of accruals is negative (-59.93) and the index is characterized by very high volatility. The highest price is observed for Hellenic Petroleum (2016), and the lowest one for OTE (2005). According to Jarque-Bera normality test, p-value is zero for all variables. That means that all variables are not normally distributed. In summary, the data for the test sample are characterized by very high volatility, making the results of the empirical study less reliable and less consistent. Because of the recession of the Greek economy and the

Table 2. Descriptive statistics

	Debt Ratio	Earning Smoothnes	Accrual	Ln Total Assets	ROE
Mean	0.5410	3.7186	-59.9321	6.0879	6.9735
Median	0.5600	0.6046	-5.6661	5.9647	5.9652
Maximum	0.9113	1228.1890	847.4960	9.7627	304.4302
Minimum	0.0973	0.0116	-1749.6000	2.5997	-182.3199
Std. Dev.	0.1675	51.8851	213.1480	1.5028	24.3409
Skewness	-0.2609	23.3755	-3.6108	0.2785	3.4060
Kurtosis	2.52	551.94	20.60	2.58	52.75
Jarque-Bera	11.82	7132854.00	8503.99	11.43	59264.24
Probability	0.0027	0.0000	0.0000	0.0033	0.0000
Observations	564	564	564	564	564

significant reduction of domestic demand, the financial data of listed companies in the ASE changed to a great extent, enhancing their volatility, as result of the existence of outliers in the sample.

Regression Models

Looking at the panel model estimation results in Table 3, for the whole period sample, one can observe that the model is statistically significant, with a satisfactory coefficient of determination (R-squared). Most of the independent variables of the sample are statistically significant, and the expected signs (10year government bond yield, GDP growth, debt ratio) are consistent with the fundamental theory. The coefficient of earnings smoothness with one year lag and accruals with one year lag are not statistical significant so we cannot extract any robust conclusion related to the estimated impact, as the contribution to future firms' profitability is estimated to be close to zero.

As far as firm size is concerned, it is estimated that affects firm's profitability with a negative - on average - way. The above result may be justified by the fact that during the Greek economic crisis, large firms lost in a great extent their access to financial markets and may have been burdened with higher tax charges compared to smaller ones.

The coefficient of the 10-year Greek government bond yield is negative and statistically significant. Therefore, an increase in the borrowing cost of the Greek government seems to have a negative impact on firms' profitability in the year ahead. The above result can be characterized as an expected finding as the firms' borrowing costs is being directly affected by government long term bond yields.

The coefficient of the variable related to the economic activity of the domestic economy is positive and statistically significant as it was expected. That means that an increase in the annual growth rate of GDP will have a positive impact on the current ROE.

Last but not least, the coefficients of debt ratio and squared debt ratio are statistically significant and signs follow a reverse course, which is consistent to the methodology as described above. In order to be more specific, the positive sign of debt's ratio coefficient, combined with the negative sign of squared debt's ratio coefficient is exactly the key – point what verifies the existence of optimal maximum point. Therefore, it can be concluded that the debt ratio has a nonlinear impact on firm's profitability.

Furthermore, we calculated the turning point for the debt ratio and 95% confidence interval as being shown in Chart 1. The optimized point for debt ratio is estimated to be 52.6%, while it is estimated to be fluctuated between 44.8% and 60.4% at 95% confidence interval. Taking into consideration the above findings, we can state that the debt ratio has positive impact on firm's profitability, for firms enjoying debt ratio below 52.6%. On the contrary, debt ratio indicates negative impact on ROE for companies considered as highly levered (debt ratio above 52.6%). In extreme cases the lower level of turning point to debt ratio of Greek companies examined is estimated to be even lower than 44.8%.

As far as the first sub-period (2005-09) is concerned, which coincided with the Greek economic growth, the panel regression (Table 4) is statistical significant and most of the independent variables remain statistically significant.

The coefficients of earning smoothness and accruals – both of them with one year lag -are not statistical significant, so we cannot claim that they affect firm's profitability. The same statistical connection regards to the economic activity impact on earnings as well, in full disaccordance to the results of whole period sample. This may be explained by the fact that the Greek economy faced high growth rates during that period, especially after 2004 (Athens Olympic Games took place). This growth was mainly due to high government spending and expansion of public sector's size. However, this growth model followed in none case could be characterized as sustainable, due to absence of the necessary structural reforms and private investments. So far, non-financial corporations' profitability had never highly linked with that expansion.

The coefficient of Greek government borrowing cost is statistically significant and indicates a negative sign as it was in the case of the whole period examined. As far as the firm's size impact is concerned, our findings lead to the existence of

Table 3. Panel regression, 2005-2016

	Dependent Variable: ROE		
	(1)	**(2)**	**(3)**
Earning Smoothnes(-1)	-0.0003	-0.0003	-0.0003
	[0.9713]	[0.7502]	[0.9644]
10Y Bond Yield(-1)	**-0.1356*****	**-0.1356*****	**-0.1356*****
	[0.0003]	[0.0004]	[0.0002]
GDP Growth	**0.2492*****	**0.2492****	**0.2492*****
	[0.0006]	[0.0114]	[0.0009]
Ln Total Assets	**-7.4597*****	**-7.4597*****	**-7.4597*****
	[0.0018]	[0.0004]	[0.0000]
Accrual(-1)	0.0042	0.0042	0.0042
	[0.4209]	[0.224]	[0.3174]
Debt Ratio	**93.3410*****	**93.3410*****	**93.3410*****
	[0.0005]	[0.0001]	[0.0000]
Debt Ratio^2	**-88.7023*****	**-88.7023*****	**-88.7023*****
	[0.0007]	[0.0004]	[0.0000]
C	**32.2715****	**32.2715****	**32.2715*****
	[0.0351]	[0.0166]	[0.0018]
R-squared	0.5968	0.5968	0.5968
F-statistic	12.0732	12.0732	12.0732
Prob(F-statistic)	0.0000	0.0000	0.0000
Durbin-Watson	1.2237	1.2237	1.2237
Periods included	12	12	12
Cross-sections	51	51	51
Total panel obs	523	523	523
Method	Panel EGLS (Cross-section weights)	Panel EGLS (Cross-section weights)	Panel EGLS (Cross-section weights)
Cross-section Effects	Fixed	Fixed	Fixed
Periods Effects	None	None	None
Coef. Covariance method	Period SUR (PCSE)	White Period	Ordinary
	Coefficient	95% Confidence Interval	
Optimal Debt Ratio	0.5261	0.4480	0.6043

In [ ] there are p-values, * significant for 10% significant level, ** significant for 5% significant level and *** significant for 1% significant level.

The method of estimation is a feasible GLS specification assuming the presence of cross-section heteroskedasticity (Cross section weights).

Coefficient covariance methods used for robust standard errors: the Period SUR Panel Corrected Standard Errors *handles between period correlation (cross-section clustering), so the covariance* estimators should be robust to serial correlation, the *White period* method assumes that the errors for a cross-section are heteroskedastic and serially correlated (cross-section clustered), *robust standard errors to specific heteroskedasticity and correlation between residuals for different observations.*

The 95% confidence interval for optimal debt is calculated form the standard error of ratio of the coefficients Debt ratio/(-2*Debt ratio^2), using delta method computed analytic derivatives.

Figure 1. Non-linear relationship debt ratio vs ROE, 2005 – 2016

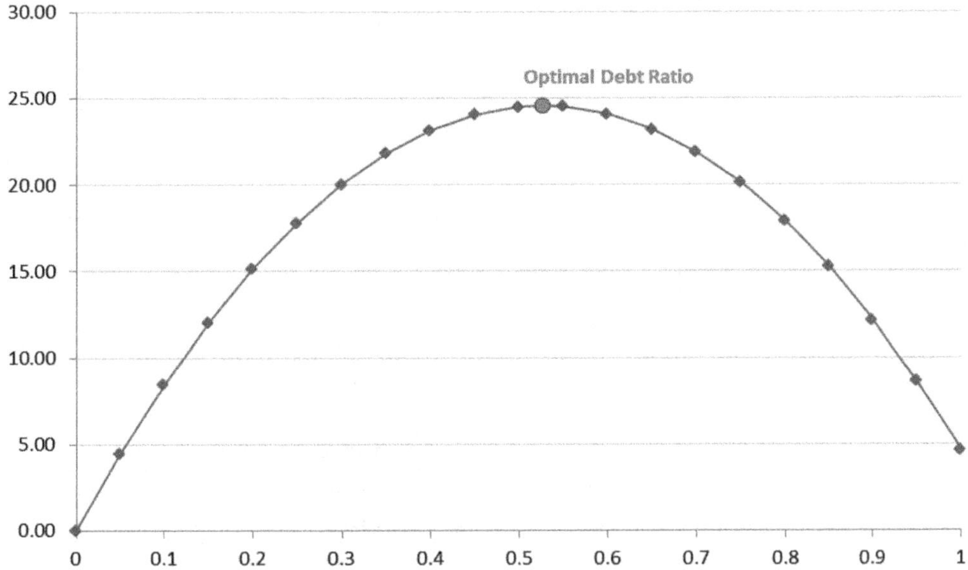

a negative effect on earnings. However, the coefficient is statistical significant at 10% confidence level.

Finally, the coefficients of debt ratio and squared debt ratio are statistically significant, but the signs are not consistent with the financial theory, as a_4 (debt ratio) is negative and a_5 (squared debt ratio) is positive. The above result implies that the optimal level of debt ratio minimizes ROE, so the debt ratio turning point (turning point minimize ROE) is totally different compared to that of the first regression (for the whole period sample 2005-16). So for the period before the beginning of the Greek crisis we find that companies which were considered as highly levered indicated better profitability compared to low levered corporations. This finding may be explained by the fact that during the period 2005-09, the Greek economy was growing fast, the risk sentiment was favorable and the worries regarding debt crisis and corporate defaults were being priced at low level by markets.

The results of the econometric model of the period of the big recession (second sub-period of the sample) of the Greek economy are being presented at Table 5. The panel model remains statistically significant and the coefficient of determination (R-squared) is higher compared to the whole sample, indicating that during the Greek economic crisis the independent variables fit to firms' profitability better.

As far as the coefficient of earning smoothness and accruals with one year lag is concerned, the statistical results are found to be similar as indicated for the whole period sample. However, the coefficient of GDP growth is statistically different

Table 4. Panel regression 2005-2009

	Dependent Variable: ROE		
	(1)	(2)	(3)
Earning Smoothnes(-1)	0.0017	0.0017	0.0017
	[0.9114]	[0.4145]	[0.9132]
10Y Bond Yield(-1)	**-6.4915****	**-6.4915****	**-6.4915*****
	[0.0227]	[0.0369]	[0.0056]
GDP Growth	-0.3357	-0.3357	-0.3357
	[0.5773]	[0.5712]	[0.4981]
Ln Total Assets	**-8.6763***	**-8.6763***	**-8.6763***
	[0.0828]	[0.0983]	[0.0516]
Accrual(-1)	-0.0037	-0.0037	-0.0037
	[0.6623]	[0.479]	[0.6297]
Debt Ratio	**-375.8700*****	**-375.8700*****	**-375.8700*****
	[0.0000]	[0.0012]	[0.0000]
Debt Ratio^2	**352.6310*****	**352.6310*****	**352.6310*****
	[0.0000]	[0.001]	[0.0000]
C	**189.0796*****	**189.0796*****	**189.0796*****
	[0.0000]	[0.0000]	[0.0000]
R-squared	0.8449	0.8449	0.8449
F-statistic	12.1078	12.1078	12.1078
Prob(F-statistic)	0.0000	0.0000	0.0000
Durbin-Watson	2.3299	2.3299	2.3299
Periods included	5	5	5
Cross-sections	51	51	51
Total panel obs	175	175	175
Method	Panel EGLS (Cross-section weights)	Panel EGLS (Cross-section weights)	Panel EGLS (Cross-section weights)
Cross-section Effects	Fixed	Fixed	Fixed
Periods Effects	None	None	None
Coef. Covariance method	Period SUR (PCSE)	White Period	Ordinary
	Coefficient	95% Confidence Interval	
Optimal Debt Ratio	0.5330	0.4936	0.5723

In [ ] there are p-values, * significant for 10% significant level, ** significant for 5% significant level and *** significant for 1% significant level.

The method of estimation is a feasible GLS specification assuming the presence of cross-section heteroskedasticity (Cross section weights).

Coefficient covariance methods used for robust standard errors: the Period SUR Panel Corrected Standard Errors *handles between period correlation (cross-section clustering), so the covariance* estimators should be robust to serial correlation, the *White period* method assumes that the errors for a cross-section are heteroskedastic and serially correlated (cross-section clustered), *robust standard errors to specific heteroskedasticity and correlation between residuals for different observations.*

The 95% confidence interval for optimal debt is calculated form the standard error of ratio of the coefficients Debt ratio/(-2*Debt ratio^2), using delta method computed analytic derivatives.

Figure 2. Non –linear relationship debt ratio vs. ROE, 2005 – 2009

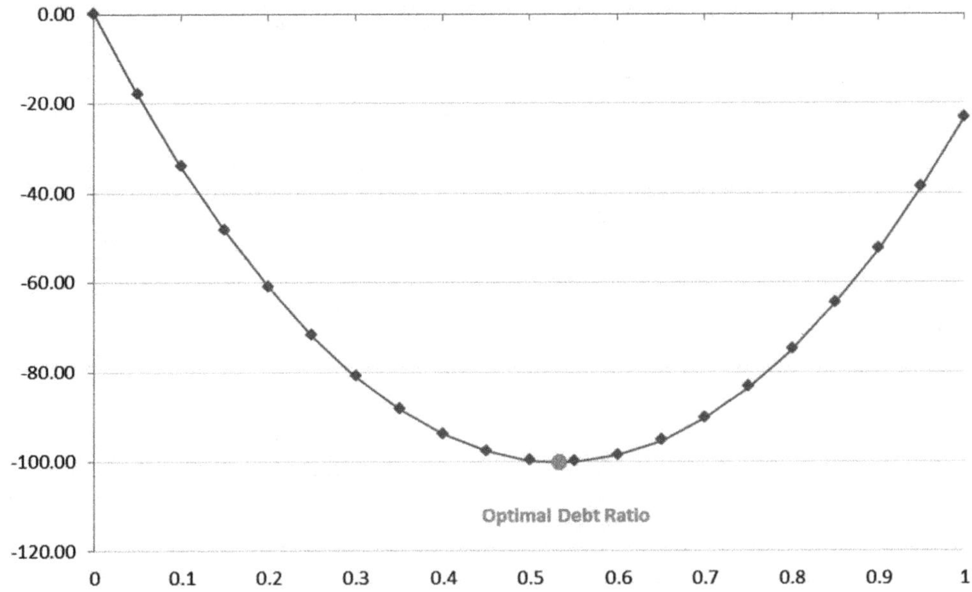

compared to the whole period sample. This finding may be justified by the fact that the Greek economy during the period of 2010-16 suffered remarkable contraction, while the companies registered some profits, mainly due to well diversified business activities and high exposure to foreign markets. The coefficient of Greek government bond yield has statistical significant negative impact on firm's profitability outlook. However, the magnitude of the impact is lower during the period of the economic crisis compared to the whole period sample.

Finally, debt ratio impact on ROE still places, the non-linear relationship. The coefficients of debt ratio and squared debt ratio are consistent with the financial theory. Regarding the optimal debt ratio, it is estimated to be 40.9% at 95% confidence interval is fluctuated between 34.1% and 47.8%. The turning point decreased considerably during the period 2010-16 compared to the whole period sample, mainly due to elevated downside risks for Greek economy and business activity and to the restricted funding and the highly cost of borrowing as resulted by the deep continuous economic crisis.

7. CONCLUSION

This study examined the course and the impact of specific variables on the profitability of companies listed on the ASE. More specifically, it is examined the impact of

Table 5. Panel regression 2010-2016

	Dependent Variable: ROE		
	(1)	(2)	(3)
Earning Smoothnes(-1)	0.0569	0.0569	0.0569
	[0.5344]	[0.4329]	[0.5689]
10Y Bond Yield(-1)	**-0.0714*****	**-0.0714*****	**-0.0714*****
	[0.0014]	[0.0082]	[0.0003]
GDP Growth	-0.0928	**-0.0928***	**-0.0928***
	[0.1299]	[0.0777]	[0.0775]
Ln Total Assets	-1.2784	-1.2784	-1.2784
	[0.5783]	[0.5848]	[0.4904]
Accrual(-1)	-0.0029	-0.0029	-0.0029
	[0.1542]	[0.2161]	[0.2569]
Debt Ratio	**76.7660*****	**76.7660*****	**76.7660*****
	[0.0003]	[0.0000]	[0.0000]
Debt Ratio^2	**-93.7895*****	**-93.7895*****	**-93.7895*****
	[0.0000]	[0.0000]	[0.0000]
C	-1.0808	-1.0808	-1.0808
	[0.9398]	[0.9392]	[0.9244]
R-squared	0.7880	0.7880	0.7880
F-statistic	18.9123	18.9123	18.9123
Prob(F-statistic)	0.0000	0.0000	0.0000
Durbin-Watson	1.7138	1.7138	1.7138
Periods included	7	7	7
Cross-sections	51	51	51
Total panel obs	348	348	348
Method	Panel EGLS (Cross-section weights)	Panel EGLS (Cross-section weights)	Panel EGLS (Cross-section weights)
Cross-section Effects	Fixed	Fixed	Fixed
Periods Effects	None	None	None
Coef. Covariance method	Period SUR (PCSE)	White Period	Ordinary
	Coefficient	95% Confidence Interval	
Optimal Debt Ratio	0.4092	0.3406	0.4779

In [ ] there are p-values, * significant for 10% significant level, ** significant for 5% significant level and *** significant for 1% significant level.

The method of estimation is a feasible GLS specification assuming the presence of cross-section heteroskedasticity (Cross section weights).

Coefficient covariance methods used for robust standard errors: the Period SUR Panel Corrected Standard Errors *handles between period correlation (cross-section clustering), so the covariance* estimators should be robust to serial correlation, the *White period* method assumes that the errors for a cross-section are heteroskedastic and serially correlated (cross-section clustered), *robust standard errors to specific heteroskedasticity and correlation between residuals for different observations.*

The 95% confidence interval for optimal debt is calculated form the standard error of ratio of the coefficients Debt ratio/(-2*Debt ratio^2), using delta method computed analytic derivatives.

Figure 3. Non-linear relationship debt ratio vs. ROE, 2010 – 2016

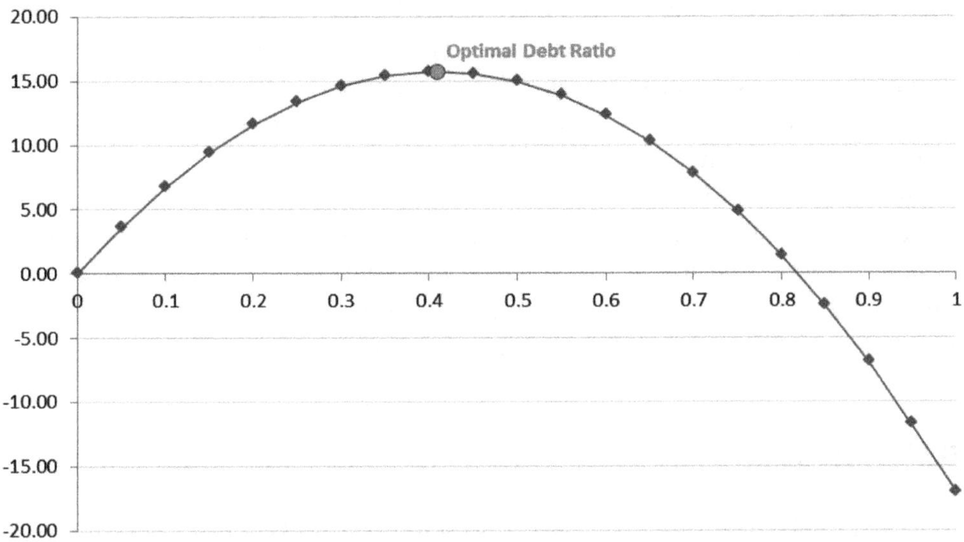

firms' size, financial leverage, accruals, earnings smoothness, GDP growth of the Greek economy and Greek government's borrowing cost on the ROE of listed companies in the ASE for the period from 2005 to 2016. The sample examined is being divided in two sub – period, due to radical changes occurred to the Greek economy, meaning form a period of stable and significant expansion to the collapse of the Greek economy and the intermediation of global institutions (EC/IMF/ECB), in order to avoid the bankruptcy of the Greek sovereign and banking sector.

Panel regression models were applied in order to estimate the effect of independent variables on ROE, taking into account the existence of heteroskedasticity and autocorrelation. More specifically, an increase in the borrowing cost of the Greek government seems to have a negative impact on firms' profitability in the year ahead.

As far as the two sub - periods are examined, the preceding empirical results lead to very interesting conclusions. For the first sub – period which takes place before the beginning of sovereign crisis in Greece (2005 – 2009), the coefficients of debt ratio and squared debt ratio are statistically significant, but the signs are not consistent with the financial theory, as a result of the fast growing, of the Greek economy and the favorable economic environment. The above finding coincides with the fact that the default risk of Greek corporates due to high leverage was priced at a very low level by capital markets.

This situation, looks to change dramatically, during the second sub – period, characterized as the period of the deep recession (2010 – 2016) for the Greek economy. More specifically, during the aforementioned period, the coefficients of debt ratio and squared debt ratio are consistent with the financial theory. This result implies that corporates financial leverage could affect profitability negatively beyond a critical debt level. The optimal debt ratio is estimated to be 40.9%. The turning point has been decreased considerably during the period 2010-16 compared to the whole period sample (52.6%), mainly due to increased downside risks for Greek economy and corporations.

The above-mentioned findings are considered vitally important in making financial decisions. Many corporations face a dilemma concerning the optimal financial leverage, the size of the company and the quality of earnings in order to maximize shareholders' wealth. Managers should take this study into account in order to increase the profitability of their companies.

REFERENCES

Abor, J. (2005). The effect of capital structure on profitability: An empirical analysis of listed firms in Ghana. *The Journal of Risk Finance*, *6*(5), 438–445. doi:10.1108/15265940510633505

Ağca, Ş., & Celasun, O. (2012). Sovereign debt and corporate borrowing costs in emerging markets. *Journal of International Economics*, *88*(1), 198–208. doi:10.1016/j.jinteco.2012.02.009

Akbar, S., Rehman, S. U., & Ormrod, P. (2013). The impact of recent financial shocks on the financing and investment policies of UK private firms. *International Review of Financial Analysis*, *26*, 59–70. doi:10.1016/j.irfa.2012.05.004

Akben-Selcuk, E. (2016). Factors affecting firm competitiveness: Evidence from an emerging market. *International Journal of Financial Studies*, *4*(2), 9. doi:10.3390/ijfs4020009

Akintoye, I. R. (2008). Sensitivity of Performance to Capital Structure. *European Journal of Soil Science*, *7*, 1.

Alesina, A., de Broeck, M., Prati, A., & Tabellini, G. (1992). Default Risk on Government Debt in OECD Countries. *Economic Policy*, *15*(15), 427–463. doi:10.2307/1344548

Arcand, J. L., Berkes, E., & Panizza, U. (2015). Too Much Finance? *Journal of Economic Growth*, *20*(2), 105–148. doi:10.100710887-015-9115-2

Arteta, C., & Hale, G. (2008). Sovereign debt crises and credit to the private sector. *Journal of International Economics*, *74*(1), 53–69. doi:10.1016/j.jinteco.2007.05.008

Ayele, G. A. (2012). *Factors Affecting profitability of insurance companies in Ethiopia: Panel evidence*. Addis Ababa University.

Barbiero, F., Brutscher, P.-B., Kolev, A., Popov, M., & Wolski, M. (2016). *Misallocation of investment in Europe: Debt overhang, credit market distress, or weak demand?* European Investment Bank.

Barnea, A., Ronen, J., & Sadan, S. (1975). The implementation of accounting objectives: An application to extraordinary Items. *The Accounting Review*, *50*, 58–68.

Beck, N., & Katz, J. N. (1995). What to Do (and Not to Do) With Time-series Cross-section Data. *The American Political Science Review*, *89*(3), 634–647. doi:10.2307/2082979

Beck, T., Buyukkarabacak, B., Rioja, F. K., & Valev, N. T. (2012). Who Gets the Credit? And Does It Matter? Household vs. Firm Lending across Countries. *The B.E. Journal of Macroeconomics*, *12*(1), 1–46. doi:10.1515/1935-1690.2262

Beidleman, C. R. (1973). Income smoothing: The role of management. *The Accounting Review*, *48*, 653–667.

Benito, A., & Hernando, I. (2007). Firm behavior and financial pressure: Evidence from Spanish Panel Data. *Bulletin of Economic Research*, *59*(4), 283–311. doi:10.1111/j.0307-3378.2007.00266.x

Bhattacharya, U., Daouk, H., & Welker, M. (2003). The world price of earnings opacity. *The Accounting Review*, *78*(3), 641–678. doi:10.2308/accr.2003.78.3.641

Borensztein, E., Cowan, K., & Valenzuela, P. (2007). *Sovereign Ceilings Lite? The Impact of Sovereign Ratings on Corporate Ratings in Emerging Market Economies*. IMF Working Paper No. 07/75.

Burja, C. (2011). Factors influencing the companies' profitability. *Annales Universitatis Apulensis Series Oeconomica*, *13*(2), 215–224.

Celasun, O., & Agsa, S. (2009). *How Does Public External Debt Affect Corporate Borrowing Costs In Emerging Markets?* IMF Working Paper.

Chaney, P. K., & Lewis, C. M. (1995). Earnings management and firm valuation under asymmetric information. *Journal of Corporate Finance*, *1*(3-4), 319–345. doi:10.1016/0929-1199(94)00008-I

Charitou, S., Elfani, M., & Lois, P. (2010). The Effect of Working Capital Management on Firm's Profitability: Empirical Evidence From An Emerging Markets. *Journal of Business & Economics Research*, *8*(12), 63–68. doi:10.19030/jber.v8i12.782

Checherita, C., & Rother, P. (2010). *The impact of high and growing government debt on economic growth an empirical investigation for the euro area*. ECB Working Paper Series No 1237.

Christopoulos, A., Dokas, I., & Matzaris, D. (2013). The estimation of corporate liquidity management using artificial neural networks. *International Journal of Financial Engineering and Risk Management*, *1*(2), 193–210. doi:10.1504/IJFERM.2013.055849

Daskalakis, N., & Psillaki, M. (2008). Do country or firm factors explain capital structure? Evidence from SMEs in France and Greece. *Applied Financial Economics*, *18*(2), 87–97. doi:10.1080/09603100601018864

Dechow, P., Kothari, S., & Watts, R. (1998). The relation between earnings and cash flows. *Journal of Accounting and Economics*, *25*, 133–168. doi:10.1016/S0165-4101(98)00020-2

Dechow, P. M. (1994). Accounting Earnings and Cash Flows as Measures of Firm Performance: The Role of Accounting Accruals. *Journal of Accounting and Economics*, *18*(1), 3–42. doi:10.1016/0165-4101(94)90016-7

Dechow, P. M., & Dichev, I. D. (2002). The quality of accruals and earnings: The role of accrual estimation errors. *The Accounting Review*, *77*(s1), 35–59. doi:10.2308/accr.2002.77.s-1.35

Dechow, P. M., Ge, W., & Schrand, C. (2010). Understanding earning quality: A review of the proxies, their determinants and their Consequences. *Journal of Accounting and Economics*, *50*(2-3), 344–401. doi:10.1016/j.jacceco.2010.09.001

Deloof, M. (2003). Does Working Capital Management Affect Profitability of Belgian Firm? *Journal of Business and Accounting*, *30*(3-4), 573–587. doi:10.1111/1468-5957.00008

Dhawan, R. (2001). Firm size and productivity differential: Theory and evidence from a panel of US firms. *Journal of Economic Behavior & Organization*, *44*(3), 269–293. doi:10.1016/S0167-2681(00)00139-6

Dogan, M. (2013). Does Firm Size Affect the Firm Profitability? Evidence from Turkey. *Research Journal of Finance and Accounting*, *4*, 53–59.

Dong, H., & Su, T. (2010). The relationship between working capital management and profitability: A Vietnam case. *International Research Journal of Finance and Economics*, *49*, 62–71.

Eljelly, A. (2004). Liquidity-Profitability Tradeoff: An empirical Investigation in an Emerging Market. *International Journal of Commerce and Management, 14*(2), 48–61. doi:10.1108/10569210480000179

Eriotis, N., Vasiliou, D., & Ventoura-Neokosmidi, Z. (2007). How firm characteristics affect capital structure: An empirical study. *Managerial Finance, 33*(5), 321–331. doi:10.1108/03074350710739605

Fara, M., & Supartika, N. (2016). Factors affecting profitability of small medium enterprises (SMEs) firm listed in Indonesia Stock Exchange. *Journal of Economics, Business and Management, 4*(2), 132-137.

Gebauer, S., Setzer, R., & Westphal, A. (2017). *Corporate debt and investment: a firm level analysis for stressed euro area countries.* Working paper Series, No 2101, European Central Bank.

Gill, A., Biger, N., & Mathur, N. (2010). The relationship between working capital management and profitability: Evidence from the United States. *Business and Economic Journal*, 1-9.

Giovanis, E., & Ozdamar, O. (2014). *Determinants of Profitability: Evidence from US Firms*. Facoltà di Economia, Università degli Studi di Verona.

Gitman, L. J., & Zutter, C. J. (2012). *Principles of Managerial Finance* (13th ed.). Addison Wesley.

Goddard, J., Tavakoli, M., & Wilson, J. O. S. (2005). Determinants of profitability in European manufacturing and services: Evidence from a dynamic panel model. *Applied Financial Economics, 15*(18), 1269–1282. doi:10.1080/09603100500387139

Gurbuz, A. O., Aybars, A., & Kutlu, O. (2010). Corporate governance and financial performance with a perspective on institutional ownership: Empirical evidence from Turkey. *Journal of Applied Managerial Accounting Research, 8*, 21–38.

Hayajneh, O. S., & Yassine, F. L. A. (2011). The impact of Working Capital Efficiency on Profitability – an Empirical Analysis on Jordanian Manufacturing Firms. *International Research Journal of Finance and Economics, 66*, 67–76.

Jandik, T., & Makhija, A. K. (2005). Debt, Debt Structure and Corporate Performance after Unsuccessful Takeovers: Evidence from Targets that Remain Independent. *Journal of Corporate Finance, 11*(5), 882–914. doi:10.1016/j.jcorpfin.2004.04.002

Kalemli-¨Ozcan, S., Laeven, L., & Moreno, D. (2015a). *Debt Overhang, Rollover Risk and Investment in Europe*. ECB and University of Maryland.

Karaduman, H. A., Akbas, H. E., Ozsozgun, A., & Ducer, S. (2010). Effects of Working Capital management on profitability: The Case for selected companies in the Istanbul Stock Exchange (2005-2008). *International Journal of Economics and Finance Studies*, *2*, 47–54.

Katsampoxakis, I., Basdekis, H., & Anathreptakis, K. (2015). How firm and market characteristics affect profitability: An empirical study. *International Journal of Corporate Finance and Accounting*, *2*(1), 67–83. doi:10.4018/IJCFA.2015010104

Kim, H., Heshmati, A., & Aoun, D. (2005). Dynamics of Capital Structure: The Case of Korean Listed Manufacturing Companies. *Asian Economic Journal*, 275–302.

Kohlscheen, E., & O'Connell, S. A. (2008). *Trade Credit and Sovereign Debt*. Department of Economics, University of Warwick.

Krishnamurthy, A., & Vissing-Jorgensen, A. (2010). *The Aggregate Demand for Treasury Debt*. Working paper. Northwestern University.

Lazaridis, I., & Tryfonidis, D. (2006). Relationship Between Working Capital Management and Profitability of Listed Companies in Athens Stock Exchange. *Journal of Financial Management and Analysis*, *19*, 1.

Leuz, C., Nanda, D., & Wysocki, P. D. (2003). Earnings management and investor protection: An international comparison. *Journal of Financial Economics*, *69*(3), 505–527. doi:10.1016/S0304-405X(03)00121-1

Li, M. Y. L., & Hwang, N. C. R. (2011). "Effects of Firm size, Financial Leverage and R&D Expenditures on Firm Earnings: An Analysis Using Quintile Regression Approach", A Journal of Accounting. *Finance and Business Studies*, *47*(2), 182–204.

Liargovas, P., & Skandalis, K. (2010). Factors affecting firm competitiveness: The case of Greek industry. *European Industrial Journal*, *2*, 184–197.

Martinez, J. V., & Sandleris, G. (2008). *Is It Punishment? Sovereign Defaults and the Decline in Trade*. Universidad Torcuato Di Tella, Working Paper.

Martinez-Carrascal, C., & Herrando, A. (2008). *The impact of financial position on investment: An analysis for non-financial corporations in the Euro Area*. ECB Working Paper Series, 943.

Mathuva, D. M. (2010). The influence of working capital management components on corporate profitability: A survey on Kenyan listed firms. *Research Journal of Business Management*, *4*(1), 1–11. doi:10.3923/rjbm.2010.1.11

McConnell, J. J., & Servaes, H. (1995). Equity ownership and the two faces of debt. *Journal of Financial Economics, 39*(1), 131–157. doi:10.1016/0304-405X(95)00824-X

McInnis, J. (2010). Earnings smoothness, average returns, and implied cost of equity capital. *The Accounting Review, 85*(1), 315–341. doi:10.2308/accr.2010.85.1.315

Modigliani, F., & Miller, M. H. (1958). The cost of capital, corporate finance and the theory of investment. *The American Economic Review, 48*(3), 261–297.

Modigliani, F., & Miller, M. H. (1963). Corporate Income Taxes and Cost of Capital: A correction. *The American Economic Review, 53*(3), 433–443.

Myers, J., Myers, L., & Skinner, D. (2007). Earnings momentum and earnings management. *Journal of Accounting, Auditing & Finance, 22*(2), 249–284. doi:10.1177/0148558X0702200211

Narware, P. C. (2010). Working Capital Management: The Effect of Market Valuation and Profitability in Malaysia. *International Journal of Business and Management, 5*, 11.

Nazir, M. S., & Afza, T. (2009). Impact of aggressive working capital management policy in firms profitability. *The IUP Journal of Applied Finance, 15*(8), 19–30.

Padachi, K. (2006). Trends in Working Capital Management and its Impact on Firm's Performance: An Analysis of Mauritian Small Manufacturing Firms. *International Review of Business Research Papers, 2*, 45–58.

Pal, R., & Ferrando, A. (2010). Financing constraints and firms cash policy in the euro area. *European Journal of Finance, 16*(2), 153–171. doi:10.1080/13518470903075748

Pervan, M., & Visic, J. (2012). Influence of firm size on its business success. *Croatian Operational Research Review, 3*, 213–223.

Qiu, M., & La, B. (2010). Firm Characteristics as Determinants of Capital Structures in Australia. *International Journal of the Economics of Business, 17*(3), 277–287. doi:10.1080/13571516.2010.513810

Raheman, A., Afza, T., Qayyum, A., & Bodla, M.A. (2010). Working Capital Management and Corporate Performance of Manufacturing Sector in Pakistan. *International Research Journal of Finance and Economics,* (47).

Ramasamy, B. (2005). Firm size, ownership and performance in the Malaysian palm oil industry. *Asian Academy of Management Journal of Accounting and Finance, 1*, 81–104.

Rayan, K. (2008). *Financial leverage and firm value*. Gordon Institute of Business Science, University of Protoria.

Richardson, S. A., Sloan, R. G., Soliman, M. T., & Tuna, A. I. (2001). *Information in Accruals About the Quality of Earnings*. SSRN.

Rose, A. K. (2005). One Reason Countries Pay Their Debts: Renegotiation and International Trade. *Journal of Development Economics*, *77*(1), 189–206. doi:10.1016/j.jdeveco.2004.03.006

Russell, D., & MacKinnon, J. G. (1993). *Estimation and Inference in Econometrics*. Oxford University Press.

Salman, A. K., & Yazdanfar, D. (2012). Profitability in Swedish SME firms: A quantile regression approach. *International Business Research*, *5*(8), 94–106. doi:10.5539/ibr.v5n8p94

Singh, J. P., & Pandey, S. (2008). Impact of working Capital Management in the Profitability of Hindalco Industries Limited. *Icfai University Journal of Financial Economics*, *6*(4), 62–69.

Sloan, R. (1996). Do stock prices fully reflect information in accruals and cash flows about future earnings? *The Accounting Review*, *71*, 289–315.

Srinivasan, R., Lilien, G. L., & Shridhar, S. (2011). Should Firms Spend More on Research and Development and Advertising During Recessions? *Journal of Marketing*, *75*(3), 49–65. doi:10.1509/jmkg.75.3.49

Stierwald, A. (2009). *Determinants of firm profitability-The effect of productivity and its persistence*. Melbourne Institute of Applied Economic and Social Research, The University of Melbourne.

Tailab, M. M. (2014). Analyzing Factors Effecting Profitability of Non-Financial U.S. Firms. *Research Journal of Finance and Accounting*, *5*, 17–26.

Teruel, P. L., & Solano, P. M. (2007). Effects of working capital management on SME profitability. *International Journal of Management Finance*, *3*(2), 164–177.

Trueman, B., & Titman, S. (1988). An explanation for accounting income smoothing. *Journal of Accounting Research*, *26*, 127–139. doi:10.2307/2491184

Verma, S. (2013). Profitability of commercial banks after the reforms: A study of selected banks in India. *International Journal of Research in Finance and Marketing*, *3*, 2.

Vermeulen, P. (2002). Business fixed investment: Evidence of a financial accelerator in Europe. *Oxford Bulletin of Economics and Statistics*, *64*(3), 217–235. doi:10.1111/1468-0084.00020

Vijayakumar, A. (2011). The determinant of profitability: An empirical investigation using Indian automobile industry. *International Journal of Research in Commerce and Management*, *2*(1), 58–64.

Vijayakumar, A. (2011). An empirical study of firm structure and profitability relationship: The case Of Indian automobile firms. *International Journal of Research in Commerce and Management*, *1*(2), 100–108.

Wald, J. K. (1999). How Firm Characteristics Affect Capital Structure: An International Comparison. *Journal of Financial Research*, *22*(2), 161–187. doi:10.1111/j.1475-6803.1999.tb00721.x

White, H. (1980). A Heteroskedasticity-Consistent Covariance Matrix and a Direct Test for Heteroskedasticity. *Econometrica*, *48*(4), 817–838. doi:10.2307/1912934

Wooldridge, J. (2002). *Econometric analysis of cross section and panel data*. The MIT Press.

Yazdanfar, D. (2013). Profitability determinants among micro firms: Evidence from Swedish data. *The International Journal of Managerial Finance*, *9*(2), 150–160. doi:10.1108/17439131311307565

Zeitun, R., Temimi, A., & Mimouni, K. (2017). Do financial crises alter the dynamics of corporate capital structure? Evidence from GCC countries. *The Quarterly Review of Economics and Finance*, *63*, 21–33. doi:10.1016/j.qref.2016.05.004

Chapter 2
Interactions Between Macroeconomic Variables and Stock Market Indices:
Evidence From Germany, Denmark, and Spain, Including the Period of Crisis

Apostolos G. Christopoulos
National and Kapodistrian University of Athens, Greece

Nikolaos Demiroglou
Panteion University of Social and Political Sciences, Greece

Ioannis G. Dokas
Democritus University of Thrace, Greece

ABSTRACT

The relationship between the performance of capital markets and changes in several macroeconomic variables has worried many researchers over time. This chapter focuses on two main areas: 1) the analysis of the behavior of per capita consumption and private investment expenditure using the model ARMA (m, n), and the impact of economic crisis on them, and 2) the examination of causal relationships between key macro-variables and selected key stock exchange indices. The analysis is carried out for the period 1995-2013 for Germany, Denmark, and Spain, which were selected on the basis of their economic position (GDP) in the European Union (E.U.). From the research, the authors found that the crisis of 2008-2009 had effects on households and businesses, which reduced their planning horizon with respect to consumption and investment. Regarding the second part of this study, the authors used the Granger causality test to find that the stock index DAX of Germany determines, to some extent, the changes in macroeconomic variables.

DOI: 10.4018/978-1-5225-6114-9.ch002

LITERATURE REVIEW

The sharp fall observed in the capital markets in the summer of 2008, was a kind of announcement of the economic cycle that will ensue for the global economy. The markets have a tendency to discount the negative or positive developments in the real economy, but the factors that lead participants in a massive liquidation of securities have not been analyzed in detail yet.

Based on the efficient markets hypothesis and the assumption of rational expectations, the asset prices are significantly dependent by variables which can describe the state of an economy. This conclusion is consistent with classical valuation models (Merton; 1973, Ross; 1976, Cox et al; 1985 etc.).

Attempting a brief historical review, it is noted that many studies have been conducted in recent decades to examine the variables that affect the capital markets or equity portfolios returns. Fama (1981), using data from the American stock market for the period 1953-1977 found empirically that stock returns depend negatively by inflation, while they are positively correlated with yields of Treasury notes and measurements for future economic activity, capital cost and the efficiency of the capital stock. Geske et al. (1983) studied the negative relation between the performance of the S&P500 and changes in short-term interest rates for the period 1947-1980, which ultimately integrates the non-expected inflation, through a process of interactions between fiscal policy and those involved in the market. Chen et. al (1986), examined the effects of expected and unexpected inflation, yields and Treasury bonds, industrial production, consumption and oil prices on stock prices, concluding that consumption was the only variable that was statistically not significant. As dependent variables we used the New York Stock Exchange (NYSE) index with equal weighting per share, weighted by market capitalization for the period into consideration from 1958 to 1984. Bong-Soo Lee (1992) examined the reverse effects. More particularly he took under consideration the weighted NYSE index after the Second World War (1947-1987) and found that stock returns are prior to the economic activity, but they cannot explain the volatility of inflation. Fama and French (1989), used data from the NYSE index for the period 1927 till 1987 to conclude that the expected returns determine significantly the observed ones which, in a significant extent, are defined by the consumption pattern, in accordance with the theories of the permanent income and life cycle (Modigliani - Brumberg; 1955 and Friedman; 1957). Specifically, during periods of growth when incomes are high relative to wealth, households increase savings desiring smooth consumption in the present and the future, which leads to a decline in interest rates and expected returns. The reverse happens in times of recession when the decline in income reduces savings. Therefore, from a theoretical aspect, the economic conditions are moving in the opposite direction in relation to the yields. Coming into the 1990s, Fama (1990) found empirically that a great part of the volatility of stock returns depends mainly on forecasts of the future activity and the expected returns of the investors, suggesting the idea that financial markets discount the future status of real economy. The same year Schwert (1990), extended the research of Fama, by studying a period of 100 years from 1889 to 1988, confirming and reinforcing the above findings. It is noted that the dependent variable was the NYSE stocks' portfolio weighted by market capitalization. Poon and Taylor (1992) carried out an investigation on the influence of macroeconomic variables on the Financial Times All Share Index of England for the period 1965-1989, which showed that the trends of major macroeconomic variables had no effect on the stock returns of English firms. At the level of small open economies, a research was accomplished by Gjerde and Sættem (1999). More specifically, they examined the nominal yields of the weighted index of the Oslo Stock Exchange (Norway) for the period 1974-1994. They applied VAR models to find that there is a significant adjustment of stock prices in changes of inflation and the oil prices. In 2000s, a critical part of research focused on the responses by financial markets in the quotes of prices for key macroeconomic indices. Flannery and Protopapadakis (2002) took into consideration 17 announcements during the period 1980-1996 considering the value weighted index NYSE, AMEX, NASDAQ to show that inflation, as represented by the Consumer Price Index (CPI) and the Producer Price Index (PPI), affects the level of yields, while news that are related to the balance of trade, employment and the housing sector affect only on volatility. In addition, announcements about the level of money supply have impact both on volatility and returns, while the level of GNP and industrial production are presented to be indifferent for investors. In the same line, Boyd et al. (2005) examined the period 1957-2000 and observed that the index S&P500 responded positively to negative announcements for employment in good times for the economy and negatively during periods of recession. On the other hand, another research by Gan et al. (2006) for the index of the 40 largest companies New Zealand (NZSE40) showed a significant influence by interest rates, money supply and real GDP, while CPI and exchange rates were not statistically significant. In more recent years, researchers have shifted towards developing countries and countries experiencing high growth rates due to significant capital inflows from the developed countries. Some of these studies are by Brailsford T., And Hooper V. (2001) who examine emerging markets, Robert Gay (2008) who examines BRICs (Brazil, Russia, India and China), Brahmasrene et al. (2007) and N. Tangjitprom (2011) who studies Thailand Stock Exchange, Buyuksalvarci (2010) who examines the Turkish capital, Yahyazadehfar et al. (2012) and Fathi et al. (2012) who study the Iranian Stock Exchange, Kimani et al. (2013) who study the Nairobi (Kenya) capital market, Attari et al. (2013) who examine the Pakistani Stock Exchange, Hussin et al. (2013) who examine the Islamic capital market using data from the index FTSE Bursa Malaysia Emas Shariah, etc.

Table 1 shows the macroeconomic variables which are present in the aforementioned literature, in a descending frequency.

In the framework of the above-mentioned literature review some critical conclusions can be identified regarding the interdependence of stock returns and changes in major macroeconomic aggregates. This paper consists of the following stages: In the first stage the process for the selection of particular EU countries and the specific period that covers our analysis are explained. The second stage includes the selection of an initial set of variables which describe national economies and may affect the global economy. In the third stage, the methodology is explained and the choice of the applied econometric tools is justified. In the fourth stage, modelling is designed using ARMA (m,n), time series for per capita consumption and investments. It is noted that consumption and investment are the main components of GDP while there are is no high correlation between them. In the fourth step, the causal relationships between the percentage changes in fundamental variables

Table 1. Macroeconomic variables in the literature

Macroeconomic Variables	Papers
Interest rate (long and short-run)	Tangjitprom (2011), Buyuksalvarci (2010), Yahyazadehfar et al. (2012), Fathi et al. (2012), Kimani et al. (2013), Attari et al. (2013), Hussin et al. (2013)
Exchange rate	Brailsford et al. (2001), Gay (2008), Brahmasrene et al. (2007), Tangjitprom (2011), Buyuksalvarci (2010), Kimani et al. (2013)
Inflation (CPI)	Brailsford et al. (2001), Tangjitprom (2012), Buyuksalvarci (2010), Kimani et al. (2013), Attari et al. (2013), Hussin et al. (2013)
Money supply	Brailsford et al. (2001), Brahmasrene et al. (2007), Buyuksalvarci (2010), Hussin et al. (2013)
Price of oil	Gay (2008), Brahmasrene et al. (2007), Buyuksalvarci (2010), Hussin et al. (2013)
Industrial production	Brahmasrene et al. (2007), Buyuksalvarci (2010), Hussin et al. (2013)
Price of gold	Buyuksalvarci (2010), Yahyazadehfar et al. (2012)
GDP	Kimani et al. (2013), Attari et al. (2013)
Real economic activity	Brailsford et al. (2001)
Unemployment	Tangjitprom (2011)
Real Estate sector	Yahyazadehfar et al. (2012)
National Income	Fathi et al. (2012)
Macroeconomic instability	Fathi et al. (2012)
Development of financial intermediation	Fathi et al. (2012)

and the main stock market indices of selected countries are examined. At the same time, we attempt to construct an econometric model which may well explain the returns of the capital markets. In the fifth stage the most significant conclusions are summarised and recommendations for further research are made.

CRITERIA FOR THE SELECTION OF STATES AND PERIOD UNDER INVESTIGATION

Criteria for Selecting the EU Member States

For the selection of the EU member states the following criteria were taken into account:

- Year of entry in the EU.
- Contribution rate to the EU-28 GDP.
- Accession to the EMU.
- Action in E.U. and/or IMF support mechanisms.

The data of the above criteria are summarized in Table 2.

Since the aim of this study is not to examine the effects of the entry into the E.U. the states that became members of the E.U. after 1990 will not be taken into account. The year 1990 is set as the beginning of the period, which is analysed in this chapter. Based on this criterion, we exclude from our analysis the following states: Austria, Bulgaria, Estonia, Cyprus, Croatia, Lithuania, Latvia, Malta, Hungary, Poland, Romania, Slovakia, Slovenia, Sweden, Czech Republic and Finland.

From the criterion of the percentages contribution to GDP of EU-28, Germany, France, the United Kingdom and Italy show double-digit number and therefore Germany is selected, since it has the highest rate of 20.9%.

Then, taking into account the currency criterion, Denmark was selected for further analysis since it remained voluntarily outside the monetary union.

By the criterion of the action to the European support mechanism, with the assistance of the IMF, Greece, Ireland, Spain, Portugal and Cyprus faced a debt crisis and possible collapse of their banking sector. From these countries Spain was selected as a major contributor to the GDP of the Eurozone by 7.8%.

Therefore, by the overall examination of the criteria adopted for the selection of the countries of EU-28, the member states selected for further analysis are Germany, Denmark and Spain.

Table 2. Criteria for the selecting the member states

EU Member State	Year of Entry	Currency	Participation Rate in the EU-28 GDP	Action in E.U. and/ or IMF Support Mechanisms
Austria	1995	Euro	2,4	NO
Belgium	1952	Euro	2,9	NO
Bulgaria	2007	Lev	0,3	NO
France	1952	Euro	15,8	NO
Germany	1952	Euro	20,9	NO
Denmark	1973	Krone	1,9	NO
Greece	1981	Euro	1,4	YES
Estonia	2004	Euro	0,1	NO
United Kingdom	1973	Pound	14,5	NO
Ireland	1973	Euro	1,3	YES
Spain	1986	Euro	7,8	YES
Italy	1952	Euro	11,19	NO
Nederland	1952	Euro	4,6	NO
Croatia	2013	Kuna	0,3	NO
Cyprus	2004	Euro	0,1	YES
Latvia	2004	Euro	0,2	NO
Lithuania	2004	Litas	0,3	NO
Luxemburg	1952	Euro	0,3	NO
Malta	2004	Euro	0,1	NO
Hungary	2004	Forint	0,7	NO
Poland	2004	Zloty	3	NO
Portugal	1986	Euro	1,3	YES
Romania	2007	Lei	1,1	NO
Slovakia	2004	Euro	0,6	NO
Slovenia	2004	Euro	0,3	NO
Sweden	1995	Krone	3,2	NO
Czech Republic	2004	Krone	1,1	NO
Finland	1995	Euro	1,5	NO

A Brief Presentation of the Selected Countries

Germany

Germany is one of the most populous countries in Europe and the most populous among the E.U. member states. Being one of the major industrialized and developed countries in the world is considered the driving force of the Union, both from a political and an economic point of view. The German economy is based mainly on its industrial and service sectors. While large geographic areas of the country are in use by farmers, only 2-3% of the population is incorporated in this sector due to the modernization of the farming sector. According to the GDP, Germany is the largest economy in the E.U. and the third largest in the world, making very high value exports annually.

Denmark

Denmark is predominantly an agricultural country because of its climate that favors crops. The combination of cooperative institutions with the modernization of the farming sector was the main factors of growth for agriculture and livestock industries. Along with these two sectors, Denmark began to develop, in a systematic way, its food, chemical, textile and electrical industry, metallurgy and shipbuilding. Oil is extracted in small quantities in the North Sea, but it is not enough to cover the country's needs. The trade balance is usually negative and it is balanced by the shipping exchange. Agricultural and livestock products are exported, as well as machinery and shipbuilding types of wind energy systems. Trade transactions are mainly made with Sweden, Germany and the United Kingdom. Finally, the unemployment rate is quite low compared to the other member states of the E.U.

Spain

Spain is a country of southwest Europe that resides in most of the Iberian Peninsula. It is considered among the most agricultural countries of Europe. Also, animal husbandry is at a high level, especially after the introduction of better farmed species, which provide rich pasturages. Spain also has a developed fishery sector with a high percentage of its production to be exported to third countries. Its industry has experienced great growth since 1986 after its entry into the E.U. The Spanish economy started by producing labour-intensive goods, moving towards more sophisticated and high readability products based on a modern industrial design.

Selection of the Examined Period

The selected time horizon includes the years from 1995 till the third quarter of 2013. This period was chosen based on the following assumptions:

1. Germany became united in 1990 after the fall of the Berlin Wall. The different socio-political system and the different production technology between East and West Germany, have led to the existence of a transitional period to obtain homogeneity as the Federal Republic of Germany, which in this study is the early 1995.
2. Details of key macroeconomic data for Spain are available by Eurostat after 1995 and therefore the time horizon had to be limited for the benefit of the best possible comparability.
3. The number of observations for each variable from 1995 until the fourth quarter of 2013 amounted to 76, decreased by one observation in the case of percentage changes. Also, by performing our analysis by the end of 2007, before the outbreak of the crisis, the number of observations is 52 (percentage changes). Therefore, the number of observations is sufficient to perform reliable statistical tests and to develop econometric models.

SELECTED VARIABLES

The selection of variables was based mainly on the frequency of their occurrence in the literature (see. Table A). Furthermore, since the index of industrial production is among the selected variables, we decided to examine separately all the variables that consist GDP rather than to use autonomously the GDP. In addition, other variables represent the labor and the money market, as expressed by the level of unemployment and interest rates respectively. Finally, the price index of crude oil has been elected, despite the fact that it is not a straight macro variable, because it affects production and thus is expected to affect capital returns.

Table 3 shows the variables used in our analysis, the source from which they were derived and their acronyms to be used in this study.

It is noted that in the third stage of the per capita consumption and investment analysis, data are not adjusted neither seasonally nor based on working days. Regarding the section that examines the interactions of macroeconomic variables on stock market returns, the calculated percentage changes are compared with the previous period, while data are adjusted based on seasonality and working days. Data are quarterly and the amounts are expressed in Euro currency (ECU before 1999).

Table 3. Selected variables

Variables	Acronyms	Source
Final consumption expenditure of households and non-profit institutions serving households (NPISH)	FCE	Eurostat
Net savings	NS	Eurostat
Gross investments	GCF	Eurostat
Index of Industrial Production	IP	OECD
Taxes less subsidies on production and imports	TOP	Eurostat
Exports of goods and services	EXP	Eurostat
Nominal unit labor costs	NLC	Eurostat*
Ανεργία	UNEM	Eurostat
Actual labor productivity	RLP	Eurostat*
Exchange rate	EXCH	Eurostat**
Short-term interest rate	STR	OECD
Long-term interest rate	LTR	OECD
Consumer Price Index	CPI	OECD
Crude Oil Price Index	OIL	IMF
Gold Price (USD)	GOLD	Bundesbank
Stock Market Indices		
DAX (Germany)	DAX	Yahoo Finance
OMX Copenhagen 20 (Denmark)	OMX	Yahoo Finance
IBEX 35 (Spain)	IBEX	Yahoo Finance

* Due to lack of data, these variables were not taken into account for Spain.

** The exchange rate refers only to Denmark, which in 1999 decided to stay outside the eurozone. Prior to 1999, we use the rate of the Danish krone with the ECU.

METHODOLOGY

Modeling of Per Capita Consumption and Investment With ARMA (m, n)

Consumption and investments are the most important components of GDP, and therefore can reflect sufficiently the diffusion time of stock market crisis on the real economy. The actual time series does not allow for reliable conclusions due to the significant volatility, especially close to times of crisis. Moreover, the non-stationarity of the time series can not provide robust results when modeling with the ARMA (m,n). It is noted that stationarity has been tested with the Augmented Dickey-Fuller test under the following test (1).

$$\Delta Yt = ay_{t-1} + x_t'd + b_1\Delta y_{t-1} + b_2\Delta y_{t-2} + \ldots + b_p\Delta y_{t-p} + u_t \quad (1)$$

The hypothesis is tested where H_0: a = 0 and H_1: a > 0.

Therefore, in order to distinguish the time series into the part of volatility - cyclicality and the part of trend we applied the filter Hodrick - Prescott. This trend can be interpreted theoretically while the cyclical part of time series can be modeled using ARMA, since it is free of a unit root. Specifically, by applying the filter the following equation (2) is minimized (Hodrick and Prescott; 1997).

$$\min_{\{g_t\}_{t=-1}^{T}} \left\{ \sum_{t=1}^{T} c_t^2 + \lambda \sum_{t=1}^{T} \left[\left(g_t - g_{t-1}\right) - \left(g_{t-1} - g_{t-2}\right) \right]^2 \right\} \quad (2)$$

where:

c_t is the cyclical component
g_t is the trend
$y_t = c_t + g_t$ is the actual time series

Finally, the model ARMA(p,q) is given by the following relationship (3):

$$X_t = c + \varepsilon_t + \sum_{i=1}^{p} \varphi_i X_{t-i} + \sum_{i=1}^{q} \theta_i \varepsilon_{t-i} \quad (3)$$

where:

p is the autoregressive term
q is the moving average term

Changes in the coefficients of the ARMA model that will occur before and after the period of crisis are expected to contribute to the investigation of the changes in the behavior of households and firms.

Germany

As mentioned in the methodology section, stationarity problems shall be tested before applying ARMA model. The Augmented Dickey - Fuller test is applied under the null hypothesis (H_0) for existence of a unit root.

The test results for the time series analysis are presented in Table 4.

Table 4. ADF test

Time Series	t-Statistic	Probability*
Gross Investments (GCF)	-2.79	0.0648
Final consumption expenditure of households and NPISH (FCE)	-0.18	0.9351

* Mac Kinnon (1996) one-sided p-values

Based on the results of Table 4, the hypothesis for the existence of unit root can not be rejected at a significance level of 5%, neither in the case of household consumption nor investments.

To address this problem, the filter Hodrick - Prescott was implemented to both time series in order to achieve a distinction between the trend and the cyclical part. This methodology has been applied by Leventides and Kollias (2014), under the optimal control of cyclical GDP through government spending, and by Stock and Watson (1986), Campbell and Mankiw (1987), Blanchard et al (1989), Malliaris and Urrutia (2005) who concluded that GDP follows a random walk with trend.

Therefore, by breaking the given time series into the cyclical part and the trend, we receive the following graphs (Figure 1).

It is observed that in Germany, the per capita consumption of households over time shows an incremental trend with relatively low volatility. On the other hand, gross investments do not clearly show a trend but present high volatility before 2002 and after 2007.

Table 5 shows the results of the application of ARMA model on the cyclical part of the macro-variables under examination. It is noted that for the selection of the most appropriate model, the AIC and the adjusted R^2 criteria were taken into account.

Regarding the cyclical part of the per capita consumption expenditure the following can be concluded:

Figure 1. HP filter on per capita consumption and investment

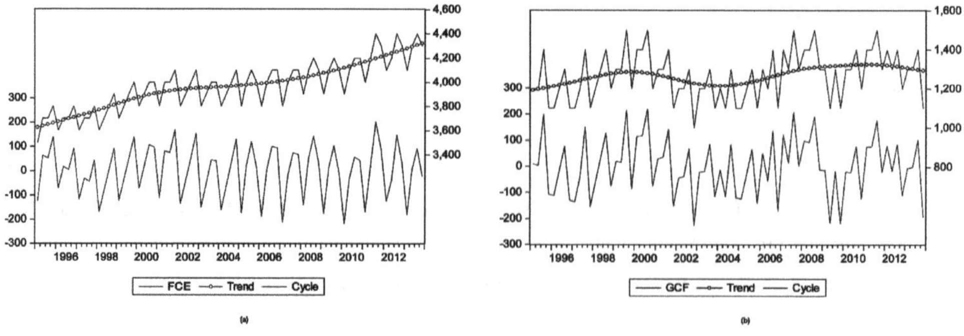

Table 5. Modelling of the circular part of the time series (with all lags)

Circular Part of Consumption Expenditure of Households and NPISH (FCEC)		Circular Part of Gross Investments (GCFC)	
Independent Variables	**Coefficients (p-Value)**	**Independent Variables**	**Coefficients (p-Value)**
C	-6.89 (0.63)	C	-8.07 (0.70)
FCEC(-1)	-0.38 (0.07)	GCFC (-1)	-0.35 (0.06)
FCEC(-2)	-0.41 (0.05)	GCFC (-2)	-0.30 (0.11)
FCEC(-3)	-0.36 (0.10)	GCFC (-3)	-0.33 (0.06)
FCEC(-4)	0.63 (0.00)	GCFC (-4)	0.64 (0.00)
MA(1)	0.75 (0.00)	MA(1)	0.82 (0.00)
MA(2)	0.74 (0.00)	MA(2)	0.75 (0.01)
MA(3)	0.76 (0.00)	MA(3)	0.68 (0.01)
MA(4)	-0.18 (0.45)	MA(4)	-0.25 (0.31)

Sequentially variables with the highest p – value are omitted.

Table 6. Modelling of the circular part of the time series (statistically significant terms)

Circular Part of Consumption Expenditure of Households and NPISH (FCEC)		Circular Part of Gross Investments (GCFC)	
Coefficients (p-Value)	**Independent Variables**	**Coefficients (p-Value)**	**Independent Variables**
C	-8.24 (0.63)	C	-13.06 (0.58)
FCEC(-1)	-0.53 (0.00)	GCFC (-1)	-0.40 (0.00)
FCEC(-2)	-0.55 (0.00)	GCFC (-2)	-0.34 (0.00)
FCEC(-3)	-0.51 (0.00)	GCFC (-3)	-0.35 (0.00)
FCEC(-4)	0.48 (0.00)	GCFC (-4)	0.62 (0.00)
MA(1)	0.94 (0.00)	MA(1)	0.96 (0.00)
MA(2)	0.92 (0.00)	MA(2)	0.92 (0.00)
MA(3)	0.94 (0.00)	MA(3)	0.96 (0.00
R^2_{adj} = 0.86, AIC = 10.24, Breusch-Godfrey LM test (4 lags – prob) = 0.66		R^2_{adj} = 0.72, AIC = 11.06, Breusch-Godfrey LM test (4 lags - prob) = 0.18	

- Current consumption (cyclical component) is positively associated with consumer spending a year ago (four quarters) and negatively with the consumption of previous quarters.
- The inclusion of the MA terms allows saying that changes in consumer spending are partly due to stochastic - behavioural factors. Alternatively, the

shocks in consumption are embodied in consumer behavior within a nine month period.

- Consumer spending is not affected by the recession years of 2008-2009 and/ or the Eurozone debt crisis, which mainly appears in the years 2011-2012. This finding is shown in Figure 1a where there is not any downward trend.

Regarding the per capita gross investment, the Chow test is applied for the period after the first quarter of 2008. We find that in the fourth quarter of 2008 there is a breakpoint in our model.

Then, another model for the period 1995Q1 - 2008Q4 is developed, which is presented in Table 7. It is mentioned that the specification of a model for the period after crisis is not possible, due to the limited number of observations (18).

Taking the above into consideration regarding the expenditure for gross investments, it is worth mentioning the following:

Box 1. Results of chow test 2008Q4

F-statistic	2.845321	Prob. F(5,62)	0.0224
Log likelihood ratio	14.87349	Prob. Chi-Square(5)	0.0109
Wald Statistic	14.22661	Prob. Chi-Square(5)	0.0142

*For the Chow test, the moving average (MA) terms are disregarded.

Table 7. Modelling the gross investment for the period 1995Q1 - 2008Q4

Circular Part of Gross Investments (GCFC) – Total Number of Variables		**Circular Part of Net Investments (GCFC) – Statistically Significant Variables**	
Independent Variables	**Coefficients (p-Value)**	**Independent Variables**	**Coefficients (p-Value)**
C	10.48 (0.50)	C	8.19 (0.57)
GCFC (-1)	-0.08 (0.37)	GCFC (-1)	-0.04 (0.02)
GCFC (-2)	-0.03 (0.79)	GCFC (-4)	0.95 (0.00)
GCFC (-3)	-0.05 (0.61)	MA(1)	0.36 (0.02)
GCFC (-4)	0.93 (0.00)	MA(2)	0.55 (0.00)
MA(1)	0.44 (0.02)	MA(3)	-0.43 (0.00)
MA(2)	0.52 (0.00)		
MA(3)	0.57 (0.01)		
MA(4)	-0.44 (0.03)		
		R^2_{adj} = 0.77, AIC = 10.92, Breusch-Godfrey LM test (4 lags - prob) = 0.19	

- The recession period 2008-2009, led to the change of the planning horizon for investments, which became more short term. Specifically, before the outbreak of the crisis, current investments depended mainly on the amount of investment a year earlier.
- The fourth quarter of 2008, can be also considered as the time when the financial crisis expanded on the real economy of Germany, as it is witnessed by the influence on the structure of per capita investments.
- It can be also seen that the integration of shocks is performed less efficiently under normal market conditions, which is shown by the lower coefficients of the moving average terms.

Denmark - Spain

In the case of Denmark and Spain, we apply the same methodology adopted for the examination of consumption and investment in Germany. The results of this analysis are shown briefly focusing on the inferences in respect to each country but also in comparison with each other. Firstly, Table 8 presents the results of Dickey – Fuller test.

Figure 2 shows the results of the Hodrick - Prescott filter application in time series of per capita consumption and investment in the cases of Denmark and Spain respectively.

From Figures 2 and 3 we can see that the per capita consumption expenditure in Denmark has a slight upward trend from 1995 to 2002, with a strongest upward trend from 2002 to the second quarter of 2008 when it began to decline.

Also, the per capita investment has increased significantly from the beginning of the examined period until the third quarter of 2006 when it began to decline gradually, with a clear downward trend to be observed since the second quarter of 2007. Substantial stabilization of investment spending can be seen since the late 2012.

Regarding Spain, both gross investment and consumption show initially a rising trend followed by a decline which is more evident in the time series of investment. However, it is worth noting that the beginning of decline in the per capita investment is found in the fourth quarter of 2006, while the decline in per capita consumption

Table 8. ADF test

Time Series	Denmark		Spain	
	t-Statistic	Probability*	t-Statistic	Probability*
Gross investment (GCF)	-1.91	0.32	-1.39	0.58
Final consumption expenditure of households and NPISH (FCE)	-1.48	0.54	-2.11	0.24

* Mac Kinnon (1996) one-sided p-values

Figure 2. Implementation of the HP filter on macro-variables of Denmark

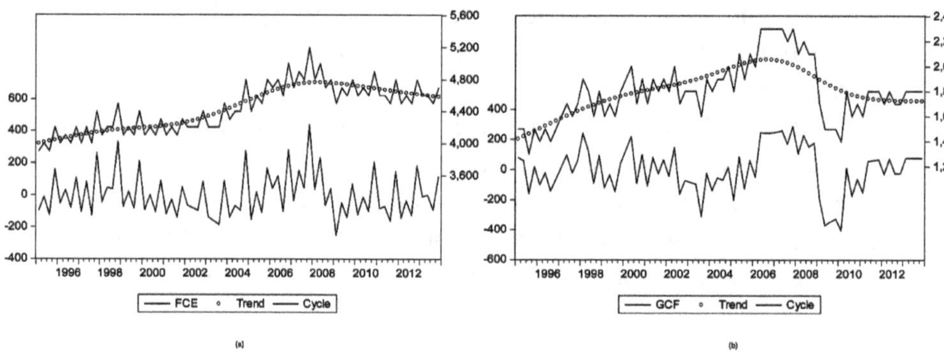

Figure 3. Implementation of the HP filter on macro-variables of Spain

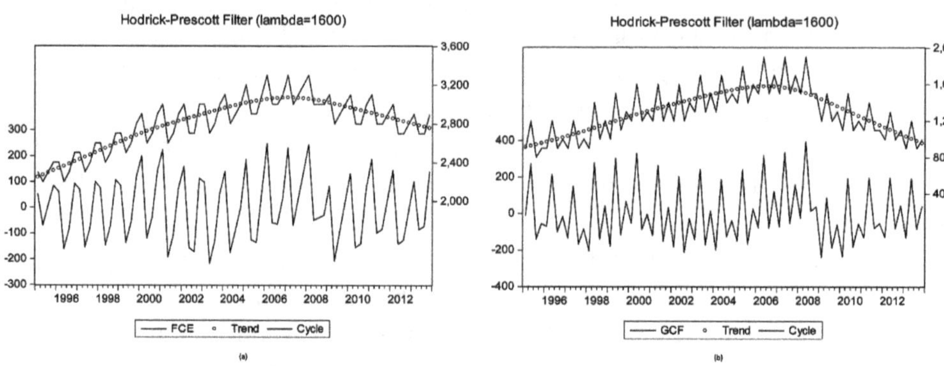

begins three 3 monthly later. Therefore, the reduction of the two most important components of the Spanish GDP is visible long before the beginning of recession of years 2008-2009.

It is worth noting that while the theory suggests that a fall in consumption leads to an increase in investment through the mechanism of savings, this does not seem to apply to Spain, where both variables are reduced simultaneously. This may be explained by an increasing capital outflow toward other economies.

Table 9 shows the ARMA results for the cyclical part of the per capita consumption expenditure of households and NPISH for Denmark and Spain.

The current consumption of households in Denmark (the cyclical part) is mainly affected by the consumption of the previous year and by shocks which observed by three quarters ago.

In the case of Spain, the constructed ARMA model contributes to the interpretation of approximately 87% of the variance of the cyclical component of consumption.

Table 9. Modelling cyclicality of consumption

Denmark		Spain	
Variables	**Coefficients (p-Value)**	**Variables**	**Coefficients (p-Value)**
C	-4,58 (0,86)	C	3,03 (0.87)
FCEC(-1)	-0.27 (0.08)	FCEC(-1)	-0.41 (0.05)
FCEC(-2)	-0.27 (0.07)	FCEC(-2)	-0.42 (0.05)
FCEC(-3)	0.27 (0.07)	FCEC(-3)	-0.43 (0.04)
FCEC(-4)	0.71 (0.00)	FCEC(-4)	0.57 (0.01)
MA(1)	0.68 (0.00)	MA(1)	0.84 (0.00)
MA(2)	0.80 (0.00)	MA(2)	0.94 (0.00)
MA(3)	0.64 (0.00)	MA(3)	0.76 (0.00)
MA(4)	-0.17 (0.39)	MA(4)	-0.05 (0.81)

Table 10. Modelling cyclicality of consumption - statistically significant terms

Denmark		Spain	
Variables	**Coefficients (p-Value)**	**Variables**	**Coefficients (p-Value)**
C	-7,26 (0,82)	C	3.26 (0.87)
FCEC(-1)	-0,36 (0,00)	FCEC(-1)	-0.45 (0.00)
FCEC(-2)	-0,37 (0,00)	FCEC(-2)	-0.47 (0.00)
FCEC(-3)	-0,37 (0,00)	FCEC(-3)	-0.47 (0.00)
FCEC(-4)	0,62 (0,00)	FCEC(-4)	0.52 (0.00)
MA(1)	0,79 (0,00)	MA(1)	0.90 (0.00)
MA(2)	0,96 (0,00)	MA(2)	0.99 (0.00)
MA(3)	0,79 (0,00)	MA(3)	0.82 (0.00)
Statistical Tests			
R^2_{adj}	0,71		0.87
AIC	11,56		10.61
Breusch-Godfrey test (autocorrelation)	0,85		0.71

More specifically, the respective current consumption expenditure seems to depend heavily on consumer behavior in the previous year and on “white noise” with three lags.

Applying the Chow test for the case of Denmark, we find a break in the structure of the model in the first quarter of 2008, where consumption has experienced a large decline. On the other hand, the Chow test identifies a break model in the fourth quarter of 2008, based on the model of Spain. The test results are given in Table 11.

Table 12 presents the best modeling for the circularity of consumption before the great shock of 2008.

We observe that by 2008, the moving average terms (MA) do not contribute significantly to the explanatory power of the model which means that consumer spending did not show great sensitivity to macroeconomic shocks. A significant dependence exists in relation to the consumption of the previous year.

Considering then the per capita gross investment we observe that the application of the filter Hodrick - Prescott does not contribute to the removal of unit root in the case of Denmark. Therefore, the first differences were calculated and the new time

Table 11. Results of Chow test

Denmark - 2008Q1			
F-statistic	2.77	Prob. F(5,62)	0.02
Log likelihood ratio	14.53	Prob. Chi-Square(5)	0.01
Wald Statistic	13.87	Prob. Chi-Square(5)	0.02
Spain – 2008Q4			
F-statistic	2.29	Prob. F(5,62)	0.05
Log likelihood ratio	12.18	Prob. Chi-Square(5)	0.03
Wald Statistic	11.43	Prob. Chi-Square(5)	0.04

Table 12. Modelling cyclical part of consumption for the period 1995Q1 - 2007Q4 and 1995Q1 - 2008Q3 respectively

Denmark		Spain	
Variables	**Coefficients (p-Value)**	**Variables**	**Coefficients (p-Value)**
C	17.32 (0.36)	C	7,20 (0,51)
FCEC(-1)	-0.02 (0.85)	FCEC(-1)	-0,09 (0,49)
FCEC(-2)	-0.03 (0.78)	FCEC(-2)	-0,06 (0,60)
FCEC(-3)	-0.04 (0.72)	FCEC(-3)	-0,12 (0,28)
FCEC(-4)	0.99 (0.00)	FCEC(-4)	0,93 (0,00)
MA(1)	0.31 (0.12)	MA(1)	0,43 (0,06)
MA(2)	0.48 (0.01)	MA(2)	0,44 (0,05)
MA(3)	0.34 (0.06)	MA(3)	0,36 (0,07)
MA(4)	-0.42 (0.03)	MA(4)	-0,55 (0,01)

Table 13. Modelling circularity of consumption in period 1995Q1 - 2007Q4 (statistically significant terms)

Denmark		Spain	
Variables	**Coefficients (p-Value)**	**Variables**	**Coefficients (p-Value)**
C	8.64 (0.50)	C	5.53 (0.35)
FCEC(-4)	0.99 (0.00)	FCEC(-4)	1.00 (0.00)
MA(2)	0.59 (0.00)	MA(1)	0.33 (0.01)
MA(4)	-0.43 (0.01)	MA(4)	-0.51 (0.00)
Statistical Tests			
R^2_{adj}	0.76		0.86
AIC	11.49		10.68
Breusch-Godfrey test (autocorellation)	0.19		0.12

series gfcp was set up. Note that in this case, modeling with the ARMA model did not obtain particularly good results as it is shown in Table 14. On the other hand, in the case of Spain, the application of the ARMA model obtained more robust results.

The terms with the highest p-value are removed successively until statistically significant coefficients occur (backward elimination process).

Both in the case of Denmark and in the case of Spain, the current investment is significantly dependent to its value or the percentage change of its value (in the case of Denmark) on the previous year. However, the changes in investment in Denmark

Table 14. Modeling of per capita gross investment

Denmark		Spain	
Variables	**Coefficients (p-Value)**	**Variables**	**Coefficients (p-Value)**
C	0,01 (0,73)	C	3.85 (0.84)
GCFP(-1)	-0,24 (0,80)	GCFC(-1)	-0.23 (0.05)
GCFP(-2)	-0,13 (0,89)	GCFC(-2)	-0.23 (0.05)
GCFP(-3)	-0,37 (0,60)	GCFC(-3)	-0.24 (0.04)
GCFP(-4)	0,49 (0,52)	GCFC(-4)	0.76 (0.00)
MA(1)	-0,05 (0,96)	MA(1)	0.65 (0.00)
MA(2)	0,23 (0,69)	MA(2)	0.91 (0.00)
MA(3)	0,56 (0,37)	MA(3)	0.67 (0.00)
MA (4)	-0,65 (0,48)	MA (4)	-0.04 (0.82)

Table 15. Modeling of per capita gross investment: Statistically significant terms

Denmark		Spain	
Variables	**Coefficients (p-Value)**	**Variables**	**Coefficients (p-Value)**
C	0.01 (0.58)	C	4.15 (0.83)
GCFP(-3)	-0.37 (0.00)	GCFC(-1)	-0.24 (0.01)
GCFP(-4)	0.59 (0.00)	GCFC(-2)	-0.24 (0.01)
MA(2)	0.20 (0.00)	GCFC(-3)	-0.26 (0.00)
MA(3)	0.56 (0.00)	GCFC(-4)	0.74 (0.00)
MA (4)	-0.57 (0.00)	MA(1)	0.67 (0.00)
		MA(2)	0.94 (0.00)
		MA(3)	0.69 (0.00)
R^2_{adj} = 0.42, AIC = -2,44, Breusch-Godfrey LM test (4 lags - prob) = 0,22		R^2_{adj} = 0.91, AIC = 10.79, Breusch-Godfrey LM test (4 lags - prob) = 0,61	

appear to be due to factors that are not included in the ARMA model, a conclusion which comes up from the low R^2. On the other hand, 91% of the variance in gross investments (cyclical part) of Spain is explained by the value of the previous year and shocks that have been observed in the economy over the last three quarters.

Applying the Chow test for dates close to the time when the global crisis erupted, it is found that there is a "break" in the model of Denmark during the third quarter of 2008, while in Spain it takes place in the fourth quarter of 2008, as shown by the relevant Table 16.

Re-examining the two models to the aforementioned periods (2008Q3 and 2008Q4) for Denmark and Spain respectively, we obtain the results shown in Table 17.

The terms with the highest p-value are removed successively until statistically significant coefficients occur (backward elimination process).

Table 16. Results of Chow test

Denmark - 2008Q3			
F-statistic	9.37	Prob. F(5,62)	0.00
Log likelihood ratio	47.51	Prob. Chi-Square(5)	0.00
Wald Statistic	43.94	Prob. Chi-Square(5)	0.00
Spain – 2008Q4			
F-statistic	2.23	Prob. F(5,62)	0.04
Log likelihood ratio	19.95	Prob. Chi-Square(5)	0.01
Wald Statistic	16.94	Prob. Chi-Square(5)	0.03

Table 17. Modeling of per capita gross investment for the periods 1995Q1 - 2008Q3 and 1995Q1 - 2008Q4

Denmark		Spain	
Variables	**Coefficients (p-Value)**	**Variables**	**Coefficients (p-Value)**
C	0.03 (0.38)	C	12,34 (0,48)
GCFP(-1)	-0.60 (0.44)	GCFC(-1)	-0,13 (0,23)
GCFP(-2)	-0.28 (0.70)	GCFC(-2)	-0,12 (0,28)
GCFP(-3)	-0.49 (0.41)	GCFC(-3)	-0,12 (0,28)
GCFP(-4)	0.20 (0.67)	GCFC(-4)	0,87 (0,00)
MA(1)	0.14 (0.86)	MA(1)	0,35 (0,10)
MA(2)	0.02 (0.97)	MA(2)	0,70 (0,00)
MA(3)	0.48 (0.26)	MA(3)	0,54 (0,00)
MA (4)	-0.40 (0.35)	MA (4)	-0,13 (0,53)

Table 18. Modeling of per capita gross investment - statistically significant terms

Denmark		Spain	
Variables	**Coefficients (p-Value)**	**Variables**	**Coefficients (p-Value)**
C	0.02 (0.07)	C	6.85 (0.71)
GCFP(-1)	-0.49 (0.00)	GCFC(-4)	0.98 (0.00)
GCFP(-3)	-0.51 (0.00)	MA(1)	0.32 (0.04)
MA(3)	0.76 (0.00)	MA(2)	0.85 (0.00)
MA (4)	-0.24 (0.02)	MA(3)	0.47 (0.00)
R^2_{adj} = 0.56, AIC = -2.78, Breusch-Godfrey LM test (4 lags - prob) = 0,32		R^2_{adj} = 0.92, AIC = 10.75, Breusch-Godfrey LM test (4 lags - prob) = 0,22	

Regarding Denmark, we observe that the inclusion of shocks into changes of investments was slower before the period of crisis, in contrast with Spain where "white noise" factors with three lags appear. An increase by approximately 0.14 units is observed in the R^2_{adj} of Denmark but again it can be concluded safely that a reliable model can be constructed. Therefore, it becomes clear that under normal market conditions, the use of autoregressive terms and moving average terms do not contribute significantly to the interpretation of changes in gross investment in Denmark. Possibly, changes in gross investment in Denmark are due to other macroeconomic variables such as exchange rates, indices of industrial production, etc. In contrast, in the case of Spain, it is observed that the current investments are linked largely to the investment expenditure of the previous year.

A general conclusion for all the investigated countries after the crisis period is the reduction of the planning horizon and the faster integration of shocks both on consumption and investment expenditures. Moreover, investments usually exhibit high sensitivity to disturbances in the economic system, while household consumption expenditure usually exhibit smoother behavior. Nevertheless, the crisis erupted in 2008, appears to significantly affect private consumption of Denmark and Spain, as it is presented from the graphs of cyclicality and trend. It is also mentioned that the use of ARMA models seems to fit better in the case of the behavior of macroeconomic variables of Spain.

Finally, in Table 16 of the Annex we can see the descriptive statistics for the selected variables for each country.

CAUSALITY BETWEEN MACROECONOMIC VARIABLES AND STOCK MARKET RETURNS

Methodology

As mentioned in the section of the variables selection, at this stage we will take into account the percentage changes of the selected variables. Most of the macroeconomic variables often exhibit a high correlation between them. So, a correlation matrix is constructed in order to reject variables with high correlation between each other, since the highly correlated variables either contribute similarly in the interpretation of the changes of the dependent variable or do not contribute at all. Also, the use of the percentage changes leads to the elimination of unit root and therefore the time series of macro variables become stationary and there is no need for the application of cointegration tests (Johansen, 1988).

At the next step, the Granger (1969) causality test is applied to examine the extent to which the dependent variable (y) is interpreted by previous values and whether the inclusion of a lagged independent variable explains most satisfactorily the observed changes. We perform a model using up to four lags where we consider that Y is Granger caused by X, when X contribute to the prediction of Y or equivalent when the regression coefficients of lags of X are statistically significant.

Specifically, the statistical program performs two regressions of the following form:

$$y_t = a_0 + a_1*y_{t-1} + \dots + a_l*y_{t-l} + b_1*x_{t-1} + \dots + b_l*x_{t-l} + e_t$$

$$x_t = a_0 + a_1*x_{t-1} + \dots + a_l*x_{t-l} + b_1*y_{t-1} + \dots + b_l*x_{t-l} + e_t$$

where

l: the number of lags.

The null hypothesis (H_0) assumes that b1 = b2 = ... = Bt = 0 based on asymptotic approximation of the normal distribution (Wald statistics).

Finally, it is noted that the aim of this study is to build a statistical model, in which the dependent variable is the percentage change of a stock index, and to investigate statistically significant macro-variables which interpret these changes.

Germany

Following the methodology of the previous paragraph, the correlation matrix (Table 4.2.1) is calculated presenting the correlations between the independent variables.

High correlation exists only between the industrial production index and the nominal labor cost. The correlation is negative indicating that the increase in nominal hourly wages has led, during the examined period, a drop-in production due to rising costs. Therefore, the nominal labor cost index (NLC) is rejected from further analysis, since this indicator appear frequently in the literature.

The results of the Granger causality test are presented in the following Table 20. More specifically, the value of F-statistic is given in the column of lags p-value is given in parentheses. When the p-value takes values lower than the significance level of 5%, the null hypothesis is rejected and thus there is interdependence between the examined variables.

Table 19. Correlations

	GOLD	CPI	FCE	GCF	IP	LTR	NLC	NS	OIL	RLP	STR	TOP	UNEM
GOLD	1.00												
CPI	0.08	1.00											
FCE	-0.04	0.04	1.00										
GCF	0.09	-0.08	-0.25	1.00									
IP	0.14	-0.22	0.05	0.44	1.00								
LTR	0.17	0.00	-0.11	0.16	0.25	1.00							
NLC	-0.17	0.19	-0.24	-0.29	-0.70	-0.26	1.00						
NS	-0.03	-0.00	-0.14	0.25	0.45	0.13	-0.39	1.00					
OIL	0.28	0.07	0.08	-0.08	0.21	0.44	-0.24	0.01	1.00				
RLP	0.00	-0.25	0.16	0.13	0.47	0.11	-0.50	-0.10	0.03	1.00			
STR	0.02	-0.07	0.16	0.27	0.52	0.22	-0.34	0.14	-0.01	0.19	1.00		
TOP	0.24	0.06	0.02	0.27	0.22	0.06	-0.18	0.12	0.11	-0.06	0.17	1.00	
UNEM	-0.15	0.16	-0.16	-0.34	-0.38	-0.15	0.07	-0.19	0.00	-0.09	-0.41	-0.27	1.00

Table 20. Granger causality test

Independent Variable	H_0	Lags			
		l = 1	l = 2	l = 3	l = 4
GOLD	GOLD does not Granger cause DAX	0.13 (0.72)	0.16 (0.85)	0,77 (0,52)	0,97 (0,43)
	DAX does not Granger cause GOLD	0.47 (0.50)	0.29 (0.75)	0,21 (0,89)	0,83 (0,51)
CPI	CPI does not Granger cause DAX	1,82 (0,18)	2,58 (0,08)	2,00 (0,12)	1,52 (0,21)
	DAX does not Granger cause CPI	0,80 (0,37)	0,51 (0,60)	0,32 (0,81)	0,73 (0,57)
FCE	FCE does not Granger cause DAX	1,26 (0,27)	0,72 (0,49)	0,58 (0,63)	1,50 (0,21)
	DAX does not Granger cause FCE	1,08 (0,30)	0,84 (0,44)	2,76* (0,05)	2,59* (0,04)
GCF	GCF does not Granger cause DAX	0.71 (0.40)	0.90 (0.41)	1.52 (0.22)	1.14 (0.35)
	DAX does not Granger cause GCF	7.55* (0.01)	4.62* (0.01)	3.66* (0.02)	3.42* (0.01)
IP	IP does not Granger cause DAX	0.04 (0.83)	1.25 (0.29)	0.62 (0.60)	0.56 (0.69)
	DAX does not Granger cause IP	7.36* (0.01)	4.43* (0.02)	3.23* (0.03)	3.24* (0.02)
LTR	LTR does not Granger cause DAX	0.58 (0.45)	1.68 (0.19)	1.20 (0.32)	0.89 (0.48)
	DAX does not Granger cause LTR	1.71 (0.19)	0.48 (0.62)	0.35 (0.79)	0.22 (0.93)
NS	NS does not Granger cause DAX	0.66 (0.42)	0.25 (0.78)	0.39 (0.76)	0.42 (0.80)
	DAX does not Granger cause NS	5.66* (0.02)	5.76* (0.00)	4.14* (0.01)	3.12* (0.02)
OIL	OIL does not Granger cause DAX	1.12 (0.29)	0.76 (0.47)	0.45 (0.72)	0.82 (0.52)
	DAX does not Granger cause OIL	0.72 (0.40)	0.77 (0.47)	0.90 (0.45)	1.28 (0.29)
RLP	RLP does not Granger cause DAX	0.00 (0.98)	0.30 (0.74)	0.22 (0.88)	0.11 (0.98)
	DAX does not Granger cause RLP	4.15* (0.04)	2.54 (0.09)	1.86 (0.14)	1.42 (0.24)
STR	STR does not Granger cause DAX	2.06 (0.16)	1.14 (0.32)	0.64 (0.59)	0.55 (0.70)
	DAX does not Granger cause STR	1.40 (0.24)	4.89* (0.01)	2.77* (0.05)	3.38* (0.01)
TOP	TOP does not Granger cause DAX	0.05 (0.82)	0.15 (0.86)	0.13 (0.94)	0.12 (0.98)
	DAX does not Granger cause TOP	0.01 (0.92)	0.02 (0.98)	0.30 (0.83)	0.31 (0.87)
UNEM	UNEM does not Granger cause DAX	2.06 (0.16)	1.67 (0.20)	1.21 (0.31)	0.99 (0.42)
	DAX does not Granger cause UNEM	4.75* (0.03)	3.26* (0.04)	2.31 (0.08)	1.70 (0.16)

* Existence of causality relations

From Table 20, we can conclude that none of the selected macroeconomic variables has an impact on the changes of the basic German stock index in the level of forecasting. From the other hand, it is observed that in several cases the course of the macroeconomic variables is determined by an upward or downward trend in the stock market. This is the case of private consumption expenditure, gross investments, net savings, the industrial production index, the short-term interest rates and unemployment.

It can therefore be concluded that both households, regarding consumption and saving, and firms concerning investment and production base their decisions on the course of the stock exchange. In short, the stock market may seem to anticipate the future state of the economy at a depth of at least one year in the light of Granger test, since it seems to cause changes in the aforementioned macroeconomic variables.

However, a regression will be applied between changes of index DAX and each independent variable, except the nominal labor cost which shows a high correlation with the index of industrial production, in order to examine whether there is a possibility of making linear prediction model of stock changes.

Table 21, presents the results of the regressions, which were run for four lags of each variable, while Table 22 was based on data of the period 1995-2008, ie before the onset of the crisis. Recall that the German economy during the onset time of crisis is defined in section 3 of this paper.

From Table 21-22, it is noted that increases in the Consumer Price Index (CPI) have a negative impact on DAX returns. On the other hand, there is a positive relationship between changes in gross investment and stock returns. Note also that the abovementioned variables remain statistically significant using data both before and after the crises.

In addition, using data for the period 1995 - 2013, the consumption expenditure (FCE) and the long-term interest rate (LTR) also seems to positively affect the performance of DAX.

Including the significant variables obtained in the two models, we take the following regression outputs:

Period 1995-2013

$$DAX = \underset{(0.14)}{2.45} - \underset{(0.04)}{2.23} * CPI + \underset{(0.02)}{0.38} * LTR + \underset{(0.69)}{1.06} * FCE\left(-4\right) + \underset{(0.10)}{0.60} * GCF\left(-3\right)$$

or removing variables that were not statistically significant.

Table 21. Regression results of the DAX index with macroeconomic variables: Period 1995Q1 – 2013Q4

Independent Variable	Lag = 0	Lag = 1	Lag = 2	Lag = 3	Lag = 4
CPI	-2.42 (0.03)*	1.57 (0.17)	-1.68 (0.14)	-0.47 (0.69)	-0.04 (0.97)
FCE	-1.84 (0.47)	2.92 (0.25)	-0.78 (0.76)	0.94 (0.72)	5.03 (0.05)*
GCF	-0.19 (0.60)	0.32 (0.39)	-0.52 (0.16)	0.80 (0.03)*	-0.46 (0.22)
GOLD	-0.12 (0.58)	-0.07 (0.74)	-0.13 (0.62)	-0.37 (0.15)	-0.36 (0.17)
IP	0.97 (0.14)	0.10 (0.88)	-0.86 (0.20)	-0.51 (0.45)	-0.28 (0.67)
LTR	0.42 (0.01)*	-0.15 (0.41)	-0.26 (0.18)	-0.26 (0.18)	-0.03 (0.89)
NS	0.08 (0.42)	0.08 (0.43)	-0.04 (0.68)	-0.08 (0.45)	0.05 (0.62)
OIL	0.02 (0.81)	0.10 (0.29)	-0.07 (0.47)	0.02 (0.85)	-0.14 (0.13)
RLP	1.65 (0.34)	-0.01 (0.99)	-1.00 (0.57)	1.08 (0.54)	-0.40 (0.83)
STR	-0.01 (0.96)	-0.14 (0.15)	-0.10 (0.29)	-0.11 (0.26)	-0.07 (0.50)
TOP	0.83 (0.13)	0.10 (0.86)	-0.20 (0.71)	-0.06 (0.92)	0.23 (0.68)
UNEM	-0.09 (0.86)	0.78 (0.15)	0.94 (0.08)	0.54 (0.34)	0.52 (0.35)

*Marked with an asterisk are the statistically significant coefficients, given the level of significance 5%. In parentheses the p-value of each coefficient is given.

$$DAX = \underset{(0.04)}{3{,}04} - \underset{(0.02)}{2.43} * CPI + \underset{(0.01)}{0.42} * LTR$$

with $R^2_{adj} = 0.12$, DWstat = 2.09, AIC = 7.85, Prob (F-stat) = 0.00

Period 1995-2008

$$DAX = \underset{(0.16)}{2.16} - \underset{(0.04)}{2.32} * CPI + \underset{(0.49)}{0.25} * GCF(-1) + \underset{(0.05)}{0.70} * GCF(-3)$$

Table 22. Results of regression on DAX index with aggregates: Period 1995Q1 - 2008Q4

Independent Variable	Lag = 0	Lag = 1	Lag = 2	Lag = 3	Lag = 4
CPI	-3,29 (0,02)*	1,70 (0,24)	-2,54 (0,08)	0,07 (0,96)	0,46 (0,76)
FCE	0,51 (0,87)	1,67 (0,59)	-0,60 (0,85)	3,02 (0,33)	4,76 (0,13)
GCF	-0,44 (0,35)	0,99 (0,04)*	-0,45 (0,35)	0,96 (0,05)*	0,57 (0,26)
GOLD	-0,26 (0,38)	-0,07 (0,83)	-0,31 (0,31)	-0,28 (0,37)	-0,36 (0,26)
IP	1,04 (0,39)	2,24 (0,17)	-0,92 (0,58)	0,92 (0,60)	-0,58 (0,75)
LTR	0,42 (0,13)	-0,19 (0,53)	0,09 (0,78)	-0,40 (0,21)	-0,32 (0,31)
NS	0,01 (0,92)	0,11 (0,40)	-0,01 (0,98)	0,01 (0,96)	0,06 (0,64)
OIL	-0,06 (0,57)	0,02 (0,88)	-0,04 (0,78)	0,25 (0,08)	-0,27 (0,06)
RLP	1,01 (0,64)	0,82 (0,71)	1,07 (0,63)	0,34 (0,89)	0,14 (0,95)
STR	0,18 (0,37)	-0,16 (0,46)	-0,15 (0,49)	-0,29 (0,18)	-0,08 (0,71)
TOP	0,95 (0,15)	0,07 (0,91)	-0,05 (0,94)	0,18 (0,79)	0,33 (0,63)
UNEM	-0,05 (0,95)	0,49 (0,48)	0,88 (0,22)	0,89 (0,23)	1,17 (0,12)

* Marked with asterisk are the statistically significant coefficients, given the level of significance 5%. In parentheses the p-value of each coefficient is given.

or removing variables that were not statistically significant.

$$DAX = \underset{(0.15)}{2.19} - \underset{(0.04)}{2.31} * CPI + \underset{(0.04)}{0.72} * GCF(-3)$$

with $R^2_{adj} = 0.10$, DWstat = 1,93, AIC = 7.92, Prob (F-stat) = 0.01

The variance of the DAX index explained by the macroeconomic variables is only 12%. The negative relationship between inflation and stock returns has been found in several studies in the past and it is also true in the case of the German capital market. In addition, the long-term interest rate can be observed directly as it is released in subsequent periods as other measurable macro-variables, so it can be used directly to predict future returns.

In conclusion, changes in several key macro-variables interpret in a small extent the changes in the main German stock index therefore it is not possible to construct a reliable model for prediction of stock returns using macro variables. Additionally, there is the risk of endogeneity in the model.

Denmark

For the case of Denmark, the same methodology is adopted as in the case of Germany. Initially, the correlation Table 23 between macroeconomic variables is presented.

High correlation of over 50%, is observed between the nominal labor costs and the real labor productivity and therefore the latter will qualify for further analysis in order to ensure better comparability with Germany.

In the Table 24, the results of the causality Granger test are presented.

In the case of Denmark, we observe stronger interactions between stock returns and changes in macroeconomic variables. The main conclusions are summarized as follows:

- Changes in crude oil prices (OIL), gold (GOLD) and exchange rate (EXCH) do not affect the returns of the stock index.

Table 23. Correlations

	Gold	CPI	EXCH	FCE	GCF	IP	LTR	NLC	NS	OIL	RLP	STR	TOP	UNEM
Gold	1.00													
CPI	-0.04	1.00												
EXCH	-0.05	-0,29	1.00											
FCE	0.16	0,13	0,06	1.00										
GCF	0.16	-0,26	0.20	0.06	1.00									
IP	-0.03	-0,17	-0.02	0.18	0.11	1.00								
LTR	0.10	0,05	0.01	0.10	0.18	0.05	1.00							
NLC	-0.08	0,17	-0.13	-0.19	-0.37	-0.18	-0.06	1.00						
NS	-0.10	-0,28	0.11	-0.14	0.35	0.42	-0.02	-0.37	1.00					
OIL	0.28	-0,04	-0.03	0.23	-0.16	0.07	0.31	-0.17	0.00	1.00				
RLP	0.11	-0,11	0.22	0.19	0.25	0.39	0.00	-0.53	0.37	0.16	1.00			
STR	-0.01	0,10	-0.13	0.12	0.23	0.16	0.36	0.06	0.01	-0.10	-0.06	1.00		
TOP	0.05	0,01	0.18	0.42	0.11	0.18	-0.11	-0.20	0.11	0.14	0.35	-0.04	1.00	
UNEM	-0.15	0,2	0.17	0.09	-0.13	-0.11	-0.14	0.05	-0.20	0.00	0.00	-0.35	-0.05	1.00

Table 24. Results of the Granger causality test

Independent Variable	H_0	Lags			
		l = 1	L = 2	l = 3	l = 4
GOLD	GOLD does not Granger cause OMX	0.90 (0.35)	0.42 (0.65)	1.76 (0.16)	1.36 (0.26)
	OMX does not Granger cause GOLD	0.05 (0.82)	0.21 (0.81)	0.14 (0.93)	0.58 (0.68)
CPI	CPI does not Granger cause OMX	1.35 (0.25)	2.95 (0.06)	2.39 (0.08)	2.43 (0.06)
	OMX does not Granger cause CPI	11.07* (0.00)	5.17* (0.01)	4.22* (0.01)	2.99* (0.03)
FCE	FCE does not Granger cause OMX	0.48 (0.49)	0.76 (0.47)	0.77 (0.52)	0.64 (0.64)
	OMX does not Granger cause FCE	6.48* (0.01)	3.47* (0.04)	3.90* (0.01)	2.81* (0.03)
GCF	GCF does not Granger cause OMX	0.99 (0.32)	2.04 (0.14)	1.29 (0.29)	1.97 (0.11)
	OMX does not Granger cause GCF	8.76* (0.00)	6.35* (0.00)	4.82* (0.00)	4.53* (0.00)
IP	IP does not Granger cause OMX	0.49 (0.49)	0.52 (0.60)	0.45 (0.72)	0.73 (0.57)
	OMX does not Granger cause IP	10.15* (0.00)	8.62* (0.00)	6.99* (0.00)	5.17* (0.00)
LTR	LTR does not Granger cause OMX	6.73* (0.01)	3.17 (0.05)	2.01 (0.12)	1.61 (0.18)
	OMX does not Granger cause LTR	0.46 (0.50)	0.18 (0.84)	0.16 (0.92)	0.16 (0.96)
NS	NS does not Granger cause OMX	0.29 (0.59)	0.28 (0.75)	0.23 (0.87)	0.12 (0.97)
	OMX does not Granger cause NS	5.75* (0.02)	6.01* (0.00)	4.16* (0.01)	4.50* (0.00)
OIL	OIL does not Granger cause OMX	1.26 (0.27)	2.14 (0.12)	1.45 (0.24)	1.34 (0.26)
	OMX does not Granger cause OIL	0.02 (0.89)	0.88 (0.42)	0.63 (0.60)	0.92 (0.45)
RLP	RLP does not Granger cause OMX	7.61* (0.01)	4.68* (0.01)	3.99* (0.01)	3.62* (0.01)
	OMX does not Granger cause RLP	8.43 (0.00)	6.32 (0.00)	4.15 (0.01)	3.56 (0.01)
STR	STR does not Granger cause OMX	4.18* (0.04)	2.01 (0.14)	1.85 (0.15)	1.70 (0.16)
	OMX does not Granger cause STR	3.35 (0.07)	4.46* (0.01)	3.70* (0.02)	3.29* (0.02)

continued on following page

Table 24. Continued

Independent Variable	H_0	Lags			
		l = 1	L = 2	l = 3	l = 4
TOP	TOP does not Granger cause OMX	0.71 (0.40)	3.93* (0.02)	2.64 (0.06)	2.07 (0.10)
	OMX does not Granger cause TOP	2.54 (0.12)	2.53 (0.09)	4.02* (0.01)	3.12* (0.02)
UNEM	UNEM does not Granger cause OMX	5.37* (0.02)	2.57 (0.08)	2.17 (0.10)	1.49 (0.22)
	OMX does not Granger cause UNEM	18.54* (0.00)	9.24* (0.00)	6.02* (0.00)	4.27* (0.00)
EXCH	EXCH does not Granger cause OMX	0.29 (0.59)	0.27 (0.76)	0.30 (0.82)	0.36 (0.84)
	OMX does not Granger cause EXCH	3.31 (0.07)	0.79 (0.46)	0.50 (0.68)	0.48 (0.75)

*Causality relations

- The CPI, which represents the inflation level, the final consumption expenditure (FCE), the gross capital formation (GCF), the industrial production (IP) and the net savings (NS) depend upon the changes in capital market and they follow them with some lag.
- In the case of real labor productivity (RLP), we observe statistically significant interactions by the side of the stock exchange index, and vice versa.
- Regarding the short-term rate (STR) and taxes on production (TOP), it is found that the stock returns initially affect the changes in taxation and interest rates, but an inverse behavior is observed in the following period.
- Unemployment (UNEM) is influenced by past stock yields, but it also has an impact on capital returns. This conclusion is particularly important in crisis periods, such as the depression of 2008-09, given that capital losses were prior to the recession in the real economy. However, the subsequent disclosure of negative announcements regarding macroeconomic indicators such as unemployment, again lead to losses in stock markets.

Table 25 shows the results of the regression between percentage changes in the IMEX and the selected macroeconomic variables.

Observing Table 25, which takes into account the period from 1995 to 2013, we find a positive relationship of stock changes with the current consumption expenditure (FCE), the actual labor productivity (RLP) with one lag, taxes on production (TOP) with one lag and unemployment. Before the onset of the crisis, the stock returns

Table 25. Results of regression of index IMEX with macro-variables: Period 1995Q1 - 2013Q4

Independent Variables	Lag = 0	Lag = 1	Lag = 2	Lag = 3	Lag = 4
CPI	-2,30 (0,01)*	0,55 (0,57)	-1,58 (0,10)	-1,45 (0,14)	1,12 (0,26)
EXCH	8.93 (0.02)	3.94 (0.33)	-0.10 (0.98)	3.65 (0.37)	0.59 (0.89)
FCE	2.00 (0.04)*	1.08 (0.27)	-0.89 (0.37)	-0.63 (0.53)	-0.44 (0.66)
GCF	0.08 (0.71)	-0.20 (0.36)	0.37 (0.09)	-0.02 (0.94)	-0.41 (0.06)
GOLD	-0.03 (0.85)	-0.18 (0.32)	-0.02 (0.91)	-0.44 (0.03)*	-0.27 (0.19)
IP	-0.23 (0.54)	0.20 (0.58)	-0.24 (0.51)	-0.03 (0.94)	-0.31 (0.42)
LTR	0.17 (0.15)	-0.28 (0.03)*	-0.15 (0.24)	0.01 (0.96)	0.14 (0.38)
NS	-0.02 (0.64)	0.02 (0.67)	-0.01 (0.84)	-0.02 (0.58)	-0.01 (0.79)
OIL	0.15 (0.04)	0.11 (0.14)	-0.10 (0.18)	-0.03 (0.67)	0.04 (0.63)
RLP	-0.44 (0.47)	1.49 (0.01)*	-0.54 (0.38)	0.61 (0.33)	-0.18 (0.77)
STR	-0.10 (0.24)	-0.20 (0.03)*	-0.13 (0.14)	-0.03 (0.71)	-0.12 (0.19)
TOP	1.06 (0.01)*	0.59 (0.19)	-1.05 (0.02)*	0.08 (0.87)	0.30 (0.53)
UNEM	0.43 (0.32)	1.04 (0.02)*	0.94 (0.03)*	0.64 (0.14)	0.49 (0.27)

were positively related with the exchange rate, industrial production and labor productivity with one lag.

Therefore, considering the recession it is concluded that consumption, as a component of active demand, plays an important role during the downward phase of the economic cycle, and does not play an important role in periods characterized by normal market conditions. The opposite occurs with changes in industrial production, which is statistically significant only before the onset of the recent crisis. Labor productivity remains statistically significant in all periods.

On the other hand, the yields of OMX index are negatively associated with CPI, changes in the price of gold and taxation with three lags, the long and the short

Table 26. Results of regression index IMEX with aggregates: Period 1995Q1 - 2008Q3

Independent Variable	Lag = 0	Lag = 1	Lag = 2	Lag = 3	Lag = 4
CPI	-2.41 (0.02)*	0.02 (0.99)	-2.26 (0.03)*	-1.07 (0.32)	1.53 (0.16)
EXCH	7.55 (0.04)*	4.88 (0.19)	0.96 (0.80)	4.22 (0.27)	0.65 (0.86)
FCE	0.51 (0.62)	0.26 (0.81)	-0.41 (0.70)	0.19 (0.86)	0.68 (0.54)
GCF	0.23 (0.35)	0.09 (0.72)	0.39 (0.11)	0.10 (0.69)	-0.34 (0.17)
GOLD	-0.25 (0.23)	-0.36 (0.09)	-0.20 (0.35)	-0.16 (0.47)	-0.16 (0.49)
IP	-0.48 (0.20)	0.76 (0.04)*	-0.23 (0.54)	0.06 (0.87)	-0.06 (0.89)
LTR	0.05 (0.81)	-0.22 (0.29)	0.17 (0.44)	-0.02 (0.93)	-0.14 (0.53)
NS	-0.03 (0.54)	0.04 (0.48)	0.03 (0.61)	-0.02 (0.66)	0.02 (0.73)
OIL	-0.07 (0.43)	0.02 (0.83)	0.07 (0.49)	0.15 (0.13)	-0.01 (0.95)
RLP	-0.82 (0.16)	1.38 (0.02)*	-0.42 (0.48)	0.76 (0.21)	-0.14 (0.82)
STR	0.11 (0.42)	-0.06 (0.68)	-0.14 (0.31)	-0.11 (0.41)	-0.25 (0.07)
TOP	0.94 (0.07)	0.72 (0.19)	-1.09 (0.05)*	0.79 (0.16)	0.55 (0.34)
UNEM	0.35 (0.46)	0.55 (0.26)	0.79 (0.12)	0.82 (0.12)	0.75 (0.16)

interest rate with one lag. During 1995 - 2008, gold and interest rates are no longer statistically significant.

Then we carry out a regression including all statistically significant variables.

Period 1995-2013

$$OMC = \underset{(0.08)}{2.21} - \underset{(0.01)}{2.33} * CPI + \underset{(0.00)}{2.85} * FCE - \underset{(0.49)}{0.08} * LTR(-1) + \underset{(0.00)}{1.77} * RLP(-1) - \underset{(0.23)}{0.11} *$$

$$STR(-1) - \underset{(0.18)}{0.89} * UNEM(-1) + \underset{(0.44)}{0.54} * UNEM(-2) - \underset{(0.06)}{0.34} * GOLD(-3)$$

Omitting each time, the no statistically significant variables according to the highest p-value, we obtain the following model.

$$OMX = \underset{(0.07)}{2.17} - \underset{(0.01)}{2.37} * CPI + \underset{(0.00)}{2.88} * FCE + \underset{(0.00)}{1.67} * RLP(-1)$$
$$- \underset{(0.05)}{0.15} * STR(-1) - \underset{(0.02)}{0.41} * GOLD(-3)$$

με $R^2_{adj} = 0.33$, DWstat = 1.84, AIC = 7.22, Prob (F-stat) = 0.00

Similarly, for the period before the economic crisis we have:

Period 1995 - 2008

$$OMX = \underset{(0.03)}{3.19} - \underset{(0.04)}{2.06} * CPI + \underset{(0.08)}{6.92} * EXCH + \underset{(0.40)}{0.32} * IP(-1)$$
$$+ \underset{(0.18)}{0.79} * RLP(-1) - \underset{(0.35)}{0.47} * TOP(-2) - \underset{(0.19)}{1.27} * CPI(-2)$$

or omitting variables that were not statistically significant.

$$OMX = \underset{(0.06)}{2.25} - \underset{(0.05)}{1.88} * CPI + \underset{(0.02)}{9.28} * EXCH + \underset{(0.03)}{1.18} * RLP(-1)$$

with $R^2_{adj} = 0.24$, DWstat = 1,73, AIC = 7.11, Prob (F-stat) = 0.00

From the above regression outputs, there is a noticeable negative relationship between stock returns and the CPI, given that high inflation reduces the real returns, while there is positive dependence with changes in labor productivity. Also, during the crisis, equity returns appear to incorporate changes in the consumer spending, in the short-term interest rate and in the price of gold. It is noted that in times of recession the preservation of consumption at high levels contributes to the non-collapse of GDP. Also, in recession periods, many investors turn to buying gold as a reserve value and monitor closely changes in interest rates since these changes reflect the level of market risk.

It is mentioned though that in the case of Denmark, as in Germany, we can not construct a reliable model for the stock market interpretation, since only 24% of the total variance of stock indices can be explained.

Spain

In Table 27 we can see the correlations between the percentage changes in key macroeconomic variables using data from Spain. Due to lack of data, the nominal labor costs (NLC), the net savings (NS) and the actual labor productivity (RLP) are not included in the tested macroeconomic variables.

There is a strong negative correlation between unemployment and industrial production and investment. This relationship shows that employment in Spain is very sensitive to economic cycles, which result in a significant decline in output and investment. This may be due to the "loose" institutional framework which governs the employment and the lack of protective measures during recessions (Garbelini et al, 2014). In addition, there is over 50% correlation between industrial production and gross investment. Therefore, in the following part of our analysis we can concentrate only on the changes in industrial production.

In the case of Spain, three variables - the consumption expenditure of households (FCE), the index of industrial production (IP) and the taxation on production and imports (TOP) - seem to develop interactions with the returns of the IBEX stock index, while it is the only one among the investigated countries in this paper where there is no evidence of interactions with inflation (CPI). Specifically, changes in consumer spending and industrial production index appear to proceed, displaying a larger lag of the capital market index, while the opposite happens in the case of taxation.

Then, in Table 29, we present the regression results between IBEX and the examined macroeconomic fundamentals of Spain and other variables (e.g. gold,

Table 27. Correlations

	GOLD	CPI	FCE	GCF	IP	LTR	OIL	STR	TOP	UNEM
GOLD	1.00									
CPI	0.02	1.00								
FCE	-0.02	0.21	1.00							
GCF	0.06	0.05	0.29	1.00						
IP	0.10	-0.06	0.49	0.58	1.00					
LTR	0.31	-0.03	0.03	-0.06	0.06	1.00				
OIL	0.28	0.03	0.07	0.05	0.20	0.30	1.00			
STR	0.10	0.09	0.24	0.30	0.30	0.25	0.05	1.00		
TOP	-0.04	-0.17	0.39	0.06	0.18	-0.06	-0.01	0.04	1.00	
UNEM	0.13	-0.04	-0.51	-0.65	-0.74	0.12	-0.13	-0.30	-0.14	1.00

Table 28. Results of Granger testing

Independent Variable	H_0	Lags			
		l = 1	l = 2	l = 3	l = 4
CPI	CPI does not Granger cause IBEX	0,73 (0,40)	0,91 (0,41)	0,97 (0,41)	0,80 (0,53)
	IBEX does not Granger cause CPI	2,21 (0,14)	2,01 (0,14)	2,42 (0,07)	2,02 (0,10)
GOLD	GOLD does not Granger cause IBEX	0.60 (0.49)	1.58 (0.21)	1.27 (0.29)	1.53 (0.20)
	IBEX does not Granger cause GOLD	0.03 (0.86)	0.57 (0.57)	0.41 (0.75)	0.29 (0.88)
FCE	FCE does not Granger cause IBEX	0,66 (0,42)	2,23 (0,12)	5,62* (0,00)	4,03* (0,01)
	IBEX does not Granger cause FCE	0,70 (0,40)	3,48* (0,04)	3,04* (0,04)	2,90* (0,03)
IP	IP does not Granger cause IBEX	3,72 (0,06)	3,17* (0,05)	3,41* (0,02)	2,89* (0,03)
	IBEX does not Granger cause IP	6,84* (0,01)	3,54* (0,03)	2,71* (0,05)	1,92 (0,12)
LTR	LTR does not Granger cause IBEX	0,58 (0,45)	1,01 (0,37)	2,17 (0,10)	1,58 (0,19)
	IBEX does not Granger cause LTR	0,11 (0,74)	0,14 (0,87)	0,21 (0,89)	0,33 (0,86)
OIL	OIL does not Granger cause IBEX	0,93 (0,34)	0,72 (0,49)	0,80 (0,50)	2,12 (0,09)
	IBEX does not Granger cause OIL	0,92 (0,34)	0,75 (0,48)	0,45 (0,72)	0,77 (0,55)
STR	STR does not Granger cause IBEX	1,93 (0,17)	1,03 (0,36)	1,11 (0,35)	1,26 (0,30)
	IBEX does not Granger cause STR	1,69 (0,20)	3,16 (0,05)	2,00 (0,12)	1,71 (0,16)
TOP	TOP does not Granger cause IBEX	1,25 (0,27)	3,84* (0,03)	2,22 (0,09)	1,66 (0,17)
	IBEX does not Granger cause TOP	2,30 (0,13)	4,37* (0,02)	3,50* (0,02)	2,52* (0,05)

* Existence of causal relations

oil, etc.) that affect the global economy. In this part, variables rejected due to high correlation are not taken into account.

In the case of Spain, the CPI does not seem to be negatively associated with the performance of the IBEX index as observed in Denmark and Germany. Positive dependencies are evident with the index of industrial production (IP) and the taxation

Table 29. Regression results of IBEX index with macro-variables for the period 1995 – 2013

Independent Variable	Lag = 0	Lag = 1	Lag = 2	Lag = 3	Lag = 4
CPI	-0.02 (0.98)	0.96 (0.39)	-1.33 (0.24)	-0.89 (0.43)	-0.33 (0.78)
GOLD	-0.11 (0.62)	-0.16 (0.45)	-0.40 (0.09)	-0.29 (0.23)	-0.44 (0.08)
FCE	1.96 (0.10)	0.90 (0.45)	2.15 (0.07)	-2.81 (0.02)*	1.78 (0.16)
IP	2.17 (0.01)*	1.37 (0.08)	-0.07 (0.93)	-0.66 (0.41)	0.12 (0.89)
LTR	-0.39 (0.06)	-0.14 (0.49)	-0.28 (0.18)	-0.55 (0.01)*	-0.23 (0.30)
OIL	-0.02 (0.82)	0.09 (0.33)	-0.06 (0.49)	-0.10 (0.26)	-0.19 (0.04)*
STR	-0.06 (0.52)	-0.12 (0.17)	-0.11 (0.24)	-0.10 (0.30)	-0.14 (0.17)
TOP	-0.20 (0.18)	-0.16 (0.28)	0.41 (0.01)*	-0.14 (0.39)	0.14 (0.38)

Table 30. Regression results of IBEX index with macro-variables for the period 1995 - 2008

Independent Variable	Lag = 0	Lag = 1	Lag = 2	Lag = 3	Lag = 4
CPI	-1.31 (0.33)	0.59 (0.67)	-1.63 (0.25)	-0.80 (0.58)	-0.07 (0.96)
GOLD	-0.24 (0.39)	-0.17 (0.55)	-0.37 (0.20)	-0.13 (0.65)	-0.41 (0.17)
FCE	2.03 (0.17)	0.85 (0.57)	3.68 (0.02)*	-4.19 (0.01)*	2.75 (0.10)
IP	2.40 (0.01)*	2.31 (0.07)	2.97 (0.03)*	0.07 (0.97)	1.61 (0.39)
LTR	-0.39 (0.13)	-0.33 (0.21)	-0.13 (0.62)	-0.50 (0.07)	-0.43 (0.13)
OIL	-0.12 (0.23)	-0.01 (0.96)	-0.01 (0.98)	0.08 (0.53)	-0.28 (0.03)*
STR	-0.15 (0.41)	-0.13 (0.49)	-0.26 (0.17)	-0.19 (0.32)	-0.43 (0.02)
TOP	-0.14 (0.47)	-0.07 (0.72)	0.58 (0.00)*	-0.37 (0.06)	0.29 (0.15)

on production (TOP). The IBEX index is also negatively related to consumption expenditure (FCE), the long-term interest rate (LTR) and the oil price index (OIL). It is worth noting that the dependence on the long rate is not statistically significant in the period before the economic crisis.

The regression equations, taking under consideration the statistically significant macroeconomic variables, are as follows:

Period 1995-2013

$$IBEC = \underset{(0.04)}{3,14} + \underset{(0.01)}{1,91} * IR + \underset{(0.11)}{0,24} * TOP(-2) - \underset{(0.04)}{0.40} * LTR(-3)$$
$$-\underset{(0.02)}{2.77} * FCE(-3) - \underset{(0.20)}{0.11} * OIL(-4)$$

Omitting consecutively the terms with the highest p-value, we get the following equation.

$$IBEC = \underset{(0.04)}{3,64} + \underset{(0.00)}{2,32} * IR - \underset{(0.02)}{0.44} * LTR(-3) - \underset{(0.00)}{3,43} * FCE(-3)$$

with $R^2_{adj} = 0.25$, DWstat = 2,32, AIC = 7.68, Prob (F-stat) = 0.00

Period 1995-2008

$$IBEC = \underset{(0.04)}{6.95} + \underset{(0.11)}{1.66} * IP + \underset{(0.09)}{2.57} * IP(-2) + \underset{(0.20)}{0.26} * TOP(-2)$$
$$-\underset{(0.43)}{1.54} * FCE(-2) - \underset{(0.02)}{4.76} * FCE(-3) - \underset{(0.08)}{0.20} * OIL(-4)$$

Removing consecutive terms with the highest p-value we get the following equation.

$$IBEC = \underset{(0.00)}{6.52} + \underset{(0.00)}{2.86} * IP - \underset{(0.00)}{1.54} * FCE(-3)$$

with $R^2_{adj} = 0.27$, DWstat = 2,34, AIC = 7.68, Prob (F-stat) = 0.00

Observing the two regression equations, relating the explanation of the IBEX variance, the following remarks can be drawn:

- The current changes in the industrial production index (IP) have a positive effect on stock market returns, both under normal market conditions but also in times of recession.
- The past consumption expenditure of households appears to adversely affect the performance of the stock market index. This can be explained mainly by savings, which is the unconsumed disposable income, and may be placed in shares.
- The long-term interest rate has statistically an important role in the period that includes both the global recession and debt crisis that broke out in Spain, but not in earlier years.

5. CONCLUSION

From the time series of per capita consumption and investment, it is found that Germany maintained its upward trend in consumer spending in the period of cricis, while at the same time there was not a corresponding upward or downward trend in investment. On the other hand, we observe a fall of both consumption and investment in Spain and Denmark.

Regarding the cyclical part of the per capita consumption and investment, the modeling with the ARMA model obtained satisfactory results, except in the case of investment expenditure in Denmark, where the R^2 was below 60%. From the analysis executed, it is concluded that the current values of variables depend primarily on their value a year ago, according to the findings of the autoregressive terms. The shocks get embodied in current consumption and investment in about three quarters, as shown by statistically significant moving average terms. Also, there is a "break" in the structure of the per capita consumption and investment mainly in the third and fourth quarter of 2008, after the collapse of Lehman Brothers and the global stock market crisis.

By the examination of causality relationships, it was found that the German index DAX Granger causes changes in private consumption expenditure, gross, net savings, the industrial production index, the short-term interest rates and unemployment. Stronger causality relationships are observed in the case of Denmark, where the OMX index Granger causes changes in the CPI, in consumer spending, gross investment, industrial production and net savings. Bidirectional relationships are observed with interest rates, taxes on production and unemployment. Finally, the Danish index IBEX seems to interact with the final consumption expenditure, industrial production and taxation.

Comparing the results of this study with previous ones, we find that inflation continues to impact negatively on stock returns, which has been established since Fama in 1981. Also, the level of industrial production affects proportionally the equity returns as was found by Chen et al (1986) for the stock index of New York. Interesting findings were also observed by Buyuksalvarci, A. (2010) on the index of the 100 largest companies in Turkey, under which the interest rate, industrial production, oil prices and the exchange rate have a negative impact on yields. In contrast, positive effect is evidence for the money supply, while the price of gold and inflation is not statistically significant. It is noted that in our study, only in the case of Spain the inflation (CPI) is not statistically significant. In short, it is concluded that any capital market presents interactions with different macroeconomic variables based on fundamental elements and the structure of each economy, while the phase of the business cycle also plays an important role. Also, the developed capital markets seem to have less response to macroeconomic shocks, probably because of better integration of information, as in the case of Germany.

Last but not least, it is noted that it was not possible to construct a reliable linear regression model to predict the stock market returns, taking as independent variables several macroeconomic variables. This conclusion derives from the fact that the R^2 did not exceed 25-35% even in periods of normal market conditions. The results were even more disappointing in the case of Germany, in which the coefficient was around 10 to 12%.

REFERENCES

Attari, M., & Safdar, L. (2013). The Relationship between Macroeconomic Volatility and the Stock Market Volatility: Empirical Evidence from Pakistan. *Pakistan Journal of Commerce and Social Sciences*, *7*(2), 309–320.

Blanchard, J. O., & Fischer, S. (1989). *Lectures in Macroeconomics*. MIT Press.

Boyd, J., Hu, J., & Jagannathan, R. (2005). The stock Market's Reaction to Unemployment News: Why Bad News is usually Good for Stocks. *The Journal of Finance*, *60*(2), 649–672. doi:10.1111/j.1540-6261.2005.00742.x

Brahmasrene, T., & Jiranyakul, K. (2007). Cointegration and Causality between Stock Index and Macroeconomic Variables in an Emerging Market. *Academy of Accounting and Financial Studies Journal*, *11*(3), 17–29.

Brailsford, T., & Hooper, V. (2001). Selecting macroeconomic variables as explanatory factors of emerging stock market returns. *Pacific-Basin Finance Journal*, *9*(4), 401–426. doi:10.1016/S0927-538X(01)00020-8

Buyuksalvarci, A. (2010). The Effects of Macroeconomics Variables on Stock Returns: Evidence from Turkey. *European Journal of Soil Science*, *14*(3), 70–83.

Campbell, J. Y., & Mankiw, N. G. (1987). Are output fluctuations transitory? *The Quarterly Journal of Economics*, *102*(4), 857–880. doi:10.2307/1884285

Chen, N.-F., Roll, R., & Ross, S. A. (1986). Economic Forces and the Stock Market. *The Journal of Business*, *59*(3), 383–403. doi:10.1086/296344

Eugene, F. (1981). Stock returns, Real Activity, Inflation and Money. *The American Economic Review*, *71*(4), 545–565.

Evsey, D. (1946). Capital Expansion, Rate of Growth and Employment. *Econometrica*, *14*(2), 137–147. doi:10.2307/1905364

Fama, E. (1990). Stock returns, Expected Returns and Real Activity. *The Journal of Finance*, *45*(4), 1089–1108. doi:10.1111/j.1540-6261.1990.tb02428.x

Fama, E., & French, K. (1989). Business Conditions and Expected Returns on Stocks and Bonds. *Journal of Financial Economics*, *25*(1), 23–49. doi:10.1016/0304-405X(89)90095-0

Fathi, S., Sameti, M., Nouri, B., & Esfahani, S. (2012). Examining the Effect of Selective Macroeconomic Variables on The Stock Exchange's Depth and Breadth (Case Study: Tehran Stock Exchange). *International Journal of Economics and Finance*, *4*(3), 97–104. doi:10.5539/ijef.v4n3p97

Flannery, M., & Protopapadakis, A. (2002). Macroeconomic factors do influence Aggregate Stock Returns. *Review of Financial Studies*, *15*(3), 751–782. doi:10.1093/rfs/15.3.751

Friedman, M. (1957). *A Theory of the Consumption Function*. Princeton University Press.

Gan, Lee, Yong, & Zhang. (2006). Macroeconomic Variables and Stock Market Interactions: New Zealand Evidence. *Investment Management and Financial Innovations*, *3*(4), 89–101.

Garbellini, N., Marelli, E., & Wirkierman, A. L. (2014). Domestic demand and global production in the Eurozone: A multi-regional input-output assessment of the global crisis. *International Review of Applied Economics*, *28*(3), 336–364. doi:10.1080/02692171.2013.872086

Geske, R., & Roll, R. (1983). The Fiscal and Monetary Linkage Between Stock Returns and Inflation. *The Journal of Finance*, *38*(1), 1–33. doi:10.1111/j.1540-6261.1983.tb03623.x

Granger, C. W. J. (1969). Investigating causal relations by econometric models and cross – spectral methods. *Econometrica*, *37*(3), 424–438. doi:10.2307/1912791

Hussin, M., Muhammad, F., Awang, S., Marwan, N., & Razak, A. (2013). The Impact of Oil Price Shocks on Islamic Financial Market in Malaysia. *Journal of Islamic Economics, Banking and Finance*, *9*(3), 53–68. doi:10.12816/0001611

John, C., Jonathan, I., & Ross, S. A. (1985). An intertemporal general equilibrium model of asset prices. *Econometrica*, *53*(2), 363–384. doi:10.2307/1911241

Kimani, D., & Mutuku, C. (2013). Inflation Dynamics on the Overall Stock Market Performance: The Case of Nairobi Securities Exchange in Kenya. *Economics and Finance Review*, *2*(11), 1 – 11.

Lee, B.-S. (1992). Causal Relations among Stock Returns, Interest Rates, Real Activity and Inflation. *The Journal of Finance*, *47*(4), 1591–1603. doi:10.1111/j.1540-6261.1992.tb04673.x

Leventides, J., & Kollias, I. (2014). Optimal Control Indicators for the Assessment of the Influence of Government Policy to Business Cycle Shocks. *Journal of Dynamics and Games*, 79 – 104.

MacKinnon, J. (1996). Numerical Distribution Function for Unit Root and Cointegration Tests. *Journal of Applied Econometrics*, *11*(6), 601–618. doi:

Malliaris & Urrutia. (2005). How big is the random walk in macroeconomic time series: Variance ratio tests. *Economic Uncertainty, Instabilities And Asset Bubbles*, 9 – 12.

Merton, R. C. (1973). An intertemporal capital asset pricing model. *Econometrica*, *41*(5), 867–887. doi:10.2307/1913811

Modigliani, F., & Brumberg, R. (1954). Utility Analysis and the Consumption Function: an interpretation of cross-section data. In K. K. Kurihara (Ed.), *Post-Keynesian Economics*. New Brunswick, NJ: Rutgers University Press.

Nopphon, T. (2011). Macroeconomic Factors of Emerging Stock Market: The Evidence from Thailand. *International Journal of Financial Research*, *3*(2), 105–114.

Øystein, G., & Frode, S. (1999). Causal relations among stock returns and macroeconomic variables in a small, open economy. *Journal of International Financial Markets, Institutions and Money*, *9*(1), 61–74. doi:10.1016/S1042-4431(98)00036-5

Poon, S. H., & Taylor, S. J. (1992). Stock returns and volatility: An empirical study of the UK stock market. *Journal of Banking & Finance*, *16*(1), 37–59. doi:10.1016/0378-4266(92)90077-D

Robert, G. (2008). Effect of Macroeconomic Variables on Stock Market Returns For Four Emerging Economies: Brazil, Russia, India, And China. *International Business & Economics Research Journal*, *7*(3), 42–56.

Robert, S. (1956). A Contribution to the Theory of Economic Growth. *The Quarterly Journal of Economics*, *70*(1), 65–94. doi:10.2307/1884513

Ross, S. A. (1976). The arbitrage theory of capital asset pricing. *Journal of Economic Theory*, *13*(3), 341–360. doi:10.1016/0022-0531(76)90046-6

Roy, H. (1939). An essay in Dynamic Theory. *Economic Journal (London)*, *49*(193), 14–33. doi:10.2307/2225181

Schwert, W. (1990). Stock Returns and Real Activity: A Century of Evidence. *The Journal of Finance*, *45*(4), 1237–1257. doi:10.1111/j.1540-6261.1990.tb02434.x

Stock, J. H., & Watson, M. W. (1986). Does GNP have a unit root? *Economics Letters*, *22*(2-3), 147–151. doi:10.1016/0165-1765(86)90222-3

Trevor, S. (1956). Economic Growth and Capital Accumulation. *The Economic Record*, *32*(2), 334–361. doi:10.1111/j.1475-4932.1956.tb00434.x

Yahyazadehfar, M., & Babaie, A. (2012). Macroeconomic Variables and Stock Price: New Evidence from Iran. *Middle East Journal of Scientific Research*, *11*(4), 408–415.

APPENDIX

Table 31. Descriptive statistics

	Germany		Denmark		Spain	
	FCE	GCF	FCE	GCF	FCE	GCF
Mean	3.967,11	1.268.42	4.435,53	1.802,63	2.803,95	1.289,47
Median	4.000,00	1.300,00	4.450,00	1.800,00	2.800,00	1.250,00
Maximum	4.400,00	1.500,00	5.200,00	2.300,00	3.300,00	1.900,00
Minimum	3.500,00	1.000,00	3.900,00	1.300,00	2.200,00	800,00
Std. Dev.	206,81	123,52	301,86	242,20	269.04	273,53
Skewness	0,05	0,02	0,19	0,39	-0,41	0,30
Kurtosis	2,44	2,14	2,15	2,70	2,53	2,37
Jarque-Bera	1,04	2,36	2,72	2,20	2,78	2,38
Probability	0,59	0,31	0,26	0,33	0,25	0,30
Observations	76	76	76	76	76	76

Chapter 3
The Impact of Capital Controls on the Use of Electronic Means of Payments (EMPs) in Greece:
Empirical Study

Nikolaos Giannopoulos
Piraeus Agency S.A., Greece

Alina Hyz
Piraeus University of Applied Sciences, Greece

ABSTRACT

The aim of this chapter is to analyze the evolution of the use of electronic means of payments (EMPs) in Greece during the years of capital controls and the prospects created for the Greek banking market and economy from their use. More generally, the authors try to analyze the level of reaction of the real economy to an extreme economic event, coupled with the subsequent development of trends. The introduction of capital controls in Greece in 2015 has led to significant changes in consumers' behavior including the evolution of the means of payment. In this study, the authors analyze initially the penetration of EMPs in Greece during the years before capital controls, then they focus on the current situation and the estimation for the future. They describe the policy followed by the state and measures taken by the Greek banks to encourage the wider use of electronic means of payments.

DOI: 10.4018/978-1-5225-6114-9.ch003

1. INTRODUCTION

The deep economic crisis that hit Greece is reflected, inter alia, in the main macroeconomic ratios, like Gross Domestic Product and unemployment and some indicators of the banking sector, like deposits, total loans and non-performing loans. Greece is characterized by borrowing problems, high public debt, serious lack of competitiveness, unsustainable social security system, particularly poor public administration and a large and wasteful public sector (Bukowski, 2011; Δημητροπούλου, et al. 2014, Karamanis, et al., 2014, Gikas, et. al. 2013, Hyz, Gikas, 2016, Hyz, et.a;. 2017).

Two and a half years have passed since capital restrictions have been imposed in Greece due to the Greek government's inability to reach an agreement with its lenders. Negative results of the five-month negotiations with the members of Eurogroup culminated in premature elections on January 2015 and the establishment of a coalition government of two parties: Coalition of the Radical Left (Syriza) and Independent Greeks (Anel). New negotiation began with the logic of debt cancellation and country disengagement from the memorandums, but the attitude of the country's partners was insurmountable on these issues, leading to a waste of time and expectations.

During this time, the Greek banks declined sharply, leading to strong concern about the ability to maintain the country's liquidity and the viability of Greek banks. On Friday, June 26, 2015, the country's prime minister announced a referendum on July 5, in response to the ensuing set-up of partners to accept their proposal within the day. Following the above events, the European Central Bank decided not to further increase the level of its Emergency Liquidity Assistance for Greek banks. In June 2015 capital controls were introduced.

As a result, the Greek government was forced to immediately close Greek banks for almost 20 days and to implement controls on bank transfers from Greek banks to foreign banks, and limits on cash withdrawals to avoid an uncontrolled bank run and a complete collapse of the Greek banking system (Samitas, Polyzos, 2015). Cash withdrawal per customer was limited to the amount of € 60 per day, or € 420 per week cumulatively, while special categories of transactions were identified which, after approval, could be circumvented.

According to the government decision, the new card operation framework (debit, credit, prepaid) was defined as shown in Table 1.

The aim of the paper is to answer the following questions:

1. What is the degree of electronic means of payments' penetration in Greece?
2. What is the Greek society's view on the new forms of payments?

Table 1.

Allowed Transactions	Unauthorized Transactions
Debit Cards	
Issuing of one card per customer	Purchases and payments to foreign companies
Withdraw up to € 60 via ATM	Transactions in foreign venues that deal with money handling
Purchases and payments in physical stores	
Purchases and payments in online stores	
Credit Cards	
Card issuance	Cash withdrawal via ATM
Purchases and payments in physical stores	Purchases and payments to foreign companies
Shopping and Payments in E-Shops	Transactions in foreign venues that are the subject of money handling
Prepaid Cards	
Card issuance and charging	Cash withdrawals via ATM
Recharging card	Purchases and payments to foreign companies
Card payment via internet banking	Purchases and payments in physical stores
Purchases and payments in physical stores	Cash out bank cash
Purchases and payments in online stores	

3. What may be the impact of the above changes on the Greek Economy in general and the banking system in particular?

The paper is structured as follows: in Section 1 we present the evolution of the use of EMPs in Greece, Section 2 presents the methodology and exhibits the results obtained from the study, and Section 3 summarises the main conclusions drawn from this research, limitations and research implications.

2. EVOLUTION IN THE USE OF ELECTRONIC MEANS OF PAYMENTS (EMPS)

According to the Cash Report (2016), Greece has the highest percentage of cash usage in all of the EU. During the last decades, the use of EMPs in Greece lags considerably behind the rest of the EU. Despite the growth recorded since 2001, Greece continues to occupy very low positions in the relevant rankings. Based on the value of transactions with EMPs per inhabitant in 2013, Greece ranked higher only compared to Croatia and Bulgaria, while in terms of the number of transactions per inhabitant Greece occupied the last position in the ranking (European Central Bank, 2017, IOBE, 2015). In order to reach the EU average for this ranking, the number of EMP transactions per inhabitant in Greece should increase by about 11 times from their 2013 level, thus the potential for further growth is significant (IOBE, 2015).

The introduction of capital controls in Greece in summer 2015, has led to significant changes in consumers' behavior. The bank holiday, the compulsory acceptance of payment cards and the daily limit on ATM withdrawals gave a significant boost to the diffusion of digital payments (IOBE, 2015). Both the value and the number of domestic transactions with payment cards issued in Greece more than doubled, month on month, in July 2015 (+103% and +105% respectively) (IOBE, 2015). Some months later and after a partial relaxation of restrictions on capital movements consumers have continued to increase the use of plastic money. The use of debit cards during the first five months of capital controls was increased by 40%, while respectively the credit cards use was increased by about 10%. In 2016, credit card payments in Greece reached a total value of approximately 4.9 billion euro (Statista, n.d.). This is an increase when compared to the 4.2 billion euro reached in 2015. Also, a survey by the Small Enterprises' Institute of the Hellenic Confederation of Professionals, Craftsmen and Merchants (IME GSEVEE, 2016) showed an increase in POS use of 20% within one year of the implementation of capital restrictions. According to this research during the period from January 2016 till the January 2017 we can observe also increase in the number of cards transactions by 1.345%, increase in the value of card payments by 136%, the number of installed POS terminals in Greece reached 600 thousand in January 2017 (see Figure 1), debit cards are 81% of the total number of active cards in circulation (11.8 million), with 1.3 million issued in the 2015-2016.

Figure 1. Number of POS terminals in Greece (2000-2016)
Source: Statista (n.d.)

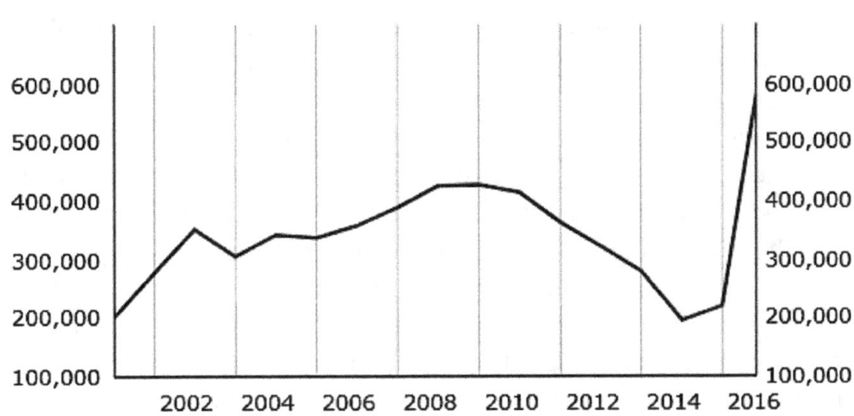

A large increase of the demand for POS terminals was caused by Greece's Law 4446/2016 amended the country's tax system providing for a person's tax-exempt income to be linked to the minimal value of spending via electronic means. This law was put in force from the beginning of 2017 and according to it what is deemed tax-free income is linked to a minimum value of expenses that a taxpayer incurs, provided that payment is effected by electronic means, depending on the individuals' level of income. A progressive scale was applied for the determination of the income tax reduction related to electronic transactions. In particular, the level of expenses that must be effected via electronic payment in order to secure the tax reduction were as follows: 1/. spending by electronic means of 10 percent of income for incomes up to 10,000 euro; 2/. 15 percent of income for incomes from 10,000.01 up to 30,000 euro and 3/. 20 percent of income for incomes exceeding 30,000 euro, with a maximum value (ceiling) of spending of 30,000 euro, regardless of income level (KPMG, 2017). In case taxpayers do not achieve the spending levels above-noted, a tax of 22 percent is imposed. The measure was aimed at tax compliance of businessmen and creating a culture of use of plastic money by citizens. In order to determine the categories of expenditure, consumer goods were taken into account from Greek Statistical Office consumer price index. From these expenditures, non-consumer expenses are deducted such as home purchase, tax payments, mortgage payments, purchase of investment products (stocks, bonds, etc.). After the introduction of this law applications for POS systems from Greek firms was doubled reached 8,000 per month. At the same time, about 80% of retail sales were realized through the POS system. In the health sector there was a significant use of plastic money in private clinics and pharmacies (20%, 40% accordingly), but on the other hand, the small penetration in doctor's offices was observed.

Finally, paragraph 3 of Article 20 of Law 3842/2010, as amended by paragraph 2 of Article 69 of Law 4446/2016, stipulated that from 22 Dec. 2015 onwards the trading threshold would be reduced from 1,500 to 500 euro, above which transactions between individuals and businesses (for the sale of goods or the provision of services) should be carried out exclusively through the use of card-based payment instruments or other electronic means of payment (as, for instance, electronic funds transfer, use of an electronic wallet, etc.).

As part of the measures taken to reduce withdrawals, the representatives of four systemic Greek banks made a proposal to the government, to implement an extra tax on cash withdrawals in order to boost the use of plastic money. The aim of the banks was the creation of disincentives, in order to make cash use unprofitable.

There are two main constraints on the further expansion of POS terminals: one of them is the high cost of terminal's installation and the second, high commissions which the firms are required to pay to banks for the use of POS. These burdens lead to an increase in business operating costs. In this context, the Greek government has expressed its willingness the cost of electronic transactions to fall below 1% in order to bring it into line with the European average. A parallel decrease also follows the cost of installing terminals, which ranged from €100 to €500, and has been dropped to €100-€150.

In the context of combating tax evasion and the need of an increase of e-payments the Ministry of Finance proceeded to the decision to the mandatory install of POS terminals by specific professional sectors which related with high tax evasion. Following these measures, the POS terminals applications for January 2017 have reached 9.000 (25% increase), twice as much as in the previous months. Ascending course follows the number of installed terminals and the corresponding value of electronic transactions. Lastly, in the context of stepping up the measure by motivating the citizens, the lottery measures were being considered, through which people doing transactions via POS, will automatically enter a lottery through which they can earn a refund.

According to a circular issued by the Ministry of Finance pursuant to article 66 of Law 4446/2016, the shops that do not display the POS terminals signs in a visible place will be penalized by the amount of €1.000. In particular, businesses should inform consumers of the existence or not of POS and the types of cards that are accepted with special marks that should be placed in a viewable position.

With the imposition of the bank holiday during the summer of 2015 and the capital controls after, the use of EMP recorded remarkable growth rates. However, even with the sharp increase that was observed under the extraordinary circumstances, the position of Greece in the rankings did not improve much, due to the large gap from most other EU countries.

3. EMPIRICAL RESEARCH

3.1 Methodology and Research Questions

The purpose of this study is to explore the views of citizens on the use of POS both before and after the imposition of capital controls, but also their general attitudes (norms and valuation) to the electronic means of payment (EMPs).

The population of this survey covers all the country's citizens. A sample of the survey consisted citizens from Athens and Thessaloniki, Mainland and island Greece, who were asked to answer the questionnaires designed for the purpose of the survey. The method followed is simple random sampling and the sample is considered representative, given that increase reliability and the generality of the exported results. The total number of citizens responded to the fill of the relevant research tool is 318. The statistical analysis of the data was carried out using the statistical program SPSS 23.

The main research questions are as follows:

1. Do the use of POS and EMPs will contribute to reducing tax evasion?
2. Were the measures taken by the Greek government and the Bank of Greece sufficient to increase the use of POS and EMPs?
3. What are the main problems faced by the consumers in their electronic transactions?
4. Do respondents believe that the use of electronic means of payment is safe?
5. In which product categories respondents prefer to use electronic means of payments?

A questionnaire was employed to collect data The type of questions contained in the questionnaire is questions of opinion or point of view. We use Likert scales (1–5), ranging from "strongly disagree" to "strongly agree" were used for all belief items to ensure statistical variability among survey responses for all items measured. The questionnaire is divided into four parts. The questions in the first section refer to the individual profile of the respondents: gender, age, place of residence, marital status, educational and professional level. The second section contains questions referring to the period prior to the implementation of capital controls, while the third section has the same questions refer to the period after the introduction of the capital controls. Finally, the fourth section contains general questions about the use of EMPs and POS.

3.2. Results

3.2.1 Chi-Square Test of Independence

3.2.1.1 Variable "Degree"

There are statistically significant results of the independence test with the independent variable "Bachelor Degree". This variable is a re-coding of the "Educational Level" variable and has two values, "Yes" and "No". The "Yes" includes "Graduate University / TEI", "Postgraduate Degree" and "Ph.D. Degree". "No" includes the values "Compulsory education" and "Secondary education". There is a statistically significant relationship between the "Bachelor Degree" variable and the following variables: "debit card before the capital controls" (Pearson X^2 =9,787, df=1 and Sig=0,002), "credit card before capital controls" (Pearson X^2 =5,139, df=1 and Sig=0,029), "using e-Banking applications before the introduction of capital controls"

Pearson X^2 =8,125, df=1 and Sig=0,004), " issue a new credit card during last year" (Pearson X^2 =34,361, df=2 and Sig=0,000), "using e-banking after the introduction of capital controls" (Pearson X^2 =38,382, df=2 and Sig=0,000), "using POS in your gas station transactions" (Pearson X^2 =9,250, df=1 and Sig=0,003), "using POS for buying electronic devices" (Pearson X^2 =4,659, df=1 and Sig=0,031),"using POS in your transactions to pay bills" (Pearson X^2 =7,352, df=1 and Sig=0,007), "using POS in your transactions for another transaction" (Pearson X^2 =7,352, df=1 and Sig=0,007), do you have a computer, tablet or smartphone with Internet access" (Pearson X^2 =22,603, df=1 and Sig=0,000), "You prefer to trade using POS or cash" (Pearson X^2 =9,009, df=2 and Sig=0,011), "You intend to increase the use of POS in the future" (Pearson X^2 =5,054, df=1 and Sig=0,033).

3.2.1.2. Variable "Gender"

There are statistically significant results of the independence test with the independent variable "Gender". There is a statistically significant relationship between the "Gender" variable and the following variables: "You were using e-Banking applications before the imposition of capital controls" (Pearson X^2 =15,093, df=1 and Sig=0,000), "You started to use e-Banking applications after the imposition of capital controls" (Pearson X^2 =11,203, df=2 and Sig=0,004), "You use POS in your gas station transactions" (Pearson X^2 =10,338, df=1 and Sig=0,001), "You use POS for buying clothes" (Pearson X^2 =7,770, df=2 and Sig=0,007), "You use POS for buying electronic devices" (Pearson X^2 =4,308, df=1 and Sig=0,042).

3.2.1.3 Variable "Marital status"

There are statistically significant results of the independent test for the independent variable "Marital status". There is a statistically significant relationship between the "Marital status" variable and the following variables: "You had debit card before the imposition of capital controls" (Pearson X^2 =28,730, df=3 and Sig=0,000), "You were using e-Banking applications before the imposition of capital controls" (Pearson X^2 =9,606, df=3 and Sig=0,022), "You started to use e-Banking applications after the imposition of capital controls" (Pearson X^2 =15,925, df=6 and Sig=0,014), "You use POS in your gas station transactions" (Pearson X^2 =21,429, df=3 and Sig=0,000), "You use POS in your transactions to pay bills" (Pearson X^2 =27,223, df=3 and Sig=0,000), "You use POS in your transactions for another transaction" (Pearson X^2 =8,116, df=3 and Sig=0,044), "Do you think that commercial banks in Greece have taken adequate measures to increase the use of POS" (Pearson X^2 =11,554, df=3 and Sig=0,009).

3.2.1.4 Variable "Occupation"

There are statistically significant results of the independent test for the independent variable "Occupation". There is a statistically significant relationship between the "Occupation" variable and the following variables: "You had debit card before the imposition of capital controls" (Pearson X^2 =26,108, df=7 and Sig=0,000), "You were using e-Banking applications before the imposition of capital controls" (Pearson X^2 =29,989, df=7 and Sig=0,000), "You started to use e-Banking applications after the imposition of capital controls" (Pearson X^2 =36,195, df=14 and Sig=0,001), "You use POS in your gas station transactions" (Pearson X^2 =67,464, df=7 and Sig=0,000), "You use POS for buying electronic devices" (Pearson X^2 =38,316, df=7 and Sig=0,000), "You use POS in your transactions to pay bills" (Pearson X^2 =25,091, df=7 and Sig=0,001), "You use POS in your transactions for another transaction" (Pearson X^2 =20,291, df=7 and Sig=0,005).

3.2.2. Testing Differences Between Means

3.2.2.1 Independence Samples T-Test

In this research study, there was only one statistically significant effect on the application of Independence t-test:

H_0: There is no statistically significant difference between the variable "Bachelor Degree" and "You were using POS for your purchases before the imposition of capital controls."

H_1: There is a statistically significant difference between the variable "Bachelor Degree" and "You were using POS for your purchases before the imposition of capital controls."

The mean of non-graduates on whether they used POS for their purchases before the imposition of the capital controls was 1.6415 (standard deviation: 0.79509) and for graduates, it was 2.0660 (standard deviation: 0.77605) (Table 2). Based on the results of Levene's Test for the Equality of Variances, there is no statistically significant difference between the two groups variances (Sig. = 0.080 > 0,05) (Table 3).

Therefore, we can assume that the two groups variances are equal (Equal Variances Assumed). Since the value of statistical significance for the t-test is less than 0.05 (Sig. = 0.000 <0.05), we reject H_0 and accept the alternative. We conclude that there is a statistically significant difference between the averages of the variables "Bachelor Degree" and" You was using POS for your purchases before the imposition of capital controls. Specifically, the results indicate that non-graduates who completed the questionnaire tend to use less the POS for their purchases before the imposition of capital controls.

Table 2.

	Bachelor Degree Graduate	N	Mean	Std. Deviation	Std. Error Mean
You used POS for your purchases before the imposition of capital controls	No	106	1,6415	0,79509	0,07723
	Yes	212	2,066	0,77605	0,0533

3.2.3 Paired Samples T-Test

This criterion was applied to determine whether there is a statistically significant difference in the use of e-banking applications before and after the imposition of capital controls. The results show that the imposition of capital controls has affected the use of e-banking (Table 4, Table 5, Table 6).

3.2.4 One-Way Analysis of Variance (ANOVA)

The results showed that:

1. There are statistically significant differences between the average age of respondents and whether they use the POS for their purchases before the imposition of capital controls.
2. There are statistically significant differences between the average age of respondents and holding a debit card before the imposition of the capital controls.

Table 3.

		Levene's Test for Equality of Variances		t-Test for Equality of Means						
		F	Sig.	t	df	Sig. (2-Tailed)	Mean Difference	Std. Error Difference	95% Confidence Interval of the Difference	
									Lower	Upper
You used POS for your purchases before the imposition of capital controls	Equal variances assumed	3,09	0,1	-4,56	316	0	-0,42453	0,09308	-0,6077	-0,2414
	Equal variances not assumed			-4,52	205,64	0	-0,42453	0,09383	-0,6095	-0,2395

Table 4.

	Mean	N	Std. Deviation	Std. Error Mean
You were using e-Banking applications before the imposition of capital controls	1,6981	318	0,4598	0,02578
You started to use e-Banking applications after the imposition of capital controls	1,9277	318	0,77691	0,04357

Table 5.

	N	Correlation	Sig.
You were using e-Banking applications before the imposition of capital controls & You started to use e-Banking applications after the imposition of capital controls	318	-0,715	0

Table 6.

		Paired Differences					t	df	Sig. (2-Tailed)
		Mean	Std. Deviation	Std. Error Mean	95% Confidence Interval of the Difference				
					Lower	Upper			
Pair 1	You were using e-Banking applications before the imposition of capital controls & You started to use e-Banking applications after the imposition of capital controls	-0,22956	1,15138	0,06457	-0,35659	-0,10253	-3,555	317	0

3. There are statistically significant differences between the average age of respondents and holding a credit card before the imposition of the capital controls.
4. There are statistically significant differences between the average age of respondents and in the use of electronic banking applications (e-Banking) before the imposition of capital controls.

5. There are statistically significant differences between the average age of respondents and whether they use the POS for their purchases after the imposition of capital controls.
6. There are statistically significant differences between the average age of respondents and holding a debit card after the imposition of capital controls.
7. There are statistically significant differences between the average age of respondents and holding a credit card after the imposition of capital controls.
8. There are statistically significant differences between the average age of respondents and if they face problems with their transactions with the use of POS.
9. There are statistically significant differences between the average age of respondents and whether they have been the victim of abuse when using POS.
10. There are statistically significant differences between the average age of respondents and whether they use POS in their Super Market transactions.
11. There are statistically significant differences between the average age of respondents and whether they use POS in their gas station transactions.
12. There are statistically significant differences between the average age of respondents and whether they use POS in buying electronic devices.
13. There are statistically significant differences between the average age of respondents and whether they use POS in their entertainment transactions.
14. There are statistically significant differences between the average age of respondents and whether they use POS in paying bills.
15. There are statistically significant differences between the average age of respondents and the availability of a computer, tablet or smartphone with Internet access.

3.2.5 Control of Research Hypothesis

1. The majority of the sample (94%) believes that the use of POS will help reduce tax evasion. Therefore the first research hypothesis is confirmed (Table 7).
2. The majority of the sample (50.3) believes that the Greek government and the National Bank of Greece received last year sufficient measures to increase the use of POS. Therefore the second research hypothesis is confirmed (Table 8)
3. There is a statistically significant difference in the use of POS for purchases of the respondents before and after the imposition of capital controls. Therefore, the third research hypothesis is confirmed (Table 9).
4. The majority of the sample (87.1%) intends to increase the use of POS in the future. Therefore the fourth research hypothesis is confirmed (Table 10).

Table 7.

		Frequency	Percent	Valid Percent	Cumulative Percent
Valid	Yes	299	94	94	94
	No	19	6	6	100
	Total	318	100	100	

Table 8.

		Frequency	Percent	Valid Percent	Cumulative Percent
Valid	Yes	160	50,3	50,3	50,3
	No	158	49,7	49,7	100
	Total	318	100	100	

Table 9.

		N	Correlation	Sig.
Pair 1	You used POS for your purchases before the imposition of capital controls & You used POS for your purchases after the imposition of capital controls	318	0,413	0

Table 10.

		Paired Differences					t	df	Sig. (2-tailed)
		Mean	Std. Deviation	Std. Error Mean	95% Confidence Interval of the Difference				
					Lower	Upper			
Pair 1	You used POS for your purchases before the imposition of capital controls & You used POS for your purchases after the imposition of capital controls	-0,94025	0,78605	0,04408	-1,02698	-0,85353	-21,331	317	0

4. DISCUSSION OF THE RESULTS, LIMITATIONS, AND RESEARCH IMPLICATIONS

The primary purpose and object of this research study are to explore the views of the Greek people for the use of POS and EMPs before and after the introduction of capital controls in Greece. For this purpose were formulated individual factors which exploring personal characteristics of respondents, the opinions of respondents in the period before the application of capital controls, the views of respondents in the period after the introduction of capital controls and general questions on the use of POS and EMPs.

The number of respondents amounts to 318, of which 166 are men and 152 women, while their ages vary fact that certifies views and opinions. The same applies to the rest demographics as the sample comes from the urban, suburban and rural area, there is diversity in marital status, education level and occupation of respondents.

On the use of POS for their purchases before the implementation of capital controls, the majority of respondents with a percentage of 76.7% said they rarely or never used the EMPs. However, the vast majority, 85.2% were debit cardholders before the implementation of capital controls while credit card had only a percentage of 39.9%. This can be explained by the distrust showed by cardholders to extend the use of their cards beyond the withdrawn cash and specifically on making purchases with direct debit devices POS.

It is important to consider the fact that until recently, very few shops and mostly large business chains had POS systems in their branches. The disadvantage that transactions with physical POS charged with bank fees and that the purchases through plastic money prevent any possibility of concealing income, make entrepreneurs and consumers reluctant to use debit and credit cards.

Percentage 30.2% of the respondents replied that used e-banking applications before the introduction of capital controls, although the 86.48% answered that they have a computer, tablet or smartphone. This can be explained by the lack of experience in the electronic payments, the citizen's reservation for computer transactions and in the preference of using cash under fear of a haircut.

Table 11.

		Frequency	Percent	Valid Percent	Cumulative Percent
Valid	Yes	277	87,1	87,1	87,1
	No	41	12,9	12,9	100
	Total	318	100	100	

Low rates of use POS before the period of capital controls, increase significantly after implementation of restrictions. Specifically, after the introduction of capital controls, the percentage of respondents who said that they always or often using POS stands at 86.8%, while it had risen the implementation of electronic banking with the service usage rate 60.7% versus 30.2% before the capital controls. This finding is probably due to the limitation of cash withdrawals from banks and the effort of the owners of capital to spend all their money on purchases - mostly luxury - so do not lose their deposits.

Increasing show the percentages of citizens who issued debit and credit card after the start of capital controls as a result of the limitation of withdrawals and the new tax bill for the tax-free "building".

Important reference should be made, in that there were statistically significant differences - before and after the imposition of capital controls – the use of POS, the card issuing (debit and credit), as well as the use of electronic banking.

Interestingly presents that the vast majority of respondents with a percentage of 89.3%, believe that the use of POS is safe, response that can be explained by the too high percentage of responses "problems in their dealings with the POS rarely or never" (93.7%) and "have never been the victim of fraud using POS" (92.8%).

As regards the areas in which respondents use EMPs, first option is the supermarket with a share of 89.3%, followed by the gas station with a percentage of 70.4%, bill payments with a rate of 67.6%, buying clothing with 55%, buying electronic items with a percentage of 26.4% and a low rate of 11% reported using EMPs for fun. Finally, a 44% uses the POS in various other transactions. These percentages can be explained by age, marital status and occupation, as they were found statistically significant differences between them, but also by the fact that large and famous companies, customers feel the prestige and safety of the transactions provided by these brand names (hypermarket, electronic goods, clothing - footwear).

The vast majority (94%) consider that the POS help reduces tax evasion. The respondents seem to be divided on whether they believe that the Greek government and the National Bank have taken sufficient measures over the last year to increase the use of POS, while for the same question a 60% considers that only commercial banks received adequate measures. This opinion supported by the bank advertisements, the information and the returning points from markets. On the contrary, the Greek government showed delayed reflexes to institutionalize measures for retailers and all the productive sectors.

Characteristic is that after a long delay POS terminal installation has become compulsory for the majority of retail businesses, especially in sectors with a tradition of tax evasions such as restaurants, bars and the self-employed.

Regarding the preference of respondents for the form of payment, only 10.7% said they prefer to pay using only POS and 12.9% using only cash. The majority, with 76.4% said they prefer to pay with both ways. This probably depends on the type of each transaction.

Almost all respondents with 98.7% believe that the imposition of capital controls has led to increased use of POS and the majority of them with 87.1% intend to increase the use of POS in the future.

The results of the survey present the reality of the Greek society and economy following the implementation of capital controls, which led to a large increase in the use of plastic money. While this may be restrictive for most citizens, it also helps to reduce tax evasion and expedite the end of capital controls.

It has been more than a year since the start of capital controls, and in that time it has changed a lot in the use of money in Greece, as the restrictions on capital transactions created a new reality as a reference for the transactions of citizens and businesses. Greece was a country where the majority of transactions carried out using bank notes, while electronic transactions had limited use. Today there is a major shift, artificially created due to extraordinary events, which translates into an increase in the use of electronic transactions. POS is one of the most popular alternative transaction methods that were previously used mainly for credit card payments. The change we see today in our daily lives with citizens to use their cards even for small payments raises many questions.

It would be very interesting to carry out a corresponding survey in Cyprus for the period of the imposition of capital controls and to compare the results with this survey.

One possible limitation is the cross-sectional nature of the study. It is however very difficult, to find a large sample of respondents and to have them participate in a longitudinal study. Finally, we did not include in our analysis personality variables which play an important role in explaining attitudes towards the use of EMPs. Future studies may address these issues and provide greater insight into the task of explaining and predicting EMPs' use.

REFERENCES

Δημητροπούλου, Δ., Κοτσομανώλη-Φιλιππάκη, Α., Χαραμπάκης, Ε., & Αγγέλης, Γ. (2014). Η Χρηματοδότηση των Ελληνικών Επιχειρήσεων προ και κατά τη διάρκεια της Κρίσης, Οικονομικά Δελτία, Τεύχος 39, Τράπεζα της Ελλάδος

Bukowski, S. (2011). Economic and Monetary Union - Current Fiscal Disturbances and the Future. *International Advances in Economic Research, 17*(3), 274–287. doi:10.100711294-011-9310-7

ECB. (2017). *The use of cash by households in the euro area*. Retrieved from https://www.ecb.europa.eu/pub/pdf/scpops/ecb.op201.en.pdf

G4S. (2016). *Update G4S Cash Report Europe 2016*. Retrieved from https://www.thefutureofcash.com/userfiles/files/the-future-of-cash-2016a.pdf

Gikas, G., Hyz, A., & Tagkas, P. (2013). The Experience of Greece from its participation in the Eurozone. *Management Insight. The Journal of Incisive Analysers, 9*(1).

Hyz, A., & Gikas, G. (2016). CAMELS and Greek banking sector performance during the crisis. An analysis and review of the evidence. *Acta Universitatis Lodziensis. Folia Oeconomica, 5*(316).

Hyz, A., Kalandonis, P., & Stavroulakis, D. (2017). Management of working capital - The Achilles heel of small and medium enterprises (SMEs). The case of Greece. *Central European Review of Economics and Finance, 2017*(2).

IME GSEVEE. (2016). *Economic Climate Trends*. Retrieved from http://www.imegsevee.gr/pressrelease/1085-ime-gsevee-survey-february-2016--biannual-representation-of-economic-climate-in-small-enterprises-

IOBE (Foundation for Economic & Industrial Research). (2015). *Digital payments and tax revenues in Greece*. Retrieved from http://iobe.gr/docs/research/en/RES_05_F_21102015_REP_EN.pdf

Karamanis, K., & Hyz, A. (2014). Flexible working and Unemployment in Greece: An Analysis and Review of the Evidence. *International Journal of Academic Research in Business and Social Sciences, 4*(10).

KPMG. (2017). *Greece – New Law Amends Income Tax System*. Retrieved from https://home.kpmg.com/xx/en/home/insights/2017/04/flash-alert-2017-073.html

Samitas, A., & Polyzos, S. (2016). Freeing Greece from capital controls: Were the restrictions enforced in time? *Research in International Business and Finance, 37*, 196–213. doi:10.1016/j.ribaf.2015.11.005

Statista. (n.d.). *Banks and Financial Services*. Retrieved from https://www.statista.com/markets/414/topic/459/banks-financial-services/

Chapter 4
The Information Content of Tax Loss Carryforwards Before and During the Global Financial Crisis:
Evidence From Greece

Chytis Evangelos
Technological Educational Institute of Epirus, Greece

Filos Ioannis
Panteion University, Greece

Gkouma Olympia
Panteion University, Greece

ABSTRACT

Tax loss carryforwards are a valuable asset because they usually reduce a company's future tax payments. This chapter investigates the importance of deferred tax assets from tax loss carryforwards (DTA_TLC) by sector and index (FTSE/ASE) for the period before and after the outbreak of the financial crisis (2005-2012). In the non-banking industry, the DTA_TLC cover on average half (1/2) of the total deferred tax assets (DTAs) and one-fifth (1/5) of income before taxes (IBT). The telecommunications industry accounts for the largest DTA_TLC components, while the chemicals sector for the smallest. On average, the companies listed in the FTSE/ASE 20 report DTA_TLC five times larger than those of the FTSE/ASE 40. In the banking sector, until 2009 DTA_TLC constituted a small part of total assets and IBT. In contrast, after 2010, DTAs include significant components of DTA_TLC, as a consequence of the private sector involvement (PSI) and the financial crisis.

DOI: 10.4018/978-1-5225-6114-9.ch004

INTRODUCTION

In many tax jurisdictions, the losses occurred by a company, are eligible to be carried forward in the future and be offset against future taxable profits. Under the condition that future taxable profits will be available in the future, this tax provision leads to less tax payable in the future.

According to the International Accounting Standards (IAS 12 & US SFAS 109)[1], in the case that a company suffers losses that are recognised by the tax authorities (TLC), the recognition of an asset in respect of taxes that will be saved in the future years as a consequence of the unused tax losses (DTA is permitted. A Deferred Tax Asset (DTA) is recognized for the tax losses computed for tax purposes, to the extent that taxes arising from taxable profits will be saved in the future[2]. The deferred tax asset is intended to be offset against future tax liabilities and therefore the remeasurement of this asset is required at the end of each reporting year. The DTA that is estimated, at the end of the reporting year, that will not be utilized in the future, is reduced and charged immediately to profit or loss.

The Deferred Tax Assets (DTA) had zero to minimal importance for the international accounting practice and research, until the adoption of US GAAP US SFAS 109 by the FASB in 1992. The previous setting (APB No 11/1967) although it provided the compulsory calculation of Deferred Taxes in the form of comprehensive allocation and the split of deferred taxes in long term and short term in the statement of financial position, it explicitly prohibited the recognition of deferred tax asset in carry forward losses. The application of SFAS No 109 contributed to the flexibility of Deferred Tax Assets recognition criteria (including DTA on carryforward losses) and at the same time imposed the regular impairment test of deferred tax assets (DTA Valuation Allowance). Since mid-90s a research mobility was developed around DTA.

Many studies focus on whether investors perceive the Deferred Tax Assets from carried forward losses (DTA_TLC) as assets valued by the capital market (Amir et al., 1997; Ayers, 1998; Amir & Sougiannis, 1999; Zeng, 2003; Kumar and Visvanathan, 2003; Bauman and Bauman, 2002; Bauman and Das, 2004). The findings of these studies are often conflicting. The issue of tolerable threshold in the determination of recoverable amount of DTA and the movement in the valuation allowance sparked numerous discussions in the research community (Miller & Skinner, 1998; Behn et al., 1998; Visvanathan, 1998; Bauman et al., 2001; Burgstahler et al., 2002; Schrand & Wong, 2003; Chao et al., 2004; Frank & Rego, 2006; Christensen et al., 2008; Herbohn et al., 2010). The research results do not provide sufficient evidence that the valuation allowance is used systematically as mean of earnings management. Furthermore, the studies indicate that the accounting treatment generally follows the criteria and guidance provided by SFAS No.109[3].

According to SFAS No. 109 and International Accounting Standard IAS 12, the recognition of Deferred Tax in the Assets arising from tax losses carried forward (DTA_LC) is permitted to the extent that it is probable that future taxable profit will be available against which the unused tax losses and unused tax credits can be utilized (more likely than not criterion). In other words, the probability of future taxable profits should exceed 50% and the reasonability of the assumptions used should be provable.

TAX LOSSES CARRIED FORWARD AND ACCOUNTING STANDARDS

Tax Losses Carried Forward According to Greek GAAPS

In Greece, the applicable tax legislation is included in the Income Tax Code (L. 4172/2013, Article. 27, para. 1,), which states that in the event of the result of the tax year is a loss, this loss may be carried forward and be offset against taxable profits of the future five (5) consecutive tax years. The loss of the earlier year is offset in priority over subsequent year loss.

The specific provision (par. 2, Article 27) stated that, the debit difference[4] arising against the company from the exchange of Greek government bonds or corporate bonds guaranteed by the Greek government, under the participation in the program of rescheduling Greek Debt (PSI), is deducted from the gross income in thirty (30) equal annual installments commencing from year that the exchange of securities occurred, regardless of their retention period. Recently the complementary art. 27^{A} was issued, which stated that the income tax attributable to: a) the amortised debit difference of PSI and provisions for doubtful debts and b) the cumulative credit risk provisions and losses of legal entities regulated by Bank of Greece as at December 31, 2014, for which DTA has been or will be recognized in accordance with IFRS, is considered under certain conditions, as receivable against Greek State.

The specific provisions have significantly affected the computation and the recoverability of Deferred Tax Assets from Carried forward Losses, particularly as regards the banking sector.

Tax Losses Carried Forward According IAS 12

In accordance with IAS 12.34, a Deferred Tax Asset shall be recognized for the carryforward of unused tax losses and unused tax credits to the extent that it is probable that future taxable profit will be available against which the unused tax losses and unused tax credits can be utilized. The existence of unused tax losses constitutes strong evidence that future taxable profit may not be available. In this case, the recognition of a Deferred Tax Asset (DTA) in respect of losses carried forward is primarily prohibited by the standard.

Therefore, when an entity has a history of recent losses, the entity recognizes a deferred tax asset arising from unused tax losses or tax credits only to the extent that the entity has sufficient taxable temporary differences or if this is not the case, the standard requires other convincing evidence that sufficient taxable profit will be available against which the unused tax losses or unused tax credits can be utilized by the entity, according to IAS 12.35.

The standard does not define the time period that the investigation of history of recent losses should cover. According to SFAS 109/A100 methodology, the time period should cover the latest three years, including the most recent. The cumulative loss during this period should exceed the total profit. Depending on the industry sector and the general economic environment, the time period under investigation could be longer or shorter[5]. However, a reasonable period should reflect the taxable profits' growth trend.

The standard does not provide clear definition on the term "strong evidence". According to IAS 12.36, an entity considers the following criteria in assessing the probability that taxable profit will be available against which the unused tax losses or unused tax credits can be utilized:

- Whether the entity has sufficient taxable temporary differences relating to the same taxation authority and the same taxable entity, which will result in taxable amounts against which the unused tax losses or unused tax credits can be utilized before the right to offset against tax liabilities expire,
- Whether it is probable that the entity will have taxable profits before the unused tax losses or unused tax credits expire,
- Whether the unused tax losses result from identifiable causes which are unlikely to recur,
- Whether tax planning opportunities are available to the entity that will create taxable profit in the period in which the unused tax losses or unused tax credits can be utilized.

To the extent that it is not probable that taxable profit will be available against which the unused tax losses or unused tax credits can be utilized, the deferred tax asset is not recognized.

Furthermore, according to IAS 12.56: "The carrying amount of a deferred tax asset shall be reviewed at the end of each reporting period. An entity shall reduce the carrying amount of a deferred tax asset to the extent that it is no longer probable that sufficient taxable profit will be available to allow the benefit of part or all of that deferred tax asset to be utilized. Any such reduction shall be reversed to the extent that it becomes probable that sufficient taxable profit will be available". According to IAS 12.36, in the event that the unused tax losses result from identifiable causes which are unlikely to recur, this alone constitutes convincing evidence.

The management's argument that the non – recognition of the deferred tax asset (DTA) may negatively impact on the market, is not generally accepted. In addition, the usually optimistic management estimates cannot constitute convincing evidence and therefore these should be analyzed further.

The Probability Criterion

The definition and interpretation of the term "when it is probably" has been subject of debate between academic society, authors, auditors and supervisory authorities. In the framework of the convergence project of IFRS and US GAAP, IASB has clarified its argument that the term "probable" is the same with the term "more likely than not". This argument negates the prevailing view, up to now, that the probability criterion according to IFRS corresponded to a significantly higher percentage[6] than the US GAAP 50%. However, even if the criterion of probability higher than 50% is assumed, this alone is not enough to provide a clear, objective and generally applicable answer to whether and when there will be sufficient taxable profits in the future.

Based on the scenario in Table 1, it is expected that the temporary tax-deductible differences will be utilized by 53.3%. Taking into account the probability distribution and the "best estimate" rationale provided by IAS 37.39, the average 60% could be elected.

The determination of the probability criterion has an impact on the Deferred Tax Asset measurement process. In accordance with IAS 12.24, the Deferred Taxed should be recognised at the original value and subsequently be remeasured based on the provisions of IAS 12.56. The above procedure in not applicable on first time adoption of the standard. In this occasion, especially with regard to Deferred Tax Assets, these should preferable be presented net.

Table 1. Probability distribution: "Probably: criterion satisfied

Scenario	Utilisation Rate	Estimated Probability	Weighted Value
A	100%	33.3%	33.3%
B	60%	33.3%	20.0%
C	0%	33.3%	0.0%
Expected Value			53.3%

The standards provide guidance on IAS 12.56 stating that carrying amount of Deferred Taxes should be reduced to the extent that it is probable to be utilised in the future[7]. Similar rationale is indicated by the American GAAP SFAS 109 (Impairment Approach). The accounting treatment requires the valuation allowance to be presented on a contra-account.

The estimated probability of sufficient future taxable profits against which the unused tax losses may be utilised depend more on subjective rather than objective criteria that involve largely the estimates and intentions of management. If the assessment of the probability of the scenario occurring changes significantly, the expected value may even reach zero.

The same applies for the "best estimate" approach, referred above.

In the respective case, the most likely scenario is zero recovery. The expected value stands at 37.3% and the recognition of Deferred Tax does not qualify due the subjective judgement of management. This fact proves that such a criterion leaves much room for maneuver and could lead to manipulation of financial statements. Ultimately, the matter to focus should not be on the probability of each scenario to occur but to whether such criteria may be perceived as objective.

It should be also emphasized that the above described methodology is applicable only to the Deferred Tax Assets. The recognition of Deferred Tax Liabilities does not require probable future profits.

Table 2. Probability distribution: Expected value < 50%

Scenario	Utilisation Rate	Estimated Probability	Weighted Value
A	100%	33.3%	33.3%
B	49%	33.3%	16.3%
C	0%	33.3%	0.0%
Expected Value			49.7%

Table 3. Probability distribution: Best estimate

Scenario	Utilisation Rate	Estimated Probability	Weighted Value
A	100%	25%	25.0%
B	49%	25%	12.3%
C	0%	50%	0.0%
Expected Value			37.3%

According to IAS 12.28, it is probable that taxable profit will be available when there are sufficient taxable temporary differences relating to the same taxation authority and the same taxable entity which are expected to reverse:

1. In the same period as the expected reversal of the deductible temporary difference or
2. In periods into which a tax loss arising from the deferred tax asset can be carried back or forward.

In such circumstances, the deferred tax asset is recognised in the period in which the deductible temporary differences arise.

When there are insufficient taxable temporary differences relating to the same taxation authority and the same taxable entity, in accordance with IAS 12.29, the deferred tax asset is recognised to the extent that:

1. It is probable that the taxable entity will have sufficient taxable profit relating to the same taxation authority, in the same period as the reversal of the deductible temporary difference (or in the periods into which a tax loss arising from the deferred tax asset can be carried back or forward) or
2. Tax planning opportunities[8] are available to the entity that will ensure taxable profit in appropriate periods for the Deferred Tax Assets utilisation.

More specifically, the carrying amount of a deferred tax asset shall be reviewed at the end of each reporting period. The standard provides that an entity shall reduce the carrying amount of a deferred tax asset to the extent that it is no longer probable that sufficient taxable profit will be available to allow the benefit of part or all of that deferred tax asset to be utilised. Any such reduction shall be reversed to the extent that it becomes probable that sufficient taxable profit will be available. Furthermore, an entity reassesses at the end of each reporting period in accordance with IAS 12.37, unrecognised deferred tax assets that qualify for recognition in the current period. The entity recognises a previously unrecognised deferred tax asset to the extent that it has become probable that future taxable profit will allow the deferred tax asset to be recovered[9].

The assessment of Deferred Tax Asset value and recoverability is associated with the expected tax rates enacted in future periods (IAS 12.46) and with impending changes in legislation regarding the period of time that carried forward losses are available to the offset against tax liabilities (e.g. the offsetting period is extended from 5 years to 30 years).

Figure 1. Deferred tax asset recognition process

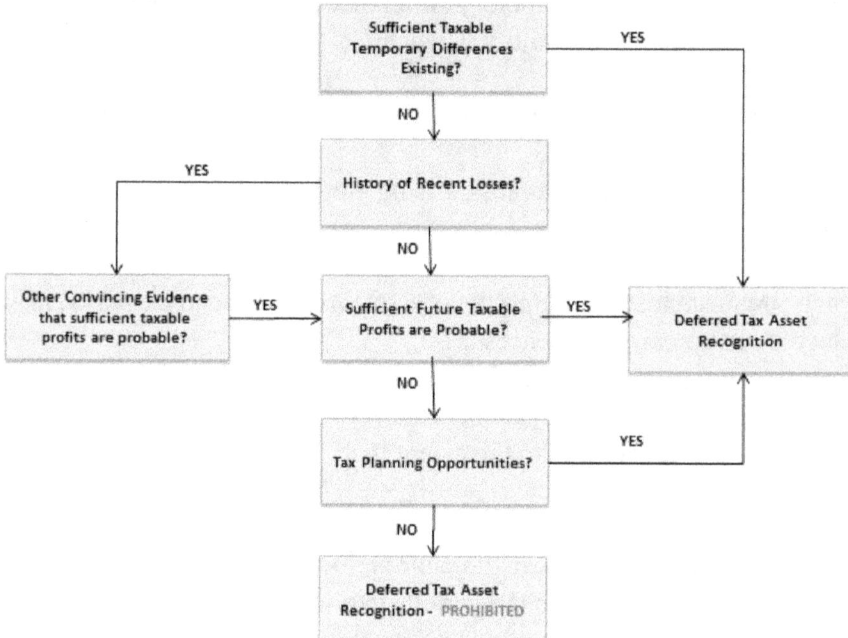

DEFERRED TAX ASSETS ARISING FROM CARRIED FORWARD LOSSES ON FIRMS' STATEMENT OF FINANCIAL POSITION

The research sample includes the total population of ASE listed firms, which belonged to one of the internationally certified indices (FTSE/ASE 20, FTSE/ASE Mid 40 & FTSE/ASE 80) for the period 2005-2012.

The majority of observations comes from the Non-Banking/Industry Sector. The Industry sector constitutes 90% (913 observations) while Banking sector constitutes 10% (98 observations) of the total 1.011 observations included in the research.

The dataset was principally hand-collected. The notes to the annual consolidated financial statements for the years ended in the period 2005-2012 consisted the source of the dataset. During the respective period, there was full and compulsory adoption of IAS/IFRS by the listed firms.

In general, the Non-Banking Sector entities present mainly Deferred Tax Liabilities. However, it is observed that, by the end of year 2012, the Deferred Taxes attributable to carried forward losses consist on average the second (2nd) most significant figure and have been tripled in comparison with the year 2006.

In the Banking Sector, the Deferred Tax Assets amounted to € 6.7 billion and account for 184.16% of the Negative Equity. It is worth mentioning that, one third

(1/3) of the Banking Sector entities, have recognized Deferred Tax Assets (DTA) that, for the first time, exceed the 3% of their Total Assets. These DTAs are associated with impairment of the Loan portfolios', the value of Investments and Securities, the valuation of Derivatives and the Accounting Losses that resulted from the application of the PSI which correspond to 87% of the Total Deferred Tax Assets.

The segregation in the presentation of findings between Banking and Non-Banking sector is due to the different accounting events that have caused the respective losses that have been carried forward.

The tables presented below analyze the Deferred Tax Assets from carried forward losses by index and by sector and the major findings derived from the listed firms.

Table 4 illustrates the Deferred Tax Assets from unused tax losses compared to the Total Assets, Total Equity and Profit/Loss for the years 2005-2012 for the Non-Banking Sector Entities. In addition, it presents the ratio of DTA from unused tax losses movement to Total DTAs movement and the percentage movement of Net DTA/DTL from year to year.

Approximately 41% of total Non-Banking Sector Entities (377 out of 913) have recognized Deferred Tax Assets (DTA) arising from unused tax losses that cover on average 44,62% of Total Deferred Tax Assets and 20% of Profit/Loss before tax on the time period 2005-2012.

Table 4. Distribution and fluctuations of DTAs arising from unused tax losses in total assets, equity, and profit/loss for the year (non-banking sector)

Year	Firm Years	DTA_LC / Total Assets (%)	DTA_LC / Equity (%)	DTA_LC/ Profit-Loss before tax(%)	DTA_LC / Total DTA (%)	D(DTA_LC) / D(Total DTA) (%)	D(DTA_LC) / D(Total DT) (%)
2005	35	0,15%	0,36%	3,33%	13,27%	8,85%	-11,34%
2006	38	0,25%	0,60%	4,96%	35,57%	-671,56%	898,13%
2007	44	0,41%	0,97%	6,87%	46,49%	134,14%	-17,87%
2008	51	0,50%	1,32%	22,01%	50,13%	62,65%	62,75%
2009	53	0,51%	1,31%	**16,11%**	41,60%	-469,66%	-22,98%
2010	53	**0,58%**	1,69%	**-145,37%**	53,68%	240,08%	36,95%
2011	53	**0,60%**	1,92%	-18,75%	52,33%	-44,59%	-6,87%
2012	50	0,56%	1,67%	55,91%	50,08%	27,16%	14,85%
Total	**377**	**0,46%**	**1,22%**	**20,02%**	**44,62%**	**61,84%**	**-89,30%**

It should be emphasized that, in the years 2009-2010, the percentage of DTA arising from unused tax losses has risen dramatically from 16% of Profit before tax in year 2009 to 145% of Loss in the year 2010. This is attributable mainly to the shrinking of profitability and the turn from profits before tax € 1.9 billion in year 2009 to loss € 0.2 billion and € 1.5 billion in 2010 and 2011 respectively.

Nevertheless, this fact is not associated with recognition of Deferred Tax Assets (DTAs) in respect of these losses. It is noted that, the DTAs represent 0,6% of Total Assets in both years 2010 and 2011 while at the same time DTAs arising from unused tax losses consist more than 50% of the Total Deferred Tax Assets.

Approximately 50% of the listed firms included in the indices FTSE/ASE 20 & 40 have recognized DTAs in respect of unused tax losses that represent more than 80% of Total DTAs from unused tax losses.

The listed firms included in the index FTSE/ASE 20 have recognized on average € 21.9 million on DTAs representing five (5) times higher level compared to those included in the FTSE/ASE 40 and have noted a maximum value of € 91.5 million.

Table 6 illustrates the allocation of DTAs from unused tax losses by sector.

The Telecommunications Sector has recorded the highest DTAs (€ 20.6 million) on average while the Chemicals Sector has recorded the lowest DTAs (€ 0.48 million) on average.

Table 5. illustrates the allocation of DTAs from unused tax losses by market index

In €	FTSE/ASE 20	FTSE/ASE Mid 40	FTSE/ASE SmallCap 80, FTSEMSFW	FTSEA, FTSEGT	ΑΟΜ	Non Indexed	Total
Firm Years without DTA_LC	48	101	196	26	146	20	537
Firm Years with DTA_LC	54	99	116	18	69	20	376
Total Observations	**102**	**200**	**312**	**44**	**215**	**40**	**913**
(%)	**53%**	**50%**	37%	41%	32%	50%	41%
Total DTA_LC	1.182.306.031	433.596.670	168.162.351	35.205.355	67.040.190	102.379.915	1.988.690.512
(%)	**59%**	**22%**	8%	2%	3%	5%	100%
Average	**21.894.556**	**4.379.764**	1.449.675	1.955.853	971.597	5.118.996	5.289.071
Standard Deviation	22.073.635	5.390.912	2.216.171	2.111.592	1.273.064	6.065.567	11.347.901
Minimum	278.000	4.256	1.000	5.701	18.521	23.000	1.000
Median	16.968.078	2.492.000	584.640	1.552.500	533.723	1.675.500	1.191.183
Maximum	91.515.000	28.631.476	12.490.378	8.960.137	5.902.227	17.326.256	91.515.000

Furthermore, the Telecommunications Sector has recorded the firmest years with DTAs arising from unused tax losses (100%), mainly due to Hellenic Telecommunications Organization (HTO S.A.), followed by Raw Materials Sector (75%) and Health Care (74%).

Below is the corresponding analysis of the Deferred Tax Assets from carried forward losses (DTA_LC) for the Banking Sector. It should be noted that he analysis of the Banking Sector has not included the DTA_LC categories that have been significantly affected by the financial crisis from 2010 onwards, due to comparability

Table 6. Distribution of deferred tax assets arising from unused tax losses by sector (excluding banking sector)

In €	Firm Years without DTA_LC	Firm Years with DTA_LC	(%) Firm Years	Total DTA_LC	% to Total DTA_LC	Average	Standard Deviation	Minimum	Median	Maximum
Real Estate	10	12	55%	28.061.000	1%	2.338.417	1.433.993	23.000	2.032.000	4.704.000
Insurance	4	3	43%	1.556.000	0%	518.667	418.729	37.000	723.000	796.000
Industrial Goods and Services	85	29	25%	181.398.366	9%	6.255.116	7.170.526	191.911	1.122.237	22.222.511
Retail	18	19	51%	23.436.198	1%	1.233.484	1.631.470	56.754	511.000	5.902.227
Construction and Materials	39	57	59%	574.944.488	30%	10.086.745	20.941.773	3.677	1.600.000	91.515.000
Media	18	14	44%	73.339.618	4%	5.238.544	3.276.957	1.859.773	4.140.306	13.744.285
Oil and Gas	12	9	43%	70.197.633	4%	8.618.269	16.840.948	122.044	390.383	46.416.000
Personal and Household Goods	69	18	21%	26.602.035	1%	1.477.891	1.516.646	255.070	864.362	5.280.000
Raw Materials	14	42	75%	184.712.793	10%	4.397.924	4.999.626	4.256	2.895.248	17.348.364
Travel and Leisure	19	10	34%	32.538.080	2%	3.253.808	2.098.238	244.150	2.975.500	8.033.000
Technology	37	38	51%	197.838.430	10%	5.206.274	7.306.237	1.000	460.000	28.631.476
Telecommunications	0	7	100%	144.100.000	7%	20.585.714	9.503.233	8.600.000	20.900.000	36.000.000
Food and Beverage	58	33	36%	198.610.896	10%	6.018.512	10.797.122	2.005	847.615	38.100.000
Health Care	7	20	74%	32.436.000	2%	1.621.800	2.692.413	37.000	865.500	12.481.000
Utilities	20	8	29%	93.589.000	5%	11.698.625	30.133.974	25.000	89.000	86.040.000
Chemical	25	10	29%	4.790.356	0%	479.036	329.213	151.860	379.530	1.086.226
Financial Services	21	12	36%	69.182.575	4%	5.765.215	8.408.367	301.000	2.823.080	30.983.000
Total	**457**	**341**	**43%**	**1.937.333.468**	**100%**	**5.681.330**	**11.822.099**	**1.000**	**1.371.744**	**91.515.000**

purposes. These categories concern impairment of the Loan portfolios', the value of Investments and Securities, the valuation of Derivatives and the Accounting Losses that resulted from the application of the PSI.

In respect of the Banking Sector (not taking into account the financial crisis consequences as described above), the DTAs arising from unused tax losses (DTA_LC) account for much lower portion of Total Assets, Equity and Profit/Loss before tax (P/L_BT) compared to the other sectors. In time period (2005-2012), the DTA_LC represent 1.16% of Total Equity, 6.11% of P/L_BT and 8.68% of Total DTA.

It should be emphasized that, in the years 2009-2010, the ratio of DTA arising from unused tax losses to Profit/Loss before tax has risen dramatically from 12% to 42% while DTA_LC account for 17% and 22% of the Total Deferred Tax Assets respectively. This fact is attributable to the significant shrinkage of profitability, from profits € 4.7 billion in year 2008 to € 2.5 billion (2009) and € 1.0 billion in 2010 which has resulted in an increase of DTA_LC from € 1.4 billion (2009) to € 2.1 billion in 2010.

In the contrary to the Industry Sector, the Banking Sector entities have recognized Deferred Tax Assets in respect of the unused tax losses in a great extent.

Table 7. Distribution and fluctuation of DTAs arising from unused tax losses in total assets, equity and profit/loss for the year (banking sector)

Year	Firm Years	DTA_LC / Total Assets (%)	DTA_LC / Equity (%)	DTA_LC/ Profit-Loss before tax(%)	DTA_LC / Total DTA (%)	D(DTA_LC) / D(Total DTA) (%)	D(DTA_LC) / D(Total DT) (%)
2005	8	0,02%	0,35%	1,96%	4,62%	4,62%	4,72%
2006	7	0,01%	0,20%	0,93%	3,36%	34,02%	-4,01%
2007	8	0,02%	0,30%	1,43%	8,25%	-32,83%	-19,64%
2008	9	0,06%	0,92%	5,33%	**17,08%**	40,92%	29,09%
2009	9	0,07%	0,89%	**12,27%**	**22,13%**	-64,72%	-541,41%
2010	10	0,09%	1,28%	**42,12%**	21,11%	24,33%	19,88%
2011	6	0,05%	4,60%	-0,45%	3,73%	-6,97%	-5,13%
2012	4	0,11%	-8,44%	-5,56%	4,86%	6,41%	14,78%
Total Banking Sector	**61**	**0,06%**	**1,16%**	**-6,11%**	**8,68%**	**5,54%**	**5,89%**
Total Non - Banking Sector	**377**	**0,46%**	**1,22%**	**20,02%**	**44,62%**	**61,84%**	**-89,30%**

Table 8 illustrates the allocation of DTAs from unused tax losses of the Banking Sector firms by market index.

In respect of the Banking Sector, it is noted that 84% of total observations included in the FTSE/ASE 20 has recognized DTAs for unused tax losses while the respective percentage for the entities included in the FTSE/ASE 40 is just 20%. The cumulative DTAs arising from unused tax losses, recognized by the entities included in the FTSE/ASE 20 (€ 1.5 billion), represent 93% of the Total DTAs arising from unused tax losses. The entities included in the index FTSE/ASE 20 have recognized on average (€ 32,5 million) on DTAs arising from unused tax losses representing three (3) times higher level compared to those included in the FTSE/ASE 40 and have noted a maximum value of € 289 million.

CONCLUSION

The empirical research of Deferred Tax position of ASE listed companies has derived the following conclusions:

Table 8. Distribution of deferred tax assets arising from unused tax losses by trade index (banking sector)

In K€	FTSE / ASE 20	FTSE / ASE Mid 40	FTSE/ASE SmallCap 80, FTSEMSFW	FTSEA, FTSEGT	ΑΟΜ	Non Indexed	Total
Firm Years without DTA_LC	9	12	9	0	6	1	37
Firm Years with DTA_LC	47	3	1	3	5	2	61
Total Observations	56	15	10	3	11	3	98
(%)	**84%**	**20%**	10%	100%	45%	67%	62%
Total DTA_LC	**1.528.217**	32.152	23.367	1.983	59.753	763	1.646.235
(%)	93%	2%	1%	0%	4%	0%	100%
Average	**32.515**	**10.717**	23.367	661	11.951	382	26.987
Standard Deviation	54.733	8.479	23.367	610	9.106	347	49.185
Minimum	102	1.450	23.367	207	100	136	100
Median	11.622	12.616	23.367	422	11.940	382	9.646
Maximum	**289.484**	18.086	23.367	1.354	23.367	627	289.484

- In the non-banking/industry sector, the DTA_TLC account on average for half (1/2) of the total Deferred Tax Assets (DTAs) and for one fifth (1/5) of Income Before Taxes (IBT).
- The Telecommunications industry accounts for the largest DTA_TLC components, while the Chemicals sector for the smallest.
- On average, the companies listed in the FTSE/ASE 20 report DTA_TLC five times higher than those of the FTSE/ASE 40.
- In the banking sector, from 2006 to 2009, DTA_TLC constituted a small part of Total Assets and IBT. In contrast, after 2010 DTAs include significant components of DTA_TLC, as a consequence of the Private Sector Involvement (PSI) and the financial crisis.
- The companies of the index FTSE/ASE 20 represent 93% of the total allocation of DTA_TLC, which is on average three times higher than those in the FTSE/ASE 40.

The utilisation of unused tax losses carried forward depend on the probability of sufficient taxable profits generated in the future. The estimated probability of sufficient future taxable profits against which the unused tax losses may be utilised depend more on subjective rather than objective criteria that involve largely the estimates and intentions of management. In the occasion that an entity presents a history of recent losses, the recognition of DTA_TLC must be justified based on the strict requirements of IAS 12.

At this point, the role of external auditors is of particular significance. The auditor should assess the management's estimates and issue the audit opinion with emphasis of matter regarding the uncertainties that raise doubts on the entity's ability to continue as a "going concern", unless the management take measure with the aim to improve the financial results and the liquidity of the entity.

With regard to supervisory authorities, it would be fair to establish a general framework of the methods and models that document and support the existence of adequate tax planning to avoid troubleshoot failures and intentional recognition of irrevocable tax assets.

REFERENCES

Amir, E., Kirschenheiter, M., & Willard, K. (1997). The Valuation of Deferred Taxes. *Contemporary Accounting Research*, *14*(4), 597–622. doi:10.1111/j.1911-3846.1997.tb00543.x

Amir, E., & Sougiannis, T. (1999). Analysts' Interpretation and Investors' Valuation of Tax Carryforwards. *Contemporary Accounting Research*, *16*(1), 1–33. doi:10.1111/j.1911-3846.1999.tb00572.x

Ayers, B. C. (1998). Deferred tax accounting under SFAS No. 109: An empirical investigation of its incremental value-relevance relative to APB No. 11. *The Accounting Review*, 195–212.

Bauman, C. C., & Bauman, M. P. (2002). The deferred tax asset valuation allowance and earnings quality. *Review of Accounting and Finance*, *1*(1), 72–87. doi:10.1108/eb026980

Bauman, C. C., Bauman, M. P., & Halsey, R. F. (2001). Do firms use the deferred tax asset valuation allowance to manage earnings? *The Journal of the American Taxation Association*, *23*(s-1), 27–48. doi:10.2308/jata.2001.23.s-1.27

Bauman, M. P., & Das, S. (2004). Stock market valuation of deferred tax assets: Evidence from internet firms. *Journal of Business Finance & Accounting*, *31*(9-10), 1223–1260. doi:10.1111/j.0306-686X.2004.00573.x

Behn, B. K., Eaton, T. V., & Williams, J. R. (1998). The determinants of the deferred tax allowance account under SFAS No. 109. *Accounting Horizons*, *12*(1), 63–78.

Burgstahler, D., Elliott, W. B., & Hanlon, M. (2002). *How firms avoid losses: Evidence of use of the net deferred tax asset account.* Working Paper, University of Washington.

Chao, C. L., Kelsey, R. L., Horng, S. M., & Chiu, C. Y. (2004). Evidence of earnings management from the measurement of the deferred tax allowance account. *The Engineering Economist*, *49*(1), 63–93. doi:10.1080/00137910490432683

Christensen, T. E., Paik, G. H., & Stice, E. K. (2008). Creating a bigger bath using the deferred tax valuation allowance. *Journal of Business Finance & Accounting*, *35*(5-6), 601–625. doi:10.1111/j.1468-5957.2008.02092.x

Chytis, E., Koumanakos, E., & Siriopoulos, C. (2013). Deferred Tax Positions under the prism of financial crisis and the effects of a corporate tax reform. *12th Annual Conference of the Hellenic Finance and Accounting Association (HFAA), organized by the Department of Accounting and Finance of the University of Macedonia.*

EFRAG. (2013). *EFRAG and the FRC issue the Feedback Statement on the Discussion Paper Improving the Financial Reporting of Income Tax*. Retrieved from http://www.efrag.org/Front/n1-1102/EFRAG-and-the-FRC-issue-the-Feedback-Statement-on-the-Discussion-Paper--Improving-the-Financial-Reporting-of-Income-Tax.aspx

Frank, M. M., & Rego, S. O. (2006). Do managers use the valuation allowance account to manage earnings around certain earnings targets? *The Journal of the American Taxation Association*, *28*(1), 43–65. doi:10.2308/jata.2006.28.1.43

Herbohn, K., Tutticci, I., & Khor, P. S. (2010). Changes in Unrecognised Deferred Tax Accruals from Carry-Forward Losses: Earnings Management or Signalling? *Journal of Business Finance & Accounting*, *37*(7-8), 763–791. doi:10.1111/j.1468-5957.2010.02207.x

IASB. (2014). *IAS 12 Income Taxes: Recognition of Deferred Tax Assets for Unrealised Losses*. Retrieved from http://www.ifrs.org/Current-Projects/IASB-Projects/Pages/IASB-Work-Plan.aspx

IASB/FASB. (2006). *A Roadmap for Convergence between IFRSs and US GAAP-2006-2008-Memorandum of Understanding between the FASB and the IASB*. Retrieved from http://www.ifrs.org/Use-around-the-world/Global-convergence/Convergence-with-US-GAAP/Documents/MoU.pdf

IFRS. (n.d.). *IAS 12 Income Taxes*. Retrieved from http://www.ifrs.org/Current-Projects/IASB-Projects/Income-Taxes/Pages/Income-taxes-research-project.aspx

Kumar, K. R., & Visvanathan, G. (2003). The information content of the deferred tax valuation allowance. *The Accounting Review*, *78*(2), 471–490. doi:10.2308/accr.2003.78.2.471

Miller, G. S., & Skinner, D. J. (1998). Determinants of the valuation allowance for deferred tax assets under SFAS No. 109. *The Accounting Review*, 213–233.

Schrand, C. M., & Wong, M. H. (2003). Earnings management using the valuation allowance for deferred tax assets under SFAS no. 109. *Contemporary Accounting Research*, *20*(3), 579–611. doi:10.1506/480D-098U-607R-5D9W

Visvanathan, G. (1998). Deferred tax valuation allowances and earnings management. *Journal of Financial Statement Analysis*, *3*, 6–15.

Zeng, T. (2003). The valuation of loss carryforwards. *Canadian Journal of Administrative Sciences/Revue Canadienne des Sciences de l' Administration*, *20*(2), 166-176.

ENDNOTES

1 http://www.ifrs.org/current-projects/iasb-projects/income-taxes/Pages/Income-Taxes.aspx
http://www.fasb.org/summary/stsum109.shtml

2 The precondition for this treatment is the existence of evidence of sufficient future taxable profits.

3 For a review of these studies, refer to Graham et al., 2012

4 Debit difference is defined as the difference between the nominal value of securities issued in exchange and the historical cost of these securities. In the specific occasion that, the loss that occurred by the securities valuation following the acquisition which has not been offset against reserve of art. 38 of L. 2238/1994, the acquisition cost is considered.

5 This was the reason that IASB decided against the strict determination of the three-year cumulative loss period.

6 Usually probability > 75%.

7 The carrying amount of a deferred tax asset shall be reviewed at the end of each reporting period. An entity shall reduce the carrying amount of a deferred tax asset to the extent that it is no longer probable that sufficient taxable profit will be available to allow the benefit of part or all of that deferred tax asset to be utilised.

8 Tax planning opportunities are actions that the entity would take in order to create or increase taxable income in a particular period before the expiry of a tax loss or tax credit carryforward.

9 For instance, an improvement in trading conditions may make it more probable that the entity will be able to generate sufficient taxable profit in the future for the deferred tax asset to meet the recognition criteria. Another example is when an entity reassesses deferred tax assets at the date of a business combination or subsequently.

Chapter 5
A Comparative Analysis on International Portfolio Flows to Asian Stock Markets With a Nonlinear Perspective

Ayben Koy
Istanbul Commerce University, Turkey

ABSTRACT

After the Asian financial crisis was solved by International Monetary Fund in late 1997, the recovery in Asian economies begun by 1999. Most of the countries affected by the crisis needed to change their exchange rate policies. This chapter brings insight on how the international portfolio flows to Asian stock markets are affected from the shocks on EUR/USD parity. The weekly observations between 01/01/2010 to 21/04/2017 belong to India, Indonesia, Philippine, South Korea, Thailand, Malaysia, and Vietnam. Use of Markov regime switching vector autoregressive models presents the relationship according to the different regimes of the markets in the study. The results indicate that (1) the international portfolio flows through Asian stock markets are governed by a long run, nonlinear relation; (2) the shocks on EUR/USD parity have positive effects on the countries' portfolio flows except Malaysia; and (3) the responses to the shocks vary according to the market regimes or according to the countries.

DOI: 10.4018/978-1-5225-6114-9.ch005

INTRODUCTION

Beginning in the summer of 1997, a series of currency declines spread through Asian markets and were followed with decreasing stock markets. The crisis called the Asian Financial Crisis or Asian Contagion had been solved by International Monetary Fund in late 1997. Most of the countries affected from the crisis needed to change their exchange rate policies (Calvo and Reinhart, 2002). The effect of the crisis had been seen in the developed markets too. However, the inevitable transition from the fixed exchange rate policy to the flexible rate policy made the markets unprotected under fluctuating currencies. This change has also been a part of international markets' liberalizations. By the monetary policy of central banks following the last global crisis and European crisis, which aimed to increase the economic activity for example in USA the interest rates had reached zero lower bound and lowered yields on government bonds, caused high liquidity in international markets, and high portfolio flows to the emerging markets (EMs) were seen. Large external financing needs and risk premiums of EMs took the attention of international investors. Moreover, emerging economies, which have a high growth rate compared to the world average, are attracting these markets in terms of international investors. After the European Central Bank (ECB) announced the extended asset purchase programme (EAPP) in 2015, increases in portfolio flows to EMs were expected too (Georgiadis and Grab, 2015). The Asian countries, which have experienced sharp currency depreciations, gave an opportunity to -the risk premiums of the international investors to rise (Sangare, 2016). In particular, the exchange rate, interest rate and asset returns are the primary factors for portfolio investments which aim to go back to the home country with high returns. Moreover, recent international finance theory suggests that exchange rates are influenced by capital flows as much as by current account balances and long-term interest rates. Because having the highest average 6.5 GDP growth rate (Estimate; 2015=6.8; 2016=6.4; Projection; 2017=6.5. (imf.org)) above other country groups, the studies on Emerging and Developing Asia have got an increasing interest among academicians.

In the sample period between 01/01/2010-21/04/2017, USD had got a stronger appearance not only against EMs' currencies but also against Euro, too. In most of the researches, foreign exchange is used as an indicator effecting international portfolio flows to the countries' capital markets. Actually, foreign exchange volatility of a country is an indicator which only affects that country's variables. The goal of our study is to provide a comparative evaluation on the relationship between EUR/USD parity and the international portfolio flows with a nonlinear perspective. The mutual switching mechanism of the international portfolio flows through Asian stock markets (India, Indonesia, Philippine, South Korea, Thailand, Malaysia and Vietnam) between 01/01/2010 to 21/04/2017 is firstly investigated. Secondly, a model including EUR/USD parity and the portfolio flows is described. After analyzing the portfolio flows as a whole, the relationships between EUR/USD parity and portfolio flows are analyzed in models by time series duals.

LITERATURE REVIEW

There is a wide literature investigating the factors effecting capital flows tend towards EMs (Culha, 2006; Yıldız, 2012; Onyeisi et al, 2016). There are many factors effecting the capital flows, which are related to the properties of home country or the properties of the host country or both of them. These factors are also divided into push factors and pull factors. Factors such as tax legislation, trust in law and justice, political stability of the country where the investment is made are as important factors as the variety of financial instruments, transaction volume and market depth. One of the pull factors attracting capital flows is liberalization. An effective liberalization policy would increase international portfolio flows to EMs (Bekaert & Harvey, 2000; Bekaert, Harvey & Lumsdaine, 2002). However, the increases of international portfolio flows cause fragility. Mishra et al. (2014) have evidence that EMs, which had tightened restrictions on inflows, experienced minimal market reactions to The Federal Reserve System (FED) announcements in the period between 2013 to 2014.

Another important pull factor is market integration. The information in international financial markets would affect a high integrated stock market more than a low integrated one. In a high integrated EM, foreign speculators would affect volatility and return as well (Bekaert & Harvey, 1997). The behavior of portfolio flows before or after crisis is another related subject. Ahmed and Zlate (2014) studied the pre-crisis (2002-2008) and post crisis (2009-2012) periods for Brazil, Indonesia, South Korea, Taiwan and Thailand. One of the results is, the actual cumulative net inflows have been found growing at a consistently faster pace than the pre-crisis model would have predicted. The study has got also evidence on the sensitivities of flows to policy rate differentials and to risk aversion are different in the post-crisis period.

Baek (2006) analyze international portfolio flows to Asian and Latin American economies on the relationship between different push and pull factors. The evidence indicates the portfolio flows to Latin American economies are more related with positive economic conditions as economic growth, on the other hand portfolio flows to Asian markets are more volatile and speculative.

The relationship between exchange rates and international portfolio flows has been studied many times for EMs. In some studies, exchange rate is analyzed as only one factor among many macroeconomic variables in a relationship with international portfolio flows (Brooks et al, 2004; Chaban, 2009; Sethi, 2012; Waqas et al.,2015) and the main purpose of others were investigating exchange rate-portfolio flows relationship (Rujiravanich, 2013; Caporale et al., 2017). The studies as Brooks et al. analyze the international flows both as foreign direct investment and portfolio flows.

Some of the selected studies on Asia markets are Ghosh and Herwadkar's (2009), Sethi (2012), Ehlers and Takats (2013), Rujiravanich (2013) and Waqas et al. (2015). International portfolio flows to Indian markets have been found to be the causes of the changes in equity prices and the changes in exchange rates in Ghosh and Herwadkar's (2009) study. Although the short-term relationship between the net international portfolio flows and asset prices and exchange rates are positive, the short-term relationship between the interest rates are found negative in the study.

In another study on India, Sethi (2012) has found a dynamic relationship between international portfolio flows and macroeconomic variables of India. In a following study, Rujiravanich (2013) investigated the negative relationship between exchange rates and international portfolio flows in Thailand. However, there is a long and positive relationship between equity prices and foreign portfolio investments.

Studying with a cumulative sixteen EMs data including Asia markets, Ehlers and Takats (2013) have evidence that the shock to capital inflow would result in a higher share price and appreciation in the exchange rate, and an unexpected exchange rate shock would increase the international portfolio outflows. In a study analyzing South Asia, Waqas et al. (2015) find relationships between macroeconomic variables and international portfolio flows. They conclude that lower volatility in international portfolio flows is associated with higher interest rates, depreciation in exchange rates, foreign direct investments, lower inflation and higher growth rates.

Caporale et al. (2017) is a good example using Markov Regime Switching (MRS) models for India, Indonesia, Pakistan, Philippines, South Korea, Taiwan and Thailand over the period 1993:01–2015:11. High and low volatility regimes are indicated with a markov switching approach in the study. The evidence shows that, low volatility and high volatility of exchange rates in these economies are related with international portfolio flows to both stock market and bond market except Philippines.

DATA AND MODEL

The weekly international portfolio flows in USD to the stock markets in India, Indonesia, Philippine, South Korea, Thailand, Malaysia and Vietnam are analyzed between 01/01/2010 to 21/04/2017. Data is taken from Bloomberg and calculated as differences. To compare how markets are affected from shocks in international markets, the EUR/USD parity is used.

We used Multivariate Markov Regime Switching Vector Autoregressive (MMS-VAR) model to define the nonlinear relationship between multiple variables. In the MRS model, the regime of the economy is described by a state variable with probabilities and durations. Switching between different states (regimes) of the economy is in a Markov chain process. The economy might be in a recession regime or a growth regime. By analyzing the observed time series variable (yt), the regime of the economy (st) which cannot be directly observed, can be identified.

The MRS model has a time series process (yt) dependent on an unobservable regime variable (st) that represents the probability of being in a particular state (Krolzig, 2000):

$$f(y_t|Y_{t-1};X_t;\,\Theta_1) \text{ if } s_t = 1 \tag{1}$$

$$p(y_t|Y_{t-1};X_t;\,s_t) = \{\,f(y_t|Y_{t-1};\,X_t;\,\Theta_m) \text{ if } s_t = m$$

Xt: exogenous variables; Θ_m is the parameter vector associated with regime *m*.

The regime-generating process in MRS models is defined by the transition probabilities (Krolzig 2000).

$$p_{ij} = \mathrm{P_r}(s_{t+1} = j|s_t = i);\ \sum_{j=1}^{m} Pij = 1\ ;\ \mathrm{i,j} = \{1,..,\mathrm{m}\} \tag{2}$$

s_t follows an ergodic M-state Markov process with a transition matrix:

$$\mathbf{P} = \begin{vmatrix} p_{11} & \cdots & p_{1m} \\ \cdots & \cdots & \cdots \\ p_{m1} & \cdots & p_{mm} \end{vmatrix} \tag{3}$$

The transition probabilities of switching between two states are:

$\mathrm{P}(s_{t+1}=1|s_t = 1) = p_{11,}$

$\mathrm{P}(s_{t+1}=2|s_t = 1) = p_{12,}$

$P(s_{t+1}=1|s_t = 2) = p_{21,}$

$P(s_{t+1}=2|s_t = 2) = p_{22}$. (4)

The probability of which regime is in operation at time t conditional on the information at time t= - 1 only depends only on the statistical inference on st−1:

$$\Pr(s_t|Y_{t-1};X_t;S_{t-1}) = \Pr(s_t|s_{t-1}) \quad (5)$$

The ergodic probabilities for a two-state model which give information being in any state are given as (Bildirici 2010):

$$P_r\left(s_t = 1\right) = \frac{1-p_{22}}{1-p_{11}-p_{22}} \ , \ P_r\left(s_t = 2\right) = \frac{1-p_{11}}{1-p_{11}-p_{22}} \quad (6)$$

The Markov switching model of conditional mean (MSM) and the Markov switching intercept (MSI) model are the two main types of MRS models which Hamilton (1989) first implemented to analyze business cycles. In the MSM model, the regime switches according to the conditional mean (μt), while in the MSI model, the regime switches according to the constant (cst). There is a third model that has proven to be strong in explaining financial time series is the Markov switching intercept and heteroskedasticity (MSIH) Model. These models are as follows:

MSM Model: $y_t - \mu_t = \phi(y_{t-1} - \mu_{t-1}) + u_t$ (7)

MSI Model: $y_t - c_{st} = \phi y_{t-1} + u_t$ (8)

MSIH Model: $y_t - c_{st} = \phi y_{t-1} + u_{t+} \Omega^{1/2}$ (9)

ϕ is an n x n matrix of regime-dependent autoregressive coefficients.
u_t is an (n*1) unobservable zero mean white noise vector process.
y_{t-1} is lagged values of dependent variable.
Matrix $\Omega^{1/2}$ represents the factor applicable to state s_t in a state-dependent Choleski factorization of the variance covariance matrix of variable (y) Ω s_t.

$$\Omega\, s_t = Var[y_t | \kappa_{t-1}, s_t] ; \tag{10}$$

κ_{t-1}: denotes time t-1 information of all past observations and states.

A two-state bivariate Matrix $\Omega^{1/2}$ is (Guidolin 2016):

$$\Omega st = \begin{vmatrix} \sigma^2_{1,s_t} & \sigma^2_{12,s_t} \\ \sigma^2_{12,s_t} & \sigma^2_{2,s_t} \end{vmatrix} \tag{11}$$

The basic p lagged VAR(p) model process is:

$$y_t = c + [A_1 y_{t-1} + \ldots + A_p y_{t-p}] + u_t ; \tag{12}$$

An is (n*n) coefficient matrices

The general form of a Markov-switching vector autoregressive (MS-VAR) model is (Krolzig 1998, 2000):

$$y_t = c(s_t) + [A_1(s_t) y_{t-1} + \ldots + A_p(s_t) y_{t-p}] + u_t \tag{13}$$

A VAR with regime shifts in the mean is called a MSM(M)-VAR(p):

$$y_t = \mu(s_t) + A_1(s_t)(y_{t-1} - \mu(s_{t-1})) + \ldots + A_p(s_t)(y_{t-p} - \mu(s_{t-p})) + u_t \tag{14}$$

$u_t \sim NID(0, \Sigma(s_t))$

If the regime shifts affect the intercept of the VAR, this is called a MSI(M)-VAR(p):

$$y_t = c(s_t) + A_1(s_t) y_{t-1} + \ldots + A_p(s_t) y_{t-p} + u_t \tag{15}$$

The transition in the MSI-VAR, is smooth comparing to the MSM-VAR model. These models are the subclass of MS-VAR models. (Krolzig 1998, 2000).

If the regime shifts affect the intercept of the VAR and the model includes a variance covariance matrix, this is called a MSIH(M)-VAR(p) process:

$$y_t = c(s_t) + A_1(s_t) y_{t-1} + \ldots + A_p(s_t) y_{t-p} + u_t + \Omega_{1/2} \tag{16}$$

EMPIRICAL ANALYSIS

In this study, the mutual switching mechanism of the international portfolio flows through Asian stock markets (India, Indonesia, Philippine, South Korea, Thailand, Malaysia and Vietnam) are firstly investigated (Model 1). We applied autoregressive models with different numbers of regimes (2 or 3) and different lags to our data. Taking linearity as our null hypothesis, and following Davies' (1987), we consider a p-value less than 0.05 to constitute a statistically significant rejection of the null hypothesis. Among the several models that have been found, the model that best explains the nonlinear relationship is MSIH(3)-VAR(2), which has one of the minimum Akaike criterions' (AIC) (-39.8114), Hannan-Quinnn criterions' (HQ) (-38.9497) and Schwarz criterions' (SIC) (-37.6401). It has a large log-likelihood ratio test (7.753.2651) that signifies the maximum likelihood estimate of the transition possibilities for the Markov model. The regime switching mechanism in the MSIH model is specified by the intercept (I) and volatility/heteroskedasticity (H).

Model 2 includes EUR/USD parity and the international portfolio flows. Among all nonlinear models with large LR linearity, the best explaining one is MSIH(3)-VAR(1). This model with three regimes has got a large log-likelihood (8,184.9001), a minimum Akaike criterions' (-42.0153), a minimum Hannan-Quinnn criterions' (-41.1842) and a minimum Schwarz criterions'(-39.9208).

After analyzing the portfolio flows as a whole, the relationships between EUR/USD parity and portfolio flows are analyzed in models by time series duals. The models 3 to 9 all are selected as explained for the first model and second model. They have p-value's less than 0.05 which statistically significant rejection of the null hypothesis of Davies' (1987). Having large log-likelihood ratios and minimum AIC, HQ and SIC criterions'. All of these seven models are MSIH(3)-VAR(2).

The coefficients of Model 1 are shown in Table 2. The estimation procedure implemented in the "Ox Metrics program" identifies regime 1 (recession), regime 2 (moderate growth) and regime 3 (expansion) of the model. In the first regime and second regime, the constants of all indices are negative. In the third regime, the constants of all countries' are positive except Indonesia and Thailand.

Table 3 shows the coefficients of Model 2. In the first regime, the constants of all indices are negative. In the second regime and the third regime, the constants differ as positive or negative. Model 1 and Model 2 indicate that international portfolio flows through Asian stock markets are governed by a long run relation and switch between three regimes together. After adding EUR/USD parity as an indicator to the model, some signs of coefficients have been changed from positive to negative, or from negative to positive.

Table 1. Information criterions, Model 1-9

		Model	Log-Likelihood	AIC	HQ	SIC	LR Linearity	DAVIES (5%)
Model 1	Asia Countries	MSIH(3)-VAR(2)	7,753.2651	-39.8114	-38.9497	-37.6401	10,060.7656 (0.000)	0.0019
Model 2	Asia Countries & Eur/USD	MSIH(3)-VAR(1)	8,184.9001	-42.0153	-41.1842	-39.9208	8,700.4049 (0.000)	0.0000
Model 3	India & Eur/USD	MSIH(3)-VAR(2)	4,596.9473	-24.1053	-23.9857	-23.8040	1,396.1901 (0.000)	0.0000
Model 4	Indonesia & Eur/USD	MSIH(3)-VAR(2)	4,510.6425	-23.6498	-23.5303	-23.3485	2,521.2779 (0.000)	0.0000
Model 5	Malaysia & Eur/USD	MSIH(3)-VAR(2)	4,620.2805	-24.2284	-24.1088	-23.9271	1,057.4891 (0.000)	0.0000
Model 6	Philippine & Eur/USD	MSIH(3)-VAR(2)	4,451.1679	-23.3360	-23.2164	-23.0347	2,792.9635 (0.000)	0.0000
Model 7	South Korea & Eur/USD	MSIH(3)-VAR(2)	4,542.2535	-23.8166	-23.6971	-23.5154	1,641.7682 (0.000)	0.0000
Model 8	Thailand & Eur/USD	MSIH(3)-VAR(2)	4,467.9713	-23.4247	-23.3051	-23.1234	2,264.9427 (0.000)	0.0000
Model 9	Vietnam & Eur/USD	MSIH(3)-VAR(2)	1,930.5217	-10.0394	-9.9149	-9.7331	1,408.4789 (0.000)	0.0000

As shown in Table 4, the signs (positive or negative) of constants in different regimes differ among the models. While the constants of all regimes' in Model 3 (India) and Model 8 (Thailand) are negative (India:-0.00046, -0.00015, -0.00451; Thailand: -0.00058, -0.00198, -0.13238), the constants of EUR/USD parity (India: 0.04160, 0.85403; Thailand: 0.31099, 0.00672) for both models do not have any comparison. Moreover, the international portfolio flows to India stock market are affected very strongly (0.85403) from the change in the value of parity two weeks ago.

The constants in the first and second regime both in Model 4 (Indonesia) and Model 6 (Philippine) are positive (Indonesia: 0.31537, 0.00042; Philippine: 0.00056, 0.27809). The test results indicate that both the two stock markets are affected positively from the first lag of EUR/US parity, even they are affected negatively from the second lag (Indonesia: 0.68452, -0.82551; Philippine: 0.63127, -0.44213). The negative effect of the parity is also seen for the international portfolio flows to Malaysia in the first lag (-0.30606, 0.17466) and South Korea in the second lag (0.41633, -0.41588).

	India	Indonesia	Malaysia	Philippine	S. Korea	Thailand	Vietnam
SE (Reg. 3)	0.03790	0.21327	0.02174	0.35094	0.00543	0.00625	43.64185
SE (Reg. 2)	0.00149	0.00193	0.00312	0.00315	0.00225	0.00207	3.43364
SE (Reg. 1)	0.00744	0.00597	0.00237	0.00257	0.05844	0.16035	1.49214
Vietnam_2	0.00001	0.00001	-0.00001	0.00001	0.00001	0.00000	0.0136
Vietnam_1	0.00000	-0.00000	0.00001	-0.00003	-0.00002	0.00001	0.00242
Thailand_2	-0.00048	0.00098	-0.00058	-0.00095	-0.01159	0.00196	-0.16608
Thailand_1	-0.0072	0.00331	-0.00052	-0.00406	0.00045	-0.00021	-0.62959
S. Korea_2	0.00301	0.00891	-0.00470	0.02769	-0.00600	-0.00073	-18.34784
S. Korea_1	0.00065	-0.00193	-0.00219	0.00020	-0.00337	0.01227	-0.43257
Philippine_2	-0.00072	-0.00071	0.00032	0.00602	0.00019	-0.00123	0.98836
Philippine_1	-0.00090	-0.00007	0.00205	-0.00012	0.00055	-0.00129	-0.57565
Malaysia_2	0.00225	0.00072	0.00648	-0.00368	-0.00070	-0.00891	0.09571
Malaysia_1	0.04777	0.00175	0.03213	0.00573	-0.07579	-0.00386	35.36777
Indonesia_2	-0.00092	-0.00227	-0.00067	-0.00037	-0.00030	-0.00332	0.87985
Indonesia_1	0.00069	-0.00049	0.00170	0.00309	0.00158	0.00088	0.52040
India_2	0.00445	-0.00249	0.02365	-0.066077	0.00762	0.00773	14.25299
India_1	0.00123	-0.00259	0.00664	0.00440	0.00404	0.00757	30.05994
Constant (Reg. 3)	0.00005	**-0.03955**	0.00299	0.06817	0.000533	**-0.00275**	6.05262
Constant (Reg. 2)	**-0.00035**	**-0.00060**	**-0.00054**	**-0.00068**	**-0.00047**	**-0.00045**	**-0.57576**
Constant (Reg. 1)	**-0.00267**	**-0.00112**	**-0.00035**	**-0.00059**	**-0.00870**	**-0.02955**	**-0.58421**

Table 2. Coefficients, model 1

Table 3. Coefficients, model 2

	Constant (Reg. 1)	Constant (Reg. 2)	Constant (Reg. 3)	India_1	I Indonesia_1	Malaysia_1	Philippine_1	S. Korea_1	Thailand_1	Vietnam_1	EUR/USD_1	SE (Reg. 1)	SE (Reg. 2)	SE (Reg. 3)
India	**-0.00164**	**-0.00038**	**-0.00067**	0.00141	0.00077	0.04361	-0.00085	-0.00118	-0.00165	-0.00000	0.00120	0.00565	0.00121	0.03681
Indonesia	0.02805	**-0.00057**	**-0.00014**	-0.00287	-0.00038	0.00689	0.00029	-0.00094	0.00334	0.00002	0.02527	0.18484	0.00217	0.00417
Philippine	**-0.00037**	0.01558	**-0.00220**	0.01997	-0.03946	0.00177	-0.00017	-0.01038	0.01184	-0.00003	-0.01870	0.00264	0.16855	0.00971
S. Korea	**-0.00685**	**-0.000036**	**-0.00029**	0.00998	0.00168	-0.11536	0.00074	-0.00482	0.00063	0.00001	0.01432	0.05323	0.00185	0.00389
Thailand	**-0.00163**	**-0.00057**	**-0.03032**	0.00742	0.00112	0.01885	-0.00130	0.01254	-0.00041	0.00000	0.00654	0.00688	0.00186	0.16116
Malaysia	**-0.00048**	**-0.00037**	0.00228	0.00526	0.00166	0.02649	0.00003	-0.00034	-0.00056	0.00000	0.01236	0.00200	0.00261	0.02138
Vietnam	**-0.39117**	**-0.44994**	5.01863	26.13682	0.23364	32.65662	-0.84929	-3.98008	-1.28834	-0.00007	8.57071	1.96765	2.63833	42.34236
EUR/ USD	0.00196	**-0.00186**	0.00189	0.02734	-0.00712	0.02193	-0.00099	0.05737	-0.00390	-0.00001	0.02730	0.01371	0.01359	0.01198

Table 4. Coefficients, model 3-9

		Constant (Reg. 1)	Constant (Reg. 2)	Constant (Reg. 3)	NPI _1	NPI_2	EUR/USD _1	EUR/USD _2	SE (Reg. 1)	SE (Reg. 2)	SE (Reg. 3)
Model 3	India NPI	-0.00046	-0.00015	-0.00451	-0.00006	0.00217	**0.04160**	**0.85403**	0.00075	0.00265	0.05361
	EUR/USD	-0.00002	0.00001	0.00004	0.00032	-0.00087	0.01842	-0.02775	0.00014	0.00013	0.00014
Model 4	Indonesia NPI	0.31537	0.00042	-0.00056	-0.00057	-0.00232	**0.68452**	**-0.81551**	0.54311	0.01141	0.00121
	EUR/USD	-0.00002	0.00002	-0.00001	-0.00008	0.00004	0.02210	-0.04528	0.00011	0.00016	0.00013
Model 5	Malaysia NPI	-0.00039	-0.00046	0.00779	-0.00034	-0.00323	**-0.30606**	**0.17466**	0.00054	0.00299	0.03607
	EUR/USD	-0.00001	-0.00001	-0.00004	0.00025	-0.00060	-000171	-0.01758	0.00012	0.00015	0.00009
Model 6	Philippine NPI	0.00056	0.27809	-0.00058	-0.00024	0.006388	**0.63127**	**-0.44213**	0.00665	0.66571	0.00087
	EUR/USD	0.00001	0.00005	-0.00002	-0.00001	0.00000	0.00791	-0.03540	0.00014	0.00014	0.00013
Model 7	S. Korea NPI	-0.05018	0.00019	-0.00047	-0.00397	-0.00522	**0.41633**	**-0.41588**	0.13547	0.00560	0.00112
	EUR/USD	-0.00005	0.00003	-0.00002	0.00056	-0.00040	0.00560	-0.03709	0.00009	0.00015	0.00013
Model 8	Thailand NPI	-0.00058	-0.00198	-0.13238	-0.00020	-0.00004	**0.31099**	**0.00672**	0.00091	0.00899	0.32506
	EUR/USD	-0.00001	-0.00001	0.00004	0.00175	-0.00001	0.26343	-0.03445	0.00014	0.00014	0.00012
Model 9	Vietnam NPI	-0.49381	-0.33455	17.31825	-0.00229	0.00919	**466.69021**	**42.062402**	0.94129	5.03468	74.46686
	EUR/USD	-0.00001	0.00000	0.00004	0.00000	-0.00000	0.008274	-0.0317	0.00014	0.00012	0.00010

As the amount of international portfolio flows to Vietnam stock market is very low, the constants of EUR/USD parity in Model 9 are not comparable with other models (466.69021, 42.062402). Vietnam may not be included in the further studies' samples.

Transition probability represents the likelihood that the indices will stay in the original regime or switch to another regime. According to the matrix of Transition Probabilities, the maximum probabilities are seen from switching any regime to Regime 2 in Model 1 and Model 2 (Model 1: 0.7014, 0.6826, 0.7571; Model 2: 0.6848, 0.6520, 0.5892). The probabilities of switching from any regime to Regime 1 are prominently high for Model 3, 8 and 9 (India, p_{11}:0.4351, p_{21}:0.7517, p_{31}:0.9752; Thailand, p_{11}:0.5953, p_{21}:0.9037, p_{31}:1; Vietnam, p_{11}:0.5914, p_{21}:0.8712, p_{31}:0.9907). Switching from any regime to Regime 3 have got strong probabilities in Model 4, 6 and 7 (Indonesia, p_{13}:0.9923, p_{23}:0.9226, p_{33}:0.7546; Philippine, p_{13}:0.8728, p_{23}:0.8181, p_{33}:0.4833; South Korea, p_{13}:0.6764, p_{23}:0.9174, p_{33}:0.6467).

In the 7,33 years' period, the greatest number of observations with the highest probability and longest duration are seen in Regime 2 for Model 1 and Model 2. While the matrix of transition probabilities and regime properties are evaluated together, the mutual switching behavior of international portfolio flows in Asia tends to go to regime 2.

The highest number of observations, probability and duration are seen in Regime 1 for Model 3, 5, 8 and 9; in Regime 3 for Model 4, 6 and 7. The durations of models in different regimes are between 1 to 4 weeks.

The impulse response tests of Model 3-9 are shown in the following figures. The responses of international portfolio flow to the EUR/USD parity shocks should be grouped as;

Table 5. Matrix of transition probabilities, model 1-2

		Regime 1	Regime 2	Regime 3
Asia Countries	Regime 1	0.0985	**0.7014**	0.2001
	Regime 2	0.1837	**0.6826**	0.1338
	Regime 3	0.0981	**0.7571**	0.1449
Asia Countries & EUR/USD	Regime 1	0.1704	**0.6848**	0.1448
	Regime 2	0.1748	**0.6520**	0.1732
	Regime 3	0.3089	**0.5892**	0.1019

Table 6. Matrix of transition probabilities, model 3-9

			Regime 1	Regime 2	Regime 3
Model 3	India	Regime 1	**0.4351**	**0.4451**	0.1197
		Regime 2	**0.7517**	0.2318	0.0164
		Regime 3	**0.9752**	0.0247	0.0000
Model 4	Indonesia	Regime 1	0.0000	0.0077	**0.9923**
		Regime 2	0.0000	0.0774	**0.9226**
		Regime 3	0.0219	0.2235	**0.7546**
Model 5	Malaysia	Regime 1	**0.4206**	**0.4729**	0.1064
		Regime 2	**0.5851**	**0.4149**	0.0000
		Regime 3	**0.7676**	0.2324	0.0000
Model 6	Philippine	Regime 1	0.1187	0.0085	**0.8728**
		Regime 2	0.1819	0.0000	**0.8181**
		Regime 3	**0.4643**	0.0524	**0.4833**
Model 7	South Korea	Regime 1	0.0000	0.3236	**0.6764**
		Regime 2	0.0000	0.0826	**0.9174**
		Regime 3	0.0339	0.3194	**0.6467**
Model 8	Thailand	Regime 1	**0.5953**	0.3534	0.0493
		Regime 2	**0.9037**	0.0962	0.0000
		Regime 3	**1**	0	0
Model 9	Vietnam	Regime 1	**0.5914**	0.3377	0.0708
		Regime 2	**0.8712**	0.1288	0.0000
		Regime 3	**0.9907**	0.0093	0.0000

Table 7. Regime properties, model 1-2

			Number of Observation	Probability	Duration
Model 1	Asia Countries	Regime 1	60	0.1577	1.11
		Regime 2	264	0.6964	3.15
		Regime 3	55	0.1458	1.17
Model 2	Asia Countries & EUR/USD	Regime 1	74	0.1949	1.21
		Regime 2	246	0.6486	2.87
		Regime 3	60	0.1565	1.11

Table 8. Regime properties, model 3-9

			Number of Observation	Probability	Duration
Model 3	India	Regime 1	222	0.5838	1.77
		Regime 2	129	0.3407	1.30
		Regime 3	28	0.0755	1.00
Model 4	Indonesia	Regime 1	6	0.0173	1.00
		Regime 2	73	0.1917	1.01
		Regime 3	300	0.7909	4.08
Model 5	Malaysia	Regime 1	193	0.5110	1.73
		Regime 2	165	0.4346	1.71
		Regime 3	21	0.0544	1.00
Model 6	Philippine	Regime 1	128	0.3376	1.13
		Regime 2	14	0.0357	1.00
		Regime 3	237	0.6267	1.94
Model 7	South Korea	Regime 1	10	0.0243	1.00
		Regime 2	98	0.2583	1.09
		Regime 3	271	0.7174	2.83
Model 8	Thailand	Regime 1	262	0.6932	2.47
		Regime 2	104	0.2726	1.11
		Regime 3	13	0.0342	1.0
Model 9	Vietnam	Regime 1	260	0.6853	2.45
		Regime 2	101	0.2662	1.15
		Regime 3	18	0.0485	1.00

Figure 1. Impulse response tests, India

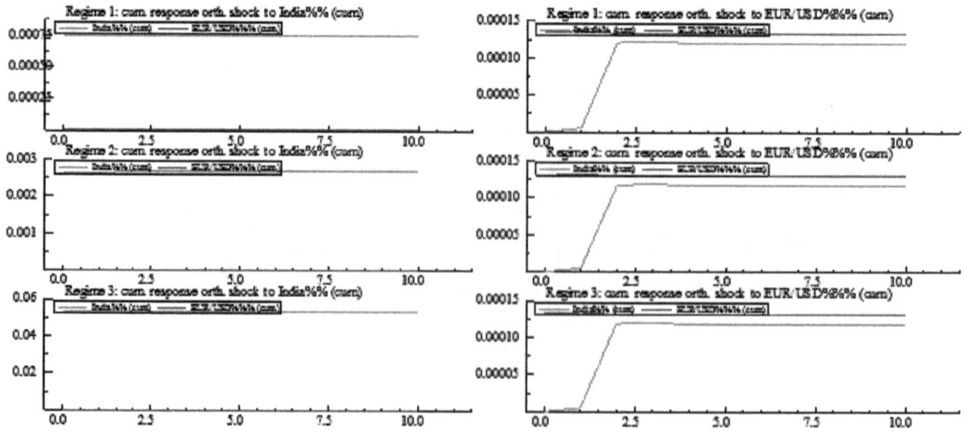

Figure 2. Impulse response tests, Indonesia

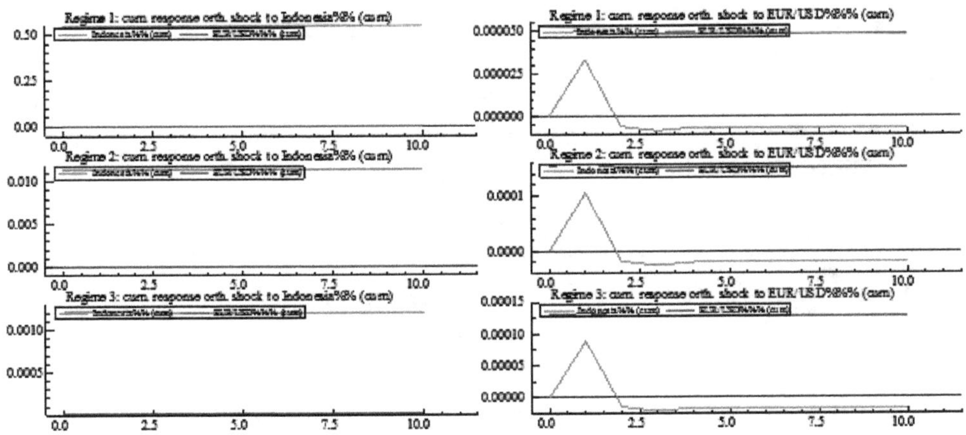

Figure 3. Impulse response tests, Malaysia

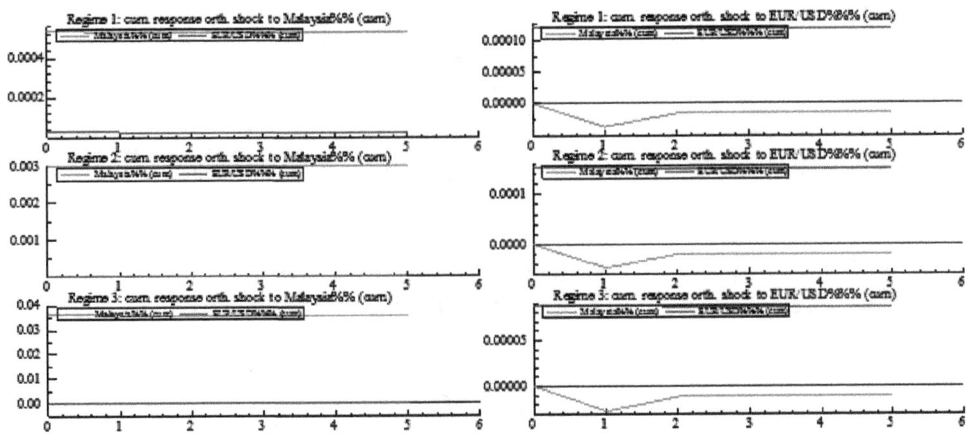

First Group: India, Thailand, Vietnam

Following quick and prominent positive responses (increasing) of the international portfolio flows to the one standard deviation's shocks on EUR/USD parity, nearly all of the responses become permanent in all regimes. The rising periods of the responses to the shocks for India are 2.5 weeks, for Thailand 2 weeks and for Vietnam 1 week. The powers of the responses in different regimes do not change too much for India and Thailand, except Vietnam. The response of the international portfolio flows in stock market in Vietnam in the third regime is smaller than the first and second regimes.

Figure 4. Impulse response tests, Philippine

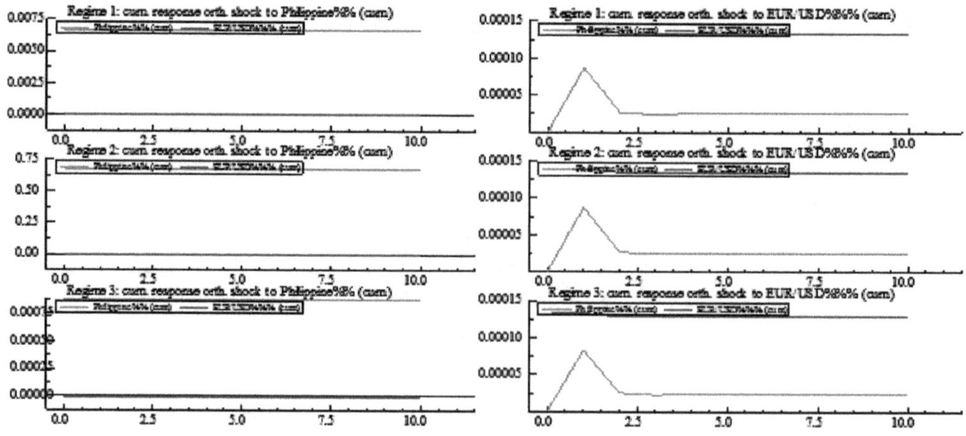

Figure 5. Impulse response tests, South Korea

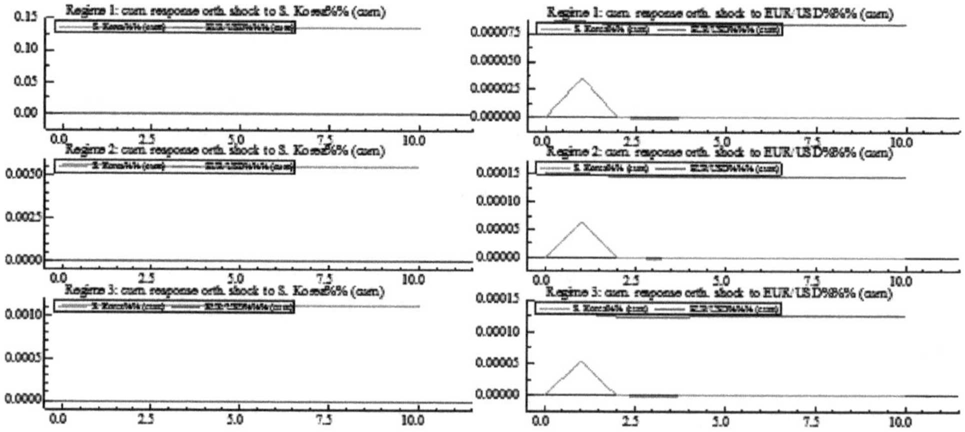

Second Group: Indonesia, Philippine, South Korea

The responses of the international portfolio flow in the second group are seen as a fast increase and a following decrease to nearly the beginning point in the first 2.5 weeks. However, there is a small negative permanent impact of the shock on Indonesia and positive permanent impact on Philippine.

Figure 6. Impulse response tests, Thailand

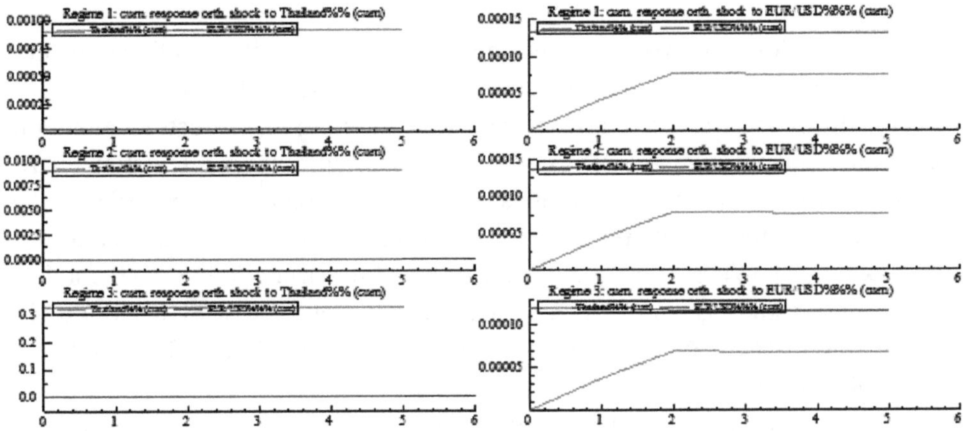

Figure 7. Impulse response tests, Vietnam

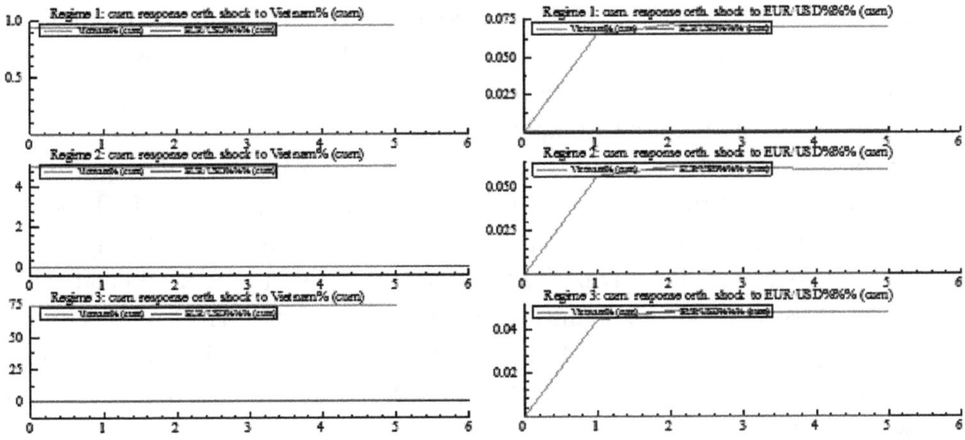

Third Group: Malaysia

The international portfolio flows in the stock market of Malaysia behaves differently from all the other countries'. If one standard deviation's shock is applied to EUR/USD parity, the response of international portfolio flows in Malaysia is shown as decrease in the first week, increase in the second week and a small permanent negative effect in the following weeks. Additionally, the negative effect is stronger in the second regime and the third regime from the first regime.

CONCLUSION

High portfolio flows to EMs have been shown up by the monetary policy of central banks following the next global crisis and European crisis. Mostly, large external financing needs and risk premiums of EMs took international investors' attention. The Asian countries, which have experienced sharp currency depreciations, gave a rise to the risk premium opportunities of the international investors, too. In this paper, how the international portfolio flows to Asian stock markets affected from the shocks on EUR/USD parity is analyzed by Multivariate MMS-VAR models. The goal of our study is to provide a comparative evaluation that EUR/USD parity is used. EUR/USD parity is an indicator which shows the effects of FED and ECB money politics either.

The mutual switching mechanism of the international portfolio flows through Asian stock markets (India, Indonesia, Philippine, South Korea, Thailand, Malaysia and Vietnam) between 01/01/2010 to 21/04/2017 is firstly investigated in the study. Secondly, a model including EUR/USD parity and the portfolio flows is described. It draws attention that all of the powerful models explaining relationships point out MSIH model that is specified by the intercept (I) and volatility/heteroskedasticity (H) with three regimes. These three regimes are regime 1 (recession), regime 2 (moderate growth) and regime 3 (expansion).

The first two models indicate that international portfolio flows through Asian stock markets are governed by a long run relation. The shocks on EUR/USD parity have positive effects on the countries' portfolio flows except Malaysia. Lastly, given the relation between EUR/USD parity and portfolio flows, the long run and short run effects of parity differs to countries and varies to regimes. The findings of the study that highlight the behavior of portfolio flows to Asian stock markets against EUR/USD parity shocks should act as a guidance to the international investors beyond academic contribution.

REFERENCES

Ahmed, S., & Zlate, A. (2014). Capital flows to emerging market economies: A brave new world? *Journal of International Money and Finance*, *48*, 221–248. doi:10.1016/j.jimonfin.2014.05.015

Baek, I. M. (2006). Portfolio investment flows to Asia and Latin America: Pull, push or market sentiment? *Journal of Asian Economics*, *17*(2), 363–373. doi:10.1016/j.asieco.2006.02.007

Bekaert, G., & Harvey, C. R. (1997). *Foreign speculators and emerging equity markets*. The Davidson Institute Working Paper Series, Working Paper Number 79.

Bekaert, G., & Harvey, C. R. (2000). Foreign speculators and emerging equity markets. *The Journal of Finance, 55*(2), 565–613. doi:10.1111/0022-1082.00220

Bekaert, G., Harvey, C. R., & Lundblad, C. (2002). *Growth volatility and equity market liberalization?* Unpublished working paper. Columbia, Duke and Indiana Universities.

Bildirici, M. E., Aykaç Alp, E., Ersin, Ö. Ö., & Bozoklu, Ü. (2010). *İktisatta kullanılan doğrusal olmayan zaman serisi yöntemleri*. Türkmen Kitabevi.

Brooks, R., Edison, H., Kumar, M. S., & Slok, T. (2004). Exchange rates and capital flows. *European Financial Management, 10*(3), 511–533. doi:10.1111/j.1354-7798.2004.00261.x

Calvo, G. A., & Reinhart, C. M. (2002). Fear of floating. *The Quarterly Journal of Economics, 117*(2), 379–408. doi:10.1162/003355302753650274

Caporale, G. M., Ali, F. M., Spagnolo, F., & Spagnolo, N. (2017). International portfolio flows and exchange rate volatility in emerging Asian markets. *Journal of International Money and Finance, 76*, 1–15. doi:10.1016/j.jimonfin.2017.03.002

Chaban, M. (2009). Commodity currencies and equity flows. *Journal of International Money and Finance, 28*(5), 836–852. doi:10.1016/j.jimonfin.2008.08.004

Çulha, A. A. (2006). A Structural VAR Analysis of the Determinants of Capital Flows into Turkey. *Central Bank Review, 2*, 11–35.

Davies, R. B. (1987). Hypothesis Testing when a Nuisance Parameter is Present Only Under the Alternatives. *Biometrika Trust, 74*(1), 33–43.

Franses, P. H. H. & Dijk, D. (2000). *Nonlinear Time Series Models in Empirical Finance*. Cambridge University Press.

Georgiadis, G., & Grab, J. (2015). *Global Financial Market Impact of the Announcement of the ECB's Extended Asset Purchase Programme*. Federal Reserve Bank of Dallas Globalization and Monetary Policy Institute. Working Paper No. 232

Ghosh, S., & Herwadkar, S. (2009). Foreign Portfolio Flows and their Impact on Financial Markets in India. *Reserve Bank of India Occasional Papers, 30*(3), 51-72.

Guidolin, M. (n.d.). *Modelling, Estimating and Forecasting Financial Data under Regime (Markov) Switching*. Lecture 7. Department of Finance. Bocconi University. Retrieved from http://didattica.unibocconi.it/mypage/dwload.php?nomefile=Lecture_7_-_Markov_Switching_Models20130520235704.pdf, 30.03.2016.

Hamilton, J. D. (1989). A New Approach to the Economic Analysis of Nonstationary Time Series and the Business Cycle. *Econometrica*, *57*(2), 357–384. doi:10.2307/1912559

International Monetary Fund. (2017). *World Economic Outlook Update*. Retrieved from http://www.imf.org/en/Publications/WEO/Issues/2017/07/07/world-economic-outlook-update-july-2017

Krolzig, H. M. (1998). *Markov Switching Vector Autoregressions: Modelling, Statistical Inference, and Application to Business Cycle Analysis*. Berlin: Springer-Verlag.

Krolzig, H. M. (2000). *Predicting Markov-switching vector autoregressive processes*. Oxford University Working Paper 2000W31.

Mishra, P., Moriyama, K., N'diaye, P. M. B. P., & Nguyen, L. (2014). *Impact of Fed Tapering Announcements on Emerging Markets*. IMF Working Paper. WP/14/109.

Onyeisi, O. S., Odo, I. S., & Anoke, C. I. (2016). Foreign Portfolio Investment and Stock Market Growth in Nigeria. *Developing Country Studies*, *6*(11), 64–76.

Rujiravanich, N. (2013). Impacts of Foreign Portfolio Investment Flows on Stock Prices and Exchange Rate *in* Thailand after Asian Financial Crisis. *Economics and Public Policy*, *4*(8), 1–20.

Sangara, İ. (2016). External shocks and exchange rate regimes in Southeast Asia: A DSGE analysis. *Economic Modelling*, *58*, 365–382. doi:10.1016/j.econmod.2016.06.004

Sethi, N. (2012). Inflows and Their Macroeconomics Impact in India a VAR Analysis. *The Romanian Economic Journal*, *46*, 93–142.

Waqas, Y., Hashmi, S. H., & Nazır, M. I. (2015). Macroeconomic factors and foreign portfolio investment volatility: A case of South Asian countries. *Future Business Journal*, *1*(1-2), 65–74. doi:10.1016/j.fbj.2015.11.002

Yıldız, A. (2012). Yabancı Portföy Yatırımlarını Etkileyen Faktörlerin Belirlenmesi. *Atatürk Üniversitesi İktisadi ve İdari Bilimler Dergisi*, *26*(1), 23–37.

Chapter 6
Banks, Stock Markets, and Growth Relationships in the EU28 Countries

Andreas G. Georgantopoulos
Panteion University of Political and Social Sciences, Greece

Ioannis Filos
Panteion University of Political and Social Science, Greece

Evangelos I. Poutos
Hellenic Open University, Greece

ABSTRACT

This chapter examines the impact of banks and stock markets on economic growth for a panel that includes the 28 EU member states. The originality of this study lies in that it tests these relationships by employing sub-regional panels based on the geographical distribution of EU countries and by clustering EU member states in Eurozone and non-Euro countries. Results support the stock market-led growth hypothesis only for the case of the full sample panel. Furthermore, both the full panel results and Eurozone panel results fail to support the bank credit-led growth hypothesis. These results are inconsistent with other studies, which however employ only full regional panels.

DOI: 10.4018/978-1-5225-6114-9.ch006

1. INTRODUCTION

The relationships between the financial system (banking sector and financial sector) and economic growth, puzzles academics, scholars and practitioners for more than a century. The literature on this subject provides exhaustive evidence that support the significance of the financial system-growth nexus dating back to the studies of Schumpeter (1911, 1934), who suggests that the financial intermediary sector plays a significant role to the productivity growth and technological advance by the allocation of savings to firms.

The literature evolved with a rapid pace, especially during the last two decades, and can be divided into two groups. The first group of studies deals with the impact of stock market development on economic growth by employing stocks traded, market capitalisation or turnover ratio as proxies. The second group of literature concentrates on the relationships between banking sector developments, as measured by credit and liquid liabilities, and economic growth. Regardless of the proxies and regions/countries employed, both strands of this literature are in consensus that the financial system promotes economic growth, although presenting different characteristics and significance levels across regions/countries. Moreover, this literature further expanded by employing measures of trade, namely, trade openness (the sum of imports and exports) and exports documenting not only the significant impact of trade on economic growth (see Shahbaz, 2012; Georgantopoulos and Tsamis, 2011; Yanikkaya, 2003; Baldwin and Forslid, 1998) but also the linkages between financial development and trade (Bordo and Rousseau, 2012; Taylor and Wilson, 2011; Baltagi et al., 2009; Hur et al., 2006).

This study aims to assess the impact of banking and financial sector developments on economic growth for a full panel of the 28 European Union member countries (EU28) over the period 1996-2016. This paper contributes to the existing pool of literature in three ways. First, this is the only study that focuses on the EU28 (Croatia became the 28th member state of the European Union on 1st of July 2013). Other studies deal with the financial system and growth nexus (see Section 2) either by employing data relating to a single country or by using too many and mixed panel data making it difficult to analyse in depth one particular region that presents similar financial attributes. Moreover, several studies include EU countries in panel data with other non-EU countries. Therefore, this study argues that EU member states, present different financial characteristics than non-EU countries, mainly due to the close economic and political cooperation that EU member states benefit. The European Union operates through a network of independent institutions[1]. Although the EU is not a single country yet, a consolidated economic and political environment has been created for its member states. In this vein, scientific conclusions could be much more accurate dealing with these countries apart from other non-EU countries when employing panel data analysis.

The second contribution of this study is that for the first time in this literature, the full EU sample is divided into a panel of Eurozone countries and non-euro countries. The European Economic and Monetary Union (EMU) is a term for the group of procedures and policies aimed to link the economic systems of all EU member states. Both the 19 Eurozone states and the 9 non-euro states are EMU members. However, a Member State needs to comply with several economic and fiscal criteria before being able to adopt the Euro as a national currency, becoming in this way a full member of the Eurozone. Therefore, the Eurozone countries enjoy an advanced stage of not only economic and trade but also monetary integration, binding the Eurozone countries tighter to each other than the rest of the non-Euro countries that have not adopted the euro currency yet. Furthermore, this study divides the full EU regional sample into four sub-regional panels (Northern, Southern, Western and Eastern EU countries) based on the geographical scheme for Europe, as created by the Statistics Division of the United Nations[2]. This is the first study that considers these sub-regions, while examining the growth nexus. We support the argument that EU neighbouring countries present more similar characteristics, which can be attributed not only to the closer trade and economic relationships, but also due to cultural and social similarities. Hence, by forming the aforementioned sub-groups of EU member states, more homogenous samples can be created and therefore we are allowed to expect more accurate empirical results. Overall, this paper assumes that these empirical findings should deviate from the results drown from the full EU sample panel due to the significant differences between the EU member states, namely in culture, currency, social structure as well as business ethics.

Third, this study examines the short-run relationships between financial sector, banking sector and economic growth[3]. There are very few studies (Georgantopoulos et al., 2015; Narayan and Narayan, 2013; Loayza and Ranciere, 2006; Kaminsky and Reinhart, 1999) that deal with these short-run relationships. However, four factors could be numbered that motivate this study to focus on a short-run timeframe: (i) the rapidly changing economic environment; since the beginning of the EU in 1957, then called European Economic Community (EEC), when the six founding member states, namely, Belgium, France, Italy, Luxembourg, the Netherlands, and West Germany signed the Treaty of Rome, numerous territorial, economic, political and social transformations have taken place, leading to a significantly expanded, and more stabilised and integrated European Union. Therefore, the risk of reaching to ambiguous and misleading results, could be higher when dealing with long period panel data in the case of the EU, (ii) the concern that averaging data leads to information loss and to rigid model that omits the cross-country heterogeneity parameter (Loayza and Ranciere, 2006), (iii) the possibility that negative effects can occur on economic growth if the banking sector is over-liberalised in the short-run, urge this study to focus on investigating the short-run relationships between the selected variables, and (iv) the data limitation problem that researchers face when choosing to work on balanced cross-country panels. Statistical validity is further ensured by employing extensive tests of misspecification and re-specifications of the empirical modes employed, such as to test the potential existence of a non-linear relationship between growth and its determinants. As Samargandi et al. (2015) point out, there are very few papers that consider a non-monotone relation between financial, banking and economic development. To this respect, it is important to assess whether there is a maximum above which financial and/or banking depth start having an adverse impact on growth.

The rest of the paper is structured as follows; Section 2, reviews the related literature. Section 3, introduces the data, the selected determinants of growth and the methodology applied in this study. Section 4, presents the summary statistics and empirical results, while Section 5, provides the concluding remarks and policy implications.

2. LITERATURE REVIEW

Since the early contributions of Bagehot (1873) on the relationships between the financial system and industrialization for the case of England as well as Schumpeter's (1911, 1934) as described briefly in the introductory section, numerous studies are published on this topic, focusing on the multi-faceted empirical aspects of this relationship. This section limits the discussion only to a contemporary body of empirical literature and puts emphasis on studies that are more closely related to this study in terms of data analysis and methodological application.

The literature provides contradictory evidence regarding the impact of the financial system and its components, namely, stock markets and banks on economic growth. Several studies propose that when banks and stock markets operate under a well-functioning economic environment, they can both boost growth and efficiently allocate resources through the reduction of information loss and transaction costs. King and Levine (1993a) examined the impact of various financial system indicators (liquid liabilities to GDP, claims on the non-financial private sector to GDP and private credit). Their study uses cross-sectional data for 80 developed and developing countries, concluding that all four indicators have a statistically significant and positive impact on growth (for related studies, see also, Bencivenga et al., 1995; Bencivenga and Smith, 1991). However, these studies also indicate that financial system can also slow economic growth since the continuously increasing resource allocation, which is associated to higher return on deposits, may lead eventually to lower interests on deposits. Therefore, in case sufficiently large externalities occur, that are associated with savings and investment, financial system will slow economic growth.

Moreover, the literature on the financial system-growth nexus is divided on whether the financial sector and banking sector are substitutes, compliments or whether banks overcome markets and vice versa as more significant stimulus of growth. Levine et al. (2000) investigate the impact of financial intermediary variables, namely, private credit and liquid liabilities on economic development for a cross-country panel of 74 countries and for a cross-section panel of 71 countries employing the Arellano and Bond (1991) GMM methodology. They conclude that the selected proxies of financial intermediation have significant and positive impact on economic development. Cole et al. (2008) assess the relations between banking sector's stock returns and economic growth for a panel of 38 countries through the application of system-GMM models. This research proposes that banking sector stock returns have more significant and positive impact on their panel of developing markets than on the panel comprised of mature markets.

Boyd and Prescott (1986) find that banks play a key role in reducing the loss of information leading to more efficient allocation of resources, while other studies propose that the financial sector underperforms in terms of resource allocation compared to the banking sector (Bhide, 1993; Stiglitz, 1985). Another group of studies stress that stock markets overcome banks in promoting economic growth. These theories emphasize that the financial sector is not only free from the monopolistic and conservative environment that the banking sector impose to the economy but also encourages innovation and competition stimulating growth in more effective ways. Shen and Lee (2006) suggest that only stock market development significantly impacts growth, by employing simple Ordinary Least Squares (OLS) and two-stage OLS procedures for a panel of 48 countries (see also, Allen and Gale, 2000).

Some other studies propose that both banks and stock markets are key growth factors, since these two components of the financial system improve in different ways the diffusion of information and allocation of resources. Levine and Zervos (1998) examine the relationship between banking sector development, stock market development and growth for a cross-section panel of 45 countries. They conclude that both components of the financial system are significant predictors of growth. Bittencourt (2012) find that financial development significantly impacts growth by employing time series and panel data for four Latin American countries, while Campos et al. (2012) in their research for the case of Argentina, they also conclude that financial development impacts growth in a statistically significant and positive way (see also, Zhang et al., 2012; Hasan et al., 2009; Beck and Levine, 2004).

Moreover, recent studies dispute on the positive relationship between financial system and growth; Anwar and Sun (2011) employ GMM estimator on annual data for the period (1970-2007) concluding that the impact of financial development on economic growth is statistically insignificant for the case of Malaysia. Overall, the majority of the literature on this topic suggests that financial system and its components (banks and stock markets) significantly influence economic growth. Owen and Temesvary (2014) conclude that the impact of the banking system on economic development is heterogeneous not only across different countries but also across different types of bank lending (foreign and domestic). Furthermore, Beck et al. (2014) assess the impact of size and the degree of financial intermediation on economic growth and growth volatility, concluding that financial intermediation has a positive impact on economic development and reduces growth volatility in the long run. Loayza and Ranciere (2006) investigate the short and long-run finance-growth relations based on a dataset of 75 countries from 1960 to 2000. They support the existence of positive long-run and negative short-run relationships between the growth of the financial sector and economic development.

Finally, much of the current literature suggests that the finance–growth relationship is non-monotonic, with the impact of financial deepening on growth becoming negative once a certain threshold is reached (Cecchetti and Kharroubi, 2012; Arcand et al., 2012; Deidda and Fattouh, 2002). Easterly et al. (2000) conclude that there is a concave relationship between financial growth and the volatility of economic development. Law and Singh (2014) assess whether the financial system has a positive impact on economic development after a country's financial growth exceeds a certain threshold level, finding that private sector credit promotes growth only up to a certain point beyond which this positive impact becomes negative.

Another strand of literature focuses on assessing the impact of fiscal policy on economic growth. The traditional theory supports that government purchases financed through deficit is not an efficient policy in order to significantly promote growth mainly because it discourages private investments and usually it leads to distortions in financial and product markets. However, the related literature is divided, with some studies favouring the hypothesis of a significantly adverse effect of high fiscal deficits on economic development (Gupta et al., 2005; Easterly and Rebelo, 1993;), while another group of empirical studies fail to trace any significant and negative effect (Miller and Russek, 1997; Levine and Renelt, 1992), or present findings of a positive relation (Barro and Redlick, 2011). Nevertheless, Baldacci et al. (2004) and Adam and Bevan (2005) managed to find non-linear effects on output level, implying that low levels of fiscal deficits can be growth-enhancing. Afonso and González-Alegre (2008), in their study on EU-15 member states and for the period 1970–2006, support the positive relation between financial deficits and economic growth, while similar findings are also presented by Morgese-Borys et al. (2008) based on a dataset of 12 new-EU members and for the period from 1994 to 2005.

3. DATA ANALYSIS AND METHODOLOGY

3.1. Data Analysis

This study uses balanced panel data for the 28 member states of the European Union[4] (EU28) for the period 1996-2016. However, the EU member states present significant differences, such as, currency dissimilarities, cultural and social differences, as well as intensity of economic cooperation, although all 28 countries enjoy full and equal membership in the EU. To assess these differences, this study divides the full EU28 panel data set, based on two features; (i) national currency, creating two sub-sets of panel data, namely, Eurozone countries, which are EU member states that have adopted the Euro (€) as their national currency, and non-Euro EU countries[5], and (ii) geographical distribution, as proposed by the United Nation's Statistics Division, in four sub-regional panel data sets, namely, Northern, Southern, Western and Eastern EU countries[6]. The hypothesis behind this categorisation is that due to the various dissimilarities within the European family, investigating only the full regional EU data set, may lead to ambiguous results and conclusions. To accept this hypothesis, significantly different empirical results and conclusions are expected when running the models for the full EU28 panel data set and for the above sub-sets.

This study employs the following variables in the estimation procedure: Economic growth (GGDP), gross fixed capital formation as a percentage of GDP (GFCF), inflation (INFL), trade openness as a percentage of GDP (OPEN), market capitalization of listed companies as a percentage of GDP (MCAP), bank's domestic credit as a percentage of GDP (CREDIT), stocks traded as a percentage of GDP (STOCKS) and the general-public deficit as percent of GDP (DEFICIT). All data are derived from the World Development Indicators (WDI), a reliable World Bank database.

Market capitalization and stocks traded are used as proxies for the financial sector development. The literature reveals four functions of the financial sector, which are considered to promote economic growth; (i) financial intermediaries enable savings to be placed into long-term assets, which are more productive than short-term assets (Bencivenga and Smith, 1991), (ii) financial markets enable investors to diversify risk and promote liquidity. In the absence of financial markets, investors constrained by liquidity shocks are forced to liquidate long-term investments, hurting economic growth (Obstfeld, 2004), (iii) the financial sector provides better corporate control (Nieuwerburgh et al., 2006), and finally, (iv) stock markets are able to deliver evaluation and monitoring services more efficiently than individual investors, ensuring an efficient allocation of funds over the life of investment projects, due to acquiring information in advance (King and Levine, 1993b).

However, a sharp rise of the stock markets may occur as a result of speculative pressure and generalised euphoria caused by the financial liberalisation (Singh, 1997; Keynes, 1936). This bull market situation increases interest rates rapidly due to higher market risk, freezing investments and hurting economic growth as a consequence (Federer, 1993). Moreover, Devereux and Smith (1994) argue that risk diversification in trading activities may cause savings' rates to decline, harming economic growth, while the same result may occur due to the use of market manipulation strategies through in-excess stock trading (De Long et al.,1989). Finally, Fry (1997) concludes that stock markets are proving to be weak intermediaries between households and businesses.

This study considers bank's domestic credit as a proxy for the banking sector development, which is consistent with the literature. Several studies use this variable, as indicator of the banking sector development. One reason is due to the availability of data for a large number of countries. Banks compared to stock markets, intermediate differently, since equity funding is associated with business performance. However, negative effects on growth may arise not only from financial intermediation but from bank intermediation also. Banks tend to allocate credit considering primarily transaction costs and the risk of default and ignoring the expected return on investment, shrinking the average investment efficiency. Interest rates decline, since investments with lower returns can now become profitable in favouring current consumption against future consumption leading to a severe decline in savings' rates with significantly negative social implications (for a thorough research see Solow, 1957[7]).

Beyond the selected proxies of the financial system, three additional potential factors of growth are also included as variables, namely, capital formation, trade openness and inflation. The literature provides exhaustive evidence on the relationships between these variables and economic growth. However, with the exception of capital formation, where there is a general consensus in the relevant theory regarding its positive impact on growth, the literature provides opposing views for the last two selected variables. For example, Grossman and Helpman (1992) conclude that trade openness has a positive effect on new technology through the imports of goods and services. When new technology is applied in the domestic production process, productivity raises and becomes more efficient having a direct positive impact on economic growth. In a similar way, Levine and Renelt (1992) argue that through trade openness countries are exposed to a greater variety of profitable investment opportunities promoting indirectly economic growth.

Inflation, on the other hand, is regarded by a number of studies as a significant growth factor. Given the assumption that money and capital are substitutes, a rise in inflation will increase to cost of holding money leading to a shift from money to capital, causing a decline in interest rates and thus increasing investments and growth

(Mundell, 1965; Tobin, 1965). Other studies argue that inflation increases the cost of investment, which in turn disrupts rational decision making and hurts productivity growth (De Gregorio, 1993; Fischer, 1993; Stockman, 1981). Furthermore, an increase in inflation may lead investors either to stall their investments (Pindyck and Solimano, 1993) or even encourage capital flight due to uncertainty (see Fischer, 1993).

Finally, an increase strand on the literature focuses on the effect of public deficit. A number of recent examples (such as Italy, Greece, Ireland, Spain and Portugal) demonstrate that public deficit can affect the evolution of market economies. Various studies conclude that government purchases financed through deficit have a negative impact on growth by introducing distortions in product and financial markets and by crowding out private investment. The opposite view argues that deficit-financed government purchases are not necessarily damaging for economic development, as, higher public spending could potentially raise an economy's productive capacity, improve quality of products and increase total supply (Barro, 1991).

3.2. Methodology

To assess the relationships between the components of the financial system and economic growth in panels, this study employs the Arellano and Bond Generalised-Method-of-Moments (GMM) estimator[8]. Therefore, the cross-country growth regression is of the following form:

$$y_{i,t} = a_0 y_{i,t-1} + BX'_{i,t} + \gamma M'_{i,t} + \eta_t + \varepsilon_{i,t}, i = 1,...,N, t = 1,...,T \tag{1}$$

where, y refers to real GDP growth rate; α_0,β and γ are parameters to be estimated; X represents the set of macroeconomic explanatory variables, namely, gross fixed capital formation as a percentage of GDP, trade openness as a percentage of GDP, inflation and public deficit as a percentage of GDP; M is a vector of financial and banking sector development, employing stocks traded as a percentage of GDP, market capitalization as a percentage of GDP and bank's domestic credit as a percentage of GDP as proxies; η stands for the unobserved country specific effect; ε is the error term; while i and t represent country and time period, respectively[9].

Moreover, Arellano and Bond (1991) propose to difference Equation (1) in order to solve the underlying problem of correlation between the dependent variable and the error term and eliminate country specific effects. Although differencing eliminates the country specific effects and $E(\varepsilon_{i,t} - \varepsilon_{i,t-1}) = 0$, however, $(y_{i,t-1} - y_{i,t-2})$ is not independent of $(\varepsilon_{i,t} - \varepsilon_{i,t-1})$. The Arellano and Bond method solves this problem by employing two or more lags of the first difference of the growth rate as instruments.

In regards with $(X_{i,t} - X_{i,t-1})$ and $(M_{i,t} - M_{i,t-1})$ this study assumes that financial system variables and control variables are predetermined considering that $E(X_{i,t}, \varepsilon_{i,s}) \neq 0$ and $E(M_{i,t}, \varepsilon_{i,s}) \neq 0$ for $s < t$ but zero for $s \geq t$. Therefore, for these predetermined variables, one or more lagged levels are orthogonal to the differenced error term and thus form valid instruments for the respective first differenced explanatory variables.

This study does not limit its methodological applications only to Arellano and Bond (1991) GMM estimator. The reasons are threefold: First, the country specific relationships between the financial system development and economic growth also present significant research interest. However, the cross-country effect is eliminated in the AB-GMM estimator. Second, differencing may exacerbate the bias due to measurement errors in variables by decreasing the so called "signal-to-noise ratio" (see Griliches and Hausman, 1986). Finally, a third reason is to cross-check the robustness of the differenced GMM estimator. To address these issues, this study also estimates this model employing the system dynamic panel data estimator presented by Arellano and Bover (1995) and Blundell and Bond (1998)[10]. The system-GMM estimator combines in a system the regression in differences with the regression in levels. The instruments for the differenced estimator rest the same as above. However, the instruments for the regression in levels are the lagged differences of the corresponding variables. These are regarded as appropriate instruments under the assumption that although there may be correlation between the levels of the explanatory variables and the country-specific effect in Equation (1), there is no correlation between the differences of these variables and the country-specific effect (Arellano and Bover, 1995).

Besides accounting for the specified dynamics, the GMM estimators have one additional virtue; they accommodate the possible endogeneity between growth and its determinants by means of appropriate instruments (through the inclusion of lags of regressors as instruments). All regressions include the lagged values of the controls that are normally used in the literature that studies the link between financial development and economic growth such as initial GDP, trade openness, inflation and public deficit (see Arcand et al, 2012, Adam and Bevan, 2005). One more decision to be made is the choice between the one-step and the two-step estimators for both the differenced and the system GMM estimators. Arellano and Bond (1991) and Blundell and Bond (1998) argue that the asymptotic inferences based on the one-step estimator are more reliable in the sense that they have correct empirical size distributions. Considering the above argument, this study employs the one-step estimator, which is in line with recent studies that utilize this methodology (see Narayan and Narayan, 2013; Cole et al., 2008).

Finally, it should be noted that the consistency of the GMM estimator lies on the validity of the assumption that the error terms are not serially correlated, as well as on the validity of the instruments. To address these issues, two commonly used diagnostic tests are employed, namely, the Sargan test and the Arellano and Bond (1991) test for autocorrelation. The Sargan test of over-identifying restrictions, tests the overall validity of the instruments by assessing whether the instruments are uncorrelated with the error terms in the estimated equation. The null hypothesis in this case is that the instruments as a group are exogenous. The second test examines the null hypothesis that the error terms are not serially correlated. This study reports only the test statistic and p-values for AR(2) because it is able to detect possible autocorrelation in levels. Therefore, failure to reject the null hypothesis for both tests implies robustness of the model. However, problems such as heterogeneity of parameters and cross-section dependence can generate bias and inconsistency for the estimators, even if the endogeneity problem has been solved. The non-linear nature of the model may resolve a large portion of the heterogeneity of the parameters (Teles and Mussolini, 2014). Therefore, we apply quadratic terms of the estimation parameters to capture non-linear relationships.

4. EMPIRICAL RESULTS

4.1. Summary Statistics

Table 1 reports some selected descriptive statistics, namely, mean, standard deviation (St. Dev.), skewness, kurtosis and coefficient of variation (CV) for all variables employed in this study, namely, economic growth (GGDP), gross fixed capital formation as a percentage of GDP (GFCF), inflation (INFL), market capitalization as a percentage of GDP (MCAP), bank's domestic credit as a percentage of GDP (CREDIT), stocks traded as a percentage of GDP (STOCKS), and the general-public deficit as percent of GDP (DEFICIT). The full sample of the 28 countries of the European Union (EU28) is categorized based on two characteristics; (i) whether an EU member state has adopted the Euro as a national currency (Panels B and C), and (ii) according to the geographical distribution of EU28 member states, based on the geographical scheme, as created by the United Nations' Statistics Division (Panels from D to G).

Overall, Table 1 reveals a wide variation across the variables and the panels created. Due to space considerations, the following summary statistics analysis is limited to the economic growth and the proxies of the financial system development. Beginning with economic growth, and assessing the currency based grouping of data (Panels B and C), the highest average growth rate is reported for the non-Euro countries (2.89%). On the other hand, calculations for the sub-regional panels (Panels D-G) show that Northern countries acquire the first place in terms of average growth (3.46%), followed by Eastern EU countries (3.05%). Southern and Western EU countries present similar average growth rates (2.04% and 2.05% respectively). The coefficient of variation suggests that non-Euro countries' average growth is marginally more volatile than Eurozone countries (1.39% and 1.32%, respectively), while in sub-regional panels, Southern EU countries are the most volatile (1.46%), followed by Northern (1.37%), Eastern (1.18%) and Western EU countries (1.09%).

To assess briefly the summary statistics for the key explanatory variables, significant disparities exist across all panels. Regarding market capitalization as a percentage of GDP, Eurozone countries present higher average market capitalization than non-Euro countries (57.81% and 41.55% respectively) while for the case of sub-regional panels the average market capitalization varies from a low of 16.93% in Eastern EU countries to a high of 79.85% in Western EU countries. Moreover, the average of bank's domestic credit as a percentage of GDP is by far higher in Eurozone countries (547.03%) than in non-Euro countries (75.31%), while for the sub-regional data, Southern countries acquire the first place in terms of average with an impressively high average credit of 1027.49%, followed by Western EU countries (133.31%), Northern EU countries (101.76%) and Eastern EU countries (around 49%). The average of stocks traded as a percentage of GDP appears higher in Eurozone countries (38.84%) than the non-Euro countries (31.39%), while for the case of sub-regional data averages from 7.77% in Eastern EU countries to around 54% in Northern EU countries. As it concerns public deficit, Northern EU countries have the lowest value, compared to Southern EU economies that present the highest deficit. Moreover, Non-euro economies are in a better position considering the public deficit, compared to Eurozone countries. Finally, an overview on skewness and kurtosis statistics indicate that data do not follow a normal distribution.

4.2. Overall Results for the Full Panel of EU28 Member States

Table 2 presents the estimation results for the full sample of the EU28 member states. As analyzed in the previous section, this study employs both the differenced (D-GMM) and system (S-GMM) GMM estimators[11]. Therefore, columns 2-4 report the results from the application of the differenced-GMM estimator, while columns 5-7 tabulate the results from the system-GMM estimator. For each GMM estimator, three models are reported to assess the impact of the key explanatory variables (MCAP, CREDIT and STOCKS) on economic growth separately. Moreover, four core explanatory variables (GFCF, OPEN and INFL, DEFICIT) are included in all six models. Due to space considerations, only statistically significant non-linear relationships are included in the following tables.

Table 1. Descriptive statistics

	GGDP	GFCF	INFL	OPEN	MCAP	CREDIT	STOCKS	DEFICIT
Panel A: Full Sample of EU28 Countries								
Mean	2.664	21.565	6.754	107.813	51.421	361.711	35.914	-2.264
St. Dev.	3.627	4.055	49.396	50.675	46.342	1728.595	50.238	3.687
Skewness	-1.125	0.707	20.423	1.545	1.681	7.115	2.166	-1.552
Kurtosis	7.226	4.005	43.601	6.554	6.927	55.470	24.788	8.962
CV	1.361	0.188	7.313	0.470	0.901	4.779	1.399	-0.614
Panel B: Eurozone Countries								
Mean	2.513	21.680	2.855	114.914	57.809	547.030	38.844	-2.248
St. Dev.	3.318	3.902	2.301	59.990	46.814	2199.686	47.962	3.923
Skewness	-0.679	0.791	3.295	1.228	1.868	5.446	1.753	-1.974
Kurtosis	5.885	4.763	24.762	4.752	8.321	33.055	6.034	10.957
CV	1.32	0.179	0.805	0.522	0.809	4.021	1.235	-0.573
Panel C: Non-Euro Countries								
Mean	2.898	21.388	12.780	96.837	41.547	75.308	31.386	-2.196
St. Dev.	4.057	4.284	78.504	28.038	43.926	53.517	53.382	3.128
Skewness	-1.539	0.627	12.783	0.501	1.457	1.181	2.695	-0.354
Kurtosis	7.984	3.135	37.171	2.831	4.068	3.655	12.421	1.152
CV	1.399	0.201	6.142	2.194	1.057	0.711	1.701	-0.709
Panel D: Northern EU Countries								
Mean	3.460	20.929	3.246	106.351	64.551	101.757	54.016	-0.843
St. Dev.	4.726	4.811	3.833	37.071	53.281	60.491	63.793	4.316
Skewness	-1.488	0.904	3.053	0.589	1.009	0.491	1.635	-2.667
Kurtosis	7.614	3.909	15.462	2.264	3.937	2.326	6.489	14.395
CV	1.366	0.229	1.181	0.349	0.825	0.594	1.181	-0.195
Panel E: Southern EU Countries								
Mean	2.043	21.776	3.126	88.328	42.835	1027.497	30.838	-3.679
St. Dev.	3.001	3.562	1.696	38.763	27.506	3143.395	43.611	3.483
Skewness	-1.125	0.192	1.552	1.041	1.244	3.528	1.833	-1.563
Kurtosis	4.137	2.694	6.501	3.029	4.891	14.669	5.733	7.127
CV	1.469	0.163	0.543	0.439	0.642	3.059	1.414	-1.056
Panel F: Western EU Countries								
Mean	2.051	20.314	1.892	131.051	79.852	133.314	46.694	-1.523
St. Dev.	2.256	1.828	0.824	76.728	53.023	30.102	49.207	2.123
Skewness	-0.371	0.077	0.275	1.157	1.441	1.015	1.738	0.573
Kurtosis	4.896	2.448	3.614	3.462	6.299	3.930	6.825	1.728
CV	1.099	0.089	0.435	0.585	0.664	0.226	1.053	-0.717

continued on following page

Table 1. Continued

	GGDP	GFCF	INFL	OPEN	MCAP	CREDIT	STOCKS	DEFICIT
Panel G: Eastern EU Countries								
Mean	3.046	23.385	21.130	112.504	16.931	48.997	7.767	-2.546
St. Dev.	3.606	4.534	105.756	35.538	11.572	19.091	8.568	3.297
Skewness	-1.136	0.218	9.413	-0.044	0.718	0.149	1.328	-0.074
Kurtosis	4.376	3.234	17.557	1.980	3.020	3.782	4.080	1.338
CV	1.183	0.193	5.005	0.314	0.683	0.389	1.103	-0.772

Note: GGDP: Economic growth; GFCF: gross fixed capital formation as a percentage of GDP; INFL: inflation; OPEN: trade openness as a percentage of GDP; MCAP: market capitalization of listed companies as a percentage of GDP; CREDIT: bank's domestic credit as a percentage of GDP; STOCKS: stocks traded as a percentage of GDP; DEFICIT: the general-public deficit as percent of GDP.

Column 2 of Table 2 present the results for the first differenced-GMM estimator model (D-GMM1), which includes market capitalization (MCAP) as a proxy of the financial sector development. Estimations show that MCAP has a statistically significant and positive impact on economic growth (GGDP) at the 5% significance level. Gross fixed capital formation (GFCF) also appears to have a positive and significant effect on growth, which is in line with the Theory, however at the weakest accepted significance level (10%). The last variable in Model 1 that reports significance is trade openness (OPEN), influencing growth in a positive way at the 1% significance level. Moving on to Model 2 (D-GMM2), similar results are presented regarding GFCF, since it appears to promote growth at the 10% significance level, while trade openness also effects economic growth in a positive way at the 1% significance level. However, Model 2 fails to trace significance for the case of bank's domestic credit (CREDIT). Model 3 (D-GMM3) presents similar results for GFCF and OPEN, since both are indicated as significant growth factors at the 10% and 1% significance levels respectively. Finally, Model 3 of D-GMM failed to trace significant relationships between stocks traded (STOCKS) and GGDP. The growth effect of a deficit-financed increase is negative. The quadratic term is negative, showing a non-linear relationship (see also Tamai, 2014). Romero-Avila and Strauch (2008), controlling for both sides of the government budget, present results showing negative responses of GDP growth to fiscal variables in general in a panel of EU countries for 1990–2005. Adam and Bevan (2005) examined the relationship between fiscal deficits and economic growth using a panel data of 45 developing countries over the period 1970–1999. They showed that the net growth effect of the fiscal deficit is growth reducing (growth-enhancing) if the fiscal deficit is greater (less) than 1.5% of GDP.

The results for the system-GMM estimator (S-GMM) are very similar to those from the D-GMM estimator. GFCF and OPEN appear to significantly promote growth across all three models of the S-GMM estimator. Significant and positive results are also documented in the case of MCAP (at the 5% level). Finally, S-GMM estimator failed to report significant relationships between CREDIT, STOCKS and GGDP. These findings are also in accordance to D-GMM results. Overall, the results from the application of both the differenced-GMM and the system-GMM estimators for the full panel of the EU28 member states are similar across all six models. Regarding the financial sector developments, namely, market capitalization and stocks traded, only MCAP has significant and positive effect on economic growth. Moreover, these models failed to report significant relationships between the banking sector variable (bank's domestic credit) and growth. Therefore, we are obliged to accept the null hypothesis of no significant impact of CREDIT on GGDP. De Gregorio and Guidotti (1995) obtain a similar weak relationship in high-income countries. They attribute this to the fact that financial development in such countries occurs mainly outside of the banking system.

Finally, the last two rows of Table 2, report the results from the examination of two commonly used diagnostic tests; (i) the Sargan test, under the null that the instruments employed are exogenous, and (ii) the AR(2) test, under the null of no autocorrelation in relation with the differenced residuals. Both tests are found to be insignificant across all models of the D-GMM and S-GMM estimators. Therefore, these results support the robustness of all six models.

4.3. Results From Eurozone and Non-Euro Panels

The first division of the full sample of EU28 member states is based on whether these EU countries have adopted the Euro as their national currency, or not yet (for more details on this segmentation, see Section 3.1.). Table 3 presents the results for the Eurozone panel derived from the application of the three models of the differenced-GMM estimator. Results for the banking and stock market variables across all three models of the D-GMM estimator imply that only MCAP has a significant and positive impact on GGDP at the 1% significance level. On the other hand, results for the macroeconomic determinants of growth, report significant and positive results for the cases of GFCF and OPEN, while INFL turns out to be statistically insignificant across all three models. Therefore, overall results for the Eurozone panel are similar to those obtained from the full panel of EU28 countries (for comparison, see Table 2). We find that public deficit - as well as its quadratic term - has a strong negative effect on growth. For the Eurozone countries, a debt-stabilization rule that could act as a threshold could be interpreted in the context of the Maastricht Treaty.

Table 2. D-GMM and S-GMM results for the full sample of EU28 countries

	D-GMM1	D-GMM2	D-GMM3	S-GMM1	S-GMM2	S-GMM3
GFCF	0.537*	0.405*	0.795*	0.080**	0.075**	0.093***
GFCFQ2	-0.122	-0.147	-0.153	-0.043	-0.039	0.028
INFL	-0.052	-0.055	-0.092	-0.023	-0.027	-0.122
OPEN	0.632***	0.537***	0.513***	0.014**	0.013**	0.014**
DEFICIT	-0.321*	-0.355*	-0.457**	-0.328*	-0.345**	-0.368**
DEFICITQ2	-0.152*	-0.157*	-0.155*	-0.045	-0.078*	-0.123*
MCAP	0.057**			0.007**		
CREDIT		0.001			0.001	
CREDITQ2		-0.012*			-0.005*	
STOCKS			0.010			0.011
Sargan test	5.509	5.874	5.762	63.472	13.984	14.454
AR(2)	-0.077	-0.179	-0.132	-0.237	-0.131	-0.187

Note: GGDP: Economic growth; GFCF: gross fixed capital formation as a percentage of GDP; GFCFQ2: gross fixed capital formation as a percentage of GDP square; INFL: inflation; OPEN: trade openness as a percentage of GDP; DEFICIT: the general-public deficit as percent of GDP; DEFICITQ2: the general-public deficit as percent of GDP square; MCAP: market capitalization of listed companies as a percentage of GDP; CREDIT: bank's domestic credit as a percentage of GDP; CREDITQ2: bank's domestic credit as a percentage of GDP square; STOCKS: stocks traded as a percentage of GDP. The coefficients of the time and country dummies have been omitted from the regression output but are available by the authors upon request. AR (2): Arellano-Bond test that examines the existence of 2nd degree of serial autocorrelation in the residuals under the null hypothesis of no autocorrelation; Sargan test: The test of over-identifying restrictions to test instrument validity under the null hypothesis that the selected instruments are valid. (***), (**), and (*) indicate 1%, 5% and 10% significance levels, respectively. This note also applies to subsequent tables.

Table 3. D-GMM results for Eurozone countries

	D-GMM1	D-GMM2	D-GMM3
GFCF	1.115***	0.672**	0.974**
GFCFQ2	0.323	0.145	0.157
INFL	0.354	0.565	0.412
OPEN	0.212***	0.129**	0.152**
DEFICIT	-0.472**	-0187**	-0.324**
DEFICITQ2	-0.383**	-0.295**	-0.117***
MCAP	0.079***		
CREDIT		0.001	
CREDITQ2		0.042	
STOCKS			0.145
Sargan test	53.432	19.589	41.381
AR(2)	-0.475	-0.321	-0.452

Table 4 displays the results from the non-Euro countries panel. Regarding the macro variables, significant and positive results are reported for GFCF at the 5% significance level in Models 1 and 2 and at the 1% significance level in Model 3 of the D-GMM estimator. GFCFQ2 remains highly significant and positive in every regression where only non-Euro countries are involved. Reflecting very different sectoral structures and patterns of structural change in Eurozone and non-euro countries, our results show that the role of structural change in determining economic growth is stronger in the case of non-euro countries. In addition, the persistently significant GFCFQ2 term further highlights that the growth effect of structural change is nonlinear (Ding and Knight, 2009). OPEN appears to strongly promote growth at 1% significance level across all three models. This result is consistent with several theoretical predictions and empirical findings in the literature, linking trade with technology transfers, institutional quality and geographical factors (for instance, Easterly and Levine, 2001). The influence of DEFICIT remains significant. Moreover, significant results are tabulated for the banking and financial sector development indicators, since MCAP significantly promotes growth at the 5% level, while CREDIT has a statistically significant but negative effect on GGDP. Over the last twenty years financial sectors have grown rapidly. If the downward bias increases with the size of the financial sector, it is not surprising to find a vanishing effect of financial depth on economic growth (Arcand et al, 2012). The quadratic term of CREDIT has a negative and significant coefficient. For a number of countries in our sample, the size of the financial sector may be too large with respect to the socially

Table 4. D-GMM results for non-Euro countries

	D-GMM1	**DGMM-2**	**D-GMM3**
GFCF	0.882**	0.889**	1.305***
GFCFQ2	0.364***	0.235***	0.172***
INFL	0.254	0.210	0.209
OPEN	0.341***	0.452***	0.298***
DEFICIT	-0.932***	-0.519***	-0.597**
DEFICITQ2	-0.373*	-0.853**	-0.749**
MCAP	0.121**		
CREDIT		-0.234**	
CREDITQ2		-0.261***	
STOCKS			0.162
Sargan test	24.734	4.508	5.964
AR(2)	0.027	0.014	0.010

optimal level. Hence, increasing CREDIT can have a negative marginal effect on GDP growth. Overall, these results present some similarities to those derived from the full EU28 panel and the Eurozone countries panel, however, with the exception of the banking sector determinant, in the sense that this is the first time so far in this study that significance is documented for the case of CREDIT, as a proxy of banking sector development.

Eurozone economies have concurrently been confronted in recent decades with common transnational developments that have transformed their national financial markets and allowed them to converge. These countries have implemented numerous common regulatory changes, motivated by the need to achieve the level of harmonization required for the establishment of a single, competitive market for financial services. During the last few years, on the other hand, most non-Euro countries, with the collaboration and assistance of international financial institutions, have taken concrete and far-reaching measures to reform their financial institutions and markets. The main differences between the applied financial policies in these two panels and the diverse financial reformations employed, can be attributed to the different institutional and financial management that is demanded by the adoption (or not) of the common European currency.

4.4. Results From Sub-Regional Panels

The second division of full EU28 panel data, is based on the United Nations geographical scheme (for more details, see Section 3.1.). Therefore, this study divides the EU28 member states in Northern, Southern, Western and Eastern EU sub-regional panels. Table 5 presents the results from the Northern EU countries and for the three models of the differenced-GMM estimator. MCAP is the only proxy of financial sector development that is found to have a weakly significant and positive effect on growth, while the only proxy employed to measure the banking sector contribution on growth, namely, CREDIT, has a significant (at the 5% level) but negative effect on GGDP. Ang and McKibbin (2007) attribute this negative relation to the expansion in credit along with a lack of regulatory control and monitoring from the bankers. This may result in an inappropriate selection of projects, which could show up as an adverse impact of financial development on economic growth. Financial deepening appears to have a negative effect on growth beyond a certain threshold, which is different from the predominant view that financial development and economic growth are positively linked.

Results for the macroeconomic determinants of growth, imply that OPEN is the only variable that has a statistically significant impact on growth at the 1% level across all three models of the D-GMM estimator. These findings are different from those obtained from the previous panels, mainly, due to the fact that these are the

Table 5. D-GMM results for Northern EU countries

	D-GMM1	DGMM-2	D-GMM3
GFCF	0.701	0.432	0.751
GFCFQ2	0.425	0.157	0.531
INFL	0.451	0.412	0.589
OPEN	0.572***	0.737***	0.681***
DEFICIT	0.247**	0.152**	0.442**
DEFICITQ2	-0.122***	-0.088**	-0.042**
MCAP	0.074*		
CREDIT		-0.145**	
CREDITQ2		-0.272**	
STOCKS			0.078
Sargan test	5.845	4.052	4.412
AR(2)	-0.088	-0.085	-0.089

only results that imply non-significance for the case of GFCF. All counties in the sample are developed, in terms that physical capital tends not to be important any more. Neoclassical growth theory asserts that long-run growth cannot be sustained through capital deepening alone (Solow, 1957), as diminishing returns to physical capital set in, and what is required to overcome this is the complementary effect of human capital and/or public capital in production. Another interesting deviation is that no proxy of the financial sector is reported as a significant growth factor. DEFICIT's influence is also different compared to the previous panels. In particular, deficit effect may have opposite flow if financed by external loans at market rates. Low uncertainty regarding the state of the economy can be taken to imply that a higher current deficit will pay off in the future, through resource-enhancing effects, and that the government's determination to ensure stable debt dynamics is beyond doubt. The quadratic term remains negative and statistically significant.

The results from the Southern EU sub-regional panel are displayed in Table 6. These findings are unique in this study, since this is the first time that all macroeconomic determinants of growth have a significant effect on GGDP. GFCF positive and significant effect (at the 1% level) on growth revisits, while INFL and OPEN significantly promote GGDP at the 5% significance level, for all three models of the D-GMM estimator. Considering that the southern EU countries experienced sharper recession relative to the non-Euro countries this fact alone can be seen as evidence of the legal and politico-institutional disparities that this panel presents. The negative relationship between growth and public deficit is driven by the fact

Table 6. D-GMM results for Southern EU countries

	D-GMM1	DGMM-2	D-GMM3
GFCF	0.763***	0.755***	0.617**
GFCFQ2	0.347	0.432	0.348
INFL	0.605**	0.655**	0.654**
OPEN	0.321**	0.159**	0.194**
DEFICIT	-0.652**	-0.517***	-0.543***
DEFICITQ2	-0.178**	-0.143***	-0.125***
MCAP	-0.025		
CREDIT		0.154	
CREDITQ2		0.042	
STOCKS			-0.019
Sargan test	7.577	7.321	7.177
AR(2)	-0.356	-0.343	-0.341

that southern EU countries lack access to international credit during recessions. An alternative class of explanations concentrates on political failures (Tornell and Lane, 1999), from political pressure for wasteful spending, (Talvi and Vigh, 2005) or from the presence of corrupt politicians (Alesina et al., 2008). On the other hand, these are the first tabulated results that imply non-significance for all the employed banking/stock market variables.

Table 7 presents the results derived from the Western EU sub-regional panel. These findings are similar to those from the Southern EU panel, in terms of the macro variables, since all three determinants of growth are found to be significant, however, at different levels of statistical significance, with the exception of negative impact of OPEN on growth. Specifically, GFCF weakly promotes growth at the 10% significance level, INFL influences GGDP in a positive way, at the highest level of significance (at the 1% level), while OPEN has a negative and significant effect on GGDP at the 5% significance level. Emphasis should be given to the fact that these are the only results that report a negative influence of trade openness on growth. This finding may appear somewhat unusual, but some of the literature points to the possibility of openness hindering growth if the appropriate planning is missing or there is specialization in the 'wrong' sector (Samargandi et al., 2015). Regarding the proxies of financial sector development, only MCAP is reported as a weakly significant growth contributor, while for the case of CREDIT, as a banking sector indicator, robust evidence of significant (at the 1% level), however, negative impact on GGDP are tabulated. Our results indicate that there exists an inverted U-shaped

Table 7. D-GMM results for Western EU countries

	D-GMM1	DGMM-2	D-GMM3
GFCF	0.682*	0.574*	0.422*
GFCFQ2	0.128	0.123	0.147
INFL	0.321***	0.452***	0.309***
OPEN	-0.120**	-0.111**	-0.153**
DEFICIT	-0.452**	-0.448**	-0.322
DEFICITQ2	0.157	0.032	0.048
MCAP	0.027*		
CREDIT		-0.134***	
CREDITQ2		-0.155***	
STOCKS			-0.023
Sargan test	18.570	3.437	12.754
AR(2)	-0.133	-0.344	-0.217

relation between CREDIT and growth. Deidda and Fattouh (2002) conclude that the relationship between financial development and economic growth is non-linear.

The results from the Eastern EU panel are reported in Table 8. Findings imply that GFCF has a statistically significant (at the 5% level) and positive impact on growth. Moreover, similar results are also reported for OPEN, since it promotes growth at the 1% significance level across all three models of the D-GMM estimator. However, non-significant estimations are found for the case of INFL. Regarding the proxies of banking/stock markets development, the respective D-GMM models (models 1 and 3) failed to trace any significant relationships with GGDP at any accepted significance level. The DEFICIT is negative while the quadratic term is statistically insignificant. High uncertainty can be taken to correspond to a situation where any existing deficits are associated mostly with excessive consumptive expenditures, rather than expenditures that will pay off in the future, and the state of the economy is not satisfactory enough to eliminate the possibility of an unsustainable public-sector position (Goulas and Zervoyianni, 2013).

5. SUMMARY, CONCLUDING REMARKS, AND POLICY IMPLICATIONS

The central objective of this study is to investigate the impact of the financial system (banking/stock markets) development on economic growth for a full sample of the

Table 8. D-GMM results for Eastern EU countries

	D-GMM1	DGMM-2	D-GMM3
GFCF	0.527**	0.632**	0.739**
GFCFQ2	0.189	0.132	0.152
INFL	0.154	0.148	0.185
OPEN	0.247***	0.283***	0.457***
DEFICIT	-0.157**	-0.263**	-0.196**
DEFICITQ2	0.108	0.092	0.047
MCAP	0.088		
CREDIT		-0.239	
CREDITQ2		0.152	
STOCKS			0.143
Sargan test	11.878	5.672	9.145
AR(2)	-0.232	-0.224	-0.252

EU28 member states, for the period 1996-2016. For this purpose, balanced panel data are employed. Moreover, this study, for the first time in this literature, divides the full EU28 panel, under two principals: (i) whether an EU member country has adopted the Euro (€) as a national currency or not, creating two sub-panels, the Eurozone panel and the non-Euro countries panel, and (ii) according to the geographical distribution of EU member states, creating four sub-regional panels (Northern, Southern, Western and Eastern EU countries panels) based on the geographical scheme designed by the United Nations (UN) Statistics Division for Europe. The motivation behind the first sample division is supported by the logical assumption, that single currency EU member states are much more economically dependent to each other than the rest of the non-Euro countries. Therefore, conclusions under this sample division should be more accurate than those when dealing with all the EU countries. The motive behind the second sample division is basically the assumption that sub-regional panels may produce more accurate results due to the greater uniformity of EU neighboring member countries not only in terms of levels of economic prosperity, but also from a cultural and social point of view, even in terms of business ethics and government intervention.

Therefore, this study goes beyond the inspiring works of Narayan et al. (2011) and Narayan and Narayan (2013). These studies assess the financial development-growth nexus for wide regional panels, one of which involves a group of mixed European countries, regardless of whether they have become full EU members or not. However, this paper concentrates not only to the European countries in general, but focuses on the EU countries, while further divides the EU region in terms of single currency and sub-regional panels. We support that the EU is a special case of multi-national union that despite promoting a close economic cooperation between the European member countries, academics, researchers and policy makers should consider that it is not yet a single country with common fiscal policy. Considering all these variations, even narrowing a European sample to an EU full sample could lead to biased results. In this spirit, we propose that further segmentation is needed in order to produce more accurate empirical results. The hypothesis tested behind this argument is that different results are expected to arise from the empirical application on the full EU countries panel and the created sub-groups.

The empirical analysis employs the differenced and system-GMM estimators. To assess the impact of the financial system components on economic growth, two proxies are used for financial sector development, namely, market capitalization and stocks traded, while bank's domestic credit is used as a proxy for the banking sector development. Results for the finance-growth nexus, suggest that the financial sector significantly promotes growth in the case of full EU28 sample, only in terms of market capitalization, since stocks traded variable is insignificant. Moreover, this impact appears fading when assessing these relationships from the division of the full EU28 panel, since the influence of stocks traded on growth continues to be insignificant in both currency and sub-regional EU28 data groups, while market capitalization significantly promotes growth only in the cases of currency-based panels and in the cases of Northern and Western sub-regional panels, however, at only 10% significance level. On the other hand, the banking-growth relationships are absent in the case of full EU28 sample, while significant and negative results are reported from the created sub-groups, with the exception of Eurozone, Southern and Eastern EU countries' panels.

This study also employs some selected macroeconomic determinants of growth, namely, inflation, gross fixed capital formation, public deficit and trade openness. Results for trade openness and gross fixed capital formation imply that both variables have a significant and positive impact on growth across all panels. These findings are in line with the vast majority of related literature, in that capital stock and openness are seen as stimuli for economic growth. The only exception from these conclusions is the case of the significant but negative effect of trade openness on growth derived from the Western EU countries sub-regional panel. Finally, inflation is found to have insignificant effect on growth across all panels, with the exceptions of Southern and Western EU countries sub-regional panels, where it is found to significantly promote growth. The overall conclusion to be drawn from the public deficits is that its effect cannot a priori be considered as the state of the economy matters. We find that public deficit - as well as its quadratic term - has a strong and negative effect on growth in almost all panels. This result has noteworthy policy implications; To the extent that the macroeconomic environment is volatile and the prospects of a number of European economies are uncertain, perceived risks associated with current fiscal deficits are likely to continue in the future, even in EU member states that do not exhibit significant debt burdens, slowing down the rate of economic development. To address this issue, it is imperative to achieve higher prospective returns from public deficits through careful deficit restructuring (Goulas and Zervoyianni, 2013).

To conclude, several implications arise from the empirical findings. First, robust empirical results imply that capital stock and trade openness are key contributors of EU's economic growth. The exception of significant and negative impact of openness on growth in the case of the Western EU countries cannot be attributed to panel heterogeneity, since all Western EU countries are developed economies. However, it could be attributed to the financial distortion caused by the severe financial crisis of 2008. Second, a prerequisite seems to be a review on the stock markets regulatory framework, since the impact of stocks traded variable on growth is totally absent across all panels. Third, the EU member states need to focus on further improving banking regulations and the credit allocation process, while restoring banking competition seems to be essential, in order for banks to become significant growth contributors, considering this study's findings, which imply that banking activity hurts growth in some EU sub-regions.

Therefore, this study implies that significant differences exist between Eurozone member states and non-Euro countries in terms of economic, political, institutional and structural development. Characteristics such as the ownership structure, the market concentration, the size and importance of different delivery channels and the presence of foreign banks vary substantially across the EU member states. This could have important consequences on financial stability, as it affects profit and risk trade-offs, cost efficiency and ultimately has a bearing on the shock-absorptive capacity of the financial system.

Finally, exhaustive empirical results derived from all panels, do not reject our hypothesis that different results may occur, when dealing with sub-regional panels - at least in the case of the European Union - where several economic and fiscal variations demand researchers to focus on more narrow data groups. Thus, our paper provides stimulus for a more disaggregate empirical analysis on the impact of bank and stock market regulations on economic development. In particular, we urge fellow researchers to empirically test the financial deepening that needs to be undertaken in order to ensure that the maximum potential benefit for the economy can be achieved through the banking sector or other growth-enhancing strategies if the appropriate finance threshold has been achieved.

REFERENCES

Adam, C., & Bevan, D. (2005). Fiscal deficits and growth in developing countries. *Journal of Public Economics*, *89*(4), 571–597. doi:10.1016/j.jpubeco.2004.02.006

Afonso, A., & González-Alegre, J. (2008). *Economic growth and budgetary components: A panel assessment for the EU*. ECB Working Paper 848.

Alesina, A., Campante, F. R., & Tabellini, G. (2008). Why Is Fiscal Policy Often Procyclical? *Journal of the European Economic Association*, *6*(5), 1006–1036. doi:10.1162/JEEA.2008.6.5.1006

Allen, F., & Gale, D. (2000). *Comparing Financial Systems*. Cambridge, MA: MIT Press.

Ang, J. B., & McKibbin, W. J. (2007). Financial liberalization, financial sector development and growth: Evidence from Malaysia. *Journal of Development Economics*, *84*(1), 215–233. doi:10.1016/j.jdeveco.2006.11.006

Anwar, S., & Sun, S. (2011). Financial development, foreign investment and economic growth in Malaysia. *Journal of Asian Economics*, *22*(4), 335–342. doi:10.1016/j.asieco.2011.04.001

Arcand, J., Berkes, E., & Panizza, U. (2012). *Too much finance?* International Monetary Fund, Research Department.

Arellano, M., & Bond, S. (1991). Some tests of specification for panel data: Monte Carlo evidence and an application to employment equations. *The Review of Economic Studies*, *58*(2), 277–297. doi:10.2307/2297968

Arellano, M., & Bover, O. (1995). Another look at the instrumental-variable estimation of error-components models. *Journal of Econometrics*, *68*(1), 29–52. doi:10.1016/0304-4076(94)01642-D

Bagehot, W. (1873). *Lombard Street* (1962 ed.). Homewood, IL: Richard D. Irwin.

Baldacci, E., Hillman, A., & Kojo, N. (2004). Growth, governance and fiscal-policy transmission channels in low-income countries. *European Journal of Political Economy*, *20*(3), 517–549. doi:10.1016/j.ejpoleco.2003.12.002

Baldwin, R. E., & Forslid, R. (1998). Trade and growth Any unfinished business? *European Economic Review*, *42*(3-5), 695–703. doi:10.1016/S0014-2921(98)00010-5

Baltagi, B. H. (2001). *Econometric analysis of panel data* (2nd ed.). Chichester, UK: John Wiley & Sons.

Baltagi, B. H., Demetriades, P. O., & Law, S. H. (2009). Financial development and openness: Evidence from panel data. *Journal of Development Economics*, *89*(2), 285–296. doi:10.1016/j.jdeveco.2008.06.006

Barro, R. J. (1991). Economic growth in a cross section of countries. *The Quarterly Journal of Economics*, *106*(2), 407–443. doi:10.2307/2937943

Barro, R. J., & Redlick, C. J. (2011). Macroeconomic effects from government purchases and Taxes. *The Quarterly Journal of Economics*, *126*(1), 51–102. doi:10.1093/qje/qjq002

Beck, T., Degryse, H., & Kneer, C. (2014). Is more finance better? Disentangling intermediation and size effects of financial systems. *Journal of Financial Stability*, *10*, 50–64. doi:10.1016/j.jfs.2013.03.005

Beck, T., & Levine, R. (2004). Stock markets, banks, and growth: Panel evidence. *Journal of Banking & Finance*, *28*(3), 423–442. doi:10.1016/S0378-4266(02)00408-9

Bencivenga, V. R., & Smith, B. D. (1991). Financial intermediation and endogenous growth. *The Review of Economic Studies*, *58*(2), 195–209. doi:10.2307/2297964

Bencivenga, V. R., Smith, B. D., & Starr, R. M. (1995). Transaction costs, technological choice, and endogenous growth. *Journal of Economic Theory*, *67*(1), 53–117. doi:10.1006/jeth.1995.1069

Bhide, A. (1993). The hidden costs of stock market liquidity. *Journal of Financial Economics*, *34*(1), 1–51. doi:10.1016/0304-405X(93)90039-E

Bittencourt, M. (2012). Financial development and economic growth in Latin America: Is Schumpeter right? *Journal of Policy Modeling*, *34*(3), 341–355. doi:10.1016/j.jpolmod.2012.01.012

Blundell, R., & Bond, S. (1998). Initial conditions and moment restrictions in dynamic panel data models. *Journal of Econometrics*, *87*(1), 115–143. doi:10.1016/S0304-4076(98)00009-8

Bond, S. R., Hoeffler, A., & Temple, J. (2001). *GMM estimation of empirical growth models*. CEPR Discussion Paper No. 3048. Centre for Economic Policy Research, London, UK.

Bordo, M. D., & Rousseau, P. L. (2012). Historical evidence on the finance-trade-growth nexus. *Journal of Banking & Finance*, *36*(4), 1236–1243. doi:10.1016/j.jbankfin.2011.11.012

Boyd, J. H., & Prescott, E. C. (1986). Financial intermediary-coalitions. *Journal of Economic Theory*, *38*(2), 211–232. doi:10.1016/0022-0531(86)90115-8

Campos, N. F., Karanasos, M. G., & Tan, B. (2012). Two to tangle: Financial development, political instability and economic growth in Argentina. *Journal of Banking & Finance*, *36*(1), 290–304. doi:10.1016/j.jbankfin.2011.07.011

Cecchetti, G., & Kharroubi, E. (2012). *Reassessing the impact of finance on growth*. BIS Working Paper No. 381. Bank for International Settlements.

Cole, R. A., Moshirian, F., & Wu, Q. (2008). Bank stock returns and economic growth. *Journal of Banking & Finance*, *32*(6), 995–1007. doi:10.1016/j.jbankfin.2007.07.006

De Gregorio, J. (1993). Inflation, taxation and long-run growth. *Journal of Monetary Economics*, *31*(3), 271–298. doi:10.1016/0304-3932(93)90049-L

De Gregorio, J., & Guidotti, P. (1995). Financial development and economic growth. *World Development*, *23*(3), 433–448. doi:10.1016/0305-750X(94)00132-I

De Long, J., Shleifer, A., Summers, L., & Waldmann, R. (1989). The size and incidence of the losses from noise trading. *The Journal of Finance*, *44*(3), 681–696. doi:10.1111/j.1540-6261.1989.tb04385.x

Deidda, L., & Fattouh, B. (2002). Non-linearity between finance and growth. *Economics Letters*, *74*(3), 339–345. doi:10.1016/S0165-1765(01)00571-7

Devereux, M., & Smith, G. (1994). International risk sharing and economic growth. *International Economic Review*, *35*(3), 535–550. doi:10.2307/2527072

Ding, S., & Knight, J. (2009). Can the augmented Solow model explain China's remarkable economic growth? A cross-country panel data analysis. *Journal of Comparative Economics*, *37*(3), 432–452. doi:10.1016/j.jce.2009.04.006

Easterly, W., Islam, R., & Stiglitz, J. E. (2000). *Explaining growth volatility*. The World Bank.

Easterly, W., & Levine, R. (2001). What have we learned from a decade of empirical research on growth? It's not factor accumulation: Stylized facts and growth models. *The World Bank Economic Review*, *15*(2), 177–219. doi:10.1093/wber/15.2.177

Easterly, W., & Rebelo, S. (1993). Fiscal policy and economic growth: An empirical investigation. *Journal of Monetary Economics*, *32*(3), 417–458. doi:10.1016/0304-3932(93)90025-B

Federer, P. (1993). The impact of uncertainty on aggregate investment spending. *Journal of Money, Credit and Banking*, *25*(1), 30–45. doi:10.2307/2077818

Fischer, S. (1993). The role of macroeconomic factors in growth. *Journal of Monetary Economics*, *32*(3), 485–512. doi:10.1016/0304-3932(93)90027-D

Fry, M. J. (1997). In favour of financial liberalization. *Economic Journal (London)*, *107*(442), 754–770. doi:10.1111/j.1468-0297.1997.tb00041.x

Georgantopoulos, A., & Tsamis, A. (2011). The Triangular Causal Links between Economic Development, FDI and Exports: Evidence from Turkey. *Middle Eastern Finance and Economics*, *15*, 66–75.

Georgantopoulos, A., Tsamis, A., & Agoraki, M. (2015). The Euro-adoption effect and the bank, market, and growth nexus: New evidence from EU panels. *Journal of Economic Asymmetries*, *12*(1), 41–51. doi:10.1016/j.jeca.2015.01.002

Goulas, E., & Zervoyianni, A. (2013). Growth, deficits and uncertainty: Theoretical aspects and empirical evidence from a panel of 27 countries. *The Quarterly Review of Economics and Finance*, *53*(4), 380–392. doi:10.1016/j.qref.2013.07.005

Griliches, Z., & Hausman, J. A. (1986). Errors in variables in panel data. *Journal of Econometrics*, *31*(1), 93–118. doi:10.1016/0304-4076(86)90058-8

Grossman, G. M., & Helpman, E. (1992). *Innovation and growth: Technological competition in the global economy*. Boston: MIT Press.

Gupta, S., Clements, B., Baldacci, E., & Mulas-Granados, C. (2005). Fiscal policy, expenditure composition and growth in low-income countries. *Journal of International Money and Finance*, *24*(3), 441–463. doi:10.1016/j.jimonfin.2005.01.004

Hasan, I., Wachtel, P., & Zhou, M. (2009). Institutional development, financial deepening, and economic growth: Evidence from China. *Journal of Banking & Finance*, *33*(1), 157–170. doi:10.1016/j.jbankfin.2007.11.016

Hur, J., Raj, M., & Riyanto, E. Y. (2006). Finance and trade: A cross-country empirical analysis on the impact of financial development and asset tangibility on international trade. *World Development*, *34*(10), 1728–1741. doi:10.1016/j.worlddev.2006.02.003

Kaminsky, G. L., & Reinhart, C. M. (1999). The twin crises: The causes of banking and balance-of-payments problems. *The American Economic Review*, *89*(3), 473–500. doi:10.1257/aer.89.3.473

Keynes, J. M. (1936). *The general theory of employment, interest, and money*. London: Macmillan.

King, R. G., & Levine, R. (1993a). Finance and growth: Schumpeter might be right. *The Quarterly Journal of Economics*, *108*(3), 717–737. doi:10.2307/2118406

King, R. G., & Levine, R. (1993b). Finance, entrepreneurship, and growth. *Journal of Monetary Economics*, *32*(3), 513–542. doi:10.1016/0304-3932(93)90028-E

Law, S. H., & Singh, N. (2014). Does too much finance harm economic growth? *Journal of Banking & Finance*, *41*, 36–44. doi:10.1016/j.jbankfin.2013.12.020

Levine, R., Loayza, N., & Beck, T. (2000). Financial intermediation and growth: Causality and causes. *Journal of Monetary Economics*, *46*(1), 31–77. doi:10.1016/S0304-3932(00)00017-9

Levine, R., & Renelt, D. (1992). A sensitivity analysis of cross-country growth regressions. *The American Economic Review*, *82*, 942–963.

Levine, R., & Renelt, D. (1992). A sensitivity analysis of cross-country growth regressions. *The American Economic Review*, *82*, 942–963.

Levine, R., & Zervos, S. (1998). Stock markets, banks and economic growth. *The American Economic Review*, *88*, 537–558.

Loayza, N. V., & Ranciere, R. (2006). Financial development, financial fragility and growth. *Journal of Money, Credit and Banking*, *38*(4), 1051–1076. doi:10.1353/mcb.2006.0060

Miller, S., & Russek, F. (1997). Fiscal structures and economic growth. *Economic Inquiry*, *35*(3), 603–613. doi:10.1111/j.1465-7295.1997.tb02036.x

Morgese-Borys, M., Polgàr, K., & Zlate, A. (2008). *Real convergence and determinants of growth in the EURO candidate and potential candidate countries: A panel data approach, ECB occasional Paper No. 86*. European Central Bank.

Mundell, R. (1965). Growth, stability and inflationary finance. *Journal of Political Economy*, *73*(2), 97–109. doi:10.1086/258999

Narayan, K. P., Mishra, S., & Narayan, S. (2011). Do market capitalisation and stocks traded converge? New global evidence. *Journal of Banking & Finance*, *35*(10), 2771–2781. doi:10.1016/j.jbankfin.2011.03.010

Narayan, K. P., & Narayan, S. (2013). The short-run relationship between the financial system and economic growth: New evidence from regional panels. *International Review of Financial Analysis*, *29*, 70–78. doi:10.1016/j.irfa.2013.03.012

Nieuwerburgh, S. V., Buelens, F., & Cuyvers, L. (2006). Stock market development and economic growth in Belgium. *Explorations in Economic History*, *43*(1), 13–38. doi:10.1016/j.eeh.2005.06.002

Obstfeld, M. (1994). Risk taking, global diversification, and growth. *The American Economic Review*, 1310–1329.

Owen, A. L., & Temesvary, J. (2014). Heterogeneity in the growth and finance relationship: How does the impact of bank finance vary by country and type of lending? *International Review of Economics & Finance*, *31*, 275–288. doi:10.1016/j.iref.2014.02.007

Pesaran, H., & Smith, R. (1995). Estimating long-run relationships from dynamic heterogeneous panels. *Journal of Econometrics*, *68*(1), 79–113. doi:10.1016/0304-4076(94)01644-F

Pindyck, R., & Solimano, A. (1993). Economic instability and aggregate investment. *NBER Macroeconomics Annual*, *8*, 259–303. doi:10.1086/654223

Romero-Avila, D., & Strauch, R. (2008). Public finances and long-term growth in Europe: Evidence from a panel data analysis. *European Journal of Political Economy*, *24*(1), 172–191. doi:10.1016/j.ejpoleco.2007.06.008

Roodman, D. (2006a). *How to Do xtabond2: An Introduction to Difference and System GMM in Stata*. Center for Global Development, Working Paper Number 103.

Roodman, D. (2006b). *A Note on the Theme of Too Many Instruments*. Center for Global Development, Working Paper Number 125.

Samargandi, N., Firdmuc, J., & Ghosh, S. (2015). Is the Relationship between Financial Development and Economic Growth Monotonic? Evidence from a Sample of Middle-Income Countries. *World Development*, *68*, 66–81. doi:10.1016/j.worlddev.2014.11.010

Schumpeter, J. (1911). *Theorie der Wirtschaftlichen Entwicklung Leipzig*. Duncker and Humblot.

Schumpeter, J. A. (1934). *The theory of economic development*. Cambridge, MA: Harvard University Press.

Shahbaz, M. (2012). Does trade openness affect long run growth? Cointegration, causality and forecast error variance decomposition tests for Pakistan. *Economic Modelling*, *29*(6), 2325–2339. doi:10.1016/j.econmod.2012.07.015

Shen, C. H., & Lee, C. C. (2006). Same financial development yet different economic growth — Why? *Journal of Money, Credit and Banking*, *38*(7), 1907–1944. doi:10.1353/mcb.2006.0095

Singh, A. (1997). Financial liberalisation, stockmarkets and economic development. *Economic Journal (London)*, *107*(442), 771–782. doi:10.1111/j.1468-0297.1997.tb00042.x

Solow, R. (1957). Technical change and the aggregate production function. *The Review of Economics and Statistics*, 70–92.

Stiglitz, J. E. (1985). Credit markets and the control of capital. *Journal of Money, Credit and Banking*, *17*(2), 133–152. doi:10.2307/1992329

Stockman, A. C. (1981). Anticipated inflation and the capital stock in a cash-in-advance economy. *Journal of Monetary Economics*, *8*(3), 387–393. doi:10.1016/0304-3932(81)90018-0

Talvi, E., & Vegh, C. (2005). Tax Base Variability and Procyclical Fiscal Policy in Developing Countries. *Journal of Development Economics*, *78*(1), 156–190. doi:10.1016/j.jdeveco.2004.07.002

Tamai, T. (2014). Public capital, deficit financing, and economic growth in a stochastic economy. *Journal of Macroeconomics*, *42*, 14–26. doi:10.1016/j.jmacro.2014.06.006

Taylor, M. A., & Wilson, F. L. J. (2011). International trade and finance: Complementaries in the United Kingdom 1870–1913 and the United States 1920–1930. *Journal of International Money and Finance*, *30*(1), 268–288. doi:10.1016/j.jimonfin.2010.10.002

Teles, K., & Mussolini, C. (2014). Public debt and the limits of fiscal policy to increase economic growth. *European Economic Review*, *66*, 1–15. doi:10.1016/j.euroecorev.2013.11.003

Tobin, J. (1965). Money and economic growth. *Econometrica*, *33*(4), 671–684. doi:10.2307/1910352

Tornell, A., & Lane, P. (1999). The Voracity Effect. *The American Economic Review*, *89*(1), 22–46. doi:10.1257/aer.89.1.22

Yanikkaya, H. (2003). Trade openness and economic growth: A cross-country empirical investigation. *Journal of Development Economics*, *72*(1), 57–89. doi:10.1016/S0304-3878(03)00068-3

Zhang, J., Wang, L., & Wang, S. (2012). Financial development and economic growth: Recent evidence from China. *Journal of Comparative Economics*, *40*(3), 393–412. doi:10.1016/j.jce.2012.01.001

ENDNOTES

1 Some of the most prominent EU institutions are the European Parliament, the Council of the European Union, the European Council, the European Commission, the European Central Bank, the Court of Auditors and the Court of Justice of the European Union.

2 The UN geographical scheme categorizes Cyprus, under the Western Asia sub-regional group. For the purposes of this study and since Cyprus is an EU member state, this country is included in the Southern sub-regional EU panel. This is the only deviation from the original UNs' composition of regions. Electronically available at: http://millenniumindicators.un.org/unsd/methods/m49/m49regin.htmhttp://millenniumindicators.un.org/unsd/methods/m49/m49regin.htm (accessed 10 May 2016).

3 Due to cross-country restrictions, our time-series dimension does not allow the estimation of long-run effects, while the evidence of long-term relationships can be obtained only when variables are integrated at the same level (Pesaran and Smith, 1995). However, for the reasons explained below, our main interest focuses on analyzing and comparing the short-run parameters.

4 The EU28 member states are: Austria, Belgium, Bulgaria, Croatia, Cyprus, Czech Republic, Denmark, Estonia, Finland, France, Germany, Greece, Hungary, Ireland, Italy, Latvia, Lithuania, Luxemburg, Malta, the Netherlands, Poland, Portugal, Romania, Slovakia, Slovenia, Spain, Sweden, and the United Kingdom.

5 The Eurozone countries are: Austria, Belgium, Cyprus, Estonia, Finland, France, Germany, Greece, Ireland, Italy, Latvia, Lithuania, Luxemburg, Malta, the Netherlands, Portugal, Slovakia, Slovenia, and Spain. The non-Euro countries are: Bulgaria, Croatia, Czech Republic, Denmark, Hungary, Poland, Romania, Sweden, and the United Kingdom.

6 The Northern EU countries are: Denmark, Estonia, Finland, Ireland, Latvia, Lithuania, Sweden, and the United Kingdom. The Southern EU countries are: Croatia, Cyprus, Greece, Italy, Malta, Portugal, Slovenia, and Spain. The Western EU countries are: Austria, Belgium, France, Germany, Luxemburg, and the Netherlands. Finally, the Eastern EU countries are: Bulgaria, Czech Republic, Hungary, Poland, Romania, and Slovakia.

7 The Solow growth model allows a dynamic view of how savings affects the economy over time. However, structural growth models omit variables that plausibly affect growth.

8 Various empirical approaches have been used to explore the relationship between finance and growth. Earlier research was based on cross-sectional data using standard OLS estimation methods (see, for instance, Levine and Zervos, 1998; King and Levine, 1993a, 1993b), receiving criticism mainly due to econometric problems.

9 To ensure the validity of our calculations we include in our models country dummies to control for country heterogeneity (see Baltagi, 2001). These dummies have been found (jointly) statistically significant in all our models. For the sake of brevity, we do not report these findings. Moreover, to control for time-effects (such as productivity changes) we use time dummies. Both the country and time effects can be seen as country-specific and period-specific components (Ding and Knight, 2009; Bond et al., 2001).

10 The Differenced and System generalized method of moments (GMM) estimators has grown rapidly in recent years. Both are general estimators designed for situations with few time periods and many individuals; independent variables that are not strictly exogenous; fixed effects; and heteroskedasticity and autocorrelation within individuals (Roodman, 2006). The flexible GMM framework accommodates unbalanced panels and multiple endogenous variables (Roodman, 2008).

11 The results from running the models of system-GMM estimator are very similar to those of the differenced-GMM estimator. For the sake of brevity, we report the results for the system-GMM estimator only for the full sample of EU28 countries. However, the remaining results are available from the author upon request.

Chapter 7
The Impact of Economic Sentiment, Consumer, Producer and Investor's Confidence Indices on Stock Returns of the Listed Companies in FTSE-20 in Greece

Constantine Cantzos
Piraeus University of Applied Sciences, Greece

Aristidis Papagrigoriou
Piraeus University of Applied Sciences, Greece

Petros Kalantonis
Piraeus University of Applied Sciences, Greece

Stefanos Theotokas
Piraeus University of Applied Sciences, Greece

ABSTRACT

This chapter examines the relationship between stock returns of companies listed in the FTSE-20 on the Athens Exchange and behavioral indicators. The research is based on the behavioral APT model, which examines stock returns' risk factors through the involvement of macroeconomic variables and behavioral indicators. The data is the closing price of 17 shares listed in the FTSE-20 index, a number of macroeconomic variables, and a series of behavioral indicators for the period of January 2001-December 2014. Regressions were conducted with dependent

DOI: 10.4018/978-1-5225-6114-9.ch007

variable stock returns of a portfolio invested equally in these 17 stocks. In addition, the research tests the existence of long-run and short-run equilibrium and causality. The change in the industrial production index along with the risk premium have a positive and significant impact on the portfolio returns. Johansen's test showed that there is a long-run equilibrium between stock returns, macroeconomic variables, and behavioral indicators. The VECM and VAR models showed that there is not long and short-run causality, not even Granger causality. No similar research has been conducted in Greece, thus it fills a literature gap.

INTRODUCTION

Overview

This study examines the effect of behavioral indicators (Consumer Confidence Index, Investor Confidence Index, Producer Confidence Index and Economic Sentiment Indicator) in stock returns of companies listed in the FTSE-20 index in Greece, in the context of the Arbitrage Pricing Theory (APT).

The economic and business environment is changing radically, due to new socio-political and economical conditions, globalisation, and rapid advances in technology and sciences. (Kennet et al., 2013). The most common approach of the association between macroeconomic variables and stock returns is the Arbitrage Pricing Theory (APT) developed by Ross (1976). Based on this theory, multiple risk factors can explain stock returns. The behavioral approach of APT is a recent concept, as only a few studies have attempted to incorporate those factors to the context of APT. One of these studies is that of Hasan (2010), who also found evidence for the significance of the Investor Confidence Index, together with macroeconomic fundamentals to explain the observed stock returns. Consequently, the effect of behavioral indicators cannot be taken into consideration while ignoring the effect of fundamental economic data within the APT.

Research Aim and Objectives

The research aim of this study can be summarized in the following sentence: "Examination of the behavioral approach of APT in Greece: The case of companies listed in the FTSE-20." To fulfill the research aim of the study, a series of research objectives have been developed that are presented below:

1. Identification of the number of risk factors for the FTSE-20 index stock returns in the period 2001-2014.
2. Examination of the effect of Greece's fundamental macroeconomic data in the FTSE-20 index stock returns in the period 2001-2014.
3. Examination of the effect of behavioral indicators in the FTSE-20 index stock returns in the period 2001-2014.

Several indicators have been suggested that capture the behavior of investors. One of those indicators includes the difference between bid and ask prices (Sewell, 2007). The bid-ask difference includes the difference between the highest price at which a buyer is willing to buy the stock and the lowest price at which the investor willing to sell the stock. Significant differences are found in assets not readily convertible into cash. Therefore, if important differences in stock are found, it practically means that the public is pessimistic about the course of the stock, as it is considered difficult to liquify (Talangi, 2004).

The basic research hypothesis to be tested includes the following:

H01: Behavioral indicators do not affect stock returns of the FTSE-20.
H1: Behavioral indicators affect stock returns of the FTSE-20.

Based on the fact that behavioral finance was created to reflect the effects on stock returns and explain the behavior of the stock market, the existence of a two-way relationship between behavioral indicators and FTSE-20 stock returns is expected.

LITERATURE REVIEW

This chapter aims to discuss the literature background on asset pricing theories, with emphasis on the Arbitrage Pricing Theory (APT). Also, studies that aim to empirically examine the application of the APT model are presented, and whether this model can be analyzed in the context of a behavioral approach.

ASSET PRICING THEORIES

The purpose of asset pricing theories is to determine the fundamental or intrinsic value of an asset[1]. Also, there is a close relationship between the fundamental value and the required rate of return for the investors[2]. The main focus of asset pricing theories is to determine the required rate of return (Skiadas, 2009).

The fundamental value of an asset should be distinguished from the price in the market. The market price is determined by the supply and demand of an asset and can therefore deviate from the fundamental value, but in the long term it will converge to that value[3].

Although the importance of most theories is found in the fundamental value, asset pricing theories are widely used to explain the observed values. Since several theories have failed to provide a sufficient explanation of prices, they were modified to better adapt to the data. In the recent years, studies have focused on the explanation of prices, rather than the determination of fundamental value. However, since the appearance of the Efficient Market Hypothesis, it seems that there is a close relationship between the fundamental value and price, indicating that the value must always be equal to the fundamental value. Therefore, in many cases there is no distinction between the determination of fundamental value and the explanation of the observed prices. In many cases are similar (Pennachi, 2007).

EFFICIENT MARKET HYPOTHESIS

The Efficient Market Hypothesis is an investment theory, with the basic idea that it is impossible to "hit the markets', because the effectiveness of the stock markets leads all available information to reflect on the observed prices. According to the framework of this theory, stock is traded on the stock exchanges at their fair prices[4], making it impossible for investors to either purchase undervalued stock or sell stock at higher prices. Thus, it would be impossible to "hit" the stock market through market timing[5] and the only way for investors to obtain higher returns is to invest their wealth in higher risk investments (Palan, 2007).

Although the Efficient Market Hypothesis is a cornerstone of modern financial theory, it is quite contradictory and often a subject of dispute among researchers. However, supporters of the theory believe that it makes no sense for investors to look for undervalued stock or to try to predict future trends in the markets, either through fundamental or through technical analysis (Ghazani and Araghi, 2014; Lalou et.al., 2016; Lee et al., 2010; Lee and Lee, 2009).

While academic researchers have found evidence to support the Efficient Market Hypothesis (Chen and Yeh, 2002; Timmermann and Granger, 2004), other arguments have been found that lead to controversy among researchers. Critics of the theory are based on events such as the collapse of the stock market in 1987, when the Dow Jones Industrial Average index (DJIA) declined by more than 20% in one day, but also mention evidence that stock prices may significantly deviate from their fair prices (Mahanov and Hudson, 2014; Urquhart and Hudson, 2013).

Efficient Market Hypothesis in the Greek Stock Market (Athens Stock Exchange- A.S.E.)

Some studies aim to specifically test the Efficient Market Hypothesis in the Greek capital market (Athens Stock Exchange). Stengos and Panas (1992) tested the Efficient Market Hypothesis in the A.S.E., with a distinction between a "weak"[6] and a "semi-strong"[7] form hypothesis, depending on information. Consequently, their findings support the "weak" and "semi-strong" form hypothesis of the efficient markets.

Dockery and Kavussanos (1996) concluded that studied the stock exchange market is not efficient. Niarchos and Alexakis (1998) have also drawn the same conclusion. Samitas (2004) rejected the weak form hypothesis of the efficiency, as well as the semi-strong form hypothesis of the secondary market in the A.S.E.

ARBITRAGE PRICING THEORY MODEL-APT

The Arbitrage Pricing Theory was suggested by Stephen Ross in 1976 and predicts a relationship between portfolio returns and asset returns through a linear combination of several independent macroeconomic variables (Giovanis, 2010).

The APT, as well as the CAPM, describes the expected return as a linear function of systematic risk, but, unlike the CAPM, it reflects the possibility that there may be more than one systematic risk factor (Koch, 2009).

The APT descriptive equation is the following (Koch, 2009):

$$E(R_i) = R_0 + \lambda_1 \cdot \beta_{i1} + \lambda_2 \cdot \beta_{i2} + \dots\dots\dots\dots + \lambda_j \cdot \beta_{ij} \tag{1}$$

$E(R_i)$ shows the expected return of the asset *i*, R_0 is the risk-free asset return, $\beta_{i1} - \beta_{ij}$ are the reaction coefficients that describe the change in asset return i for the change of a unit in *j* factor, and λ_j shows the premium for the risk associated with factor *j*.

The reaction rates that characterize an asset is calculated from a market model:

$$r_{it} = b_{i0} + b_{i1} \cdot \delta_{1t} + b_{i2} \cdot \delta_{2t} + \dots\dots\dots\dots + b_{ij} \cdot \delta_{jt} + u_{it} \tag{2}$$

where r_{it} shows the asset return *i* for the period *t*, δ_{jt} is the value of the *j* factor at the time period *t* which is common for all assets, b_{ij} is the estimated response rate of asset i to the j factor, b_{i0} is the estimated asset return i when all values are zero, and u_{it} is an error term with $E(u_{it}) = 0$ representing the residual risk (Koch, 2009).

EMPIRICAL RESEARCH OF THE APT MODEL APPLICATION

International Research

The determination of the factors included in the APT model includes at least an indirect identification. The three approaches presented below are used to identify such factors.

The first approach involves algorithmic analysis of the estimated covariance matrix of asset returns. The second approach is based on the fact that the researcher uses the estimated covariance matrix of asset returns as a starting point and decides on the selection of factors and therefore estimates the matrix.

The third approach is purely at the discretion of the investigator, since he/she mainly uses intuition to choose the factors. Then, the researcher estimates the coefficients of the factors and tests whether they explain cross-sectional variations in the estimated expected returns.

Roll and Ross (1980) found that at least three or four factors explain stock returns. On this basis, and in order to determine the factors, Chen et al. (1986) identified the macroeconomic factors affecting stock prices and concluded that the monthly growth of industrial production, changes in the risk premium and the term structure of interest rates had a statistically significant effect, rather than the unexpected inflation and the changes in the expected inflation.

Bonini et al. (2007) showed that the macro-economic factors with the greatest capacity to predict returns are spread, the G.D.P. and the inflation rate. Acikalin et al. (2008) suggested that macroeconomic factors can predict the performance of the general index. The same results were presented by Abdulrahim (2011), Zhu (2012), Kumar (2013). Rjoub et al. (2009) found that money supply, the term structure of interest rates and the risk premium are statistically significant in the unexpected inflation. Ozcan (2012) suggested that macroeconomic variables present long-run equilibrium with returns of the stock index.

Greece

Limited literature exists regarding the relationship of stock returns in A.S.E. and macroeconomic variables. The results of the study of by Niarchos and Alexakis (2000) statistically reject the Efficient Markets Hypothesis in A.S.E. Other studies applied in the Greek market supported the long relationship between stock returns and macroeconomic factors, such as the results of Dritsaki and Dritsaki-Bargiota (2005), Theophano and Sunil (2006), Spyridis et al. (2012), Chalikias (2013).

BEHAVIORAL APPROACH OF APT MODEL

Traditional pricing theories do not take the economic climate into account, which is included mainly in behavioral finance. The studies examining the impact of the Economic Sentiment Indicator on stock returns have found evidence confirming that this effect is indeed statistically significant (Brown and Cliff, 2004; Lee et al., 1991; Elton et al., 1998 ; Neal and Wheatley, 1998; Baker and Wurgler, 2007; Lemmon and Portniaguina, 2006). In other studies, however, that aimed to examine the predictive ability of the Economic Sentiment Indicator in stock returns, the results are mixed, and do not show any clear trend (Schmeling, 2009; Brown and Cliff, 2005).

Methodology

Sample and Selection Criteria

The sample of this research is drawn from companies listed in the large cap index (FTSE-20) in the A.S.E. Selection criteria of the companies include data availability for the stock prices on a monthly basis during the period January 2001-December 2014 and that the company remained listed throughout the considered period. By applying these criteria, the final sample of companies amounted to 17 which are presented in the following table:

Research Variables

The research variables, particularly the factors that affect stock returns are based on macroeconomic variables used in previous studies. The research variables are presented in the following table:

Data Analysis: Results

This chapter presents the results of the empirical analysis. Initially, descriptive statistics of the variables for the chosen period of research are presented. Then, the results of unit root, autocorrelation-heteroscedasticity tests and regression, on which the above pathologies are corrected, are presented. Finally, a Johansen cointegration test is conducted on series that are not stationary and are integrated of order one.

Table 1. Sample of companies listed in the FTSE-20

Company Sample
1. ALPHA BANK 2. BANK OF PIRAEUS 3. COCA COLA HBC (ATH) 4. CORINTH PIPE WORKS 5. DUTY FREE SHOPS 6. ELLAKTOR 7. FRIGOGLASS 8. HELLENIC PETROLEUM 9. HELLENIC TELECOM.ORG. 10. INTRALOT INTGRTD.SYSV. 11. JUMBO 12. MARFIN INV.GP.HDG. 13. METKA 14. MYTILINEOS HOLDINGS 15. NATIONAL BK.OF GREECE 16. TITAN CEMENT CR 17. VIOHALCO CB

For the cointegration relationship an error correction model is created and impulse-response functions are extracted. The stationary series were modeled in a vector autoregressive model with the purpose to conduct a Granger causality test.

Descriptive Statistics of Variables

As shown in Table 3, the returns of a portfolio invested in equal proportions in each of the 17 stocks for that period, yields on average 4.44% return. The median value is close to zero, 0.006%. This means that for the half periods the returns were positive, while for the rest were negative.

FACTOR ANALYSIS

This chapter presents the results of the factor analysis conducted by the method of maximum likelihood and a rotation the factor loading matrix, using the Varimax rotation. Varimax is a rotation that minimizes the number of variables that have large weight and makes them more interpretable factors some applications of the method are conducted by Tampouratzis et al (2014); Tampouratzis et al (2010); Skordoulis et al., (2014); Chalikias (2013); Chalikias & Kolovos (2013) e.t.c.The results are presented below:

Table 2. Research variables, measurement, and data source

Variable	Measurement	Source
Risk premium	Difference between market return (FTSE-20 index return) and risk-free interest rate (Euribor 1 month)	Yahoo finance (αποδόσειςδείκτη FTSE-20), http://www.euribor-rates.eu/euribor-rate-1-month.asp (Euribor rate)
Term structure of interest rates	Difference between returns of 10-year government bonds (long-term interest rate) and three-month Greek Treasury bills (short-term interest rate)	OECD Statistics
Industrial Production Index (MIP)	Production in the industry sector (energy, intermediate goods, capital goods, consumer durables, non-durable consumer goods, base year 2010 = 100)	Hellenic Statistical Authority
Oil price (Brent)	Brent oil prices in Euros	EIA
Gold price	Gold price per pound in Euros	http://www.indexmundi.com/commodities/?commodity=gold
Exchange rate	Euro/Dollar exchange rate	http://www.investing.com/currencies/eur-usd-historical-data
Money supply (M3)	Money supply M3	Bank of Greece
Consumer Prices (CPI)	Consumer Price Index, base year 2009=100.	Hellenic Statistical Authority
Consumer Confidence Index (CCI)	ResearchonconsumerconfidenceintheEurozonecountries, base year 2010=100.	OECD Statistics
Business Confidence Index (BCI)	ResearchonbusinessconfidenceintheEurozonecountries, base year 2010=100.	OECD Statistics
Economic Sentiment Index (ESI)	Researchonoptimism/pessimismofconsumers, producers, retailers, industryandthe construction sector about the future, base year 2010=100.	European Commission
Investor Confidence Index (Bidask)	Differencesin bid-ask prices in company stocks (average bid-ask spread price of 17 stocks for each month)	Yahoo Finance
Portfolio	Portfolio invested equally in each ofthe 17 stocks, $\sum_{i=1}^{17}\frac{1}{17}P_i$, based on monthly stock closing prices (end of month).	Yahoo Finance
Portfolio return	Returnofportfolio invested equally in each of the 17 stocks, $\sum_{i=1}^{17}\frac{1}{17}R_i$, basedonthe percentage change of monthly stock closing prices (end of month).	Yahoo Finance

Table 3. Descriptive statistics

Descriptive Statistics					
	Average	**Median**	**Maximum**	**Minimum**	**Standard Deviation**
Portfolio Return	4.440315	0.005476	64.08574	-0.3130	15.32059
BCI	99.34646	100.1400	102.4300	93.53000	2.432824
Brent	69.49683	68.58500	132.7200	18.71000	33.42767
CCI	98.63399	99.88641	101.3316	9.912420	9.929484
CPI	93.32195	93.00000	111.3000	73.60000	11.31129
ESI	99.48354	99.50000	101.8000	96.50000	1.452279
Exhrate	1.260827	1.300000	1.580000	0.849400	0.171386
Gold	370.2779	331.4950	997.6200	1.000000	250.9839
M3	170.2576	164.4730	243.7010	113.0970	37.60143
MIP	111.6930	117.7317	126.3720	87.80521	11.66528
Riskprem	-2.404	-2.135	0.034439	-5.190	1.538645
termstruct	5.710604	3.315500	34.49100	-0.892	6.636814
Bid-Ask Spreads					
ALPHA BANK	1.102	0.00023	2.752	-2.274	6.642
BANK OF PIRAEUS	1.618	0.000485	1.914	-3.007	1.654
COCA COLA HBC (ATH)	0.275347	0.000109	7.382	-7.044	2.938
CORINTH PIPE WORKS	0.021079	0.005	1.640	-0.96	0.348192
DUTY FREE SHOPS	6.10E-05	-0.12	4.900	-3.620	1.438.260
ELLAKTOR	0.046073	0	2.600	-2.180	0.549002
FRIGOGLASS	-0.005427	-0.04	7.600	-2.980	1.153
HELLENIC PETROLEUM	0.017744	-0.01	2.080	-3.640	0.727474
HELLENIC TELECOM.ORG.	0.044695	-0.03	4.540	-2.500	1.066
INTRALOT INTGRTD.SYSV.	0.071994	0.01	1.684	-4.100	2.051
JUMBO	-0.127575	8.00E-07	2.115	-2.149	5.129
MARFIN INV.GP.HDG.	-0.049268	-0.02	9.720	-4.440	1.259
METKA	-0.024146	-0.005	3.320	-2.580	0.95108
MYTILINEOS HOLDINGS	0.123054	8.50E-08	3.611	-3.285	0.81562
NATIONAL BK.OF GREECE	0.002967	1.20E-06	0.225715	-0.2322	0.056621
TITAN CEMENT CR	0.14878	-0.195	1.688	-4.190	2.469
VIOHALCO CB	0.036793	0.03	0.22	0	0.037073
BidaskA (mean)	69.61	0.10	11.260	-2.50	866.26

Table 4. Factor analysis results

	Factor Loading	
	F1	**F2**
ALPHA BANK	23.69843	-0.191618
BANK OF PIRAEUS	1.33E-16	0.204293
COCA COLA HBC (ATH)	-0.036436	0.022924
CORINTH PIPE WORKS	-0.108229	0.067524
DUTY FREE SHOPS	-0.085258	0.035573
ELLAKTOR	-0.08032	0.059420
FRIGOGLASS	-0.099287	0.049132
HELLENIC PETROLEUM	-0.0513	0.022039
HELLENIC TELECOM. ORG.	-0.081496	0.025022
INTRALOT INTGRTD. SYSV.	-0.081192	0.059558
JUMBO	-0.073967	0.039705
MARFIN INV.GP.HDG.	-0.088011	0.060239
METKA	-0.09166	0.046953
MYTILINEOS HOLDINGS	-0.110752	0.066178
NATIONAL BK.OF GREECE	-0.047537	0.121685
TITAN CEMENT CR	-0.052253	0.033365
VIOHALCO CB	0.006519	0.008553
Factor	**Variation**	**Percentage**
F1	561.7071	0.999781
F2	0.123190	0.000219
Total	561.8303	1.000000

According to the table above, the variation of the 17 stock returns is mainly explained by two factors. The first factor explains the stock returns by 99%, while the second factor of by 1%. By saving the scores of each factor, the regression of the return of each stock and the portfolio as a whole was possible, with the two factors as independent variables. It appears that only in the case of Coca-Cola's stock there is a statistically significant effect of the factor 2 on the returns ($B = 0.02$, $p = 0.02$). The results of the regressions are presented in the appendix, Tables 11-28.

UNIT ROOT TESTS RESULTS

This section presents the results of the Dickey-Fuller test. As shown in Table 29 in the Appendix, most variables, apart from some exceptions, are not stationary in levels. The variables that are stationary are the bid-ask spreads. Bid-ask spreads of Corinth Pipeworks that are integrated of order one ($p = 1.00$) and Ellaktor ($p = 1.00$) are excluded. A stationary series in level is the consumer confidence index ($p = 0.000$). It is also noted that there are two variables that are stationary in second differences. These variables include consumer price index ($p = 0.000$) and money supply ($p = 0.000$). These series are integrated of order two. This shows that most variables evolve randomly in time, as the existence of unit root means that the autocorrelation of the residuals are equal to 1 ($\rho = 1$). The next chapter presents the results of the autocorrelation-heteroscedasticity tests on the examined model.

Autocorrelation-Heteroscedasticity Test Results

This chapter presents the results of the autocorrelation-heteroscedasticity tests, which are concentrated in the following table:

The Durbin-Watson test yielded a statistic equal to 0.55, which means that the correlation coefficient of the model residuals equals to 0.73. So, there is a first order autocorrelation in the residuals. Durbin's alternative test was conducted by regressing the residuals on their 12 lags. As shown, the residuals with a time lag have a statistically significant effect (R = 0.63, $p = 0.000$), suggesting first order autocorrelation in the residuals. However, the residuals with 12 time lags also have a statistically significant effect (R = 0.18, $p = 0.02$).

As there is no dependent variable with lags in the model, it is predicted that the Breusch-Godfrey test would yield similar results. The lags selected were 12. As shown, residuals with a lag have a statistically significant effect on the model,

Table 5. Autocorrelation-Heteroscedasticity tests

Autocorrelation Tests		
	Statistic/p-Value	**Result**
Durbin-Watson (2(1-ρ))	0.55	Firstorder autocorrelationinresiduals
Breusch-Godfrey	0.00	Firstorderautocorrelationinresiduals
Heteroscedasticity Tests		
White test	0.00	Heteroscedasticity of unknown form
ARCH LM test	0.00	Heteroscedasticity ARCH (1) form

with a coefficient of 0.65 (p = 0.000). This estimation is relatively close to the estimation based on Durbin's alternative test, which confirms the existence of first order autocorrelation in the residuals. Also, residuals with 12 lags are significant at 10% significance level (B = 0.18, p = 0.10). This is compatible with the Durbin test.

Therefore, the possibility of heteroscedasticity in residuals was tested. The White test controls the null hypothesis that there is heteroscedasticity. As the probability of the test is null, this means that there is some unknown form of heteroscedasticity. Since heteroscedasticity exists, ARCH heteroscedasticity test was conducted. The null hypothesis of the test is that there is q order heteroscedasticity. For the 12 lags, the test showed that only the squared residuals with a time lag are statistically significant (B = 0.66, p = 0.000). This means that ARCH (1) heteroscedasticity exists.

An additional test was the extraction of Q-statistic with the Cumby-Huizinga test. Since ARCH form heteroscedasticity exists, a Breusch-Godfrey test was conducted, but by extracting Newey-West robust standard errors. The result showed that the residuals with a lag have a statistically significant effect on the model (B = 0.68, p = 0.000). The same applies to residuals with 12 lags (B = 0.17, p = 0.01). Estimations of the Breusch-Godfrey test and Cumby-Huizinga test are quite close; suggesting that the form of the autocorrelation observed in residuals is MA (1) and MA (12). The results of autocorrelation and heteroskedasticity tests are presented in the Appendix, tables 30-35.

This leads to the fact that in the regression to be conducted, the model should include only stationary series of the variables to remove any trend, but also to include MA (1) and MA (12) disturbances that correct this form of autocorrelation. Also, for the correction of ARCH (1) heteroscedasticity, Newey-West robust standard errors were extracted.

REGRESSION

The following table presents the regression conducted, corrected for autocorrelation and heteroscedasticity. First, the regression involved only macroeconomic variables, followed by the regression that includes behavioral indicators as well.

As shown in Table 6, the regression is overall statistically significant at 1% significance level (Prob> F = 0.01). According to the adjusted R-squared coefficient, the model explains only 8% of the volatility of portfolio returns. The effect of change in the industrial production at 5% significance level (B = 0.06, p = 0.02) is statistically significant and positive, and so is the effect of a change in risk premium (B=1.67, p = 0.0002) at 1% significance level. A risk premium increase seems to boost portfolio returns, since as long as the difference in the index returns in FTSE-20 in relation to risk-free interest rate is increased, portfolio returns increase

Table 6. Regression with correction for autocorrelation and heteroscedasticity (macroeconomic variables)

Variable	Coefficient	Standard Error	t-Statistic	Prob.
D(BRENT)	-0.020612	0.018632	-1.106237	0.2703
D(CPI,2)	-0.009995	0.069815	-0.143171	0.8863
D(EXCHRATE)	1.340797	2.532889	0.529355	0.5973
D(GOLD)	0.000303	0.000482	0.629556	0.5299
D(M3)	0.011825	0.027969	0.422812	0.6730
D(MIP)	0.064730**	0.027479	2.355607	0.0197
D(RISKPREM)	1.666060***	0.433624	3.842178	0.0002
D(TERMSTRUCT)	-0.045458	0.050900	-0.893103	0.3732
C	-0.126890	0.146731	-0.864782	0.3885
MA(1)	0.257134***	0.080403	3.198061	0.0017
MA(12)	0.233103***	0.074942	3.110456	0.0022
R-squared	0.135909	Mean dependent var		-0.108216
Adjusted R-squared	0.080519	S.D. dependent var		1.336669
S.E. of regression	1.281726	Akaike info criterion		3.397891
Sum squared resid	256.2803	Schwarz criterion		3.603268
Log likelihood	-272.7239	F-statistic		2.453654
Durbin-Watson stat	1.971223	Prob(F-statistic)		0.009488***

by 1.67%. Therefore, as long as tolerance towards risk is increased and therefore investors require a higher risk premium to invest in stock, this will tend to increase portfolio returns. Durbin-Watson statistic is 1.97, very close to 2, meaning that autocorrelation problems are corrected.

As shown in Table 7, the regression is overall statistically significant at 5% significance level as indicated by the probability of the F-test (p = 0.03). The descriptive ability of the model is also low, as it explains 7% of the volatility of stock returns. The coefficient that is statistically significant at 5% significance level is the change in the industrial production index (B = 0.07, p = 0.02). A positive change in the industrial production index by one tends to increase portfolio returns by 0.07%. Additionally, the risk premium is also statistically significant at 1% significance level (B = 1.59, p = 0.001). Similar to the previous case, reduced tolerance to risk will tend to increase portfolio returns by 1.59%. The Durbin-Watson statistic is close to 2 (1.97), suggesting that through this adjustment autocorrelation in residuals is corrected. The model including the behavioral indicators seems to have higher

Table 7. Regression with correction for autocorrelation and heteroscedacity

Variable	Coefficient	St. Error	t-Statistic	Prob.
D(BCI)	0.311042	0.512118	0.607364	0.5445
D(BRENT)	-0.024275	0.020013	-1.212963	0.2270
CCI	-0.003353	0.010038	-0.334012	0.7388
D(CPI,2)	-0.007076	0.072136	-0.098088	0.9220
D(ESI)	-0.954135	0.645802	-1.477443	0.1416
D(EXCHRATE)	1.472969	2.599731	0.566585	0.5718
D(GOLD)	0.000318	0.000494	0.643467	0.5209
D(M3,2)	0.011850	0.028938	0.409485	0.6828
D(MIP)	0.067670**	0.028240	2.396199	0.0178
D(RISKPREM)	1.587235***	0.449426	3.531696	0.0005
D(TERMSTRUCT)	-0.043747	0.051122	-0.855737	0.3935
Bidask	2.07E-05	0.000112	0.184352	0.8540
C	0.222577	1.006302	0.221183	0.8252
MA(1)	0.234497***	0.085737	2.735068	0.0070
MA(12)	0.260758***	0.077102	3.382004	0.0009
R-squared	0.148760	Mean dependent var		-0.108216
Adjusted R-squared	0.070356	S.D. dependent var		1.336669
S.E. of regression	1.288790	Akaike info criterion		3.430812
Sum squared resid	252.4689	Schwarz criterion		3.710871
Log likelihood	-271.4728	F-statistic		1.897355
Durbin-Watson stat	1.970652	Prob(F-statistic)		0.030583**

Akaike and Schwarz information criteria. This means that the model that includes only macroeconomic variables has better quality information in relation to the model that includes behavioral indicators.

LONG-RUN EQUILIBRIUM

As some of the variables are not stationary in levels, all I(1) series can be tested for some common long-term trends . Because the test is influenced by the number of lags, first their number is selected, modeling variables in vector autoregressive models with 1 lag and 1-2 lags. The Akaike and Schwarz criteria had lower value in the model with 1 lag which indicates that the test should include a time lag.

Table 8. Johansen cointegration test (1-time lag) (Number of hypothesized CE equations = 0.05)

	Eigenvalue	Trace Statistic	Critical Value	Prob.**
none	0.489592	479.4370	334.9837	0.0000
maximum 1	0.372363	367.7946	285.1425	0.0000
maximum 2	0.343423	290.4730	239.2354	0.0000
maximum 3	0.278788	220.6344	197.3709	0.0020
maximum 4	0.242922	166.3818	159.5297	0.0200
maximum 5	0.221996	120.1859	125.6154	0.1023

*The test shows that there are 5 cointegrating equations at 0.05 significance level

Based on the results of Table 8, it appears that there are at most 5 cointegrating equations. Long-run estimation of the cointegrating equation coefficients of interest are presented in Table 9.

As shown, the coefficient of Brent has a statistically significant effect (B = 0.83, t-stat=2.47), as well as inflation's (B = 53.67, t-stat = 14.31), economic sentiment indicator's (B = -10.41, t- stat = -2.52), the change in money supply (B = 16.17, t-stat = 8.81) and the term structure of interest rates (B = 1.90, t-stat = 3.02).

LONG-RUN AND SHORT-RUN CAUSALITY

As shown by the error correction model, Table 36, Appendix, the error is not statistically significant (B = -0.001, t-stat = -0.30), meaning that there is no long-run causality running from the independent variables on the dependent one. Moreover, the estimates show that there is no short-run causality, as none of the independent variables have a statistically significant effect on stock returns. However, although there is a long-run equilibrium between the variables, there is not long-run or short-run causality. For the above error correction model, the impulse-response functions of the portfolio value in unanticipated orthogonal shocks were extracted of each variable separately. The functions were extracted for a period of 12 months after the shock.

As shown above, a shock in the business confidence index will cause an increase in portfolio value and gradually lead to a new long-run equilibrium, higher than the previous. The same applies to a change in Brent oil price. At first, a shock in oil prices will lead to fluctuations in the value of the portfolio, but will gradually lead to a new equilibrium, higher than the previous. An unexpected shock in inflation will increase its value but will gradually lead to a new lower equilibrium. An increase

Table 9. Estimation of long-run cointegrating equation coefficients

Cointegrating Equation	Estimations
PORTFOLIO(-1)	1.000000
BCI(-1)	3.424075
	(2.63909)
	[1.29745]
BRENT(-1)	0.826900
	(0.33472)
	[2.47045]
D(CPI(-1))	53.66737
	(3.75019)
	[14.3106]
ESI(-1)	-10.41290
	(4.12499)
	[-2.52435]
EXCHRATE(-1)	-86.05386
	(54.6072)
	[-1.57587]
GOLD(-1)	0.005511
	(0.01707)
	[0.32290]
D(M3(-1))	16.17349
	(1.83637)
	[8.80730]
MIP(-1)	-0.179830
	(0.81793)
	[-0.21986]
RISKPREM(-1)	4.569812
	(4.26631)
	[1.07114]
TERMSTRUCT(-1)	1.902267
	(0.63051)
	[3.01703]
C	733.8068

Figure 1. Impulse-response functions (vector error correction model)

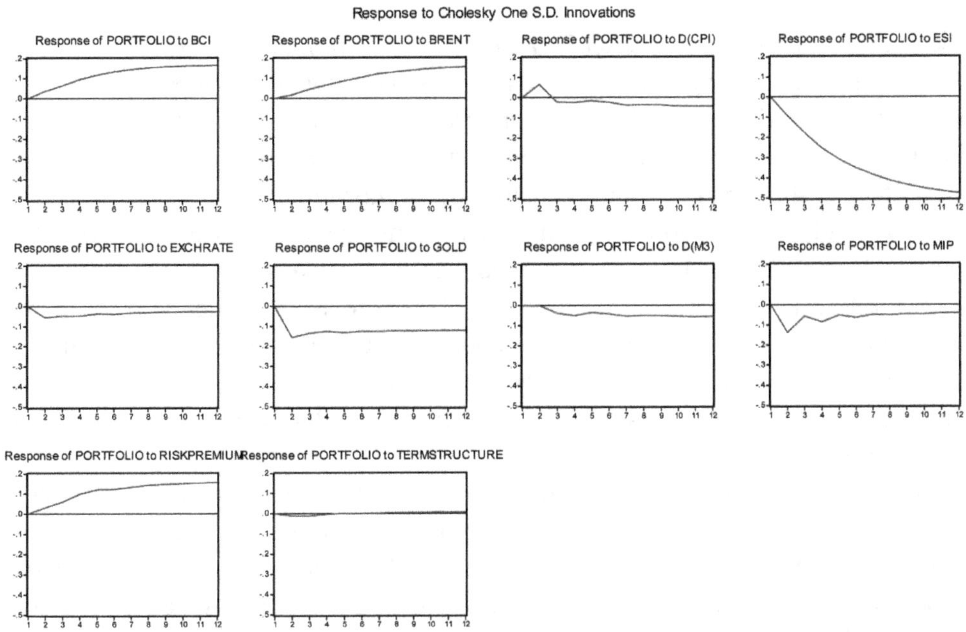

in risk premium increases the value of the portfolio and gradually leads to a new equilibrium, higher than the previous one. A shock in the exchange rate will reduce the portfolio value, and that reduction will be permanent, as the new equilibrium would be lower than the original. A shock in the economic sentiment indicator would seem to cause a particularly large reduction in portfolio value. The new equilibrium appears to be much lower than the original. Gold price and a change in the industrial production index also cause permanent changes in the portfolio value, leading to a lower equilibrium. However, a shock in the term structure of interest rates seems to cause only temporary changes in portfolio value, as it tends to return the system to its original equilibrium. The above show that while there is essentially long-run equilibrium, it is unstable. Apart from the shock in the term structure of interest rate, shocks in the other variables tend to lead the system to a new equilibrium, either higher or lower than the initial equilibrium.

SHORT-RUN EQUILIBRIUM

The vector autoregressive model included only the stationary series of variables. Those already stationary were included in levels, while the series integrated of order one were included in first differences and those integrated of order two in second differences. The reason for the creation of the model was to perform the Granger causality test, showing essentially a short-run equilibrium relationship between the variables, and the extraction of the impulse-response functions based on this model. The results of Vector Autoregressive Model are presented Table 37, Appendix.

According to the results of the Vector Autoregressive Model, shocks in the independent variables only lead to temporary changes in stock returns. In the long run, the system returns to the previous equilibrium. Therefore, the Vector Autoregressive Model suggests that by essentially introducing all variables a stable equilibrium can be achieve

As shown in Table 10, there is no short-run equilibrium between the variables, as there is no Granger causality. The null hypothesis of the test is that there is no Granger causality. This means that the independent variables cannot predict the short-run portfolio returns, as the probability of the test for all variables exceeds the 1%, 5% and 10% significance level.

Figure 2. Impulse-response functions (vector autoregressive model)

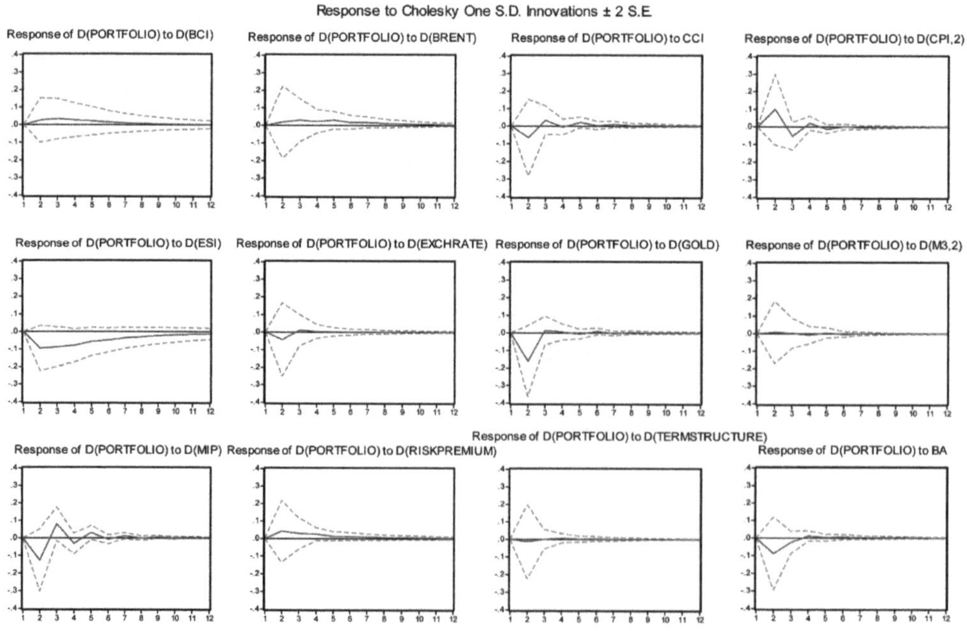

Table 10. Granger causality test

Dependent Variable: D(PORTFOLIO)			
	Chi-sq	**df**	**Prob.**
D(BCI)	0.873539	1	0.3500
D(BRENT)	0.028571	1	0.8658
CCI	0.328304	1	0.5667
D(CPI,2)	0.617824	1	0.4319
D(ESI)	2.168023	1	0.1409
D(EXCHRATE)	0.051892	1	0.8198
D(GOLD)	2.342070	1	0.1259
D(M3,2)	.068694	1	0.7932
D(MIP)	.511452	1	0.1130
D(RISKPRE)	.208972	1	0.6476
D(TERMSTRUCT)	.008716	1	0.9256
Bidask	.717669	1	0.3969
Όλες	0.35095	12	0.5852

CONCLUSION

The purpose of this study was to determine whether the behavioral indicators together with the macroeconomic variables can statistically significantly affect the stock returns listed in the FTSE-20 index in the A.S.E.

The factor analysis of the returns of all 17 stocks showed that two factors explain the variation in stock returns for this period. It is suggested that a positive change in the industrial production index tends to increase the portfolio returns. Given that some of the portfolio companies belong to the industrial sector, such an effect is considered reasonable. In particular, the production increase is considered a positive sign for investors. Therefore, they tend to buy stocks of these companies. But the increase in volume tends to increase the price of stocks and, therefore, their performance as well.

Another factor that positively affects portfolio returns is risk premium. As risk premium increases, tolerance of investors towards risk is decreased. Therefore, investors increasingly demand higher returns to invest in securities with risk in relation to risk-free assets. The largest market returns in relation to risk-free assets constitute a positive sign for investors, who invest in the FTSE-20 index stock, increasing volume and thus the value and their returns.

Consequently, these regressions showed that the two risk factors that emerged from the factor analysis include the industrial environment and the risk premium. This finding is partly compatible with that of Kumar (2013), who concluded to three risk factors, one of which is the industrial environment.

Term structure of interest rates does not seem to have any significant effect. This may happen because the term structure of interest rates is essentially a measure of alternative investment returns, excluding FTSE-20 index stock. In recent years and particularly during the crisis, both the Greek government bonds and the 3-month bills are returns with risk. So, there is some substitutability or complementarity between the returns of these three investment goods.

Money supply has no statistically significant effect. During the examination period of this study, most years include the period after the accession to the euro, which means that the monetary policy is exerted by the European Central Bank. Consequently, since the money supply is partly exogenous, it does not affect the stock returns.

For the period under examination, the competitiveness of the Greek economy does not seem to have a major influence on stock returns. The exchange rate basically captures the degree of competitiveness of the Greek economy with respect to its exports.

Johansen's cointegration test showed that a long-run equilibrium between portfolio value and the independent variables exists. In particular, Brent oil, inflation, the economic sentiment indicator, the change in money supply and the term structure of interest rates have a significant effect. Therefore, the evolution of these variables reports some common trends with the value of the portfolio.

All the effects are positive, except for the impact of the Economic Sentiment Indicator, which is negative. The positive effect suggests that if the long-run value of the portfolio has an upward trend, the price of Brent oil, inflation, changes in money supply and the term structure of interest rates will also have an upward trend. Instead, the Economic Sentiment Indicator has a downward trend. The negative effect of this indicator can be explained by the fact that the examination period includes the crisis, which contributed to a downward trend. The fact that there is a long-run equilibrium between macroeconomic variables and stock returns is also suggested by previous studies (Acikalin et al., 2008; Ozcan, 2012), as well, and the long-run equilibrium with the Economic Sentiment Indicator (Hasan, 2010).

The impulse-response functions showed that a shock in the term structure of interest rates causes only temporary changes in portfolio value. However, all other variables seem to cause permanent changes in the portfolio value, leading to a new equilibrium. However, there is no long-run and short-run causality between stock returns and macroeconomic variables and behavioral indicators. Also, portfolio returns one month before cannot predict the returns for the next month, a finding that was supported by Niarchos and Alexakis (2000). Consequently, in this context, the findings of the study are more in line with studies that prove the Efficient Market Hypothesis such that by Stengos and Panas (1992).

Further, Granger causality tests showed that none of the variables Granger causes portfolio stock returns after one month. This finding is different from those of Dockery and Kavussanos (1996), Niarchos and Alexakis (1998), Samitas (2004), Acikalin et al. (2008) and Dritsaki and Dritsaki-Bargiota (2005).

Overall, it appears that while there is evidence of long-run equilibrium, there is no short-run / long-run causality and short-run equilibrium of any kind between stock returns and explanatory variables. Only the Economic Sentiment Indicator seems to have long-run equilibrium relationship with portfolio stock returns. No other index that captures the general feeling of the public and the investors seems to significantly affect stock returns.

REFERENCES

Abdulrahim, S. (2011). *Nigerian Stock Returns and Macroeconomic variables: Evidence from the APT Model.* Retrieved 28/02/2016 from http://i-rep.emu.edu.tr:8080/jspui/bitstream/11129/186/1/Saliha.pdf

Acikalin, S., Aktas, R., & Unal, S. (2008). Relationships between stock markets and macroeconomic variables: An empirical analysis of the Istanbul Stock Exchange. *Investment Management and Financial Innovations*, *5*(1), 8–16.

Baker, M., & Wurgler, J. (2007). Investors Sentiment in the Stock Market. *The Journal of Economic Perspectives*, *21*(2), 129–151. doi:10.1257/jep.21.2.129

Bonini, S., Capizzi, V., Cipollini, A., & Erbetta, F. (2007). *The Effect of Analysts' Forecasts on Stock Market Returns: A Composite Multifactor Approach.* 10.2139/ssrn.990047

Brown, G. W., & Cliff, M. T. (2004). Investor Sentiment and the Near-term Stock Market. *Journal of Empirical Finance*, *11*(1), 1–27. doi:10.1016/j.jempfin.2002.12.001

Brown, G. W., & Cliff, M. T. (2005). Investor Sentiment and Asset Valuation. *The Journal of Business*, *78*(2), 405–439. doi:10.1086/427633

Chalikias, M.S., & Kolovos, K.G. (2013). Citizens' views in Southern Greece PART II: The contribution of forests to quality of life. *Journal of Environmental Protection and Ecology*, *14*(2), 629–637.

Chalikias, M. S. (2013a). Research of personnel selection methods in the Greek private bank sector. *African Journal of Business Management*, *7*(26), 2570–2575.

Chalikias, M. S. (2013b). Citizens' views in Southern Greece PART I: The forests' threats. *Journal of Environmental Protection and Ecology*, *14*(2), 509–516.

Dockery, E., & Kavussanos, M. G. (1996). Testing the Efficient Market Hypothesis Using Panel Data, with Application to the Athens Stock Market. *Applied Economics Letters*, *3*(2), 121–123. doi:10.1080/135048596356834

Dritsaki, C., & Dritsaki-Bargiota, M. (2005). The Causal Relationship between Stock, Credit Market and Economic Development: An Empirical Evidence for Greece. *Economic Change and Restructuring*, *38*(1), 113–127. doi:10.100710644-005-4525-3

Elton, E. J., Gruber, M. J., & Busse, A. (1998). Do Investors Care about Sentiment? *The Journal of Business*, *71*(4), 477–500. doi:10.1086/209754

Fabozzi, F., Neave, E., & Zhou, G. (2012). *Financial Economics*. John Wiley & Sons.

Ghazani, M., & Araghi, M. (2014). Evaluation of the adaptive market hypothesis as an evolutionary perspective on market efficiency: Evidence from the Tehran stock exchange. *Research in International Business and Finance*, *32*, 50–59. doi:10.1016/j.ribaf.2014.03.002

Giovanis, E. (2010). *Application of Capital Asset Pricing (CAPM) and Arbitrage Pricing Theory (APT) Models in Athens Exchange Stock Market*. GRIN Verlag.

Hasan, E. (2010). *Behavioral approach to Arbitrage Pricing Theory*. Retrieved 17/02/2016 from http://mpra.ub.uni-muenchen.de/26343/1/MPRA_paper_26343.pdf

Johansen, S. (1988). Statistical Analysis of Cointegration Vectors. *Journal of Economic Dynamics & Control*, *12*(2–3), 231–254. doi:10.1016/0165-1889(88)90041-3

Johansen, S. (1991). Estimation and Hypothesis Testing of Cointegration Vectors in Gaussian Vector Autoregressive Models. *Econometrica*, *59*(6), 1551–1580. doi:10.2307/2938278

Kennet, M., Drosos, D., & Tsotsolas, N. (2013). Special Issue: The Greek Crisis: Some Environmental and Economic initiatives and the first steps towards implementing Green Economics. *International Journal of Green Economics*, *7*(4), 315–319.

Koch, C. (2009). *The Arbitrage Pricing Theory as an Approach to Capital Asset Valuation*. GRIN Verlag.

Kumar, R. (2013). The Effect of Macroeconomic Factors on Indian Stock Market Performance: A Factor Analysis Approach. *IOSR Journal of Economics and Finance*, *1*(3), 14–21. doi:10.9790/5933-0131421

Lalou, P., Chalikias, M., Skordoulis, M., Papadopoulos, P., & Fatouros, S. (2016). A Probabilistic Evaluation of sales expansion. *5th International Symposium and 27th National Conference on Operation Research*, 109-112.

Lee, C., & Lee, J. (2009). Energy prices, multiple structural breaks, and efficient market hypothesis. *Applied Energy*, *86*(4), 466–479. doi:10.1016/j.apenergy.2008.10.006

Lee, C., Lee, J., & Lee, C. (2010). Stock prices and the efficient market hypothesis: Evidence from a panel stationary test with structural breaks. *Japan and the World Economy*, *22*(1), 49–58. doi:10.1016/j.japwor.2009.04.002

Lee, C., Shleifer, A., & Thaler, R. (1991). Investor Sentiment and the Closed-end Fund Puzzle. *The Journal of Finance*, *46*(1), 75–109. doi:10.1111/j.1540-6261.1991.tb03746.x

Lemmon, M., & Portniaguina, E. (2006). Consumer Confidence and Asset Prices: Some Empirical Evidence. *Review of Financial Studies*, *19*(4), 1499–1529. doi:10.1093/rfs/hhj038

Mahanov, V., & Hudson, R. (2014). A note on the relationship between market efficiency and adaptability – New evidence from artificial stock markets. *Expert Systems with Applications*, *41*(16), 7436–7454. doi:10.1016/j.eswa.2014.06.004

Neal, R., & Wheatley, S. M. (1998). Do Measures of Investor Sentiment Predict Returns? *Journal of Financial and Quantitative Analysis*, *333*(4), 523–547. doi:10.2307/2331130

Niarchos, N., & Alexakis, C. (1998). Stock market prices, 'causality' and efficiency: Evidence from the Athens stock exchange. *Applied Financial Economics*, *8*(2), 167–174.

Niarchos, N. A., & Alexakis, C. A. (2000). The Predictive Power of Macroeconomic Variables on Stock Market Returns: The Case of the Athens Stock Exchange. *SPOUDAI*, *50*(1/2), 74–86.

Ozcan, A. (2012). The Relationship Between Macroeconomic Variables and ISE Industry Index. *International Journal of Economics and Financial Issues*, *2*(2), 184–189.

Palan, S. (2007). *The efficient market hypothesis and its validity in today's markets*. GRIN Verlag.

Pennachi, G. (2007). *Theory of Asset Pricing*. Prentice Hall.

Rjoub, H., Tursoy, T., & Gunsel, N. (2009). The effects of macroeconomic factors on stock returns: Istanbul Stock Market. *Studies in Economics and Finance*, *26*(1), 36–45. doi:10.1108/10867370910946315

Roll, R. (1977). A Critique of the Asset Pricing Theory's Tests. *Journal of Financial Economics*, *4*(2), 129–176. doi:10.1016/0304-405X(77)90009-5

Ross, S. A. (1976). The Arbitrage Theory of Capital Asset Pricing. *Journal of Economic Theory*, *13*(3), 341–360. doi:10.1016/0022-0531(76)90046-6

Samitas, A. (2004). Testing the Efficient Market Hypothesis in The Greek Secondary Capital Market. *Zegreb International Review of Economics and Business*, *7*(1), 23–38.

Schmeling, M. (2009). Investor Sentiment and Stock Returns: Some International Evidence. *Journal of Empirical Finance*, *16*(3), 394–408. doi:10.1016/j.jempfin.2009.01.002

Sewell, M. (2007). *Behavioural Finance*. University of Cambridge.

Skiadas, C. (2009). *Asset Pricing Theory*. Princeton University Press.

Skordoulis, M., Chalikias, M., & Koniordos, M. (2014). Students' satisfaction through DREEM and LOT-R. In *Communications in Computer and Information Science. 466: Knowledge-Based Software Engineering: Proceedings of 11th Joint Conference on Knowledge-Based software Engineering*. Springer International Publishing.

Spyridis, T., Sevic, Z., & Theriou, N. (2012). Macroeconomic vs Statistical APT in the Athens Stock Exchange. *International Journal Of Business*, *17*(1), 39–64.

Stengos, T., & Panas, E. (1992). Testing the efficiency of the ASE: Some results from the banking sector. *Empirical Economics*, *17*, 239–252. doi:10.1007/BF01206285

Talangi, A. (2004). Modern Finance Versus Behavioral Finance. *Quarterly Journal of Financial Research*, 3-25.

Tambouratzis, T., Souliou, D., Chalikias M., & Gregoriades, A. (2010). Combining probabilistic neural networks and decision trees for maximally accurate and efficient accident prediction. *Proceedings of the IEEE International Joint Conference on Neural Network*, 1-8.

Tambouratzis, T., Souliou, D., Chalikias, M., & Gregoriades, A. (2014). Maximising accuracy and efficiency of traffic accident prediction by combining information mining with computational intelligence approaches and decision trees. *Journal of Artificial Intelligence and Soft Computing Research*, *4*(1), 31–42.

Theophano, P., & Sunil, P. (2006). Economic variables and stock market returns: Evidence from the Athens stock exchange. *Applied Financial Economics*, *16*(3), 993–1005.

Timmermann, A., & Granger, C. (2004). Efficient market hypothesis and forecasting. *International Journal of Forecasting*, *20*(1), 15–27. doi:10.1016/S0169-2070(03)00012-8

Urquhart, A., & Hudson, R. (2013). Efficient or adaptive markets? Evidence from major stock markets using very long run historic data. *International Review of Financial Analysis*, *28*, 130–142. doi:10.1016/j.irfa.2013.03.005

Zhu, B. (2012). The Effects of Macroeconomic Factors on Stock Return of Energy Sector in Shanghai Stock Market. *International Journal of Scientific and Research Publications*, *2*(11), 1–4.

ENDNOTES

1 The fundamental or intrinsic value is defined as the actual value of a company or an asset based on a correspondent perception of its actual value, including all aspects of a company or asset, both tangible and intangible. This value may be identical to the current market value. Therefore, investors use a range of analysis techniques in order to appraise the fundamental value of securities, aiming to find investments whose intrinsic value exceeds the current market value (Fabozzi et al., 2012).

2 The required rate of return is defined as the minimum annual return on an investment, which encourages individuals and companies to invest in a specific security or project. Investors use the required rate of return to decide where to place their wealth and companies use it to decide on the implementationof a new project or expansion (Fabozzi et al., 2012).

3 Empirically, there is reasonable evidence that the asset prices, as well as their returns differsignificantly from the fundamental value and therequired rate of return respectively short-term, but converge to the fundamental value or the required rate of return in the long-term.

4 Fair price is defined as the amount or price at which an asset is exchanged between two parties, and those two parties are aware of the relative information.

5 Market timing is defined as the attempt to forecast the future course of the market, typically by using economic data or technical indicators.

6 The weak form efficient market hypothesis is based on the fact that the only reliable information at a time t is the stock price of the previous periods. Based on this form, the market can be predicted through fundamental analysis.

7 The semi-strong efficiency assumes that stock prices include all available public information. Based on this form, neither technical nor fundamental analysis can be applied to predict the market.

APPENDIX

Table 11. Regression of factors on stock return

Dependent Variable: PORTFOLIOR				
Variable	**Coefficient**	**Std. Error**	**t-Statistic**	**Prob.**
FACTOR1	-0.385276	1.236465	-0.311595	0.7557
FACTOR2	0.080168	1.180430	0.067914	0.9459
C	4.359172	1.182459	3.686530	0.0003
R-squared	0.000619	Mean dependent var		4.361589
Adjusted R-squared	-0.011569	S.D. dependent var		15.19275
S.E. of regression	15.28038	Akaike info criterion		8.308817
Sum squared resid	38292.34	Schwarz criterion		8.364828
Log likelihood	-690.7862	Hannan-Quinn criter.		8.331551
F-statistic	0.050773	Durbin-Watson stat		2.161184
Prob(F-statistic)	0.950509			

Table 12. Regression of factors on stock return

Dependent Variable: ALPHAR				
Variable	**Coefficient**	**Std. Error**	**t-Statistic**	**Prob.**
FACTOR1	-6.531014	21.02769	-0.310591	0.7565
FACTOR2	1.237036	20.07474	0.061622	0.9509
C	74.06988	20.10926	3.683372	0.0003
R-squared	0.000610	Mean dependent var		74.11037
Adjusted R-squared	-0.011578	S.D. dependent var		258.3713
S.E. of regression	259.8627	Akaike info criterion		13.97598
Sum squared resid	11074690	Schwarz criterion		14.03200
Log likelihood	-1163.995	Hannan-Quinn criter.		13.99872
F-statistic	0.050061	Durbin-Watson stat		2.161606
Prob(F-statistic)	0.951186			

Table 13. Regression of factors on stock return

Dependent Variable: BANKOFPIRAEUSR				
Variable	**Coefficient**	**Std. Error**	**t-Statistic**	**Prob.**
FACTOR1	-0.018129	0.016650	-1.088796	0.2778
FACTOR2	-0.003576	0.015896	-0.224984	0.8223
C	-0.008415	0.015923	-0.528504	0.5979
R-squared	0.007492	Mean dependent var		-0.008331
Adjusted R-squared	-0.004612	S.D. dependent var		0.205294
S.E. of regression	0.205767	Akaike info criterion		-0.306344
Sum squared resid	6.943768	Schwarz criterion		-0.250332
Log likelihood	28.57972	Hannan-Quinn criter.		-0.283610
F-statistic	0.618975	Durbin-Watson stat		1.994683
Prob(F-statistic)	0.539749			

Table 14. Regression of factors on stock return

Dependent Variable: COCACOLAR				
Variable	**Coefficient**	**Std. Error**	**t-Statistic**	**Prob.**
FACTOR1	0.003444	0.007074	0.486916	0.6270
FACTOR2	0.016309	0.006753	2.415003	0.0168
C	0.007559	0.006765	1.117375	0.2655
R-squared	0.035738	Mean dependent var		0.007604
Adjusted R-squared	0.023979	S.D. dependent var		0.088484
S.E. of regression	0.087417	Akaike info criterion		-2.018451
Sum squared resid	1.253247	Schwarz criterion		-1.962439
Log likelihood	171.5407	Hannan-Quinn criter.		-1.995717
F-statistic	3.039117	Durbin-Watson stat		2.068829
Prob(F-statistic)	0.050582			

Table 15. Regression of factors on stock return

Dependent Variable: CORINTPIPEWORKSR				
Variable	**Coefficient**	**Std. Error**	**t-Statistic**	**Prob.**
FACTOR1	-0.019667	0.015097	-1.302744	0.1945
FACTOR2	0.001978	0.014413	0.137251	0.8910
C	0.003782	0.014437	0.261969	0.7937
R-squared	0.010347	Mean dependent var		0.003897
Adjusted R-squared	-0.001722	S.D. dependent var		0.186408
S.E. of regression	0.186568	Akaike info criterion		-0.502238
Sum squared resid	5.708466	Schwarz criterion		-0.446226
Log likelihood	44.93690	Hannan-Quinn criter.		-0.479504
F-statistic	0.857331	Durbin-Watson stat		1.890655
Prob(F-statistic)	0.426185			

Table 16. Regression of factors on stock return

Dependent Variable: DUTYFREER				
Variable	**Coefficient**	**Std. Error**	**t-Statistic**	**Prob.**
FACTOR1	0.003305	0.011136	0.296810	0.7670
FACTOR2	0.016179	0.010632	1.521815	0.1300
C	0.002443	0.010650	0.229403	0.8188
R-squared	0.014467	Mean dependent var		0.002488
Adjusted R-squared	0.002448	S.D. dependent var		0.137792
S.E. of regression	0.137624	Akaike info criterion		-1.110786
Sum squared resid	3.106206	Schwarz criterion		-1.054775
Log likelihood	95.75066	Hannan-Quinn criter.		-1.088052
F-statistic	1.203719	Durbin-Watson stat		2.111318
Prob(F-statistic)	0.302713			

Table 17. Regression of factors on stock return

Dependent Variable: ELLAKTORR				
Variable	**Coefficient**	**Std. Error**	**t-Statistic**	**Prob.**
FACTOR1	0.006610	0.011303	0.584831	0.5595
FACTOR2	0.008992	0.010791	0.833342	0.4059
C	-0.000941	0.010809	-0.087017	0.9308
R-squared	0.006302	Mean dependent var		-0.000941
Adjusted R-squared	-0.005816	S.D. dependent var		0.139281
S.E. of regression	0.139685	Akaike info criterion		-1.081054
Sum squared resid	3.199949	Schwarz criterion		-1.025042
Log likelihood	93.26798	Hannan-Quinn criter.		-1.058320
F-statistic	0.520078	Durbin-Watson stat		2.246797
Prob(F-statistic)	0.595451			

Table 18. Regression of factors on stock return

Dependent Variable: FRIGOGLASSR				
Variable	**Coefficient**	**Std. Error**	**t-Statistic**	**Prob.**
FACTOR1	-0.001023	0.011782	-0.086833	0.9309
FACTOR2	0.008309	0.011248	0.738737	0.4611
C	0.007404	0.011267	0.657143	0.5120
R-squared	0.003359	Mean dependent var		0.007442
Adjusted R-squared	-0.008795	S.D. dependent var		0.144962
S.E. of regression	0.145598	Akaike info criterion		-0.998139
Sum squared resid	3.476581	Schwarz criterion		-0.942128
Log likelihood	86.34464	Hannan-Quinn criter.		-0.975405
F-statistic	0.276400	Durbin-Watson stat		1.855321
Prob(F-statistic)	0.758862			

Table 19. Regression of factors on stock return

Dependent Variable: HELLENICPETROLEUMR				
Variable	**Coefficient**	**Std. Error**	**t-Statistic**	**Prob.**
FACTOR1	-0.004849	0.007590	-0.638868	0.5238
FACTOR2	0.009625	0.007246	1.328225	0.1859
C	0.000777	0.007259	0.106986	0.9149
R-squared	0.013035	Mean dependent var		0.000841
Adjusted R-squared	0.000999	S.D. dependent var		0.093848
S.E. of regression	0.093801	Akaike info criterion		-1.877490
Sum squared resid	1.442963	Schwarz criterion		-1.821478
Log likelihood	159.7704	Hannan-Quinn criter.		-1.854756
F-statistic	1.083000	Durbin-Watson stat		2.158422
Prob(F-statistic)	0.340987			

Table 20. Regression of factors on stock return

Dependent Variable: HELLENICTELECOMR				
Variable	**Coefficient**	**Std. Error**	**t-Statistic**	**Prob.**
FACTOR1	0.004397	0.010312	0.426361	0.6704
FACTOR2	0.008643	0.009844	0.877959	0.3813
C	0.001442	0.009861	0.146210	0.8839
R-squared	0.005792	Mean dependent var		0.001452
Adjusted R-squared	-0.006333	S.D. dependent var		0.127032
S.E. of regression	0.127433	Akaike info criterion		-1.264644
Sum squared resid	2.663242	Schwarz criterion		-1.208632
Log likelihood	108.5978	Hannan-Quinn criter.		-1.241910
F-statistic	0.477708	Durbin-Watson stat		2.110483
Prob(F-statistic)	0.621063			

Table 21. Regression of factors on stock return

Dependent Variable: INTRALOTR				
Variable	**Coefficient**	**Std. Error**	**t-Statistic**	**Prob.**
FACTOR1	-0.003982	0.011083	-0.359264	0.7199
FACTOR2	-0.000263	0.010581	-0.024818	0.9802
C	0.002273	0.010599	0.214493	0.8304
R-squared	0.000791	Mean dependent var		0.002294
Adjusted R-squared	-0.011395	S.D. dependent var		0.136195
S.E. of regression	0.136968	Akaike info criterion		-1.120332
Sum squared resid	3.076696	Schwarz criterion		-1.064320
Log likelihood	96.54773	Hannan-Quinn criter.		-1.097598
F-statistic	0.064878	Durbin-Watson stat		2.054708
Prob(F-statistic)	0.937206			

Table 22. Regression of factors on stock return

Dependent Variable: JUMBOR				
Variable	**Coefficient**	**Std. Error**	**t-Statistic**	**Prob.**
FACTOR1	-0.012086	0.009247	-1.306929	0.1931
FACTOR2	0.009942	0.008828	1.126146	0.2617
C	0.016457	0.008844	1.860899	0.0645
R-squared	0.017760	Mean dependent var		0.016562
Adjusted R-squared	0.005781	S.D. dependent var		0.114613
S.E. of regression	0.114281	Akaike info criterion		-1.482515
Sum squared resid	2.141857	Schwarz criterion		-1.426503
Log likelihood	126.7900	Hannan-Quinn criter.		-1.459781
F-statistic	1.482635	Durbin-Watson stat		2.026485
Prob(F-statistic)	0.230066			

Table 23. Regression of factors on stock return

Dependent Variable: MARFINR				
Variable	**Coefficient**	**Std. Error**	**t-Statistic**	**Prob.**
FACTOR1	0.006418	0.014617	0.439086	0.6612
FACTOR2	0.010146	0.013955	0.727031	0.4682
C	-0.002996	0.013979	-0.214335	0.8306
R-squared	0.004394	Mean dependent var		-0.002991
Adjusted R-squared	-0.007748	S.D. dependent var		0.179947
S.E. of regression	0.180643	Akaike info criterion		-0.566785
Sum squared resid	5.351642	Schwarz criterion		-0.510773
Log likelihood	50.32656	Hannan-Quinn criter.		-0.544051
F-statistic	0.361887	Durbin-Watson stat		1.908878
Prob(F-statistic)	0.696915			

Table 24. Regression of factors on stock return

Dependent Variable: METKAR				
Variable	**Coefficient**	**Std. Error**	**t-Statistic**	**Prob.**
FACTOR1	0.004529	0.010470	0.432514	0.6659
FACTOR2	0.009819	0.009996	0.982270	0.3274
C	0.004996	0.010013	0.498922	0.6185
R-squared	0.006994	Mean dependent var		0.005009
Adjusted R-squared	-0.005116	S.D. dependent var		0.129064
S.E. of regression	0.129394	Akaike info criterion		-1.234110
Sum squared resid	2.745818	Schwarz criterion		-1.178098
Log likelihood	106.0482	Hannan-Quinn criter.		-1.211376
F-statistic	0.577563	Durbin-Watson stat		2.096479
Prob(F-statistic)	0.562402			

Table 25. Regression of factors on stock return

Dependent Variable: MYTILINEOSR				
Variable	**Coefficient**	**Std. Error**	**t-Statistic**	**Prob.**
FACTOR1	-0.004683	0.012424	-0.376960	0.7067
FACTOR2	0.014631	0.011861	1.233546	0.2191
C	0.005600	0.011881	0.471303	0.6381
R-squared	0.010022	Mean dependent var		0.005683
Adjusted R-squared	-0.002051	S.D. dependent var		0.153381
S.E. of regression	0.153538	Akaike info criterion		-0.891935
Sum squared resid	3.866128	Schwarz criterion		-0.835923
Log likelihood	77.47658	Hannan-Quinn criter.		-0.869201
F-statistic	0.830135	Durbin-Watson stat		2.017764
Prob(F-statistic)	0.437814			

Table 26. Regression of factors on stock return

Dependent Variable: NATIONALBANKOFGREECER				
Variable	**Coefficient**	**Std. Error**	**t-Statistic**	**Prob.**
FACTOR1	0.004046	0.013252	0.305285	0.7605
FACTOR2	-0.011279	0.012651	-0.891544	0.3739
C	-0.007287	0.012673	-0.574964	0.5661
R-squared	0.005374	Mean dependent var		-0.007353
Adjusted R-squared	-0.006756	S.D. dependent var		0.163217
S.E. of regression	0.163768	Akaike info criterion		-0.762934
Sum squared resid	4.398459	Schwarz criterion		-0.706922
Log likelihood	66.70501	Hannan-Quinn criter.		-0.740200
F-statistic	0.443010	Durbin-Watson stat		2.060321
Prob(F-statistic)	0.642867			

Table 27. Regression of factors on stock return

Dependent Variable: TITANR				
Variable	**Coefficient**	**Std. Error**	**t-Statistic**	**Prob.**
FACTOR1	0.007567	0.007787	0.971733	0.3326
FACTOR2	0.011878	0.007434	1.597687	0.1120
C	0.002418	0.007447	0.324740	0.7458
R-squared	0.020946	Mean dependent var		0.002424
Adjusted R-squared	0.009006	S.D. dependent var		0.096670
S.E. of regression	0.096234	Akaike info criterion		-1.826269
Sum squared resid	1.518798	Schwarz criterion		-1.770257
Log likelihood	155.4935	Hannan-Quinn criter.		-1.803535
F-statistic	1.754281	Durbin-Watson stat		2.310368
Prob(F-statistic)	0.176263			

Table 28. Regression of factors on stock return

Dependent Variable: VIOHALCOR				
Variable	**Coefficient**	**Std. Error**	**t-Statistic**	**Prob.**
FACTOR1	0.005739	0.010744	0.534161	0.5940
FACTOR2	0.015340	0.010257	1.495642	0.1367
C	0.000570	0.010274	0.055465	0.9558
R-squared	0.015182	Mean dependent var		0.000599
Adjusted R-squared	0.003172	S.D. dependent var		0.132982
S.E. of regression	0.132771	Akaike info criterion		-1.182576
Sum squared resid	2.891029	Schwarz criterion		-1.126564
Log likelihood	101.7451	Hannan-Quinn criter.		-1.159842
F-statistic	1.264151	Durbin-Watson stat		1.930354
Prob(F-statistic)	0.285217			

Unit Root Test

See Table 29.

Table 29. Augmented, Dickey & Fuller, unit-root test

Dickey-Fuller Augmented Test*				
Variable	**(pvalue)**	**On First Differences (p-Value)**	**On Second Differences (p-Value)**	**Results**
Τιμές μετοχών				
Stock Value	0.83	0	-	I(1)
Bid-Ask Spread				
ALPHA BANK	0	-	-	I(0)
BANK OF PIRAEUS	0	-	-	I(0)
COCA COLA HBC (ATH)	0	-	-	I(0)
CORINTH PIPE WORKS	1	0	-	I(1)
DUTY FREE SHOPS	0	-	-	I(0)
ELLAKTOR	1	0	-	I(1)
FRIGOGLASS	0	-	-	I(0)
HELLENIC PETROLEUM	0	-	-	I(0)
HELLENIC TELECOM.ORG.	0	-	-	I(0)
INTRALOT INTGRTD.SYSV.	0	-	-	I(0)
JUMBO	0	-	-	I(0)
MARFIN INV. GP.HDG.	0	-	-	I(0)
METKA	0	-	-	I(0)
MYTILINEOS HOLDINGS	0	-	-	I(0)
NATIONAL BK.OF GREECE	0	-	-	I(0)
TITAN CEMENT CR	0	-	-	I(0)
VIOHALCO CB	0	-	-	I(0)
Μέση τιμή bid-ask	0	0	-	I(0)

continued on following page

Table 29. Continued

Dickey-Fuller Augmented Test*				
Variable	**(pvalue)**	**On First Differences (p-Value)**	**On Second Differences (p-Value)**	**Results**
Other Behavioral Indices				
BCI	0.61	0.001	-	I(1)
CCI	0	-	-	I(0)
ESI	0.34	0.0001	-	I(1)
Macrorconomic Variables				
Brent	0.23	0	-	I(1)
CPI	0.45	0.88	0	I(2)
Exchrate	0.79	0	-	I(1)
Gold	0.58	0	-	I(1)
M3	0.28	0.09	0	I(2)
MIP	0.77	0	-	I(1)
riskprem	0.33	0	-	I(1)
termstruct	0.59	0	-	I(1)

*Ho: There is unit root

Tests for Autocorrelation and Heteroscedasticity

Autocorrelation Tests

Durbin-Watson

See Table 30.

Durbin's Alternative Test

See Tables 31 and 32.

Cumby-Huizinga Test

See Table 33.

Tests for Heteroscdasticity

See Tables 34 and 35.

Table 30. Durbin-Watson test

Variable	Coefficient	Std. Error	t-Statistic	Prob.
BCI	1.426478	0.387272	3.683402	0.0003
BRENT	-0.023005	0.026366	-0.872517	0.3843
CCI	-0.009319	0.023729	-0.392732	0.6951
CPI	0.341413	0.103773	3.289986	0.0012
ESI	-0.714443	0.386322	-1.849344	0.0663
EXCHRATE	2.253631	4.364779	0.516322	0.6064
GOLD	0.002498	0.001276	1.958122	0.0520
M3	0.060536	0.024417	2.479232	0.0142
MIP	0.436200	0.072093	6.050506	0.0000
RISKPREM	-2.422305	0.314994	-7.690002	0.0000
TERMSTRUCT	-0.401458	0.053923	-7.445063	0.0000
Bidask	0.000186	0.000270	0.687462	0.4928
C	-151.5705	28.02132	-5.409116	0.0000
R-squared	0.859182	Mean dependent var		14.52987
Adjusted R-squared	0.848280	S.D. dependent var		7.537802
S.E. of regression	2.936067	Akaike info criterion		5.066242
Sum squared resid	1336.176	Schwarz criterion		5.307977
Log likelihood	-412.5643	F-statistic		78.80937
Durbin-Watson stat	**0.550956**	Prob(F-statistic)		0.000000

Table 31. Durbin's alternative test

Variable	Coefficient	Std. Error	t-Statistic	Prob.
RESIDS(-1)	0.633786***	0.082483	7.683876	0.0000
RESIDS(-2)	0.055427	0.096879	0.572120	0.5681
RESIDS(-3)	0.026417	0.096366	0.274129	0.7844
RESIDS(-4)	0.027039	0.096237	0.280962	0.7791
RESIDS(-5)	-0.050755	0.097220	-0.522065	0.6024
RESIDS(-6)	0.080674	0.099253	0.812811	0.4177
RESIDS(-7)	-0.092458	0.098766	-0.936129	0.3508
RESIDS(-8)	-0.017013	0.097206	-0.175024	0.8613
RESIDS(-9)	0.002158	0.096591	0.022339	0.9822
RESIDS(-10)	-0.107050	0.096489	-1.109442	0.2691
RESIDS(-11)	-0.148616	0.096793	-1.535400	0.1269
RESIDS(-12)	0.184971**	0.081038	2.282526	0.0239
C	-0.045154	0.155333	-0.290692	0.7717
R-squared	0.536343	Mean dependent var		-0.139568
Adjusted R-squared	0.497435	S.D. dependent var		2.708654
S.E. of regression	1.920214	Akaike info criterion		4.222406
Sum squared resid	527.2727	Schwarz criterion		4.476560
Log likelihood	-316.3476	F-statistic		13.78483
Durbin-Watson stat	1.932894	Prob(F-statistic)		0.00000***

Table 32. Breusch-Godfrey test

Breusch-Godfrey Test LM:				
F-statistic	15.25992	Probability		0.000000
Obs*R-squared	94.33364	Probability		0.000000
Dependent Variable: RESIDS				
Variable	**Coefficient**	**Std. Error**	**t-Statistic**	**Prob.**
BCI	-0.225097	0.276088	-0.815307	0.4163
BRENT	-0.000765	0.018552	-0.041243	0.9672
CCI	-0.007565	0.016910	-0.447388	0.6553
CPI	-0.159607	0.076190	-2.094852	0.0379
ESI	0.295839	0.274419	1.078058	0.2828
EXCHRATE	3.118617	3.090116	1.009223	0.3146
GOLD	-0.001074	0.000950	-1.129872	0.2604
M3	-0.002462	0.017171	-0.143409	0.8862
MIP	-0.087894	0.052915	-1.661023	0.0989
RISKPREM	0.266841	0.265345	1.005638	0.3163
TERMSTRUCT	-0.049322	0.038389	-1.284807	0.2009
Bidask	-0.000225	0.000194	-1.158297	0.2487
C	16.27492	19.74386	0.824303	0.4111
RESID(-1)	0.651583***	0.082034	7.942802	0.0000
RESID(-2)	0.095699	0.097241	0.984151	0.3267
RESID(-3)	0.010549	0.095734	0.110192	0.9124
RESID(-4)	0.073864	0.095799	0.771029	0.4420
RESID(-5)	-0.073293	0.097260	-0.753579	0.4523
RESID(-6)	0.055607	0.100041	0.555840	0.5792
RESID(-7)	-0.053095	0.099627	-0.532940	0.5949
RESID(-8)	-0.004073	0.098691	-0.041274	0.9671
RESID(-9)	-0.006790	0.098531	-0.068916	0.9452
RESID(-10)	-0.135146	0.101093	-1.336837	0.1834
RESID(-11)	-0.070471	0.100247	-0.702974	0.4832
RESID(-12)	0.147279*	0.088723	1.659983	0.0991
R-squared	0.561510	Mean dependent var		-3.74E-14
Adjusted R-squared	0.487917	S.D. dependent var		2.828614
S.E. of regression	2.024155	Akaike info criterion		4.384682
Sum squared resid	585.9002	Schwarz criterion		4.849557
Log likelihood	-343.3133	F-statistic		7.629959
Durbin-Watson stat	1.737755	Prob(F-statistic)		0.00000***

Table 33. Cumby-Huizinga test

Dependent Variable: RESIDS				
Std Error QNewey-West				
Variable	**Coefficient**	**Std. Error**	**t-Statistic**	**Prob.**
BCI	-0.103301	0.238110	-0.433837	0.6651
BRENT	0.013376	0.012668	1.055920	0.2929
CCI	0.001325	0.014484	0.091463	0.9273
CPI	0.227806	0.072507	3.141845	0.0021
ESI	0.204906	0.228983	0.894851	0.3725
EXCHRATE	-6.477583	2.812354	-2.303261	0.0228
GOLD	0.001023	0.001430	0.715697	0.4755
M3	-0.013112	0.017294	-0.758168	0.4497
MIP	0.183778	0.051818	3.546582	0.0005
RISKPREM	0.254441	0.253979	1.001817	0.3183
TERMSTRUCT	0.041665	0.027143	1.535027	0.1272
BA	3.66E-05	6.46E-05	0.566428	0.5721
RESIDS(-1)	0.683796***	0.077841	8.784526	0.0000
RESIDS(-2)	-0.037034	0.094843	-0.390476	0.6968
RESIDS(-3)	0.011956	0.100881	0.118513	0.9058
RESIDS(-4)	0.018964	0.083988	0.225798	0.8217
RESIDS(-5)	-0.045967	0.100951	-0.455345	0.6496
RESIDS(-6)	0.039217	0.101634	0.385868	0.7002
RESIDS(-7)	-0.059871	0.092541	-0.646965	0.5188
RESIDS(-8)	-0.011716	0.102497	-0.114305	0.9092
RESIDS(-9)	-0.021240	0.084814	-0.250425	0.8027
RESIDS(-10)	-0.113184	0.091735	-1.233815	0.2195
RESIDS(-11)	-0.138769	0.102088	-1.359310	0.1764
RESIDS(-12)	0.166790**	0.066373	2.512913	0.0132
C	-42.74262	17.94466	-2.381913	0.0187
R-squared	0.588388	Mean dependent var		-0.139568
Adjusted R-squared	0.512978	S.D. dependent var		2.708654
S.E. of regression	1.890287	Akaike info criterion		4.257188
Sum squared resid	468.0872	Schwarz criterion		4.745947
Log likelihood	-307.0607	F-statistic		7.802543
Durbin-Watson stat	1.918722	Prob(F-statistic)		0.000000

Table 34. White test for heteroscdasticity

F-statistic	5.966332	Probability		0.000000
Obs*R-squared	84.05635	Probability		0.000000
Dependent Variable: RESID^2				
Variable	**Coefficient**	**Std. Error**	**t-Statistic**	**Prob.**
C	839.7496	7175.894	0.117024	0.9070
BCI	130.6449	46.61529	2.802619	0.0058
BCI^2	-0.660382	0.236954	-2.786960	0.0060
BRENT	-0.455317	0.369624	-1.231838	0.2200
BRENT^2	0.000973	0.002216	0.439063	0.6613
CCI	2.392645	3.213299	0.744607	0.4577
CCI^2	-0.021045	0.029317	-0.717842	0.4740
CPI	9.546967	5.755163	1.658853	0.0993
CPI^2	-0.043861	0.029775	-1.473078	0.1429
ESI	-148.7124	137.7549	-1.079544	0.2822
ESI^2	0.761313	0.694318	1.096490	0.2747
EXCHRATE	411.3625	162.0007	2.539264	0.0122
EXCHRATE^2	-141.8099	62.96166	-2.252322	0.0258
GOLD	-0.150029	0.047819	-3.137438	0.0021
GOLD^2	0.000154	4.83E-05	3.186130	0.0018
M3	-6.470874	0.991387	-6.527091	0.0000
M3^2	0.016957	0.002483	6.829282	0.0000
MIP	-4.396415	2.853798	-1.540549	0.1256
MIP^2	0.020964	0.012845	1.632058	0.1049
RISKPREM	-16.20402	5.528328	-2.931089	0.0039
RISKPREM^2	-1.611224	0.847825	-1.900420	0.0594
TERMSTRUCT	-3.369553	0.750173	-4.491698	0.0000
TERMSTRUCT^2	0.061608	0.017622	3.496009	0.0006
Bidask	-0.038593	0.035381	-1.090803	0.2772
Bidask^2	3.27E-06	3.14E-06	1.042312	0.2990
R-squared	0.500335	Mean dependent var		7.953429
Adjusted R-squared	0.416476	S.D. dependent var		12.12761
S.E. of regression	9.264131	Akaike info criterion		7.426677
Sum squared resid	12272.85	Schwarz criterion		7.891553
Log likelihood	-598.8409	F-statistic		5.966332
Durbin-Watson stat	1.384395	Prob(F-statistic)		0.000000

Table 35. Autoregressive Conditionally Heteroscedasticity test (Lagrange Multiplier)

Έλεγχος ARCH:				
F-statistic	10.63589	Probability		0.000000
Obs*R-squared	73.57032	Probability		0.000000
Dependent: RESID^2				
Variable	**Coefficient**	**Std. Error**	**t-Statistic**	**Prob.**
C	1.926332	1.095507	1.758393	0.0808
RESID^2(-1)	0.663094	0.082512	8.036301	0.0000
RESID^2(-2)	-0.067652	0.098886	-0.684145	0.4950
RESID^2(-3)	-0.023185	0.097940	-0.236727	0.8132
RESID^2(-4)	-0.122270	0.097460	-1.254573	0.2117
RESID^2(-5)	0.134765	0.097267	1.385520	0.1681
RESID^2(-6)	0.045586	0.097901	0.465634	0.6422
RESID^2(-7)	0.010753	0.096522	0.111402	0.9115
RESID^2(-8)	-0.166062	0.092261	-1.799911	0.0740
RESID^2(-9)	0.116511	0.090793	1.283253	0.2015
RESID^2(-10)	0.140691	0.090592	1.553017	0.1226
RESID^2(-11)	0.111520	0.091386	1.220319	0.2244
RESID^2(-12)	-0.107295	0.074463	-1.440906	0.1518
R-squared	0.471605	Mean dependent var		7.309257
Adjusted R-squared	0.427264	S.D. dependent var		11.20117
S.E. of regression	8.476970	Akaike info criterion		7.192239
Sum squared resid	10275.84	Schwarz criterion		7.446393
Log likelihood	-547.9946	F-statistic		10.63589
Durbin-Watson stat	1.983929	Prob(F-statistic)		0.000000

VECM

See Table 36.

VAR

See Table 37.

Table 36. Vector Error Correction Model

Error Correction	D(PORTFOLIO)
Error Correction	-0.000676
	(0.00221)
	[-0.30512]
D(PORTFOLIO(-1))	0.133315
	(0.08155)
	[1.63485]
D(BCI(-1))	0.369562
	(0.44805)
	[0.82482]
D(BRENT(-1))	0.003164
	(0.02050)
	[0.15438]
D(CPI(-1),2)	0.072416
	(0.09181)
	[0.78877]
D(ESI(-1))	-0.821149
	(0.58475)
	[-1.40427]
D(EXCHRATE(-1))	-0.911599
	(2.95590)
	[-0.30840]
D(GOLD(-1))	-0.000873
	(0.00057)
	[-1.53930]
D(M3(-1),2)	0.009647
	(0.03550)
	[0.27175]
D(MIP(-1))	-0.053866
	(0.03412)
	[-1.57873]
D(RISKPREM(-1))	0.160268
	(0.44672)
	[0.35877]

continued on following page

Table 36. Continued

Error Correction	D(PORTFOLIO)
D(TERMSTRUCT(-1))	-0.004242
	(0.05739)
	[-0.07391]
C	-0.088972
	(0.10613)
	[-0.83831]
R-squared	0.072607
Adj. R-squared	-0.000130
Sum sq. resids	275.0516
S.E. equation	1.340792
F-statistic	0.998211
Log likelihood	-277.4564
Akaike AIC	3.499475
Schwarz SC	3.743184
Mean dependent	-0.108581
S.D. dependent	1.340705

Table 37. Vector Autoregression model

	D(PORTFOLIO)
D(PORTFOLIO(-1))	0.128435
	(0.08142)
	[1.57752]
D(BCI(-1))	0.421857
	(0.45136)
	[0.93463]
D(BRENT(-1))	0.003460
	(0.02047)
	[0.16903]
CCI(-1)	-0.006155
	(0.01074)
	[-0.57298]
D(CPI(-1),2)	0.053250
	(0.06775)
	[0.78602]
D(ESI(-1))	-0.864297
	(0.58699)
	[-1.47242]
D(EXCHRATE(-1))	-0.675109
	(2.96363)
	[-0.22780]
D(GOLD(-1))	-0.000868
	(0.00057)
	[-1.53038]
D(M3(-1),2)	0.008323
	(0.03176)
	[0.26210]
D(MIP(-1))	-0.054081
	(0.03413)
	[-1.58476]
D(RISKPREM(-1))	0.203381
	(0.44491)
	[0.45713]

continued on following page

Table 37. Continued

	D(PORTFOLIO)
D(TERMSTRUCT(-1))	-0.005347
	(0.05728)
	[-0.09336]
Bidask(-1)	-0.000103
	(0.00012)
	[-0.84715]
C	0.524606
	(1.06576)
	[0.49224]
R-squared	0.078329
Adj. R-squared	-0.000498
Sum sq. resids	273.3545
S.E. equation	1.341039
F-statistic	0.993679
Log likelihood	-276.9427
Akaike AIC	3.505333
Schwarz SC	3.767790
Mean dependent	-0.108581
S.D. dependent	1.340705

Chapter 8
The Robustness of Portfolio Optimization Models:
An Empirical Comparative Analysis

Antonis Pavlou
Technical University of Crete, Greece

Michalis Doumpos
Technical University of Crete, Greece

Constantin Zopounidis
Technical University of Crete, Greece & Audencia Business School, France

ABSTRACT

The optimization of investment portfolios is a topic of major importance in financial decision making, and many relevant models can be found in the literature. These models extend the traditional mean-variance framework using a variety of other risk-return measures. Existing comparative studies have adopted a rather restrictive approach, focusing solely on the minimum risk portfolio without considering the whole set of efficient portfolios, which are also relevant for investors. This chapter focuses on the performance of the whole efficient set. To this end, the authors examine the out-of-sample robustness of efficient portfolios derived by popular optimization models, namely the traditional mean-variance model, mean-absolute deviation, conditional value at risk, and a multi-objective model. Tests are conducted using data for S&P 500 stocks over the period 2005-2016. The results are analyzed through novel performance indicators representing the deviations between historical (estimated) efficient frontiers, actual out-of-sample efficient frontiers, and realized out-of-sample portfolio results.

DOI: 10.4018/978-1-5225-6114-9.ch008

1. INTRODUCTION

The optimization of investment portfolios seeks to maximize the return of an investment, while reducing risks as much as possible, considering the investor's risk-return profile. Nowadays portfolio optimization covers a wide range of financial assets, such as stocks, funds, bonds, commodities, currencies, and loans, whereas similar concepts and ideas are also applicable to non-financial portfolios (e.g., project portfolios).

The foundations of portfolio optimization were set by Harry Markowitz in the 1950s, through the introduction of the mean-variance (MV) model. Since then, portfolio optimization has evolved significantly in terms of modeling sophistication. Among others, one can mention the introduction of new risk-return portfolio selection criteria (Szegö, 2002), the addition of realistic features, including transaction costs and cardinality constraints (Angelelli et. al., 2008), new modeling and algorithmic approaches (Fabozzi et. al., 2010; Metaxiotis and Liagkouras, 2012; Mansini et. al., 2014), as well as the consideration of new aspects such as social responsibility and other dimensions in a multi-criteria/objective framework (Ballestero *et al.*, 2012; Xidonas *et al.*, 2012). A recent overview of research developments and trends in portfolio optimization can be found in the work of Kolm, Tutuncu and Fabozzi, (2014).

In the literature, several comparative studies have been presented for different portfolio optimization models. Some examples include the studies of Angelelli et al. (2008), DeMiguel et al. (2009), Gilli and Schumann (2011), as well as Mansini et al. (2003). Despite, however, the rich literature on comparative studies among portfolio optimization models, two main shortcomings can be identified. First, past studies have adopted a rather restrictive point of view focusing solely on the minimum risk portfolio. This approach obviously ignores other relevant efficient portfolios corresponding to different risk-return preferences that an investor may have. Moreover, the comparisons are usually performed on a bi-objective context through a single measure of risk and risk-adjusted financial criteria (e.g., the Sharpe ratio, factor models, etc.). On the other hand, optimization models adopting a multi-objective point of view have not been thoroughly examined on out-of-sample data.

This study aims to fill in these gaps in the literature, focusing on conducting a thorough analysis of the performance of efficient portfolio frontiers generated by popular portfolio optimization models. In the analysis, we consider standard bi-objective models based on different risk measures (variance, mean absolute deviation, conditional value-at-risk) as well as a multi-objective model. The comparison of the obtained frontiers is based on indicators that assess the discrepancies between estimated (historical) frontiers, the actual (future) performance of the portfolios, and a true optimal (ideal) benchmark. Empirical results are presented on a data set consisting of S&P 500 US stocks over the period 2005-2016.

The rest of the paper is organized as follows. Section 2 describes the portfolio optimization models used in the analysis as well as the proposed performance indicators. Section 3 describes the empirical setting, including the data and the testing framework used for the comparative analysis. Section 4 presents the obtained results and section 5 concludes the paper and discusses some future research directions.

2. PORTFOLIO OPTIMIZATION MODELS AND PERFORMANCE INDICATORS

In this section, we introduce the basic models used in the analysis, namely the well-known mean-variance model (MV), the mean absolute deviation model (MAD), conditional value at risk (CVaR), and a multi-objective model. Also, we describe the performance indicators used to compare the performance of the four models.

2.1 Optimization Models

The first model used in the analysis is the MV model, which is the most standard approach for portfolio optimization (Markowitz, 1952). It is a bi-objective model, seeking to minimize risk for a given level of expected return. Risk is measured by the standard deviation of portfolio returns. For a set of n assets with expected returns $\overline{r}_1,\dots,\overline{r}_n$ and covariances σ_{ij}. the MV model can be expressed as follows:

$$\min \sum_{i=1}^{n}\sum_{j=1}^{n}\sigma_{ij}x_i x_j \tag{1}$$

s.t.

$$\sum_{i=1}^{n}\overline{r}_i x_i \geq \rho \tag{2}$$

$$\sum_{i=1}^{n}x_i = 1 \tag{3}$$

$$x_i \in i = 1,\dots,n \tag{4}$$

where x_i is the proportion (weight) of capital invested in asset i, χ denotes a user-defined set of bounds for the assets' weights, and ρ is the minimum desired level for the expected return of the portfolio.

The MAD model of Konno and Yamazaki (1991), extends the MV approach by considering a different risk measure, namely the mean absolute deviation of the portfolio returns. Using historical return data $r_{i1}, r_{i2}, \ldots, r_{iT}$ for the returns of each asset i over T time periods, the MAD optimization model can be expressed in linear programming form as follows:

$$\min \sum_{t=1}^{T} y_t \tag{5}$$

s.t.

$$y_t + \sum_{i=1}^{n} (r_{it} - \overline{r}_i) x_i \geq 0 \; t = 1, \ldots, T \tag{6}$$

$$y_t - \sum_{i=1}^{n} (r_{it} - \overline{r}_i) x_i \geq 0 \; t = 1, \ldots, T \tag{7}$$

(2)-(4)

$$d_t \geq 0 \; t = 1, \ldots T \tag{8}$$

where $y_1, \ldots, y_T$ are non-negative variables representing the absolute deviation of the portfolio return in period t from its mean return.

Both the above model, assume that risk is associated with deviations from the expected level of return. Over the past two decades, the interest in financial optimization models has moved towards downside risk measures that focus on losses. Value-at-risk (VaR) is the most typical downside risk measure, representing the maximum expected losses over a given time period at a predefined confidence level (Jorion, 2006). However, VaR violates standard conditions that coherent risk measures must satisfy (Artzner *et al.*, 1999) and it is not straightforward to optimize as it is a non-convex and non-smooth function of portfolio positions, and has multiple local extrema (Krokhmal et al., 2001). To address the shortcomings of VaR, Rockafellar and Uryasev, (2002) introduced conditional VaR (CVaR), as the expected loss exceeding the VaR threshold. CVaR is a coherent risk measure (Szegö, 2002) and it can be easily optimized with linear programming as follows (Krokhmal et al., 2001):

$$\min u + \frac{1}{T\left(1-\alpha\right)}\sum_{t=1}^{T} d_t \tag{9}$$

s.t.

$$u + \sum_{j=1}^{n} r_{ti} x_i + d_t \geq 0 \; t = 1,\ldots,T. \tag{10}$$

(2)-(4)

$$d_t \geq 0, \; u \in \mathbb{R} t = 1,\ldots T. \tag{11}$$

where α is the user-defined confidence level, and u is a decision variable representing the level of VaR. In this analysis, the CVaR model is implemented at the 95% confidence level.

The last model used in this study is a multi-objective model (MOO), which combines the portfolio selection criteria of the above linear models into a three-objective model: return, MAD, and CVaR. The multi-objective formulation is based on the augmented weighted Chebyshev scalarization function approach (Steuer and Choo, 1983). The corresponding optimization model is expressed in the following form:

$$\min z - \varepsilon(f_1 - f_2 - f_3) \tag{12}$$

s.t.

$$f_1 = \sum_{i=1}^{n} \overline{r}_i x_i \tag{13}$$

$$f_2 = \frac{1}{T}\sum_{t=1}^{T} y_t \tag{14}$$

$$f_3 = u + \frac{1}{T\left(1-\alpha\right)}\sum_{t=1}^{T} d_t \tag{15}$$

$$z \geq w_1\left(f_1^* - f_1\right) \tag{16}$$

$$z \geq w_k\left(f_k - f_k^*\right)\ k = 2,3 \tag{17}$$

(3)-(4), (6)-(8), (10)-(11)

$$z \geq 0. \tag{18}$$

where f_1, f_2, f_3 are the three objectives (1-return, 2-MAD, 3-CVaR), f_k^* denotes the optimal objective function value of objective k. w_k is a positive weighting constant for objective k. z is a variable representing weighted Chebyshev distance from the ideal point $\left(f_1^*, f_2^*, f_3^*\right)$ and ε is a small user-defined constant used to exclude weakly efficient solutions. In order to construct N Pareto optimal portfolios with this multi-objective model, we randomly generate $10N$ weighting vectors and filter them to keep the N most representative ones, using the filtering algorithm described in Steuer (1986).

2.2 Performance Indicators

Given that the above described models consider different risk measures, their results are not directly comparable. To make the comparison in a meaningful manner we employ two approaches based on novel and simple indicators. The first approach is suitable for comparing efficient frontiers in a bi-objective setting, whereas the second one enables the generalization of the comparisons to a multidimensional scenario.

In both cases, two main comparisons are considered, focusing on the robustness of the portfolios' performance in terms of the differences between in-sample optimization and out-of-sample results. The first one involves the efficient frontiers derived using past (historical) data at the portfolio optimization phase (as implemented through the above models). Henceforth, these frontiers will be referred to as the *historical frontiers* (denoted by *HF*). The corresponding efficient portfolios are then tested on out-of-sample (future) data and their performances yield the *resulting frontier* (denoted by *RF*), i.e., the actual results of the investment. Finally, we also define *true efficient frontiers* (denoted by *TF*), which describe the true optimal portfolios based on the out-of-sample data. Thus, investors use historical data (*historical frontier*) seeking to obtain future results (*resulting frontier*) as close as possible to the true best choices (*true frontier*). The performance indicators used in the analysis quantify the differences between these frontiers.

2.2.1 Bi-Objective Risk-Return Indicators

The first two indicators are based on the work of Kao and Steuer (2016), who introduced them in the context of assessing the value of information used in portfolio selection. In this study, we use the indicators in a different manner, i.e., as performance measures to assess the differences described above (in-sample versus out-of-sample). Both indicators are implemented in a bi-objective risk-return setting.

First, we consider a regret indicator comparing the choices that an investor makes from efficient portfolios on frontier *HF*, against the true best results of frontier *TF*. For instance, assume a point of view focused on returns and let $\left(r_p^{true}, s_p^{true}\right)$ denote the actual (out-of-sample) return and risk (variance, MAD, or CVaR) of an efficient portfolio $p \in F$. Moreover, let $\hat{r}_p$ be the return of a portfolio on the true frontier *TF* having the same (or similar) out-of-sample risk as portfolio p. Then, the return performance indicator I for portfolio p is defined as follows:

$$I_p^{return} = \hat{r}_p - r_p^{true} \tag{19}$$

This indicator is non-negative, with higher values indicating a larger discrepancy between the actual return of portfolio p and an efficient benchmark portfolio of the same risk level.

We also compute the same indicator in terms of risk, as the risk difference between portfolios of the same return (henceforth this will be denoted as $\left(I^{risk}\right)$. In this case, however, different risk measures are used in the considered models (variance, MAD, CVaR). Consequently, this difference is not directly comparable across the different optimization models. To address this issue and make the comparisons meaningful, the computation of the indicator is normalized by the range of each risk measure among the portfolios belonging in the true efficient frontier *TF*. More specifically, let an efficient portfolio $p \in F$ and $\hat{s}_p$ be the risk measure (variance, MAD, CVaR) of a portfolio on the true frontier *TF* having the same (or similar) out-of-sample return as portfolio p. Then, the risk performance indicator I for portfolio p is defined as follows:

$$I_p^{risk} = \frac{\hat{s}_p - s_p^{true}}{R} \tag{20}$$

where R is the range of the considered risk measure in the frontier *TF*. The interpretation of this indicator is the same as the one corresponding to return.

A second indicator (denoted by D quantifies the differences between the risk-return estimates for efficient portfolios on frontier *HF* and their actual results (i.e., a robustness indicator). For instance, assume a point of view focused on return and let $\left(r_p^{est}, s_p^{est}\right)$ denote the estimated (in-sample) return and risk (variance, MAD, or CVaR) of an efficient portfolio $p \in F$. The return performance indicator D is defined for portfolio p as follows:

$$D_p^{return} = r_p^{est} - r_p^{true} \tag{21}$$

Unlike the previous indicator I the indicator D can take both positive and negative values. Negative values indicate that the actual return of a portfolio exceeds what was expected based on historical data, whereas the case $D > 0$ indicates that the actual return is lower than the expected one. Similarly, to indicator I we also compute D in terms of risk (henceforth this will be denoted as $\left(D^{risk}\right)$ following the same approach as the one described above for risk indicator (20).

2.2.2 Mean Distance Between Frontiers

While the indicators described above are intuitive and easy to use and interpret in a risk-return context, they cannot be extended to more than two dimensions. Thus, in order to enable the comparisons to a more general setting, we use the distance indicator proposed by Knowles and Corne (2002) in the context of multi-objective optimization, which enables the comparison of two frontiers A (reference frontier) and B (approximation frontier) through the following distance metric:

$$C_{AB} = \frac{1}{n_A} \sum_{x \in A} \min_{(y \in B)} \left\{ d\left(\boldsymbol{x}, \boldsymbol{y}\right) \right\} \tag{22}$$

where n_A is the number of solutions considered from frontier A and $d\left(\boldsymbol{x}, \boldsymbol{y}\right)$ is the $\boldsymbol{\lambda}$ weighted Chebyshev distance between a point $\boldsymbol{x} \in A$ and a point $\boldsymbol{y} \in B$ with weights defined as scaling constants that account for the different scales of the objectives:

$$d\left(\boldsymbol{x}, \boldsymbol{y}\right) = \max_k \left\{ \lambda_k \left(x_k - y_k \right) \right\}, \lambda_k = \frac{1}{R_k} \tag{23}$$

where R_k denotes the range of objective k in A.

The above defined indicator (22) represents the mean weighted Chebyshev distance of the solutions on frontier B from each one on frontier A (averaged over all solutions of frontier A.

For the purposes of the analysis, the comparisons described earlier for the two bi-objective indicators are also considered for this indicator, too. Therefore, the calculation of the Chebyshev distance metric is performed twice, first for the pair $\left(A, B\right) =$ *TF*, *RF*), and second for the pair $\left(A, B\right) =$ *HF*, *RF*). The former quantifies the discrepancies between the true optimal out-of-sample results (true frontier *TF*) from the actual out-of-sample results (*RF*) derived by the optimized portfolios. The latter comparison involves the difference between the historical frontier (*HF*) and the actual results (*RF*).

3. DATA AND EMPIRICAL SETTING

The analysis is based on an extensive data set involving historical data for U.S. stocks of the Standard and Poor's 500 (S&P 500) index, during a period that spans 11 years, starting from the beginning of 2005 up to the end of June 2016. The data involve all constituent stocks of S&P 500 at the end of the time period (505 stocks overall). Table 1 presents the composition of the sample by sector, whereas Figure 1 illustrates the evolution of the S&P index during the period of the analysis.

Using this dataset, the analysis is based on a series of portfolio construction and validation tests, through a rolling window approach (Gilli and Schumann, 2011). In each test, daily return data over a period of one year (~250 days) are used as in-sample estimates for portfolio optimization. At the optimization phase, the models described in the previous section are solved to derive 20 efficient portfolios. The

Figure 1. Evolution of the S&P 500 index during the period of the analysis

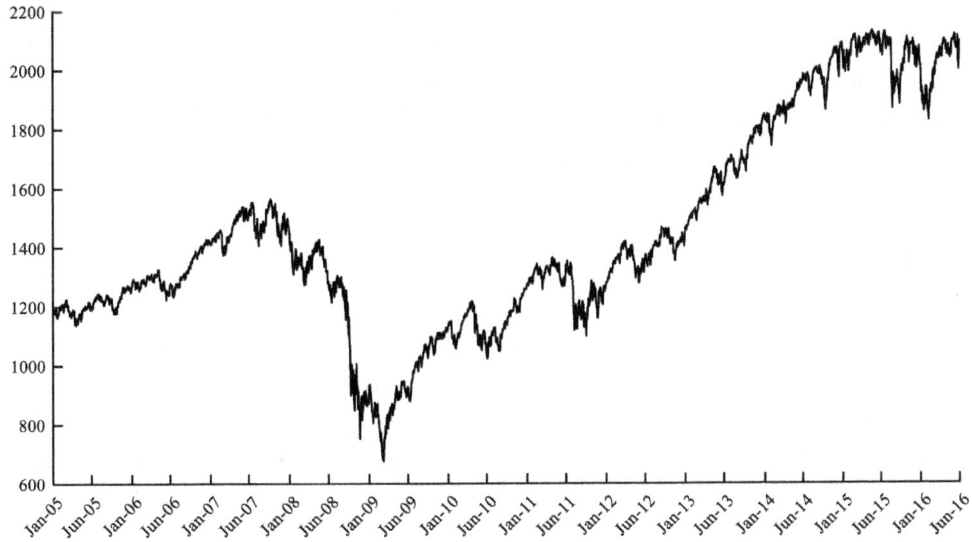

Table 1. Composition of the sample by sector

Sector	Number of Stocks	% of Total
Energy	36	7.1
Materials	25	5
Industrials	71	14.1
Consumer Discretionary	85	16.8
Consumer Staples	37	7.3
Health Care	59	11.7
Financials	65	12.9
Information Technology	65	12.9
Telecommunication Services	5	1
Utilities	28	5.5
Real Estate	29	5.7
Total	505	100.00

subsequent quarter is used for out-of-sample testing. For example, starting at the end of 2005q4, the daily data over the period 2005q1-2005q4 are used to construct 20 efficient portfolios (in-sample optimization) and 2006q1 is used for testing (out-of-sample). Then, the time window is moved one quarter ahead (2005q2-2006q1 for optimization and 2006q2 for testing) and the process is repeated until 2016q2.

This rolling window process is illustrated in Figure 2. Overall, 42 test runs are conducted. In each run, all portfolio optimization models are applied to derive historical efficient frontiers *HF* (with the in-sample optimization data), which are then examined for their out-of-sample performance (resulting frontiers, *RF*). The optimization models are also applied to the out-of-sample data to derive 20 efficient portfolios from the true frontiers *TF*.

4. RESULTS

This section presents and discusses the results obtained from the application of the optimization models following the setting described in the previous section. The discussion covers three main issues, namely the composition of the portfolios, the comparison of the models' robustness regarding the changes of the efficient frontiers over time, as well as the robustness of the results in terms of different portfolio performance criteria.

4.1 Portfolios' Composition

We start the discussion of the results with an analysis of the composition of the portfolios. Three important issues involve the size and level of diversification of the portfolios, the robustness of the portfolios' composition over time, and the similarities in the compositions of the portfolios derived with different models. The size, diversification, and robustness of a portfolio's composition are important issues for portfolio management, because they are related with the time and cost required to monitor and update a portfolio over time. On the other hand, comparing the

Figure 2. The rolling window testing process

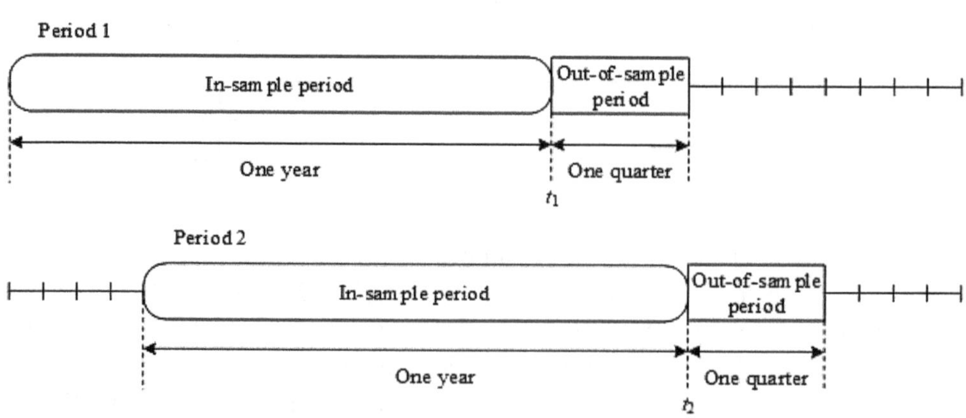

compositions of different portfolios sheds some light on their underlying differences in terms of the portfolios' structure.

Regarding the diversification of the portfolios, two simple indicators are considered. The first is the number of assets (stocks) in the portfolios and the second is the Herfindahl-Hirschman index (HHI). As the number of assets in a portfolio increases, its management (monitoring and rebalancing) becomes more difficult, time consuming, and costly. On the other hand, the HHI is used to assess the diversification of a portfolio. HHI is calculated as the sum of squares of the assets' weights ($x_{1P}, x_{2P}, \ldots, x_{nP}$. in a portfolio P .

$$HHI_P = \sum_{i=1}^{n} x_{iP}^2 \tag{24}$$

Higher HHI values indicate less diversified portfolios whereas lower values correspond to more diversified investments.

Moreover, the robustness of the compositions over time for each model is also considered. Large changes in the composition of a portfolio over time, naturally lead to higher transaction costs. To measure the changes in the composition of a portfolio between two consecutive periods t and $t+1$ we use the mean squared differences of the assets' weights:

$$CR_t = \frac{1}{n} \sum_{i=1}^{n} \left(x_{i,t+1} - x_{it} \right)^2 \tag{25}$$

Defined in this way, lower values for this indicator correspond to small changes in the composition of the portfolios from one period to the next. However, to make sure that the portfolios considered in this indicator are indeed comparable, we restrict the calculation to the minimum risk portfolios. For the MOO model, the minimum risk portfolio is defined as the one with the smallest Chebyshev distance from the minimum MAD/CVaR solution point.

Results for the above three metrics are shown in Table 2, averaged over all test runs and portfolios. It is evident that, in terms of portfolio size (number of assets), the CVaR model outperforms the rest of the models, leading to smaller portfolios. The CVaR portfolios consist, on average, of 11 stocks versus 14-16 for the portfolios derived with the other models. The differences between the models were found significant at the 1% level according to a paired-samples t-test. However, due to the smaller number of stocks in the CVaR portfolios, their level of diversification is lower (higher HHI) compared to the portfolios constructed with the other models.

Table 2. Portfolio composition indicators

	MV	MAD	CVaR	MOO
No. of assets	15	16	11	14
HHI	0.0943	0.0862	0.1275	0.1054
CR	0.0013	0.0014	0.0041	0.0021

The MAD model provides the most diversified portfolios with an average HHI index equal to 0.0862, followed by the mean-variance model ($HHI = 0.0934$), the MOO model ($HHI = 0.1054$), and finally the CVaR model ($HHI = 0.1275$). Finally, according to the CR index, the compositions of the MV and MAD portfolios are more robust over time, followed by the portfolios of the MOO model. The compositions of the CVaR portfolios, on the other hand, exhibit higher variability over time, which implies higher transaction costs.

Finally, the similarities between the assets in the portfolios constructed with different models are also examined through the Jaccard index. For a pair of portfolios p and p' the Jaccard index $J\left(p, p'\right)$ is defined as the following ratio:

$$J\left(p, p'\right) = \frac{number\ of\ stocks\ in\ both\ p\ and\ p'}{number\ of\ stocks\ in\ p\ or\ p'}$$

This measure ranges between 0 and 1 with higher values indicating higher similarity of two portfolios in terms of their constituent stocks. Table 3 reports the results for all pairwise comparisons, averaged over all efficient portfolios for each pair of models and test runs over the period of the analysis. It is evident that the portfolios of the multiobjective model (MOO) have strong similarities with the portfolios derived by the three other models, most notably with the MV and MAD portfolios, as the Jaccard index is 0.64 and 0.76 for the pairs MOO-MV and MOO-MAD, respectively. On the other hand, the similarity between the MOO-CVaR portfolios is lower (Jaccard index 0.51). The MAD-MV portfolios also have similar constituent stocks (Jaccard index 0.64), whereas CVaR portfolios are the one most dissimilar with the rest.

4.2 Robustness of Efficient Frontiers Over Time

The previous subsection focused on the analysis of issues related to the composition of the portfolios derived from different models. In this subsection as well as in subsection 4.3, we investigate the robustness of the risk-return performance of the

Table 3. Similarities between the portfolios of different models (Jaccard index)

	MV	MAD	CVaR
MAD	0.6408	-	-
CVaR	0.4679	0.3801	-
MOO	0.6436	0.7660	0.5107

portfolios using the indicators described in subsection 2.2. The two bi-objective indicators *I* and *D* (cf. section 2.2.1) are only calculated for the bi-objective models (MV, MAD, CVaR), because these indicators rely on a pure bi-objective risk-return setting. On the other hand, the more general indicator based on the Chebyshev distance metric (cf. section 2.2.2) is applied to the results of all models, as it allows the consideration of any number of objectives.

Table 4 presents the averages of all performance indicators over the 42 tests during the period of the analysis. The best results for each indicator are marked in bold. It is evident that in terms of the two bi-objective indicators, the MV model outperforms the MAD and CVaR models. More specifically, the lower value that MV portfolios achieve on indicators I^{return} and I^{risk} indicate that their out-of-sample return and risk are closer to the true best return/risk levels, as defined by the actual out-of-sample Pareto efficient portfolios (i.e., the true frontiers, *TF*). The same applies to indicators D^{return} and D^{risk} which compare the actual (out-of-sample) results of the portfolios to their historical risk-return estimates (historical efficient frontier, HF). The MAD model performs similarly to the MV model, but it is slightly inferior, whereas CVaR provides consistently less robust results. This finding regarding the CVaR model appears to be consistent with the findings of Lim et al. (2011), who derived similar results about the robustness of CVaR optimization based on simulated (randomly generated) data.

To assess the statistical significance of the differences between the results of the models for the bi-objective indicators, a paired-samples t test was conducted. The p values shown in Table 5, indicate that the differences between the results of the MV and those of MAD and CVaR are significant in terms of the two risk-based indicators (I^{risk} and D^{risk}) at the 1% significance level. Regarding the return-based indicators (I^{return} and D^{return}), the differences between MV and CVaR as well as between MAD and CVaR, are both found significant at the 1% level, whereas the differences between MV and MAD are significant only at the 10% level (p-value=0.097 for I^{return} and 0.059 for D^{return}).

Regarding the two Chebyshev distance indicators, which allow the comparison of the historical/true frontiers and actual results, the results of Table 4 show that the

Table 4. Summary of performance indicators (averages over all tests)

	I^{return}	I^{risk}	D^{return}	D^{risk}	$C_{TF,RF}$	$C_{HF,RF}$
MV	**0.0048**	**0.3382**	**0.0023**	**0.2383**	**0.4262**	0.3305
MAD	0.0049	0.3706	0.0024	0.2727	0.4343	0.3323
CVaR	0.0062	0.7176	0.0027	0.3462	0.6139	0.3555
MOO	-	-	-	-	0.4770	**0.3215**

Table 5. Paired-samples t -tests (p -values) for the differences among the models in terms of the bi-objective return/risk indicators I (above the diagonal) and D (below the diagonal)

	MV	MAD	CVaR
MV		0.097/0.000	0.000/0.000
MAD	0.059/0.000		0.000/0.000
CVaR	0.000/0.000	0.000/0.000	

Table 6. Paired-samples t-tests (p values) for the differences in the Chebyshev distance indicators ($C_{TF,RF}$ below the diagonal and $C_{HF,RF}$ above the diagonal)

	MV	MAD	CVaR	MOO
MV		0.09738	0.00000	0.00052
MAD	0.74172		0.00000	0.00129
CVaR	0.04992	0.09765		0.00000
MOO	0.23375	0.17449	0.00554	

MV model outperforms the other models in terms of the regret indicator $C_{TF,RF}$ (out-of-sample frontier versus out-of-sample results). Therefore, the actual results of the MV model are closer to the true optimal results, than the rest of the models. On the other hand, the MOO model is the best performer on the robustness indicator $C_{HF,RF}$, which implies higher robustness of this model's results over time compared to the other models. Similar to the findings discussed above for the bi-objective indicators, CVaR is found again to provide the worst results in both indicators based on the Chebyshev distance. The statistical significance of the differences between the results of the models for the Chebyshev distance indicators, was tested through a paired-samples t test. As shown in Table 6, the differences in terms of the regret indicator $C_{TF,RF}$ for the pairs (CVaR, MV) and (MOO, CVaR) are significant at the 5% significance level. Regarding the robustness indicator $C_{HF,RF}$ the MOO model performs better than the others at the 1% significance level.

4.3 Robustness Over Different Portfolio Performance Measures

To derive further insights into the relative performance of the models, we conducted a further analysis to examine the out-of-sample performance of the portfolios derived with a specific optimization model, in comparison to the true best results in terms of alternative risk measures. Given that risk is a multidimensional concept that can be expressed and measured in different ways, this part of the analysis seeks to examine how robust is the performance of portfolios derived through a specific risk-return modeling framework (e.g., MV, MAD, etc.), when compared against other performance objectives. Ideally, a portfolio optimized with a specific set of performance objectives (e.g., return and variance) would perform well even if other performance measures as considered (e.g., return and CVaR). This is particularly important for multi-objective portfolio optimization, in order to examine the information value that a combination of objectives provides compared to simpler bi-objective approaches.

The implementation of this analysis is done using the Chebyshev distance indicator $C_{TF,RF}$ to compare the out-of-sample performance of portfolios constructed through a specific optimization model, against the true Pareto frontier defined based on a different set of objectives.

Table 7 summarizes the results of these comparisons (mean differences and p values from paired-samples t tests). Each entry in this table corresponds to the comparison between the $C_{TF,RF}$ indicator for the model in row and the same indicator for the model in column, when the frontier (TF, RF is defined by the model in row. For instance, to obtain the (MV, MAD) entry, we use the true MV frontier (*TF*) derived from out-of-sample data and compare it to: (1) the actual out-of-sample mean-variance results of the MV model (leading to the calculation of $C^{\mathrm{MV}}_{TF,RF}$), and (2) the actual out-of-sample mean-variance results of the MAD model (leading to the calculation of $C^{\mathrm{MAD}}_{TF,RF}$). The (MV, MAD) entry reports the mean difference $C^{\mathrm{MV}}_{TF,RF} - C^{\mathrm{MAD}}_{TF,RF}$ (over the 42 test) and the associated p value is reported in parentheses. Naturally, one would expect that $C^{\mathrm{MV}}_{TF,RF} < C^{\mathrm{MAD}}_{TF,RF}$ because in this comparison the true frontier is defined in mean-variance terms, so the MV model should provide results closer to the true optimum than the MAD model, which is based on a different risk measure. However, this is not the case as the mean difference is slightly positive (0.002), although it is not significant. Interestingly, the results show that there are no significant differences between the three bi-objective models. The MOO model, on the other hand, performs significantly better than all the bi-objective models. For instance, the (MV, MOO) entry is slightly positive, yet significant at the 5% level (p value 0.014). This indicates that the actual (out-of-sample) returns and variances of the MOO portfolios are closer to the true mean-variance frontier than the MV portfolios. Thus, MOO portfolios provide a better approximation of the true MV frontier, than the MV portfolios themselves. The same applies to the pairs (MAD, MOO) and (CVaR, MOO); in both cases, MOO portfolios are closer to the MAD/CVaR true frontiers than the actual MAD/CVaR portfolios. On the other hand, the differences for the pairs (MOO, MV), (MOO, MAD), and (MOO, CVaR), are all negative and significant at least at the 5% level. This implies that the bi-objective efficient portfolios are not as good approximations of the multi-objective frontiers. For instance, the mean difference for the pair (MOO, MV) is -0.01 and is significant at the 1% level, thus implying that the out-of-sample return-MAD-CVaR performance of the MV portfolios is further away from the true return-MAD-CVaR frontier, compared to the portfolios optimized with these three objectives. This result for the pair (MOO, MV), combined with the above described result for the opposite comparison (MV, MOO), indicate that the MOO portfolios provide a better out-of-sample approximation of the MV frontier, whereas the MV portfolios are not good approximators of a more complex (three-objective) frontier. The same holds true for the comparisons of MOO portfolios with MAD and CVaR, thus providing empirical evidence supporting the use of MOO models for portfolio optimization, not only as conceptual tools enabling the aggregation of multiple portfolio measures, but also providing results that are robust to different optimization criteria.

Table 7. Comparison of the models in terms of their robustness over different portfolio risk measures

	MV	**MAD**	**CVaR**	**MOO**
MV	-	0.002 (0.397)	-0.003 (0.489)	0.009 (0.014)
MAD	-0.003 (0.164)	-	0.000 (0.926)	0.007 (0.022)
CVaR	0.000 (0.990)	0.002 (0.792)	-	0.014 (0.043)
MOO	-0.010 (0.008)	-0.009 (0.016)	-0.013 (0.028)	-

5. CONCLUSION

This paper presented a novel empirical comparison of popular bi-objective portfolio optimization models based on performance indicators that allow the consideration of the whole efficient frontier, rather than focusing on the minimum risk portfolio. Except for well-known bi-objective models, we also tested a multi-objective formulation through an extensive in-sample and out-of-sample evaluation protocol.

The obtained results indicate that the traditional MV model is the more robust bi-objective model, compared to other well-known approaches (MAD and CVaR). The multi-objective model was shown to be quite attractive, providing good results, which were found to be closer to the true bi-objective frontiers than the results of the bi-objective models.

This analysis can be extended towards several different directions. First, other state-of-the-art portfolio optimization models as well as simple investment strategies can be added in the analysis, together with the consideration of additional realistic scenarios and settings (transaction costs, different rebalancing periods, cardinality constrained portfolios, etc.). The investigation of the connections between the proposed performance indicators and portfolio performance measures from the financial theory is also worth the consideration. Finally, it seems promising to develop more sophisticated multi-objective models and further analyze their performance under multiple performance measures and sound data-driven testing protocols.

REFERENCES

Angelelli, E., Mansini, R., & Speranza, M. G. (2008). A comparison of MAD and CVaR models with real features. *Journal of Banking & Finance*, *32*(7), 1188–1197. doi:10.1016/j.jbankfin.2006.07.015

Artzner, P., Delbaen, F., Eber, J.-M., & Heath, D. (1999). Coherent Measures of Risk. *Mathematical Finance*, *9*(3), 203–228. doi:10.1111/1467-9965.00068

Ballestero, E., Bravo, M., Perez-Gladish, B., Arenas-Parra, M., & Pia-Santamaria, D. (2012). Socially responsible investment: A multicriteria approach to portfolio selection combining ethical and financial objectives. *European Journal of Operational Research*, *216*(2), 487–494. doi:10.1016/j.ejor.2011.07.011

DeMiguel, V., Garlappi, L., & Uppal, R. (2009). Optimal Versus Naive Diversification: How Inefficient is the 1/ N Portfolio Strategy? *Review of Financial Studies*, *22*(5), 1915–1953. doi:10.1093/rfs/hhm075

Fabozzi, F. J., Huang, D., & Zhou, G. (2010). Robust portfolios: Contributions from operations research and finance. *Annals of Operations Research, 176*(1), 191–220. doi:10.100710479-009-0515-6

Gilli, M., & Schumann, E. (2011). Optimal enough? *Journal of Heuristics, 17*(4), 373–387. doi:10.100710732-010-9138-y

Jorion, P. (2006). *Value at risk : The new benchmark for managing financial risk.* McGraw-Hill.

Kao, C., & Steuer, R. E. (2016). Value of information in portfolio selection, with a Taiwan stock market application illustration. *European Journal of Operational Research, 253*(2), 418–427. doi:10.1016/j.ejor.2016.02.011

Knowles, J., & Corne, D. (2002). On metrics for comparing nondominated sets. *Proceedings of the 2002 Congress on Evolutionary Computation, CEC 2002*, 711–716.

Kolm, P. N., Tutuncu, R., & Fabozzi, F. J. (2014). 60 Years of portfolio optimization: Practical challenges and current trends. *European Journal of Operational Research, 234*(2), 356–371. doi:10.1016/j.ejor.2013.10.060

Konno, H., & Yamazaki, H. (1991). Mean-Absolute Deviation portfolio optimization model and its applications to Tokyo Stock Market. *Management Science, 37*(5), 519–531. doi:10.1287/mnsc.37.5.519

Krokhmal, P., Palmquist, J., & Uryasev, S. (2001). Portfolio optimization with Conditional Value-At-Risk objective and constraints. *The Journal of Risk, 4*(2), 1–36. doi:10.21314/JOR.2002.057

Lim, A. E. B., Shanthikumar, J. G., & Vahn, G.-Y. (2011). Conditional value-at-risk in portfolio optimization: Coherent but fragile. *Operations Research Letters, 39*(3), 163–171. doi:10.1016/j.orl.2011.03.004

Mansini, R., Ogryczak, W., & Speranza, M. G. (2003). LP Solvable Models for Portfolio Optimization: A Classification and Computational Comparison. *IMA Journal of Management Mathematics, 14*(3), 187–220. doi:10.1093/imaman/14.3.187

Mansini, R., Ogryczak, W., & Speranza, M. G. (2014). Twenty years of linear programming based portfolio optimization. *European Journal of Operational Research, 234*(2), 518–535. doi:10.1016/j.ejor.2013.08.035

Markowitz, H. (1952). Portfolio Selection. *The Journal of Finance, 7*(1), 77–91.

Metaxiotis, K., & Liagkouras, K. (2012). Multiobjective Evolutionary Algorithms for Portfolio Management: A comprehensive literature review. *Expert Systems with Applications*, *39*(14), 11685–11698. doi:10.1016/j.eswa.2012.04.053

Rockafellar, R. T., & Uryasev, S. (2002). Conditional value-at-risk for general loss distributions. *Journal of Banking & Finance*, *26*(7), 1443–1471. doi:10.1016/S0378-4266(02)00271-6

Steuer, R. E. (1986). *Multiple Criteria Optimization: Theory, Computation and Application*. New York: John Wiley and Sons.

Steuer, R. E., & Choo, E. U. (1983). An interactive weighted Tchebycheff procedure for multiple objective programming. *Mathematical Programming*, *26*(3), 326–344.

Szegö, G. (2002). Measures of risk. *Journal of Banking & Finance*, *26*(7), 1253–1272. doi:10.1016/S0378-4266(02)00262-5

Xidonas, P., Mavrotas, G., Krintas, T., Psarras, J., & Zopounidis, C. (2012). *Multicriteria Portfolio Management*. New York: Springer. doi:10.1007/978-1-4614-3670-6

Chapter 9
Brokering Cloud Computing:
Pricing Models and Simulation Approaches

Georgia Dede
Harokopio University, Greece

George Hatzithanasis
Harokopio University, Greece

Thomas Kamalakis
Harokopio University, Greece

Christos Michalakelis
Harokopio University, Greece

ABSTRACT

Cloud computing is a rapidly evolving computational model, which has succeeded in transforming the ICT industry and the economy's production techniques by making corresponding services even more accessible to businesses, offering cost-effective solutions. The cloud broker is a new business model, derived from the necessity of finding the best provider, or the best bundle for the end user. It is a third-party business that assists clients in making the best decision in choosing the most suitable cloud provider and the most effective service bundle for their needs, in terms of performance and price. This chapter analyzes the cloud broker business model and highlights the broker's vital role and the benefits that arise from the use of its services. In that context, it describes cloud brokering and a market analysis, together with the most popular pricing models, together with a comparison among them, concluding with future directions for the expansion of the brokerage model.

DOI: 10.4018/978-1-5225-6114-9.ch009

INTRODUCTION

The contemporary transformation of the ICT industry has been achieved, to a large extend, by the introduction of cloud computing. The combination of hardware and software offers clients a more accessible and easy experience. Organizations and companies can use a more flexible strategy concerning the pricing, the "pay as you go" pricing model without any additional costs (Marston et al., 2011). Cloud computing offers a cornucopia of features that can easily adapt in any business needs. Sometimes choosing the best bundle of cloud computing services can be a very demanding task, because knowledge and experience is needed. Enterprises willing to migrate their infrastructure to the cloud are mainly concerned about the services they need, rather than who provides them (Rajkumar et al., 2009). Despite the innovative and profitable veneer cloud computing has, it also incorporates difficulties and challenges. As a consequence, the necessity of cloud brokerage was realized and the business model of cloud broker was developed. In order to provide significant assistance to the cloud computing market the cloud brokering model has emerged. The cloud broker acts as intermediary between the clients and the providers and creates a bundle of cloud services the match the need of the client.

The aim of this work is to underline the significance of cloud brokering. Cloud brokering is also a major factor that affects the rate of cloud diffusion. Due to the broker's beneficial influence, users can harvest the benefits cloud computing offers easier and with greater confidence (Buyya et al., 2009). The development of a business model has as a final purpose not only to enhance productivity and efficiency, but also τo increase the profit for all stakeholders (client, providers and broker). This paper describes some brokering algorithms that can be used. Section 2 provides a definition of cloud computing (characteristics, architecture, deployment models) while Section 3 describes the cloud brokering, its' categories and a small market analysis. The brokerage pricing models are presented in Section 4 with a comparison between them and Section 5 concludes, providing directions for future research.

CLOUD COMPUTING

According to (Mell & Grance, 2011) cloud computing is a model for enabling ubiquitous, convenient, on-demand network access to a shared pool of configurable computing resources (e.g., networks, servers, storage, applications, and services) that can be rapidly provisioned and released with minimal management effort or service provider interaction. In an easier and more comprehensive way we could define cloud as a very potent mean of optimization for business processes and minimization of costs.

At this time of its expansion cloud computing has become pretty common technology among businesses as well as government services. A short introduction to the cloud is included, for the sake of completeness. Briefly, according to (Hassan, 2011) these attributes characterize cloud computing:

- **On-Demand Computing Model:** Organizations are able to escape from complex and expensive in-house infrastructure and choose the amount of resources they require for their operation.
- **Autonomous:** Clients are separated from the technical details of the cloud services they use.
- **Predefined Quality of Service:** Cloud providers state QoS terms in their service level agreements to inform clients about expected level of service.
- **Internet-Based:** All cloud services are hosted beyond organizations and delivered over the Internet.
- **Easy-to-Use:** Cloud providers offer easy-to-use interfaces that enable clients to make use of their services.
- **Scalable:** Clients are not limited with fixed amounts of resources. They can scale up and down at free will.
- **Inexpensive:** Cloud computing offers small-and-medium-sized enterprises (SMEs) a significantly lower-cost option than building an in-house infrastructure.
- **Subscription-Based Model:** Clients subscribe to services they are interested in, and they are charged accordingly.

Cloud Computing Services and Architecture

The architecture of cloud computing starts from IaaS as a foundation and on top, SaaS (Varia, 2010). The main logic behind the hierarchy, is that on the road to the top, the user is not required to know any detail about how things work in the cloud and everything is concealed like in a Black Box. The architecture of cloud computing is graphically illustrated in Figure 1

- **Infrastructure-as-a-Service (IaaS):** IaaS provides capability to provision hardware such as CPUs, memory, storage, networks, and load-balancers. The client does not have any control of the components but can manage over operating systems, deployed applications, networking and security. According to (Marinescu, 2012) services offered by this delivery model include: server hosting, web servers, storage, computing hardware, operating systems, virtual instances, load balancing, Internet access, and bandwidth provisioning. The next architectures are based on IaaS in order to work.

Figure 1. Cloud computing architecture

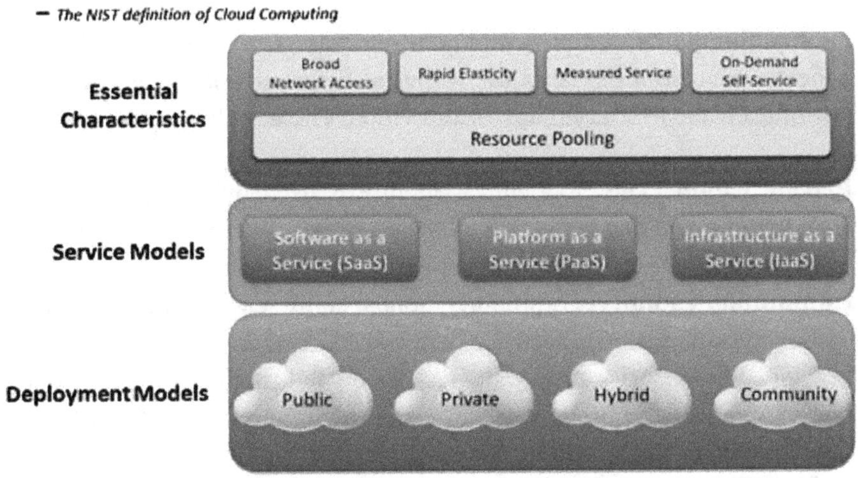

- **Platform-as-a-Service (PaaS):** Supplies users with development and administration platforms that provide on-demand access to available hardware resources. Many PaaS platforms are available to enable access to IaaS resources. PaaS is not particularly useful for portable applications, or when proprietary programming languages are used, or when the underlying hardware and software must be customized to improve the performance of the application. (Marinescu, 2012)
- **Data-as-a-Service (DaaS):** Frees organizations from buying high-cost database engines and mass storage. This service offers database capabilities for storing client information. DaaS is useful for big data analytics from enterprises and research.
- **Software-as-a-Service (SaaS):** The ultimate form of cloud resources that delivers software applications to clients in terms of accessible services. With SaaS, clients subscribe to applications offered by providers rather than building or buying them. The applications are accessible from various client devices through a thin client interface such as a web browser. If the first pillar of this paper is the cloud computing, the second is the enterprises. The cloud services offer great amount of options, so every organization can enjoy the aspects of cloud it needs.

Deployment Models

Cloud computing has different deployment models. The need for different cloud approaches comes from the need for variation between pricing, use and security demands of each separate company or individual client. (Mell & Grance, 2011)

- **Private Cloud:** The cloud infrastructure is used by a single organization. Usually private cloud is owned, managed, and operated by the organization, a third party, or some combination of them, and it may exist on or off premises.
- **Community Cloud:** A community cloud usually serves multiple organization that have same vision, exchange data and use same resources, or just need a very specific security policy. It may be owned, managed, and operated by one or more of the organizations in the community, a third party, or some combination of them, and it may exist on or off premises.
- **Public Cloud:** The cloud infrastructure is provisioned for open use by the general public. It is hosted maintained operated and located on the cloud provider's premises.
- **Hybrid Cloud:** The cloud infrastructure is a composition of two or more distinct cloud infrastructures that have been described above.

CLOUD BROKERAGE

The growing number of Cloud computing services increases the interest of consumers in comparing these services in order to choose those best adapted to their needs (Felipe, Sanchez, Felipe, Sanchez, & Diaz-sanchez, 2016). According to Gartner a cloud service broker is company or other entity that adds value to one or more (public or private) cloud services on behalf of one or more consumers of that service via three primary roles including aggregation, integration and customization brokerage. A CSB enabler provides technology to implement CSB, and a CSB provider offers combined technology, people and methodologies to implement and manage CSB-related projects. Because of the role cloud computing plays in the technology market the needs for brokering is essential as the client and the provider must communicate in a lingua franca. The broker understands the needs of the client and tries to find the best suited cloud bundle for him.

Categories of Cloud Brokering

According to (Khanna & Jain, 2015) the categorization of the brokering services splits into three:

- **Service Intermediation:** An intermediation broker provides a service that directly enhances a given service delivered to one or more service consumers, essentially adding value on top of a given service to enhance some specific capability. CSBs will offer intermediation for multiple services. Intermediation brokers also supervise pricing and billing.
- **Service Aggregation:** An aggregation brokerage service combines multiple services into one. It will ensure that all data is modeled across all components and integrated as well as ensuring the movement and security of data between the service consumer and multiple providers. Aggregation brokers usually are cloud service providers. In aggregation-style brokerages, the services brokered are bundled and do not change frequently.
- **Service Arbitrage:** Cloud service arbitrage is similar to cloud service aggregation but with one difference. The services that are being aggregated are not standard. Indeed the goal of arbitrage is to provide flexibility and opportunistic choices for the service aggregator, providing multiple e-mail services through one service provider or providing a credit-scoring service that checks multiple scoring agencies and selects the best score.

Cloud Brokering Market

"Markets and Markets Research Private Limited" predicts that the Cloud Service Brokerage market size is expected to grow from USD 4.50 Billion in 2016 to USD 9.52 Billion by 2021 and an annual growth rate up to 16.2% during the forecast period. The major drivers of this market include the proliferation of hybrid & multi-cloud environments and the enterprise need of achieving cost savings.

"Global Industry Analysts, Inc" stated that new market reports on Cloud Services Brokerage, Asia-Pacific represents the largest market worldwide, supported by the region's growing clout as the IT outsourcing hub worldwide, the emergence of cloud ready Asian countries and the growing adoption of cloud IT architecture in the enterprise sector. The United States is projected to grow at the fastest CAGR of 33.8% over the analysis period, led by the well-developed cloud ecosystem, strong early adopters' trust in the cloud, and robust sales of cloud brokerage enablement solutions as a result of the growing focus on internally handling cloud brokerage functions. Finally, Cloud Brokerage Services represents the largest market segment accounting for a majority share in total revenue, while Cloud Brokerage Enablement

Solutions represent the fastest growing market segment with revenue growing at a CAGR of 33.6% over the analysis period.

BROKERAGE PRICING MODELS

In this section, we briefly review some of the prevalent cloud brokering pricing schemes.

Description of Methodologies

Dynamic Cloud Resource Reservation

According to the Dynamic Cloud Resource Reservation (DCRR) model the cloud brokerage service reserves a great amount of resource instances (RI) - Virtual Machines (VMs) from different cloud providers and the customers take advantage of price discounts (Wang et al., 2013) The broker exploits the financial benefits of long-term instances reservations as well as the multiplexing gains. Therefore, instead of directly buying the instances from cloud providers, the customer will buy them from the cloud broker, which serves a great amount of customers demand providing on-demand instances. The DCRR model architecture is presented in Figure 2.

Figure 2 shows the architecture of the DCRR cloud brokerage service, where solid arrows show the direction of instance provisioning and dashed arrows show the direction of money flow. According to DCRR the customers purchase instances from the cloud broker in lower prices than those of cloud provider, since the broker leverages the wholesale price model and the price gap between the on-demand and the reserved instances to reduce costs for all users. Even more importantly, it can organize user requests to achieve additional cost savings with some benefits.

Figure 2. The DCRR cloud brokerage architecture

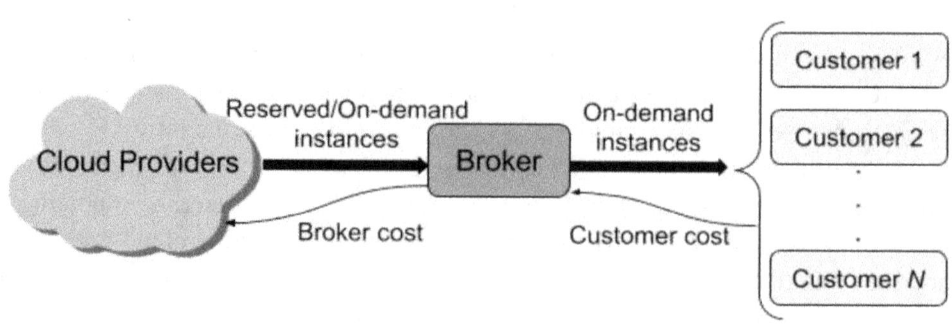

For example, better exploitation of reservation instances, which is achieved by concentrating service requirements from a large number of customers, thus limiting individual request bursts, which is considered more appropriate for reserved instances. Otherwise, users would often make individual requests, which is not economically advantageous for reserved instances. Wasted costs are also reduced due to the partial use of instances. When a customer uses a service, he is charged for the whole hour even if he uses the hour partially. On the contrary, the broker can take advantage of the single-hour charge and serves two users at the same time reducing the total cost of service in half. Finally, the broker takes the advantage of the fact that many providers offer significant discounts to customers who purchase a large number of instances. In this way, the broker reduces the costs of serving the users and increases its own revenues.

The key problem of the DCRR model for the broker is the decision on how many instances should buy in advance, how many it should launch on-demand and when it should reserve instances as the requests change dynamically over time. To meet this challenge, the problem of reserving resources is being addressed in the light of user requirements and the optimal solution comes via dynamic programming. The main types of cloud purchasing instances are on-demand instances and reserved instances.

For the case of on-demand instances, the users pay a fixed amount in each billing cycle without any commitment, while for the case of reserved instances they pay a subscription once to rent an instance / VM for a certain time period. The key issue is an optimization problem as it attempts to reduce the total cost of user requirements through the following equations (Wang et al., 2013):

$$\min_{\{r_1,\ldots,r_T\}} \cos t = \sum_{t=1}^{T} r_t \gamma + \sum_{t=1}^{T} \left(d_t - n_t\right)^{+} p \text{, } n_t = \sum_{i=t-r+1}^{t} r_i, \forall t = 1,\ldots,T$$

where refers to the total cost of reservations and n_t is the cost for on-demand requests. The problem for the broker is to dynamically decides for the reservations r_1, ..., r_t in order to reduce the total cost, where r_t denotes the number of reserved instances at time $t \geq 0$. Each r_t is efficient from time t to $t + r$-1, where r is the instance reservation period, d_t denotes total instances and n_t the number of reserved instances that are efficient at time t = 1,2, .. T, where t is associated with each billing cycle. The symbol γ denotes the subscription fee for each reserved instance and p refers to the value of the current on-demand instance for each cycle. Finally, the term $(d_t - n_t)^+$ refers to the additional on-demand instances that need to be released.

As mentioned above, the goal of the broker is to minimize the total costs (according to) as it meets all customer requests. However, this equation is described by the Curse of Dimensionality (Bellman, 2013) as the results have exponential complexity as there are a large number of possible combinations and situations for the solutions. Such problems are solved using Approximate Dynamic Programming (ADP) (Powell, 2007).

The simulation process for the performance evaluation of the above pricing model implemented in (Wang et al. 2013) was based on Google cluster usage traces. The dataset contained 180GB over a month's resource demand/usage information of 933 users on a cluster of 12,583 physical machines. Based on the results, the broker brings an aggregate cost saving at 15%, for all user demands. The benefit of the broker is different in different user groups and more specifically 40% cost saving for users with medium demand fluctuation and almost 5% for users with low demand fluctuation. Considering the individual price discount of each user, almost 70% of them can save more than 30%, while the broker can bring more than 25% price discounts to 70% of aggregated users.

Heuristics for Virtual Machine Mapping

The model of Virtual Machine Mapping Problem (VMMP) seeks to anticipate the demand for the services so that the broker can buy them in sufficient quantity but also at the right time to serve customers gaining at the same time the maximum possible profit (Nesmachnow et al., 2017).. Therefore, all the requests of the customers for VMs should be mapped to the available reserved resource instances of the broker in order to maximize its profit. In contrast to traditional brokers, the virtual broker owns a number of instances, as shown in Figure 3, and provides a variety of services to its customers at lower prices than those offered by the cloud providers (Nesmachnow et al., 2015). The large gap of price between the on-demand and the reserved instances seems to be profitable for the broker.

The broker has to distribute all the available instances based on the requirements of the customers for VMs. In the absence of other available instances, the idle on-demand resources need to be closed in order to serve the customer and thus maintaining a high level of service. However, this will result in a reduction of the profit. This problem can be formulated by defining a mapping function *f*: *VM* → *RI* that maximizes the total profit of the broker, solved according to the following optimization problem (Nesmachnow et al., 2015):

$$\max \sum_{j=1}^{m} \left[\sum_{i:f(v_i)=r_j} \left(p\left(BF\left(v_i\right)\right) - C\left(r_j\right) \right) \times T\left(v_i\right) \right] + \sum_{h:ST\left(v_h\right)>D_j\left(v_h\right)} \left(p\left(BF\left(v_h\right)\right) - COD\left(BF\left(v_h\right)\right) \right) \times T\left(v_h\right)$$

Figure 3. The VMMP architecture

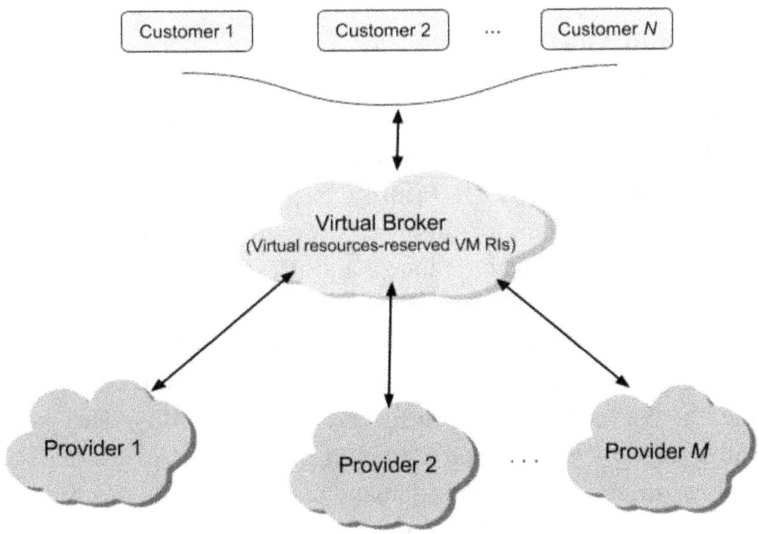

$BF(v_h)$ function considers every instance which meets or exceeds the requirements in hardware of the v_i request and selects the instance having the lowest cost on-demand. $ST(v_i)$ denotes the starting time of the v_h request based on the scheduling function f. VM=$\{v_1, \ldots v_n\}$ is the set of customers' requests for VMs and $T(v_i)$ is the time length of v_i, which have to start before the deadline $D(v_i)$, defined from the user. $RI=\{r_1, .., r_m\}$, $m<<n$ is the set of resource instances that are reserved from the broker. C is the cost function for RIs and COD the cost function for on-demand instances with $C(r_j)<<COD(r_j)$. Both functions are related to charges per hour. Moreover, $p(r_j)$ is the pricing function that defines the price the broker charges the customer per hour for the instance r_j. The broker should charge an instance r_j with lower price than the on-demand pricing of provider in order to be attractive for the customers, meaning $p(r_j)<<COD(r_j)$. The hardware requirements for each VM are denoted as $P(v_i)$:processor speed, $M(v_i)$:memory, $S(v_i)$:storage, $n_c(v_i)$:number of cores and the requests arrive in groups (i.e. per hour) A_i. The aforementioned optimization problem is subject to $M(v_i) \leq M(r_j)$, $P(v_i) \leq P(r_j)$, $S(v_i) \leq S(r_j)$ and $n_c(v_i) \leq n_c(r_j)$.

To solve the above problem, alternative scheduling heuristic algorithms are presented below using different criteria for prioritizing customer requests (Nesmachnow et al., 2013).

- **Best Fit Resource (BFR):** Each request for VM is assigned to the *RI* that best fits (the same number of cores and the closest amount of memory for the requested value), defying the time limit. It seeks to leverage the assignment of VM to those RIs that most suit, letting the most restrictive requests to run in larger RIs.

- **Earliest Finish Time (EFT):** Priority is given to requests that are completed the soonest. The availability of each *RI* determines the time of completion and as a result the basic idea of the algorithm is the execution of requests that are finished the soonest, in order to increase the availability of the *RIs*.
- **Shortest Task First (STF):** Priority is given to VMs with the shortest execution time in order to minimize the completion time. The algorithm searches the soonest inactive request and it assigns it to the lower-cost VM instance.
- **Earliest Deadline First (EDF):** Priority is given to the requests with shorter deadline (without taking into account the arrival time) and each VM is assigned to the suitable RI with the earliest availability. The purpose is to take advantage of the prompt execution of the more restrictive requests to avoid penalization of buying on-demand instances due to deadline violations.
- **Cheapest Instance (CI):** The cheapest VM RI that allows the execution of each request is selected. The basic idea is to reduce the average waiting time of VM requests. An on-demand instance is rented only if there is absolutely no reserved instance satisfying the deadline of the request.
- **MaxProfit (MaxP):** Is an algorithm of greed for profit that uses the contribution of each request to the total profit function. The request with the largest contribution is assigned to the cheapest RI that meets the hardware requirements.
- **Shortest Request to Cheapest Instance (SRCI):** The requests are sorted according to their duration and the cheapest resource that allows the execution of each one is chosen. The purpose is to maximize the profit and minimize the response time. Once the shortest requests are asked to be executed first, they will be completed earlier and the users with demands of short computing time will find that their requests are completed fast enough.

The simulation for the performance evaluation of the aforementioned algorithms in (Nesmachnow et al., 2013) is based on C programming language, using the standard stdlib library, the GNU gcc, a Xeon E5430 processor at 2.66 GHz, 8GB RAM, and the CentOS Linux 5.2, from the Cluster FING. The problem instances are defined based on information about VM requests (memory, storage, processor speed, number of cores) and the relevant data for a set of RIs from the virtual broker (available memory, storage, processor speed, number of cores, cost, pricing values). A set of 400 problem instances were solved, considering batches of 50, 100, 200, and 400 VM requests with different durations, taking into account pre-booked cloud infrastructure of 10, 20, 30, and 50 RIs for the virtual broker. The VMs include small and average machines, large machines and instances with large memory, CPU and/or storage. The results revealed that the MaxP takes a precedence over the other approaches accounting for the profit of the virtual broker, and being among the best ones in terms of QoS of the solutions.

Derivative Contracts Options

This model describes the financial method of a cloud broker using derivative contracts to purchase cheaper instances for the users and facilitate providers to predict the future demand for services. Options contracts are common types of derivatives contracts which give buyers the legal right, but not an obligation, to purchase a resource for an agreed price on some later delivery date. Derivative contracts are used by the broker as a strategy to avoid the risk for uncertainty over future demand and supply (Rogers et al., 2012). This kind of financial methods is widely used in either natural of virtual commodity and product markets.

Typically, the role of the broker is to facilitate the assignment to the demand and offer in the market. Companies that offer this kind of business services can gain a profit by charging service subscriptions and /or leveraging spreads by buying resources at lower prices and selling them at higher. The main objective is to purchase in advance long-term contracts (36 months) for resources and repack them as contracts of one month offered to customers at a higher price.

The derivative contracts model includes the following steps (Clamp et al., 2013):

- Each month the broker asks from the customers to express their needs for future resources, by selling option contracts and determine how many reserved RIs will purchase from them providers.
- Then, the customer should decide whether or not to buy additional long reserved instances (usually for 3 years).
- The next month the customers submit their demands about the instances they need, activating their contracts. If there are available RIs from previous purchases, then the broker sells them with a profit gain. Otherwise, the broker has to pay additional on-demand instances to the provider in higher prices to fulfill the obligation to the customer.

The contract options model is based on the pricing model originally developed by Wu, Zhang and Huberman (Wu et al., 2008) at the HP. In this case the customers take a discount privilege if they are able to declare a true probability of using the VMs they need in the future. Every month, each customer i estimates his own probability p_i. He then submits his p_i to the broker to buy a contract for the resources he needs. The next month the customer is charged $Used(p_i)$ if the contract is activated or otherwise $Unused(p_i)$ according to the following equations (Clamp et al. 2013).

$$U_{sed}\left(p_i\right) = 1 + \frac{k}{2} - kp_i + \frac{kp_i^{\,2}}{2} \; U_{nused}\left(p_i\right) = \frac{kp_i^{\,2}}{2}$$

According to derivative contract options, the broker observes historical resource demand of customers for reserved instances, during the previous 3 years (36 months) $H = [h_{t\text{-}36}, \ldots, h_t]$, and compares against the future resource capacity, such as the number of reserved instances that the broker has currently available $F = \{f_t, \ldots, f_{t+36}\}$ during the following 3 years. Then the deficit profile D is estimated for each forthcoming month, by subtracting historical demand from future expected demand D=F-H.

For each resource requested, a variable called Marginal Resource Utilization (MRU) is used to describe the possible utilization of an additional reserved resource over the next 3 years, based on historical demand and it is the proportion of item if $D > 0$. In addition, the broker uses another variable named threshold θ, which determines whether the broker should buy a new instance during the forthcoming 3 years. The broker has the ability to take a risk by varying the threshold value in the interval [0 1]. In case where MRU $> \theta$, the broker is advised to purchase additional reserved instances, which will very probably be utilized in the following months and this decision is expected to be profitable. On the other hand if MRU $\leq \theta$, the broker should purchase new instances on-demand, being more profitable than purchasing reserved instances in advance.

Every month clients can demand instances from the broker by exercising their options contracts. If the broker has available capacity to satisfy the demand of the client, instances are sold to clients at a higher value than the purchased one. Otherwise, the broker has to buy on-demand instances and provide them to the client in order to fulfill its obligation.

The simulation for the performance evaluation of the derivative contracts model according to (Cartlidge et al., 2013) was based on Python programming language, taking into account a set of submitting probabilities of 1000 customers with different thresholds θ, for reserved instance contract lengths of 12 and 36 months. The results revealed that in the worst case scenario the broker still makes nontrivial profit. Modifications of the operating instances of the broker, such as purchasing longer term reserved instance contracts, seem to improve profits by 30%. Considering past performance can also reward the broker with increased profits, by 36%. Taking into account ideal market conditions, where longer term contract terms are used, considering an optimum threshold, profit was increased by up to 165%.

Quantized Billing Cycles

According to Quantized Billing Cycles (QBC) the user pays the same price for an on-demand instance, regardless if the time of usage is smaller than the whole billing cycle (Saha et al., 2015). For example, a user may pay the same price using the VM for 1 hour or for a few minutes. However, this type of pricing model is not proper for customers of sporadic demand. For example, sometimes user demands for VMs are higher than the available resources and hence brokers have to purchase more resources. Given the fact that the peak of demand is transient, the resources are charged for an hour, while their use will be only for a few minutes. Consequently, the main QBS problem is the occasional customer demand and the higher the sporadic nature, the greater the loss.

This problem is addressed with a dynamic pricing approach. Increasing the sales price leads to the decrease of demand and increase of revenues. For example, in case of static pricing where there is demand for a number of resources, the revenues will be determined by a fixed interest rate. When the selling price of a VM is rising (dynamic pricing) then the demand falls, but the revenues are more. Dynamic pricing brings more profit than static. This is because in the latter case many VMs remain idle and hence they don't contribute to revenues. The basic idea behind dynamic pricing is: it is preferable to suffer a small loss of revenue for a limited time rather than buying VM and then suffering greater loss in subsequent slots due to low demand.

The optimization problem of QBS is presented below, taking into account that the user pays the broker based on per-request basis.

$$\max_{\{\gamma_t, \upsilon_t\}} P = \sum_{t=1}^{T} \left(\gamma_t d_t - \upsilon_t \right)$$

where

$$\sum_{i=t-\tau+1}^{t} \upsilon_i \geq d_t, \forall t = 1,2,\ldots,T$$

and

$$d_t = f\left(d_t^*, \gamma_t\right), \forall t = 1,2,\ldots,T$$

P is the profit to be maximized. The term $\gamma_t d_t - \upsilon_t$ is the gain at t^{th} time slot and γ_t is the selling price per time slot. The term d_t is the number of VMs need to serve a new request, υ_t is the number of VMs bought in the tth time slot, and $d_t{*}$ the actual demand. The symbol τ refers to the period of one billing cycle and $\sum_{i=t-\tau+1}^{t} \upsilon_i$ is the number of active VMs within the tth time slot. The term $d_t{*}$ is the modified demand for VMs when the selling price is equal to γ_t. The relationship relating the actual demand d_t and the modified $d_t{*}$ is based on the price-demand function $f(*)$. If $\gamma_t = \gamma{*}$, then $d_t = d_t{*}$. The revenues of selling a VM at a price $\gamma{*}$ for a billing cycle is $\gamma{*}\tau$ and if $\gamma{*}\tau > 1$ then it seems profitable for the broker, where 1 is the cost of a VM.

The above maximization problem is equivalent to the following minimization formula.

$$\min_{\{\gamma_t, \upsilon_t\}} L = \sum_{t=1}^{T} \left[\overbrace{\left(\gamma^{*} d_t^{*} - \gamma_t\, d_t\right)}^{\text{Demand Loss}} + \underbrace{\upsilon_t}_{\text{VM Loss}} \right]$$

In equation $(\gamma{*}d_t{*} - \gamma_t d_t)$ and υ_t refers to the reduction in demand and VMs respectively. In case of unexpected increase in demand $d_t{*}$ for a short time, then according to the selling prices will increase to reduce demand. In such a case the broker will suffer a small demand loss. On the other hand, the case of purchasing many VMs to support the demand hike is not the ideal solution as there is a possibility for the broker to suffer a huge VM loss in subsequent time intervals due to underutilized machines. Nevertheless, if demand is high for a long time it would be wiser to purchase the VMs. The algorithm based on belongs to the category of offline algorithms and hence it cannot be known in advance whether an increase in demand will last for a long time or not. The challenge here is to design algorithms that make decisions online based on present and past data. Such algorithms are called online.

The above algorithms described in and belong to the category of ski-rental problems. In this category the broker has to decide whether to buy or will continue to rent a resource without knowing in advance the time period of usage and future demand. If the period of usage is short then renting is preferable, while for long-term usage buying is cheaper. The ski-rental problems face the dilemma of whether to buy or rent the RIs without knowing beforehand the time period of usage. Breakeven point is used to design online algorithms, suggesting the point after which buying is better than renting.

The simulation for the performance evaluation of the proposed pricing model implemented in (Saha et al., 2015) was based on Google cluster usage traces, conducting comparative studies for the effect of demand prediction and demand threshold for switching between renting and buying. The results revealed the significant importance of demand prediction and determined the appropriate breakeven points for different thresholds.

Two-Sided Auction Mechanism

Two-sided auctions allow for many-to-many price negotiations, meaning that on the one hand there is a number of providers and on the other a number of buyers. Each side submits its bids on resources. This type of model is quite efficient in relation to unilateral auctions. However, further research is required to bridge the gap between the two sides so that both their benefits and requirements are rightly met.

The proposed model strives to meet the needs of the providers and customers as well as the broker in an attempt to attract them. This model seems to benefit all users by properly exploiting the transactions of large data services to facilitate their trade and use. This mechanism is called Two-Sided Mechanism for Trading Big Data Commodities (2-SAMBA) and determines the price each user has to pay to the broker for the resources he is going to use and the revenue the cloud provider will receive (Mashayekhy et al., 2014).

There is a set of $C = \{C_1, C_2, ..., C_m\}$ providers available to offer a large amount of resources to cloud users through a reservation system for a set of different time slots, defined as T. Each provider C_j offers a cluster to users for each time slot, reporting a minimal cost. In addition, the preferences of the providers are denoted by $a= (a_1, ..., a_m)$ where each element i denotes the minimum cost of a provider C_j. The cost of each C_j is a_j/T for each time slot. There is also a set of users U and each user i requests to use a cluster for a certain time slot and determines his bit preference as the maximum value he is willing to pay for the cluster at time t. Both users and providers report their requirements (bid and demand respectively) to the broker, who is responsible for executing and implementing the auction to determine user resource allocation and pricing. Both participants send this information to the broker a-priori, ensuring the privacy of the choices.

Based on the above, the problem of trading big data computing commodities (TBDCC) is to determine the distribution of clusters to users but also their price based on the submitted bid and demand. One mechanism for resolving this issue involves two phases:

- **Winner Determination:** The assignment of clusters to users over time is determined. If user i receives a cluster from provider C_j at time t, then the binary decision variable $x_{ij}^{t} = 1$, otherwise 0. Also, when the resources of a cloud provider C_j are allocated to a user then the binary decision variable $y_j = 1$.
- **Price Determination:** The amount of π_i^u that each user i has to pay to the broker and the amount π_j^c that each provider C_j receives from the broker. Users have almost linear utility. This is the case if the user i is granted with the resources, the utility u_i^u will be the difference between the valuation and the amount of money transferred, $u_i^u = b_t^i - \pi_u^i$ or 0 otherwise. If a provider C_j allocates a cluster to users, then its own utility will be $u_c^j = \pi_c^j - a_j$ and 0 otherwise.

The monetary payoff of the broker is defined as the total payment received by users minus the receipts of the providers, expressed by $\sum_{i \in U}^{T} \pi_i^u - \sum_{j:C_j \in C}^{T} \pi_j^c$.

When the monetary payoff is not negative, then the auction is ex-post budget balanced. This property gives the incentive to broker to set up the auction. Each participant attempts to maximize its utility. In order to promote the transactions and attract the interest of users and cloud providers this model seeks to optimize the utility for both users (customers and providers) and brokers' payoff. The phase of optimal winner determination is based on the following equation:

$$\text{Maximize} \sum_{t \in T} \sum_{i \in U} \sum_{j:C_j \in C} b_i^t x_{ij}^t - \sum_{j:C_j \in C}^{T} a_j y_j$$

where

$$\sum_{i \in U} x_{ij}^t \leq 1, \forall j : C_j \in C, \forall t \in T, \ \sum_{j:C_j \in C} \sum_{t \in T} x_{ij}^t \leq 1, \forall i \in U$$

Moreover $y_j \geq x_{ij}^t$, $x_{ij}^t = \{0,1\}$ and $y_j = \{0,1\}$. The objective function is to maximize the social welfare.

The simulation for the performance evaluation of the 2-SAMBA according to (Mashayekhy et al., 2014) is based on IBM ILOG CPLEX Optimization Studio Multiplatform Multilingual e-Assembly, C++, AMD 2.4GHz Dual Proc Dual Core,

16 GB RAM of WSU Grid System. The whole procedure includes a comparative study of SAMBA and another TBDCC algorithm called VCG-TBDCC based on Amazon request data for a total number of 350 users. The results revealed that 2-SAMBA algorithm is very fast finding solutions in less than 75 seconds, being suitable in two-sided markets with high demand. In conclusion, it turns out that 2-SAMBA is suitable for trading big data computing commodities.

Comparison of Pricing Models

In this section a comparative study of the aforementioned pricing models is presented revealing the key issues that have to be considered, when implementing each algorithm for cloud brokerage.

Considering the DCRR and the VMMP, the users receive a lower price when trading with the broker. There is no need for upfront payment for reservations and no money wasted on idle reservation instances. The broker makes profit by leveraging the wholesale model. However, the main aspect the broker has to deal with is to what extent it makes proper predictions about future demand. On the one hand the broker faces the risk to buy a pool of VMs probably not to be used in the near future. On the other hand, an incorrect estimated of future demand can lead to a lack of resources and customer service. In this case the broker will be forced to buy more expensive instances on-demand directly from cloud providers. Consequently, the result in both cases is common: profit loss.

Regarding the derivative contracts approach, it seems more profitable for the broker to purchase long-term option contracts. Moreover, the past performance of the customers benefits the broker. The main practical problem of derivative contracts is due to the inherent risk related with the unsteady nature of the cloud market. Moreover, it is very risky to take into account future probabilities of customers on demand, if we consider the case that customers may reveal a mistaken possibility and hence the broker will inaccurately forecast the reservation of the resources. In this case the broker will purchase resources that will remain unused, which results in profit loss.

As far as the QBS model is concerned, dynamic pricing turns out to make more profit than static pricing, mainly due to the underutilization of the VMs in the latter approach. The key problem that the broker has to deal with is the demand prediction and the time duration for which it has to continue to rent the VMs and the right time that the broker has to decide if purchasing the resources will be more profitable than renting.

Finally, the two-sided auction mechanism seems to be profitable for big data applications area, where there is a need to develop market mechanisms for managing, trading, and pricing big data computing services. In this case users require entire clusters for their big data applications. Such demand necessitates the design and deployment of markets for big data services in which entire clusters are the tradable goods.

Based on the aforementioned analysis and the general needs of cloud market, the pricing models for cloud brokerage offer economic benefits to both customers and providers, while at the same time being profitable for the broker.

According to pricing models adopted by the broker, presented in this book chapter, the broker reserves instances from cloud providers based on past performance of customers, using either a probability which reveals the utilization of instances for the next month or an online reservation strategy to make decisions based on history. In addition, a broker may collect tariffs from the provider market and assesses them by calculating the cost performance of each tariff always according to the priorities of customers for resources. Dynamic pricing is also presented as approach for aiming to regulate the demand on resources based on the underutilization of the VMs or minimize the service cost of the broker using dynamic programming and approximate algorithms. Moreover, the auction mechanism seems to be suitable for big data applications. In this context, the development of flexible pricing procedures is an issue of high concern, since the existing ones seem to not adequately address the pricing of cloud services.

CONCLUSION AND FUTURE OUTLOOK

This chapter gives an overview of cloud computing and its services and models, while emphasizing the need for cloud brokerage and its benefit. The most promising cloud brokerage seems to play an essential role in the increasingly complex cloud computing scenarios and in profit making in the context of future cloud market.

In the market of cloud computing, a broker functions in the same way as it does in other, real-world, markets. It matches the demands of users with supplies of providers, aiming to succeed in settling the best financial agreement between these two sides of the market. The purpose of the broker to make profits for his own offering at the same time high quality services to customers reveals a successful commodity market.

The overview of the cloud broker discussed in this book chapter focuses on the numerous benefits of this widely known business model. From a business oriented perspective, the broker assists enterprises to develop themselves, makes cost savings, creating at the same time a competitive environment with more job opportunities and challenges. Cloud brokering has a substantial potential for cloud service providers and small, upstart entrepreneurs, who gain improved profitability and new revenue opportunity.

This book chapter also emphasizes the need of pricing models adopted by the broker, presenting a review of previous literature in this area, from a cost saving perspective for the broker. These cloud brokerage pricing models serve the needs of users by providing the resources they have leased earlier to different providers either dynamically or on-demand and determining pricing according to the existed supply and demand, depending on market conditions. These approaches are based on economic strategies and algorithms taking into account the cost of resources and service quality, having the ultimate goal of maximizing profit as well as minimizing possible spending and cost savings.

As the cloud broker business model is still developed, there are several important aspects to be further explored, mainly towards the direction of developing and adopting more efficient pricing methods and the role of the broker into the reduction of costs. An important issue of future research is the development of a meta-algorithm able at forecasting future demand for more efficient pooling of resources in order to better meet the expected demand to minimum possible costs. Moreover, the possibility for a broker to adopt more than one pricing models and switch among them according to demand and recourses conditions seems to be very promising for future brokerage services. Finally, research must be extended to accommodate the SaaS and PaaS models as well, which are also expected to diffuse quickly in the coming years, raising the imperative need for new, innovative, business models.

REFERENCES

Bellman, R. (2013). *Dynamic programming*. Courier Corporation.

Buyya, R., Venugopal, S., Broberg, J., & Brandic, I. (2009). Cloud computing and emerging IT platforms: Vision, hype, and reality for delivering computing as the 5th utility. *Future Generation Computer Systems*, *25*(18), 599–616. doi:10.1016/j.future.2008.12.001

Buyya, R., Yeo, C. S., Venugopal, S., Broberg, J., & Brandic, I. (2009). Cloud computing and emerging IT platforms: Vision, hype, and reality for delivering computing as the 5th utility. *Future Generation Computer Systems*, *25*(6), 599–616. doi:10.1016/j.future.2008.12.001

Cartlidge, J., & Clamp, P. (2014). Correcting a financial brokerage model for cloud computing: Closing the window of opportunity for commercialisation. *Journal of Cloud Computing*, *3*(1), 2. doi:10.1186/2192-113X-3-2

Clamp, P., & Cartlidge, J. (2013). Pricing the cloud: an adaptive brokerage for cloud computing. In *5th International conference on advances in system simulation (SIMUL-2013)*. IARIA XPS Press.

Felipe, A., Sanchez, D., Felipe, A., Sanchez, D., & Diaz-sanchez, F. (2016). Cloud brokering: New value-added services and pricing models TELECOM ParisTech Spécialité "Informatique et Réseaux" Cloud brokering. *Nouveaux services de valeur ajoutée et politique de prix.*

Hassan, Q. F. (2011). Demystifying Cloud Security. *Crosstalk*, 6–21. Retrieved from http://www.crosstalkonline.org/storage/issue-archives/2011/201101/201101-Hassan.pdf

Iturriaga, S., Nesmachnow, S., & Dorronsoro, B. (2017). Optimizing the Profit and QoS of Virtual Brokers in the Cloud. In Cloud Computing (pp. 277-300). Springer International Publishing. doi:10.1007/978-3-319-54645-2_11

Marinescu, D. C. (2012). Cloud Computing. *Theory into Practice*, 1–403. PMID:22333270

Mashayekhy, L., Nejad, M. M., & Grosu, D. (2014, October). A two-sided market mechanism for trading big data computing commodities. In *Big Data (Big Data), 2014 IEEE International Conference on* (pp. 153-158). IEEE. 10.1109/BigData.2014.7004225

Mell, P., & Grance, T. (2011). The NIST definition of cloud computing. *NIST Special Publication*, *145*, 7. doi:10.1136/emj.2010.096966

Nesmachnow, S., Iturriaga, S., Dorronsoro, B., El-Ghazali, T., & Bouvry, P. (2013). List scheduling heuristics for virtual machine mapping in cloud systems. *VI Latin American Symposium on High Performance Computing (HPCLatam)*, 37-48.

Nesmachnow, S., Iturriaga, S., & Dorronsoro, B.IEEE. (2015). Efficient heuristics for profit optimization of virtual cloud brokers. *IEEE Computational Intelligence Magazine*, *10*(1), 33–43. doi:10.1109/MCI.2014.2369893

Powell, W. B. (2007). *Approximate Dynamic Programming: Solving the curses of dimensionality* (Vol. 703). Wiley-Interscience. doi:10.1002/9780470182963

Rogers, O., & Cliff, D. (2012). A financial brokerage model for cloud computing. Journal of Cloud Computing: Advances. *Systems and Applications*, *1*(1), 2.

Saha, G., & Pasumarthy, R. (2015, September). Maximizing profit of cloud brokers under quantized billing cycles: a dynamic pricing strategy based on ski-rental problem. In *Communication, Control, and Computing (Allerton), 2015 53rd Annual Allerton Conference on* (pp. 1000-1007). IEEE. 10.1109/ALLERTON.2015.7447117

Sean Marston, Z. L. (2011). Cloud computing — The business perspective. *Elsevier BV., 51*(1), 176–189.

Wang, W., Niu, D., Li, B., & Liang, B. (2013, July). Dynamic cloud resource reservation via cloud brokerage. *Distributed Computing Systems (ICDCS), 2013 IEEE 33rd International Conference on*, 400-409. 10.1109/ICDCS.2013.20

Wu, F., Zhang, L., & Huberman, B. A. (2008). Truth-telling reservations. *Algorithmica, 52*(1), 65–79. doi:10.100700453-007-9107-5

Chapter 10
Earnings Management and Institutional Ownership in Turkey

Aslı Aybars
Marmara University, Turkey

Levent Ataünal
Istanbul Aydin University, Turkey

ABSTRACT

Earnings management is an important factor that considerably affects the reporting quality of firms and conceivably results in suboptimal investor decisions. The presence of active institutional investors among the equity holders is generally accepted as an external control mechanism that moderates earnings management problems. This chapter aimed to evaluate the role of institutional investors on earnings management with a data of firms listed on Borsa Istanbul between 2005 and 2011. The study found a significant and negative relation between institutional ownership level and managerial discretion exercised in opportunistic management of accruals and confirmed the substantial role played by institutional investors in monitoring and disciplining corporate managers. In other words, the managers' tendency for earnings management practices is observed to be mitigated by institutional shareholdings.

DOI: 10.4018/978-1-5225-6114-9.ch010

1. INTRODUCTION

Agency theory deals with the divergence between the goals and aspirations of the principle and the agent. Opportunistic earnings management practices, which are defined as the accounting choice targeting some specific objective (Scott, 2011, pp. 423), result in agency costs causing investors to make less favorable investment decisions. The information asymmetry, or specifically, information advantage of corporate managers over the shareholders, facilitates manipulation of accounting earnings and maximize managers' utility at the expense of other stakeholders (Holthausen & Leftwich, 1983; Holthausen, 1990; Godfrey et al., 2010). The corporate managers are also inclined to distort accounting numbers solely for generating better impression on the public.

Due to the recent corporate scandals, the importance of monitoring mechanisms which assures the reliability of the reporting and related disclosures has become obvious. Governance structure and monitoring mechanisms are important determinants of level of opportunistic earnings manipulation (Dechow et al. 1996). Well-established corporate governance practices generally mitigate agency costs stemming from the separation of ownership and control. Institutional investors' equity and their active involvement in management are accepted as an external control mechanism in restraining the degree of opportunistic accruals.

The study aims to provide evidence for the role of institutional investors on earnings management based on two main hypotheses; active monitoring hypothesis and managerial myopia induced by short-term oriented institutional investors. The remainder of the study is organized as follows: The following section provides a literature overview on the topic. In the third section, the hypotheses are defined. The fourth section explains data, sample and the methodology. Fifth section presents the findings and last section concludes.

2. LITERATURE REVIEW

Earlier researchers focusing on the link between institutional ownership and earnings management mostly employed variables based on research and development expenditures (R&D) as proxies of managerial discretion (Graves, 1988; Hill & Hansen, 1989; Hansen & Hill, 1991; Baysinger et al. 1991; Eng, 1995; Bushee, 1997; Majumdar & Nagarajan, 1997; Bushee, 1998). It is presumed that increases or decreases in R&D expenses are utilized as a tool in managing earnings. However, recently new variables besides R&D related proxies are introduced.

Rajgopal and Venkatachalam (1997) using institutional investor ownership percentage and the number of institutional owners as explanatory variables together with a set of control variables found a negative relationship between institutional ownership and earnings management. Using a similar model, Rajgopal, et al. (1999) validated the significant and negative impact of institutional ownership on the selected proxy of managerial discretion. Some other researchers also confirmed the negative relationship between institutional investors and the intensity of earnings management. Chung et al. (2002) revealed the substantial role of institutional owners in discouraging managers to engage in earnings management while incentives to increase or decrease company profits were existed. Koh (2003) claimed that the relationship between earnings management and institutional ownership was non-linear. Liu (2005) showed that managers manipulated earnings upwards as the level of transient institutional ownership increased. With a concurrent study, Mitra and Cready (2005) verified the monitoring role of institutional owners in constraining accounting flexibility using a dataset of 824 firms listed on NYSE (New York Stock Exchange). A similar study on S&P 100 Index also verified that institutional ownership reduced earnings management by means of discretionary accruals (Cornett et al. 2008).

The studies related to earnings management in Turkey revealed inconsistent results. Besides, studies in Turkey is mostly limited with uncovering and assessing the amount of these discretionary accounting practices (Atik, 2009; Atik & İsmail, 2011; Ayarlıoğlu, 2007; Duman, 2010). Using quarterly data Karaibrahimoğlu (2010) found evidence on significance of corporate governance practices in mitigating earnings management. Adıgüzel (2012) verified the effect of internal corporate governance practices in mitigating earnings management in non-family-owned firms. Effective internal audit and the number of board meetings are found to be restraining amount of earnings manipulated. Given limited number and scope of studies in Turkey, this study aimed to provide further evidence on the relationship between earnings management and institutional ownership in Turkey.

3. METHODOLOGY

The moral hazard and adverse selection problems arising from principle-agent conflicts can be mitigated by close monitoring. The opportunistic approaches of agents who are benefiting from the information asymmetry can be restrained by corporate governance mechanisms which are mostly demanded by institutional owners. Effective mechanisms established to deal with potential opportunistic managerial behavior can reduce associated moral hazard and adverse selection problems. Institutional owners, who are generally better informed and more sophisticated than the individual investors, facilitate aligning interests of owners and managers. It is also argued that that institutional investors, contrary to board of directors, are more willing to use their ownership rights for monitoring and disciplining managers and more likely to prevent managers from utilizing discretionary accruals as a mean of earnings management. Thus, they force managers act in line with shareholders' interest (Cornett et al., 2007, Chung et al. 2002). This study first tests whether higher level of shares held by institutional investors leads to lower level of earnings management or not.

On the other hand, institutional investors also tend to be passive investors overreacting to information and excessive trading as they frequently aim to reach short-term targets. They tend to liquidate their equity stakes in firms with poor performance rather than engaging in actions to improve firm performance (Duggal & Millar, 1999, Graves, 1988). Eventually, institutional investors are more likely to focus on current earnings rather than long term earning potential (Porter, 1992). This myopic investment approach reduces the monitoring efficiency of institutional investors.

Institutional investors face certain barriers in exercising their managerial power. They are namely, relationship oriented, regulatory, and information processing barriers. As dependence on business relationships is increased, power obtained from ownership stakes is decreased. Although pension funds, mutual funds, and endowments and foundations are more active in governance, banks and insurance companies which have potential business relationships are less likely to involve in managerial actions and eventual conflicts. The second obstacle is related to regulatory framework, which may prevent institutional owners exercising their power. Lastly, as the number of the firms in which these investors actively oversee increases, managerial involvement is reduced due to increased information costs (David and Kochhar, 1996).

4. DATA AND THE SAMPLE

The data used in the study covers the period between 2005 and 2011. Even though the sample is comprised of all publicly listed companies on BIST during the seven-year observation period, companies that has any missing data are deducted from the sample to have a balanced panel. Consistent with the literature, the sample excludes financial companies, as they are subject to a different set of regulations which may distort discretionary accrual estimations (Koh, 2003). Furthermore, at least ten observations per year are required in an industry to ensure efficiency in abnormal accrual calculation (Hsu & Koh, 2005). The industries that do not meet this criterion are also taken out of the sample. Besides, as some variables requires estimation of year to year changes, data for the year 2005 is used only to estimate variables of 2006, and not included in the final estimations. Thus, the final sample is consisted of 177 firms in Manufacturing, Wholesale and Retail Trade, and Technology industries. Computations are done using the Stata software package.

Table 1 gives variables employed in the analysis. This study adopted the performance adjusted industry based modified Jones Model, based on Kothari et al. (2005) for estimating abnormal accruals which proxy for the level of earnings management. The regression based approach, which uses current or previous year's ROA as an additional regressor in the cross-sectional version of the Modified Jones Model, is used to calculate the dependent variable of the models. Even though cross-sectional and time series models are analogous, there is a basic difference in the specification of parameter estimates. Former model uses firm specific parameters as opposed to industry and year (or quarter) specific parameters used in the latter model (Bartov et al. 2001).

Two different methods have been proposed in literature for estimating total accruals, balance sheet approach and cash flow approach. The balance sheet method

Table 1. Variables and definitions

Variable	Abbreviation	Definition
Dependent Variables		
Absolute value of discretionary accruals	ABSDAC	Absolute value of discretionary accruals estimated by Kothari, Leone and Wasley (2005) model at year *t* for firm *i*
Explanatory Variables		
Institutional ownership	INST	The ratio of the number of shares that are held by institutional investors to total shares outstanding at year *t* for firm *i*
Square of institutional ownership	$INST^2$	Square of the ratio of the number of shares that are held by institutional investors to total shares outstanding at year *t* for firm i
Control Variables		
Firm size	LNASST	Natural log of total assets at year *t* for firm *i*
Leverage	LEVR	The ratio of total debt to total assets at year *t* for firm *i*
Return on Assets	ROA	The ratio of net income to total assets at year *t* for firm *i*
Auditor quality	AUDQ	A dummy variable equal to unity if firm *i* is being audited by one of the Big Four Auditors at year *t*, and otherwise equal to zero
Profit vs. Loss firm	LOSS	A dummy variable equal to unity if a firm *i*'s net income is below zero for year *t*, and otherwise equal to zero
Cash flow from operations	CFOASST	The ratio of cash flow from operations to total assets at year *t* for firm *i*
Liquidity	CASHR	The ratio of total cash and cash equivalents to current liabilities at year *t* for firm *i*

utilizes the changes in consecutive balance sheet accounts, and total accruals are computed as the change in non-cash current assets minus change in liabilities minus depreciation and amortization expense. Hribar and Collins (2002) and Hansen (1999) criticized this indirect method of total accrual calculation. They claimed that the results of the studies which use succeeding balance sheet amounts to estimate accruals are contaminated by substantial measurement error. If the researchers do not account for non-operating events, such as mergers/acquisitions, divestures or foreign currency translations, the results may lead into spurious deduction. Therefore, this study utilized the direct cash flow approach and total accruals are estimated as the difference between net income before extraordinary items and cash flow from operations following Xie, (2001); Hsu and Koh (2005) and Lin and Manowan (2012).

After calculating total accruals, performance adjusted cross-sectional industry based modified Jones (1991) Model is estimated each year for each industry by the below regression:

$$\frac{TA_{it}}{A_{it-1}} = \beta_0 + \alpha_i \left[\frac{1}{A_{it-1}}\right] + \beta_{1i} \left[\Delta REV_{it} - \frac{\Delta REC_{it}}{A_{it-1}}\right] + \beta_{2i} \left[PPE_{it} / A_{it-1}\right] + \beta_{3i} ROA_{it} + \varepsilon_{it} \quad (1)$$

where:

$TA_{it} = total\ accruals\ in\ year\ t\ for\ firm\ i;$

$\Delta REV_{it} = revenues\ in\ year\ t\ less\ revenues\ in\ year\ t-1\ for\ firm\ i;$

$\Delta REC_{it} = net\ receivables\ in\ year\ t\ less\ net\ receivables\ in\ year\ t-1;$

$PPE_{it} = gross\ plant, property\ and\ equipment\ in\ year\ t\ for\ firm\ i;$

$ROA_{it} = return\ on\ assets\ in\ year\ t\ for\ firm\ i;$

$A_{it-1} = total\ assets\ in\ year\ t-1\ for\ firm\ i;$

$\varepsilon_{it} = error\ term\ for\ firm\ i\ in\ year\ t$

Above equation estimates total accruals as the change in revenues while adjusting for change in receivables and the level of property, plant, and equipment. Current period ROA is added to the model in line with some of the prior studies (Kothari et al. 2005; Adıgüzel, 2012). According to Kothari et al. (2005) including ROA in the model decreases the probability that estimated discretionary accruals are systematically non-zero, which would otherwise result in invalid inferences regarding accrual behavior. The estimated coefficients in Equation 1 are used to obtain the coefficients for the below equation (2) to approximate amount of nondiscretionary accruals.

$$NDAC_{it} = \alpha_i \left(1 / A_{it-1}\right) + \beta_{1i}\left[\left(\Delta REV_{it} - XREC_{it}\right) / A_{it-1}\right] + \beta_{2i}\left[\left(PPE_{it}\right) / A_{it-1}\right] + \beta_{3i} ROA_{it} \quad (2)$$

where;

NDACit = Nondiscretionary accruals for firm i in year t;

The discretionary accruals (DAC) is calculated as the difference between total accruals and nondiscretionary accruals with the below equation (3);

$$DAC_{it} = TA_{it} - NDAC_{it} \quad (3)$$

As only the magnitude of adjustments matters (Rajgopal & Venkatachalam, 1997), the study utilized the absolute value of discretionary accruals (ABSDAC), rather than positive or negative DAC. Table 2 presents model estimation by ordinary least squares (OLS) method.

In accordance with prior studies (Bushee, 1998; Rajgopal et al. 1999; Koh, 2003; Hsu & Koh, 2005; Mitra & Cready, 2005; Koh, 2007; Cheng & Reitenga, 2009; Wahal & McConnell, 2000), the proportion of shares held by institutional investors to total outstanding shares is used as one of the proxies of institutional ownership (INST). To explore the existence of a potential non-linear relationship between institutional investors and discretionary accruals, the square of institutional ownership ratio ($INST^2$) is also used as an additional proxy. A concave relation is expected in which institutional ownership is not related to the to earnings management at very low levels (Koh, 2003). When the level of institutional ownership is high, suggesting a long-term investment perspective, a negative association between the variables is anticipated since the monitoring of institutional investors is expected to act as a limiting factor that restrains managerial accounting discretion.

Size, leverage, financial performance, auditor quality, being in profit or loss, the level of cash flow from operations and liquidity are used as control variables. Natural log of total assets (LNASST) is adopted as a proxy for firm size. Firm size is expected to have some relation with the chosen variables as previously suggested by some authors (Bushee,1998; Mitra, 2002).

Managers are inclined to manipulate financial reporting to avoid the violation of covenants stated in firms' debt agreements (Dichev & Skinner, 2002; Defond and Jiambalvo, 1994). The managers of firms with the risk of covenant breach generally attempt managing earnings (Koh, 2003). Therefore, leverage is expected to positively

Table 2. Yearly accrual model parameters based on industry classification

Variable	2006			2007			2008		
	B			β			β		
	M[1]	W[2]	T[3]	M	W	T	M	W	T
$1/A_{it-1}$	-630218	1119474	2917929	-697061	2795207	-864752	617542	5171061	-1708107
$(\Delta REV_{it}-\Delta AR_{it})/A_{it-1}$	0.0369679	-0.0263529	0.2500612	-0.0047510	0.0815472	0.2034227	-0.0597786	0.0441135	0.0690721
PPE_{it}/A_{it-1}	-0.0970183	-0.0863028	0.1591070	-0.0828579	0.0633885	0.1953376	0.1302244	-0.0709516	0.1172318
ROA_{it}	0.6820215	0.5450072	1.9959730	0.2696876	1.7868570	0.6072717	-0.0760069	-0.3529141	3.7489590
Adj. R^2	0.4011***	0.3447**	0.6436*	0.1621***	0.1121	0.0626	0.0045	0.0507	0.5654*
Variable	2009			2010			2011		
	β			β			β		
	M	W	T	M	W	T	M	W	T
$1/A_{it-1}$	-706359	268258	1047414	-646508	3674566	-2328430	1190696	302079	1209665
$(\Delta REV_{it}-\Delta AR_{it})/A_{it-1}$	0.0535408	0.0234360	-0.0314628	-0.0239895	-0.2131556	1.1859260	0.1220534	-0.1184526	0.0912950
PPE_{it}/A_{it-1}	-0.1239156	-0.0622188	-0.2616300	-0.0626651	0.0095781	-0.2898144	0.0014978	-0.1222087	-0.3153770
ROA_{it}	-0.4393021	0.7293484	1.2580420	-0.0798041	1.5115160	-0.6485374	-0.2403188	0.5940320	1.2998630
Adj. R^2	0.0878***	0.1833*	0.4965	-0.0109	0.5003***	0.5715*	0.0968***	0.4348***	0.8634***

1. Manufacturing Industry; 2. Wholesale and Retail Trade; 3. Technology
*, **, *** indicate significance at the 10%, 5%, and 1% levels, respectively

affect abnormal accruals. The study controlled for leverage with the ratio of total debt to total assets ratio (LEVR). Firms with extreme levels of profitability (most or least profitable) are generally more inclined to engage in discretionary accruals (McNichols, 2000). Mitra (2002) suggested that high discretionary adjustments were correlated with firm performance. Thus, a variable to control for this relationship is included in the regressions (ROA, return on assets).

A dummy variable (AUDQ), is employed to control for whether one of Big Four Auditors[1] is the company's auditor in line with the studies of Koh (2003), Ebrahim, (2004), Hsu and Koh (2005), Lin et al. (2009), Baxter and Cotter (2009), Adıgüzel, (2012). A dummy variable (LOSS) is used to account for the impact of losses on discretionary accruals, since a positive association between earnings management practices and the incidences of loss is verified by some authors (Baxter and Cotter, 2009; Prawitt et al. 2009).

Firms tend to smooth temporary fluctuations in their cash flows by accruals (Dechow, 1994). Although a negative correlation is expected between cash flow fluctuations and accruals, this negative relation is expected to decline over longer measurement periods due to difficulty of matching problems. As emphasized by Hsu and Koh (2005), if a firm's cash flow from operations is high, its accruals would be low, which is also true for the opposite. Cash flow from operations scaled down by total assets (CFOASST) is used to control this phenomenon.

Accounting discretion in earnings management is regarded to be positively influenced by the firms' liquidity position. Changes in working capital or cash flows from operations result in changes in a company's liquidity position. As changes in operating cash flows are already incorporated in accrual determination, the impact of liquidity on discretionary accruals is controlled by use of cash ratio (CASHR).

5. METHODOLOGY

As the collected data had both cross-sectional (firms) and time dimensions, panel data methodology is adopted to analyze the data at hand. Breusch and Pagan (1979) test states that when the assumptions of homoscedastic disturbances and fixed coefficients are not fulfilled, invalid inferences may result due to biases in estimated standard errors, and OLS estimation may lead to substantial loss in efficiency. The model developed in this study is tested for heteroskedasticity with the Breusch-Pagan test. When the test results in small p-value, GLS (generalized least squares) method should be used. The proposed model is also tested for serial correlation (autocorrelation). Autocorrelation results in consistent but inefficient estimates of regression coefficients and biased standard errors (Baltagi, 2001). Wooldridge test is utilized to detect the existence of serial correlation. The test revealed that serial correlation did not exist.

First regression equation below (4) assessed whether institutional investors act as an external control mechanism in mitigating managers' ability to opportunistically manage accruals

$$\begin{aligned}ABSDAC_{it} &= \beta_0 + \beta_1 INST_{it} + \beta_2 LNASST_{it} + \beta_3 LEVR_{it} + \beta_4 ROA_{it} \\ &+ \beta_5 AUDQ_{it} + \beta_6 LOSS_{it} + \beta_7 CFOASST_{it} + \beta_8 CASHR_{it} + \varepsilon_{it}\end{aligned} \tag{4}$$

The second model includes (Equation 5) the square of the percentage of shares that are held by institutional investors in line with the studies of Koh (2003) and Hsu and Koh (2005). This model aimed to evaluate the existence of potential variations in the relationship between the absolute value of discretionary accruals and institutional shareholding. The influence exerted by institutional investors may be varying with the percentage of the shareholding.

$$ABSDAC_{it} = \beta_0 + \beta_1 INST_{it} + \beta_2 INST^2_{it} + \beta_3 LNASST_{it} + \beta_4 LEVR_{it} + \beta_5 ROA_{it} + \beta_6 AUDQ_{it} + \beta_7 LOSS_{it} + \beta_8 CFOASST_{it} + \beta_9 CASHR_{it} + \varepsilon_{it} \quad (5)$$

6. RESULTS

Table 3 presents the results of GLS (generalized least squares) estimations for the aggregate effect of institutional ownership on the absolute value of discretionary accruals. Industry dummies (denoted by the utilization of I in parenthesis) are included whenever appropriate. As the significant variables are same with and without industrial dummies (MGLS and MGLS (I)), the former model is chosen for the evaluation of findings.

The hypothesized monitoring role of institutional shareholders is found to be highly significant. The tendency of managers to engage in aggressive earnings management practices seem to be restrained by the existence of institutional investors. Institutional investors exert their influence mainly by application of corporate governance practices. It is argued that sophisticated investors caused monitoring and disciplining of corporate managers and eventual reduction in agency costs (Mitani, 2010). It is also found that firm size significantly but negatively influenced earnings management in line with the studies of Bushee (1997), Rajgopal and Venkatachalam (1997), Rajgopal et al. (1999), Mitra (2002), Mitra and Cready (2005), Koh (2007), Baxter and Cotter (2009), Smith and Watts (1992). As suggested by Rajgopal et al. (1999), managerial opportunities in accounting discretion is reduced in larger firms because of close oversight of security analysts. Thus, relatively higher information transparency in larger firms is found to alleviate managers' discretionary behaviors.

The increase in the level of accrual management with the increase in firms' leverage is expressed by the positive and significant coefficient of the variable LEVR. This finding is anticipated since, it was also revealed in previous empirical studies which exhibited that risk of debt covenant violations triggered use of slack in accounting choices (Defond & Jiambalvo, 1994; Koh, 2003; Lin et al. 2009). Firms try to manipulate accounting numbers to avoid the probability of financial distress (Smith & Stulz, 1985). Financial performance has also been shown to affect discretionary accruals. Profitable firms are more inclined to engage in income increasing discretionary accruals, whereas less profitable firms tend to engage in income increasing discretionary accruals (McNichols, 2000).

ROA is found to be positively and significantly related to ABSDAC which is also justified by the Dechow et al. (1995). They argued the importance of controlling for financial performance while studying earnings management. However, there is no consensus in literature on the effect of inclusion of financial performance related

Table 3. The results of regressions

Dependent Variable: ABSDAC				
Explanatory and Control Variables	Estimated Coefficients (z-Value)			
	1st Model		2nd Model	
	MGLS	MGLS(I)	MGLS	MGLS(I)
INST	-0.0213	-0.0174	-0.0499	-0.0394
	(-2.89)***	(-2.35)**	(-2.22)**	(-1.74)*
INST²			0.0327	0.0248
			(1.35)	(1.03)
LNASST	-0.0040	-0.0041	-0.0041	-0.0041
	(-2.49)**	(-2.56)**	(-2.53)**	(-2.59)***
LEVR	0.0820	0.0827	0.0814	0.0820
	(8.02)***	(8.02)***	(7.95)***	(7.93)***
ROA	0.2801	0.2865	0.2823	0.2874
	(7.88)***	(8.05)***	(7.93)***	(8.07)***
AUDQ	-0.0012	-0.0020	-0.0020	-0.0026
	(-0.29)	(-0.49)	(-0.47)	(-0.63)
LOSS	0.0126	0.0106	0.0120	0.0103
	(2.11)**	(1.76)*	(2.01)**	(1.71)*
CFOASST	-0.2156	-0.2223	-0.2152	-0.2218
	(-9.06)***	(-9.37)***	(-9.04)***	(-9.35)***
CASHR	0.0106	0.0097	0.0106	0.0096
	(3.52)***	(3.25)***	(3.52)***	(3.24)***
INDUSTRY	No	Yes	No	Yes
Constant	0.1227	0.1326	0.1278	0.1369
	(4.12)***	(4.28)***	(4.26)***	(4.38)***
Number of observations	1010	1010	1010	1010
Number of groups	174	174	174	174
Wald chi²	180.28	187.87	181.82	188.93
Prob > chi²	0.0000	0.0000	0.0000	0.0000

*p<0.10; **p<0.05; ***p<0.01

control variable. Lin et al. (2009) documented a negative and significant relation between ROA and abnormal accruals, whereas Adıgüzel (2012) verified both insignificant and significant but negative relationship between ROA and the absolute value of discretionary accruals. Managers of firms at loss are also found to engage in accruals management (significant coefficient of the dichotomous variable LOSS). Other studies provided similar results (Baxter and Cotter, 2009; Prawitt et al. 2009).

Confirming the studies of Koh (2007), Chung et al. (2002) and Lin and Manowan (2012), the expected negative relationship between the control variable cash flow from operations to assets ratio (CFOASST) is verified by the significant and negative coefficient revealed. The results validated the contention that firms that have high (low) levels of cash flow from operations will have low (high) levels of accruals. Likewise, firms with low levels of accruals is expected to have less discretionary accruals than those with high levels of accruals. (Hsu & Koh, 2005).

The positive and significant relationship between firms' liquidity (CASHR) and earnings management practice are consistent with the prediction that managers of firms with higher levels of liquidity express more discretion in managing accruals. This relationship is also demonstrated in the studies of Mitra (2002), and Mitra and Cready (2005). Contrary to the expectation, being audited by one of the Big Four Auditors do not seem to have any effect on managerial incentives to adjust reported earnings, which is in conformity with the prior studies of Chtourou et al. (2001), Adıgüzel (2012), and Koh (2007).

The result of the second model is in line with the first model. However, the insignificant coefficient of $INST^2$ rejects the existence of nonlinear relationship. Thus, these findings reject the argument of co-existence of the differential impact of transient and long-term oriented institutions in the portfolio firms' earnings management practices. Consequently, it is appropriate to conclude that no variation is observed as to the direction of the relationship in the link between institutional shareholding and the absolute value of discretionary accruals as the level of ownership varies. The reported linear association has been confirmed by the various other studies in literature (Rajgopal & Venkatachalam, 1997; Rajgopal, et al. 1999; Mitra & Cready, 2005; Koh, 2007). The control variables LNASST, LEVR, ROA, LOSS, CFOASST, and CASHR are found to be statistically significant. Their magnitude and signs are in line with those of the previous model. High quality auditing, which is proxied by a dummy variable of being audited by one of the Big Four Auditors, is not found to have any influence on managerial incentives of earnings management.

It is not right to reach a direct conclusion from the negative relationship between earnings management and the level of institutional stockholding, since the drivers of the results require further analysis. As initially hypothesized, it is possible that the monitoring role of institutional shareholders have mitigated discretionary choices of managers regarding corporate earnings. However, it is also possible that due to the clientele effect, institutional investors might have disproportionately invested in firms with certain characteristics. Thus, what is inferred from the study is affected by the existence of certain exogenous factors which may be drivers of institutional investment in those firms that display a low level of accrual management. This ambiguity of causal relationship is addressed with a similar methodology suggested in the studies of Wahal and McConnell (2000), Mitra (2002), and Mitra and Cready (2005).

Two-stage least squares (2SLS) regression is employed to deal with the impact of clientele effect, which can affect the association between accounting flexibility and institutional ownership. INST is regressed on firm-specific factors that attract institutional investors to the firm's shareholding structure in the first-stage panel data model as given in the equation (6) below:

$$INST_{it} = \beta_0 + \beta_1 LNMVE_{it} + \beta_2 LEVR_{it} + \beta_3 ROA_{it} + \beta_4 AUDQ_{it} + \beta_5 DIVYIELD_{it} + \beta_6 MVBV_{it} + \beta_7 RDSALES_{it} + \varepsilon_{it} \quad (6)$$

where;

$LNMVE_{it}$ = Natural log of market value of equity in year *t* for firm *i;*
$DIVYIELD_{it}$ = The ratio of dividend per share to price per share in year *t* for firm *i;*
$MVBV_{it}$ = The ratio of market value of equity to book value of equity in year *t* for firm *i;*
$RDSALES_{it}$ = The ratio of net income to total assets in year *t* for firm *i;*

and all other variables are defined same as before. The estimated intercept and coefficients from the first-stage regression are used to compute the value of PINST that proxied for predicted value of institutional ownership based on exogenous factors. Accordingly, the value of UNEXPINST is generated as the difference between the actual value of institutional ownership and predicted value of institutional ownership denoted by INST and PINST, respectively. The equation can be demonstrated as in Equation 7 below:

$$UNEXPINST_{it} = INST_{it} - PINST_{it} \quad (7)$$

To differentiate between the significance of monitoring and clientele effects on accrual management, the second stage regression is estimated with the below equation (8):

$$ABSDAC_{it} = \beta_0 + \beta_1 LNASST_{it} + \beta_2 LEVR_{it} + \beta_3 ROA_{it} + \beta_4 AUDQ_{it} + \beta_5 LOSS_{it} + \beta_6 CFOASST_{it} + \beta_7 CASHR_{it} + \beta_8 PINST_{it} + \beta_9 UNEXPINST_{it} + \varepsilon_{it} \quad (8)$$

where;

$PINST_{it}$ = Predicted value of institutional ownership estimated from the intercept and coefficients of Equation 6 in year *t* for firm *i;*

$UNEXPINST_{it}$ = Unexpected value of institutional ownership not determined by firm-specific exogenous factors in year *t* for firm *i;*

and all other variables are defined and denoted as before.

In the second regression, PINST and UNEXPINST replace INST in Equation 4. PINST stands for institutional investment influenced by firm-specific factors other than ABSDAC. UNEXPINST stand for some part of the ABSDAC-driven institutional ownership. Therefore, these variables represent a causal relationship and a partial clientele effect, respectively. These two variables should not be correlated as they proxy for different dimensions of institutional shareholding. Based on prior studies (Mitra & Cready, 2005), the coefficient of both PINST and UNEXPINST is expected to be negative. A negative coefficient of PINST eliminates the potential influence of ABSDAC on INST, and leads us conclude on the clear monitoring role of institutional investors that mitigate earnings management activities of managers.

The negative and significant coefficient of PINST (Table 4) eliminates the possibility of ABSDAC influencing PINST. Additionally, the significant and negative coefficient of UNEXPINST provides support for a partial clientele effect with the coefficient being less than that of PINST, but still demonstrating the dominance of the causal relationship. Regarding the findings related to the coefficients of PINST and INST, (Table 3 and 4) PINST is documented to have a more robust negative relationship with ABSDAC than INST of the first model with the coefficients being -0.0493 and -0.0213, respectively. Thus, the monitoring role of institutional investors is found to be the dominant factor of the overall negative relationship between ABSDAC and INST in the main model of the study. Accordingly, only a partial influence can be attributed to the tendency of institutional investors to divert their portfolios to firms with lower accrual management practices.

7. CONCLUSION

Earnings management practices is a long-debated issue. The agents might act in their own self-interest rather than that of the principal. The mismatch between the goals and desires of the principle and the agent results in conflict of interest which brings in agency costs. Corporate governance practices that alleviate agency costs

Institutional investors are the main element of the conceptual framework of the hypotheses generated in this study. The rise in the level of institutional ownership and accompanying degree of activism result in this specific class of investors' acting as an external control mechanism. Concentration of shares in the hands of institutional

Table 4. The results of the two-stage least squares analysis of institutional monitoring influence on earning management

Dependent Variable: ABSDAC			
Explanatory and Control Variables	**Coefficient Estimates**	**Standard Errors**	**z-Statistics**
LNASST	-0.0063	0.0022	-2.90***
LEVR	0.1018	0.0070	14.51***
ROA	0.3747	0.0181	20.73***
AUDQ	0.0014	0.0040	0.35
LOSS	0.0246	0.0029	8.46***
CFOASST	-0.1826	0.0139	-13.08***
CASHR	0.0088	0.0016	5.48***
PINST	-0.0493	0.0234	-2.11**
UNEXPINST	-0.0106	0.0059	-1.78*
constant	0.1699	0.0360	4.73***
Number of observations		982	
Number of groups		171	
Wald $chi^2(9)$		2108.67	
Prob > chi^2		0.0000	

*p<0.10; **p<0.05; ***p<0.01

owners is considered to mitigate agency costs stemming from earnings management practices. Consequently, the current study is founded on the interrelation among the concepts of earnings management, institutional investors, and corporate governance within the framework provided by agency theory.

The study verified that aggregate institutional ownership provided negative influence on managerial discretion exercised in opportunistic management of accruals. Thus, the managers' tendency to engage in earnings management practices is found to be mitigated by institutional shareholdings demonstrating the influence of investor sophistication in monitoring and disciplining corporate managers in line with the findings of previous studies in literature. Secondly, it is also shown that the active monitoring role played, and myopic behavior induced by institutional investors are mutually exclusive within the Turkish context. No variation in the relation between the main variables is expected as the level of institutional ownership changes. Additional analyses performed demonstrated the existence of an only partial influence of clientele effect. Overall negative relationship between absolute value of discretionary accruals (ABSDAC) and institutional ownership (INST) mainly occurred due to the monitoring role of institutional investors.

REFERENCES

Adıgüzel, H. (2012). *The effect of internal corporate governance structure to the earnings management practice in Turkey* (Ph.D. Thesis). Marmara University Institute of Social Sciences.

Atik, A. (2009). Detecting income-smoothing behaviors of Turkish listed companies through empirical tests using discretionary accounting changes. *Critical Perspectives on Accounting*, *20*(5), 591–613. doi:10.1016/j.cpa.2008.01.003

Atik, A., & Ismail, T. H. (2011). Ethical perceptions on earnings manipulation in Turkey: An exploration of differences in preparers' and users' perspectives. *Research Journal of Finance and Accounting*, *2*(3), 169–186.

Ayarlıoğlu, M. A. (2007). *Kar Yönetimi Uygulamaları ve İstanbul Menkul Kıymetler Borsası'nda Test Edilmesi* (Ph.D. Thesis). Hacettepe University Institute of Social Sciences.

Baltagi, B. H. (2001). *Econometric analysis of panel data* (2nd ed.). John Wiley & Sons, Ltd.

Bartov, E., Gul, F. A., & Tsui, J. S. L. (2001). Discretionary-accruals models and audit qualifications. *Journal of Accounting and Economics*, *30*(3), 421–452. doi:10.1016/S0165-4101(01)00015-5

Baxter, P., & Cotter, J. (2009). Audit committees and earnings quality'. *Accounting and Finance*, *49*(2), 267–290. doi:10.1111/j.1467-629X.2008.00290.x

Baysinger, B. D., Kosnik, R. D., & Turk, T. A. (1991). Effects of board and ownership structure on corporate R&D strategy. *Academy of Management Journal*, *34*(1), 205–214. doi:10.2307/256308

Breusch, T. S., & Pagan, A. R. (1979). A simple test for heteroscedasticity and randon coefficient variation. *Econometrica*, *47*(5), 1287–1294. doi:10.2307/1911963

Bushee, B. J. (1997). *Institutional investors, longterm investment and earnings management* (Ph.D. Thesis). University of Michigan.

Bushee, B. J. (1998). The influence of institutional investors on myopic R&D investment behavior. *The Accounting Review*, *73*(3), 305–333.

Cheng, C. S. A., & Reitenga, A. (2009). Characteristics of institutional investors and discretionary accruals. *International Journal of Accounting and Information Management, 17*(1), 5–26. doi:10.1108/18347640910967717

Chtourou, S. M., Bedard, J., & Courteau, L. (2001). *Corporate governance and earnings management*. Retrieved from http://ssrn.com/abstract=275053

Chung, R., Firth, M., & Kim, J.-B. (2002). Institutional monitoring and opportunistic earnings management. *Journal of Corporate Finance, 8*(1), 29–48. doi:10.1016/S0929-1199(01)00039-6

Cornett, M. M., Marcus, A. J., Saunders, A., & Tehranian, H. (2007). The impact of institutional ownership on corporate operating performance. *Journal of Banking & Finance, 31*(6), 1771–1794. doi:10.1016/j.jbankfin.2006.08.006

Cornett, M. M., Marcus, A. J., & Tehranian, H. (2008). Corporate governance and pay-for-performance: The impact of earnings management. *Journal of Financial Economics, 87*, 357–373. doi:.jfineco.2007.03.00310.1016/j

David, P., & Kochhar, R. (1996). Barriers to effective governance by institutional investors: Implications for theory and practice. *European Management Journal, 14*(5), 457–466. doi:10.1016/0263-2373(96)00039-4

Dechow, P. M. (1994). Accounting earnings and cash flows as measures of firm performance: The role of accounting accruals. *Journal of Accounting and Economics, 18*(1), 3–42. doi:10.1016/0165-4101(94)90016-7

Dechow, P. M., Sloan, R. G., & Sweeney, A. P. (1995). Detecting earnings management. *The Accounting Review, 70*(2), 193–225.

Dechow, P. M., Sloan, R. G., & Sweeney, A. P. (1996). Causes and consequences of earnings manipulations: An analysis of firms subject to enforcement actions by the SEC. *Contemporary Accounting Research, 13*(1), 1–36. doi:10.1111/j.1911-3846.1996.tb00489.x

DeFond, M. L., & Jiambalvo, J. (1994). Debt covenant violation and manipulation of accruals. *Journal of Accounting and Economics, 17*(1-2), 145–176. doi:10.1016/0165-4101(94)90008-6

Dichev, I. D., & Skinner, D. J. (2002). Largesample evidence on the debt covenant hypothesis. *Journal of Accounting Research, 40*(4), 1091–1123. doi:10.1111/1475-679X.00083

Duggal, R., & Millar, J. A. (1999). Institutional ownership and firm performance: The case of bidder returns. *Journal of Corporate Finance*, *5*(2), 103–117. doi:10.1016/S0929-1199(98)00018-2

Duman, H. (2010). *Kamunun Aydınlatılması İlkesi Kapsamında Kazanç Yönetimi Uygulamalarının Finansal Raporlama Kalitesi ve Şirket Performansı Üzerine Etkisi: İMKB'de Bir Uygulama* (Ph.D. Thesis). Selçuk University Institute of Social Sciences.

Ebrahim, A. M. (2004). *The effectiveness of corporate governance, institutional ownership, and audit quality as monitoring devices of earnings management* (Ph.D. Thesis). Graduate School Newark, State University of New Jersey.

Eng, L. L. (1995). *The implications of managerial incentives and institutional ownership for firms' research and development (R&D) investments* (Ph.D. Thesis). University of Michigan.

Godfrey, J., Hodgson, A., Tarca, A., Hamilton, J., & Holmes, S. (2010). Accounting theory (7th ed.). John Wiley & Sons Australia, Ltd.

Graves, S. B. (1988). Institutional ownership and corporate R&D in the computer industry. *Academy of Management Journal*, *31*(2), 417–428. doi:10.2307/256557

Hansen, G. A. (1999). *Bias and estimation error in discretionary accrual models.* Working Paper, Penn State University. Retrieved from http://ssrn.com/abstract=192748

Hansen, G. S., & Hill, C. W. L. (1991). Are institutional investors myophic? A time-series study of four technology-driven industries. *Strategic Management Journal*, *12*(1), 1–16. doi:10.1002mj.4250120102

Hill, C. W. L., & Hansen, G. S. (1989). Institutional holdings and corporate R&D intensity in research intensive industries. Academy of Management Best Papers Proceedings, 17-21.

Holthausen, R. W. (1990). Accounting method choice: Opportunistic behavior, efficient contracting, and information perspectives. *Journal of Accounting and Economics*, *12*(1-3), 207–218. doi:10.1016/0165-4101(90)90047-8

Holthausen, R. W., & Leftwich, R. W. (1983). the economic consequences of accounting choice implications of costly contracting and monitoring. *Journal of Accounting and Economics*, *5*(2), 77–119. doi:10.1016/0165-4101(83)90007-1

Hribar, P., & Collins, D. W. (2002). Errors in estimating accruals: Implications for empirical research. *Journal of Accounting Research*, *40*(1), 105–134. doi:10.1111/1475-679X.00041

Hsu, G. C.-M., & Koh, P.-S. (2005). Does the presence of institutional investors influence accruals management? Evidence from Australia. *Corporate Governance*, *13*(6), 809–823. doi:10.1111/j.1467-8683.2005.00472.x

Jones, J. J. (1991). Earnings management during import relief investigations. *Journal of Accounting Research*, *29*(2), 193–228. doi:10.2307/2491047

Karaibrahimoğlu, Y. (2010). *The role of corporate governance on earnings management: Quarterly evidence from Turkey* (Ph.D. Thesis). İzmir University of Economics.

Koh, P.-S. (2003). On the association between institutional ownership and aggressive corporate earnings management in Australia. *The British Accounting Review*, *35*(2), 105–128. doi:10.1016/S0890-8389(03)00014-3

Koh, P.-S. (2007). Institutional investor type, earnings management and benchmark beaters. *Journal of Accounting and Public Policy*, *26*(3), 267–299. doi:10.1016/j.jaccpubpol.2006.10.001

Kothari, S. P., Leone, A. J., & Wasley, C. E. (2005). Performance matched discretionary accrual measures. *Journal of Accounting and Economics*, *39*(1), 163–197. doi:10.1016/j.jacceco.2004.11.002

Lin, L., & Manowan, P. (2012). Institutional ownership composition and earnings management. *Review of Pacific Basin Financial Markets and Policies*, *15*(4), 1250022. doi:10.1142/S0219091512500221

Lin, T., Hutchinson, M., & Percy, M. (2009). The role of audit committee and institutional investors in constraining earnings management: Evidence from Chinese firms listed in Hong Kong. *Proceedings of Accounting & Finance Association of Australia & New Zealand Annual Conference,* 1-40.

Liu, A. Z. (2005). *The role of financial analysts and institutional investors in the numbers game.* Retrieved from http://ssrn.com/abstract=705385

Majumdar, S. K., & Nagarajan, A. (1997). The impact of changing stock ownership patterns in the United States: Theoretical implications and some evidence. *Revue d'Economie Industrielle, 82*(1), 39–54. doi:10.3406/rei.1997.1686

McNichols, M. F. (2000). Research design issues in earnings management studies. *Journal of Accounting and Public Policy, 19*(4-5), 313–345. doi:10.1016/S0278-4254(00)00018-1

Mitani, H. (2010). *Additional evidence on earnings management and corporate governance.* Financial Research and Training Center Discussion Paper Series. DP 2009-7.

Mitra, S. (2002). *The impact of institutional stock ownership on a firm's earnings management practice: An empirical investigation* (Ph.D. Thesis). Louisiana State University and Agricultural and Mechanical College.

Mitra, S., & Cready, W. M. (2005). Institutional ownership, accrual management, and information environment. *Journal of Accounting, Auditing & Finance, 20*(3), 257–286. doi:10.1177/0148558X0502000304

Porter, M. E. (1992). Capital disadvantage: America's failing capital investment system. *Harvard Business Review*, 65–82. PMID:10121317

Prawitt, D. F., Jason, L. S., & Wood, D. A. (2009). Internal audit quality and earnings management. *The Accounting Review, 84*(4), 1255–1280. doi:10.2308/accr.2009.84.4.1255

Rajgopal, S., & Venkatachalam, M. (1997). *The role of institutional investors in corporate governance: An empirical investigation.* Research Paper, 1436.

Rajgopal, S., Venkatachalam, M., & Jiambalvo, J. (1999). *Is institutional ownership associated with earnings management and the extent to which stock prices reflect future earnings?* SSRN Working Paper Series.

Scott, W. R. (2011). *Financial accounting theory* (6th ed.). Pearson Prentice Hall.

Smith, C., & Watts, R. (1992). The investment opportunity set and corporate financing, dividend, and compensation policies. *Journal of Financial Economics, 32*(3), 263–292. doi: X (92)90029-W10.1016/0304405

Smith, C. W., & Stulz, R. M. (1985). The determinants of firms' hedging policies. *Journal of Financial and Quantitative Analysis, 20*(4), 391–405. doi:10.2307/2330757

Wahal, S., & McConnell, J. J. (2000). Do institutional investors exacerbate managerial myopia? *Journal of Corporate Finance*, *6*(3), 307–329. doi:10.1016/S0929-1199(00)00005-5

Xie, H. (2001). The mispricing of abnormal accruals. *Accounting Review, 76*(3), 357-373. Doi: . 2001.76.3.35710.2308/accr

ENDNOTE

1 The Big Four Auditing firms operating in Turkey at the time of the study are named as Deloitte, Ernst & Young, KPMG, and PWC.

Chapter 11
Measuring Compliance With IFRS Mandatory Disclosure Requirements:
Some Evidence From Greece

Apostolos Ballas
Athens University of Economics and Business, Greece

Christos Tzovas
Athens University of Economics and Business, Greece

Nicos Sykianakis
Piraeus University of Applied Sciences, Greece

Constantinos Vassilakopoulos
Athens University of Economics and Business, Greece

ABSTRACT

This chapter examines Greek firms' compliance with IFRS mandatory disclosure requirements for the years 2006 and 2008. Using a checklist based on the IFRS disclosure requirements, a compliance score was calculated for each sample firm. Two methods of measuring compliance are used: the dichotomous method and the partial compliance method. By adopting both approaches proposed in literature for measuring compliance, the authors enhance the robustness of the findings of this study, while they provide empirical evidence concerning the extent to which the two approaches provide significantly different results. Further, they investigated firms' characteristics that are hypothesized to be related with disclosure compliance. It appears that closely held firms exhibit higher compliance rate. In addition, there is a positive association between the engagement of a Big-4 international auditing firm and disclosure compliance. Firms' profitability, leverage, and size do not explain disclosure compliance. The authors found that the two methods of measuring compliance do not produce significantly different results.

DOI: 10.4018/978-1-5225-6114-9.ch011

1. INTRODUCTION

International Financial Reporting Standars (IFRS henceforth) adoption has been hypothesised to improve reporting standards, while their uniform adoption allows for greater comparability. As a result firms' information IFRS implementation improves firm's information environment and contributes toward a lower cost of capital (Sunder, 2007; Bova and Pereira, 2012). However, recent research has shown that the overall comparability effect of mandatory IFRS adoption is marginal (Cascino and Gassen, 2015), and that costs exceed the benefits of reporting under IFRS (Fox et al. 2015). In case of Greece, previous research has indicated that Greek accountants and auditors believe that the introduction of IFRS will improve the quality of financial statements prepared by Greek firms. They believe that the implementation of IFRS improves the understandability, relevance, reliability and comparability of financial statements (Karamanis and Papadakis, 2008; Naoum et al. 2011).

This study investigates Greek companies' compliance to disclosure requirements provided by IFRS and the factors that may explain compliance. The published financial statements of a sample of 58 Greek firms have been examined. In order to enhance the robustness of the findings of this study the compliance rate has been calculated by employing two approaches proposed in the literature, i.e. the commonly used dichotomous approach and the alternative partial compliance unweighted approach. Previous research found that the two methods can produce significantly different results (see, Street and Gray, 2001; Tsalavoutas et al. 2010; Mazni and Marizah, 2013; Rajhi, 2014).

Within this study we examine the disclosure compliance with the most important disclosure items of all IFRS. Many prior studies have examined the disclosure compliance with specific IFRS. As a result the total number of disclosure items that are examined in this study is significantly higher comparing to disclosure items examined in previous studies. Given the characteristics of the Greek business environment, this study investigates disclosure compliance in a country outside the Anglo-Saxon accounting paradigm. In Greece, as in many European countries (e.g. France, Italy), most firms' ownership structure is highly concentrated (Nobes and Parker, 2000; Rodosthenous, 2012), while the main providers of funds for Greek companies are banks. Furthermore, in Greece there is a close linkage between tax accounting and financial reporting. These factors are generally not associated with high disclosure compliance and high quality published financial statements (Nobes and Parker, 2000). In fact Greek companies appear to engage in some of the most extreme earnings management practices in the world (see, Bhattacharya et al., 2003; Leuz et al., 2003). Therefore, we would expect that the compliance of Greek firms with the IFRS disclosure requirements would not be particularly high.

Our findings indicate that the average compliance rate under the dichotomous approach is 75%, while under the partial compliance unweighted method the compliance rate is 71.2%. Similarly to previous research (Tsalavoutas et al. 2010; Mazni and Marizah, 2013; Rajhi, 2014) we found that the partial compliance method produces lower aggregate compliance scores. However, in our case, the observed relationship is not statistically significant.

The findings of statistical analysis suggest that ownership structure and the type of the external auditor applied are significant factors explaining compliance. Leverage, size and profitability appear to have less explanatory power. The results were similar under the two methods employed in this study for measuring disclosure compliance.

The rest of this paper is organised as follows. In Section 2 we present the hypothesis tested within this paper. In section 3 the sample and the research design followed in this article are described. Section 4 reports the results of the empirical investigation. Section 5 summarizes and concludes the paper.

2. MEASURING COMPLIANCE AND HYPOTHESIS

With respect to the measuring of firms' disclosure compliance two are the main approaches proposed in the literature. The most common approach, known also as the "dichotomous approach", adopts an unweigheted disclosure index (see Ali et al. 2004).The disclosure compliance of a company is depicted as the value a compliance ratio computed for each firm. The compliance ratio is the ratio of what a company disclosed in its annual report to what it is obliged to disclose for each category of disclosure. Thus, disclosure ratio under the dichotomous approach has been calculated as follows:

$$C_j = \frac{T = \sum_{i=1}^{n} di}{M = \sum_{i=1}^{m} di} \tag{1}$$

where:

C_j = the total compliance score for each company and $0 \leq C_j \leq 1$
T = is the total number of items disclosed (di) by company j
M = the maximum number of applicable disclosure items for company j that could have been disclosed

This approach gives equal weight to the specific items required to be disclosed by all standards. As a consequence, it gives greater weight to standards that require more items to be disclosed (Tsalavoutas et al. 2010). Although, this method has been employed in most studies examining disclosure compliance, it appears to have the serious limitation that does not treat each standard equally (Tsalavoutas et al. 2010). Given that some standards require a large number of items to be disclosed while others a few items, the standards that require more items to be disclosed are not treated equally with these standards that require few items to be disclosed (Al-Shiab, 2008).

An alternative approach proposed in the literature is the "partial compliance unweigheted method" (see Street and Gray, 2001; Al-Shiab 2008). This approach is based on the assumption that each standard is of equal importance and gives equal weight to each standard (Tsalavoutas et al. 2010). Under this approach, the compliance rate of each entity is measured by adding the degree of each standard and the diving the total by the number of standards applicable to each company.

Under the "partial compliance unweigheted method" the compliance with each standard is calculated separately. Then the sum of these compliance scores (*X*) is divided by the total number of applicable standards (*R*) for each sample firm *j*. Thus the compliance score for each firm is calculated as follows:

$$PCj = \frac{\sum_{i=1} Xi}{Rj} \quad (2)$$

where PCj is the total compliance score for each company and $0 \leq PCj \leq 1$

Prior empirical evidence suggests that the two methods can produce different results. Street and Gray (2001) found different significant associations under each method between disclosure compliance and a number of independent variables. Tsalavoutas et al. (2010) found that the two methods produce significantly different results. Similarly, Mazni and Marizah, (2013) found that the partial compliance method produces significantly lower aggregate compliance scores. The partial compliance method will produce a more conservative estimate of the aggregate compliance scores. On the other hand, the dichotomous method will give more weight to standards with more disclosure items. Rajhi (2014) provides evidence that the partial compliance approach provide significantly different score from the dichotomous approach. In particular, the dichotomous approach provides a higher compliance score than the partial compliance approach. On the basis of the findings of prior studies we formulated the following hypothesis:

H: The dichotomous method produces significantly different compliance scores from the partial compliance method.

To test the hypothesis, both the dichotomous and the partial compliance methods are applied to the compliance scores, which are derived from a disclosure checklist, which include the most important disclosure items of all IFRS. For each category of disclosure it has determined which elements should be disclosed. Subsequently it has been examined whether the sample firms made the appropriate disclosures in their annual report. For each item of disclosure there are three possibilities: the information item is disclosed in the annual reports (OK); the information item is not disclosed item in the annual reports because it is not applicable in the particular company (non-applicable NA); the information item is not disclosed item in the annual reports despite the fact it is applicable in the particular company and this company should disclose it (non-mentioned, NM). An issue with scoring disclosures in financial statements is whether or not an undisclosed information item is applicable to a sample firm. Several measures have been proposed in literature for dealing with this issue. Cooke (1989) proposed annual reports to be thoroughly examined before they were scored in order to determine whether the undisclosed information items were indeed inapplicable to the companies. Alternatively, the applicability of some items was determined by logical reasoning (Owusu-Ansah, 2000). For instance, it is sensible to expect a firm to disclose its accounting policy for securities valuation, if it owns a portfolio of securities. Both measures were adopted in this study.

In order to test the hypothesis, we examined whether the two methods provide significantly results in respect to the impact of various factors upon firms' disclosure compliance. In particular, we investigated the impact of the following factors:

- Leverage
- Ownership structure
- Corporate size
- Profitability
- Auditor type

Leverage and Disclosure Compliance

The creditors of highly leveraged firms have strong incentives to prompt their management to disclose more information (Amran et al., 2009). The highly leveraged firms tend to be more speculative and riskier while the debt-holders have greater power over the financial structure of such firms (Oliveira et al. 2011). On the other hand, it has been argued that creditors can obtain the information they need by sources other than annual reports (Leuz et al. 2004). Bank credit plays a dominant role in the financing of Greek business corporations. Banks developed a close relationship with many companies, while in certain cases they own part of their share capital. Thus, banks may directly obtain any relevant financial information, without having to rely upon publicly disclosed data. Consequently, the importance of public accounting information may further diminish. Within this context, the demand for disclosure compliance may not be high.

Prior research provides mixed evidence respecting the association between leverage and firms' disclosure compliance. Al Mutawaa and Hewaidy (2010) found no evidence that disclosure compliance is associated with the level of leverage. Md Khokan Bepari et al. (2014) examining the impact that global financial crisis had upon Australian firms compliance with IFRS 36 found that leverage is not significantly associated with compliance level. Simmilary, Atanasovski's (2015) findings suggest that leverage does not affect firm's compliance. On the other hand, Demir and Bahadi (2014) found that compliance is negatively associated with the level of leverage. Yet, Alanezi and Albuloushi (2011) found that Kuwaiti companies with higher level of leverage have higher level of compliance.

Ownership Status and Disclosure Compliance

Firms' disclosure compliance may be related with their ownership structure (Soderstrom and Sun, 2007). In more concentrated ownership structures there is less need for corporate disclosures since the major shareholders can actively monitor and control firms' management (Klassen, 1997; Birt et al., 2006). Within this context, lower disclosure compliance is expected for closely held firms. On the other hand, in the more diffused ownership structures small shareholders may face difficulties in monitoring firms' management (Barako et al., 2006). As a consequence, higher level of disclosure can be expected from widely-held firms. As mentioned above the ownership structure of most Greek firms is highly concentrated, particularly in the form of family ownership. In most cases, the owners are actively involved in their companies' administration by occupying important posts within the organizational structure of their firms (Sykianakis, 2004; Tzovas, 2006). Managers can communicate information regarding firm's performance directly to their superior owner-managers without having to rely upon financial statements. Under these circumstances, there are no strong incentives for firms to provide high quality financial disclosures.

In addition to information provision, national legal rules can be an additional mechanism that that contributes in the protection of shareholders' interests from opportunistic, self-interested and managerial behaviour (Florou and Galarniotis 2007). Greek legislation provides significant protection to shareholders' interests since the voting and dividend rights provided by the Greek legislation are quite significant. In particular, La Porta et al. (1998) found that Greece is one of only 11 (out of 49) countries that "impose genuinely one-share one-vote rules". Furthermore, is one of only seven (out of 49) countries, where firms have the legal obligation to pay as dividends a certain proportion of their profits. As a consequence, the role of accounting information as protection mechanism of shareholders' interest may not be crucial. Within this context, the demand for more accounting information may not be particularly high.

However, when ownership is concentrated to few controlling shareholders a conflict of interest may arise between them and minority shareholders (Setyadi et al. 2011). When large shareholders control firms they may pursue policies that aim to increase their benefits at the expense of minority shareholders (Shleifer and Vishny, 1997). Jensen and Meckling (1976) argue that convergence of interest can occur between outside investors and large shareholders when outside investors believe that large shareholders aim to maximize firm value. In this case outside investors will impose fewer contractual constraints in the firm. Within this context the larger shareholders will not have strong incentives to manipulate and/or withhold information. On the contrary they will have incentives to maintain level of disclosure consistent with the maximisation of the value of the firm. As a consequence, the association between owners' holdings and disclosure will be positive (Oliveira et al. 2011).

Prior research provides mixed evidence respecting the association between ownership structure and firms' disclosure compliance. Atanasovski's (2015) found that firms' compliance with IFRS 7 disclosure requirements is associated with ownership concentration. Mazni et al. (2015) found that family control is negatively related to disclosure for Malaysian firms. Similarly, the findings of Bova and Pereira (2012) suggest that greater foreign ownership leads to greater IFRS compliance. On the other hand, Alanezi and Albuloushi (2011) found that ownership diffusion does not explain Kuwaiti companies' disclosure compliance.

Corporate Size and Disclosure

Firm's size is a variable that can explain the quality of firm's disclosures (Cooke, 1989). Larger firms are more likely to be subject of political attention and scrutiny, and as a consequence to face higher political costs (Watts and Zimmerman, 1986). By providing extensive disclosures, larger firms aim to reduce their political costs (Moses, 1987; Ndubizu & Tsetsekos, 1992; Ali & Kumar, 1994; Iatrides, 2008). In addition, larger firms are usually characterised by diffused-ownership and a separation of management and ownership. Within this context, larger firms are expected to face higher agency costs. By disclosing more accounting information larger firms aim to reduce their agency cost (Zimmerman, 1983). Furthermore, the financial statements of larger firms are more likely to be thoroughly examined and analysed by financial analysts and shareholders. As a result, considerable pressure is exercised to larger firms to improve the quality of their disclosure (Hossain and Adams, 1995). Besides, larger firms are expected to possess the resources that are necessary for the preparation of an event such as the introduction of IFRS (Jones and Higgins, 2006). Al Mutawaa and Hewaidy (2010) found that company size has a positive and statistically significant association with IAS-required disclosures. Miihkinen (2012) found larger firms are more likely to report quantitative risk information. However, Md Khokan Bepari et al. (2014) found that firm size is associated with the compliance levels only when the industry effects are not controlled for. Alanezi and Albuloushi (2011) found firm's size is not associated with Kuwaiti companies' disclosure compliance.

Profitability and Disclosure

The compliance of a firm to the disclosure requirements is affected by the profitability of the firm (Palmer, 2008). When the introduction of a new or a revised accounting standard is expected to adversely affect firms' profitability, firms are more concerned about issues relating to the implementation of the new standard and the way they will communicate to their shareholders their continuing underlying profitability (Jones and Higgins, 2006). According to agency theory the managers of profitable firms will disclose financial information to the external users of accounts in order to advance their interests. They will disclose detailed information in order to continue in their positions and their compensation arrangements. On the basis of the political costs theory, it can be argued that the firms with large political visibility will have an incentive to disclose more information in order to justify the level of their profits (Inchausti, 1997). Within this context, it is expected that the more profitable firms will have higher compliance rates than the less profitable firms (Inchausti, 1997; Palmer, 2008). According to signalling theory the more profitable firms are more likely to provide the market with more and better accounting information (Verrecchia, 1983; Dye, 1985; Trueman, 1986; Jung Kwon, 1988; Miller, 2002). Thus their disclosure compliance it is expected to be high. It should be pointed, however, that a number of studies have not confirm the positive association between the quality of disclosure and the company's profitability (Lang and Lundholm, 1993; Wallace and Naser, 1995; Raffournier 1995; Alanezi and Albuloushi, 2011; Miihkinen, 2012;Atanasovski, 2015). On the other hand, Md Khokan Bepari et al. (2014) found that firm's profitability is positively associated with the compliance levels.

Auditor Type

The level of disclosure compliance is associated with the type of external auditors appointed (Street and Gray, 2001; Glaum and Street, 2003; Ali et al. 2004; Setyadi et al., 2011). In particular, it is argued that there is a positive association between the engagement of Big-4 international auditing firms and the level of a firm's disclosure compliance. The choice of external auditor is a mechanism that aims to minimize agency costs. The companies audited by the major auditing firms have significant agency costs and they attempt to reduce these costs by employing the major auditing firms (Setyadi et al., 2011). Tsalavoutas and Evans (2010) found that only companies with non-Big-4 auditors faced significant impact on net profit and liquidity on transition to IFRS. Chalmers and Godfrey (2004) argue that, in order to maintain their reputation and to avoid reputational costs, the larger and well-known auditing firms are more likely to demand higher levels of disclosure. Furthermore, the major international auditing firms have greater knowledge about IAS (Lopes and Rodrigues, 2007). In fact, Tsalavoutas and Evans (2010) found that the Greek firms that had experienced a smooth transition to IFRS, were the firms that were audited by Big-4 international auditing firms. Simmilary, Demir and Bahadi (2014) found that level of compliance of Turkish firms with IFRSs disclosures is positively related to firms being audited by Big 4 auditing firms. In the same line, Atanasovski (2015) found that sample firms' compliance with IFRS 7 disclosure requirements is associated with auditor type. Yet, Al Mutawaa and Hewaidy (2010) found that auditor-type has no impact upon firms disclosure compliance.

3. RESEARCH DESIGN

Sample Selection

The financial statements of a sample of Greek listed non-finance firms for the financial years 2006 and 2008 were examined. The year 2006 was the second year of compulsory application of IFRS for Greek firms. In order to smooth the progress of adoption of IFRS by Greek firms, in the first year of IFRS application (i.e. 2005), a number of exceptions were (unofficially) granted to firms with respect to the disclosures that they should include in their financial statements. These exceptions were over and above the exceptions allowed by IFRS1 for the first time adoption of IFRS. Therefore, if the present analysis was based on the 2005 financial statements, its results may not be indicative of the actual compliance of Greek firms. From 2009 onwards IFRS were subject of continuous revisions, while a number of revisions that had been decided in earlier periods became effective gradually after 2009. Thus, we decided to restrict our analysis in the financial statements of the periods 2006 and 2008.

Data Source

The disclosures included in published financial statements of sample of 58 Greek firms have been examined. The sample does not include firms from the following sectors: banks, insurances, real estate and financial services. The firms included in the sample of listed firms were chosen from the following sectors, as these are defined by the Athens Stock Exchange: oil and gas, chemicals, basic resources, construction and materials, industrial goods and services, food and beverage, personal and household goods, health care, retail, media, travel and leisure, telecommunications and utilities. Thus, firms from all the major sectors of the Greek economy were included in the sample. The focus of this paper is compliance with the disclosure requirements of all IFRS; this would require testing whether a firm complies with more than 1,500 items, which are not necessarily applicable in all sectors. Furthermore, checking the compliance of a company with all such requirements would be open to substantial bias because the authors could not be certain whether a disclosure requirement was pertinent to the specific company. On the other hand, there is a question regarding which are the most important disclosures. For this reason, this study uses the disclosures included in the proposal (as it then was) for a Standard for Small and Medium Sized Entities. This document supposedly focuses on the most important disclosure items. The total number of information items that were examined in this study is more than 400, which is significantly higher comparing to disclosure items examined in previous studies. For instance, Glaum and Street (2003) used an IAS disclosure checklist containing 153 items and a US GAAP one contained 144 items. Hodgdon et al. (2008) employed a disclosure list made up from 209 disclosure items and Setyadi et al. (2011) used a 29 item index.

Independent Variables

The present study uses five independent variables in order to explain the disclosure compliance (dependant variable) of the sample firms: size, leverage, profitability, ownership structure and auditor type. Two metric variables were considered as measures of size. The first one is equity (EQUITY), which is depicted by the end of year total equity of the reporting firm. The second variable is assets (ASSETS) and it is measured by the logarithm of a firm's total assets. Profitability is depicted by three metric measures of profitability; income, Return on Equity (ROE) and Return on Assets (ROA). Income (PROFITS) is measured by net income after tax at the end of the fiscal year for each firm. ROE is the ratio of total income after tax divided by the average of equity. It should be noted that in the case where equity is negative this variable is not defined. The last measure of profitability is ROA, which comprises the ratio of income divided by the average of assets. Leverage (LEV) is measured by the debt ratio of each firm in the sample. The debt ratio is calculated as the proportion of total debt to total assets.

A dummy variable has been used in order to indicate the ownership status of the sample firms. The dummy variable takes the value 1 when the firm is characterised by concentrated ownership and 0 otherwise. In order to determine the ownership structure of a firm a combination of criteria has been employed based upon the proportion of share capital owned by major shareholders and the composition of the board of directors. In particular, if three shareholders control 70% or more of firm's share capital the firm is characterised as a closely-held firm, and three shareholders control 50% or more of firm's share capital the firm is characterised as a closely-held firm, and one shareholder owns 20% or more than of share capital and no other shareholder owns more than 5% of share capital the firm is characterised by concentrated ownership. When none of the above criteria are met, the sample firm is characterised as a firm with diffused ownership. Finally, the remaining firms are categorised as closely held ones only if a firm meets at least one of the above criteria and one or more of the major shareholders participate in the board of directors.

A dummy variable has been used in order to indicate the type of the external auditor employed. The dummy variable takes the value 1 when the auditing firm is a Big-4 firm and 0 otherwise.

Table 1 presents the definitions of the independent variables.

Research Method

The statistical analysis has been conducted for both measures of disclosure compliance presented above on an individual year basis (i.e. year 2006 and year 2008) and for the pooled-sample as well. The univariate analysis aiming to examine the association between the compliance rate and each individual independent variable has been followed by a multivariate analysis. The multivariate analysis aims to identify the accumulated effect of the independent variables on the compliance ratio of the sample-firms. In particular, it has been examined the association between the disclosure compliance of the sample firms with the firms' size, leverage, profitability, ownership status and the type of the external auditor employed.

For the purposes of the multivariate analysis the following model has been estimated for each of periods 2006 and 2008 and for the pooled sample as well.

$$CR = C + (\beta 1 \text{ X } ASSETS) + (\beta 2 \text{ X } ROE) + (\beta 3 \text{ X } LEV) + (\beta 4 \text{ X } OWNS) + (\beta 5 \text{ X } AUDTYPE) \quad (3)$$

where CR = compliance rate, other variables as defined in Table 1.

Table 1. Independent variables

Variable	Description	Variable Name
Measures of Size		
Equity	the end of year total equity of the	EQUITY
	reporting firm	
Assets	logarithm of total assets	ASSETS
Measures of Profitability		
Income	the after tax income	PROFITS
ROE	income divided by equity*	ROE
ROA	income divided by assets	ROA
Leverage		
Debt ratio	total debt to total assets	LEV
Ownership Structure		
Ownership structure	concentrated vs. diffuse ownership	OWNS
	of share capital	
Auditor Type		
Auditor type	Auditor type is measured by the	AUDTYPE
	presence of Big-4 auditors	

*It should be noted that in the case where equity is negative the variable ROE is not defined

4. RESULTS

Descriptive Statistics

Descriptive statistics for the firms in the pooled sample for years 2006 and 2008 are provided in Table 2. The average compliance rate under the "dichotomous approach" is 75%, while under the "partial compliance unweighted method" the compliance rate is 71.2%. It should be noted that the average compliance rate under the "dichotomous approach" for the year 2006 is 74.91%, while under the "partial compliance unweigheted method" the compliance rate is 70.9%. For 2008 the average compliance rate under the "dichotomous approach" is 75.55% and under "partial compliance unweighted method" the compliance rate is 71.57%. These results indicate that about a quarter of the required items are not disclosed by the firms in the sample on average.

Table 2. Descriptive statistics for pooled sample (2006-2008)

Variables	Mean	Median	Max	Min	Std. Dev.
Compliance rate - Dichotomous approach(%)	75.2	76.4	91.9	49.0	9.2
Compliance rate -PC unweighted method (%)	71.2	73.8	92.3	42.0	11.5
ASSETS	687,104.9	102,991.0	14,000,007.0	11,782.0	2,358,292.0
EQUITY	242,061.5	32,102.4	5,078,431.0	-78,954.7	836,132.6
PROFITS	14,202.0	1.420.5	730,800.0	-305,879.0	96,579.3
ROA (%)	1.4	2.1	30.5	-61.5	9.4
ROE (%)	4.8	5.7	103.7	-105.6	20.0
Leverage (%)	60.0	62.9	142.3	5.9	20.6

Compliance Rate - Dichotomous Approach (%): is measured by the total compliance score for each company divided by the total number of items disclosed.

Compliance Rate - PC Unweighted Method (%): is measured by the sum of the compliance scores for each standard divided by the total number of applicable standards (*R*) for each sample firm.

Assets: is measured by the logarithm of the total assets of firm *i* in fiscal year *t*.

EQUITY: is measured by the end of year total equity of firm *i* in fiscal year *t*.

PROFITS: is measured by net income after tax at the end of the fiscal year *t* for firm *i*.

ROE: Return on equity of company *i* for fiscal year *t*. It should be noted that that in the case where equity is negative the variable ROE is not defined.

ROA: is measured by the net income of firm *i* divided by the average of assets for firm *i* at period *t* and period *t-1*.

Leverage: Debt ratio of firm *i* in fiscal year *t*.

The observed compliance rate raises some questions regarding audit quality and the enforcement of regulations in Greece especially since the financial statements of the companies in our sample were not qualified for inadequate disclosure.

Previous research has indicated that two methods for measuring disclosure compliance produce significantly different results (see Tsalavoutas et al. 2010; Mazni Abdullah and Marizah Minhat, 2013; Manel Rajhi, 2014). In our sample, the compliance rate under the "partial compliance unweighted method" is lower comparing to the compliance rate under the "dichotomous approach". It has been examined the association between the results provided by the two methods. The results of the Spearman's correlation test suggest that the results provided by the two methods employed for measuring disclosure compliance are correlated. In particular, for 2006 the value of the Spearman's correlation rho is 0.87 (significant at 5%), while for 2008 the value of the Spearman's correlation rho t is 0.95 (significant at 5%). These results suggest that the two methods do not produce significantly different results. This finding is not in line with the findings of previous research who found that the two methods produce significantly different results.

Under both measures of disclosure compliance the disclosure compliance of the sample firms for year 2006 does not differ significantly from the disclosure compliance for year 2008 (Table 3). The lack of improvement in the disclosure compliance suggests that the experience those Greek firms might have acquired regarding the implementation of IFRS did not affect significantly their compliance with IFRS disclosure requirements.

Univariate Analysis

In Table 4 the results of the univariate analysis concerning the association between the disclosure compliance and the independent variables for each individual year and for the pooled-sample are presented.

Corporate Size and Disclosure

As it can be seen in Table 4, for 2006 firms' size as measured by the log of total assets is associated with disclosure compliance under both approaches used in order to measure the dependent variable. When size is measured by total equity the association is significant only under the "dichotomous approach". For year 2008 there is a positive but not significant association between both measures of compliance and both measures of size. For the pooled-sample the association between the variables of interest does not appear to be significant. Overall, these findings provide weak evidence in that the rate of compliance is higher for bigger firms. These findings are not in line with the findings of previous research that found a significant association between the two variables (see, Inchausti, 1997; Oliveira et al. 2011; Setyadi, 2011). Within the context of Greece, Florou and Galarniotis (2007) found that corporate governance quality increases with firms' size. On the other hand, they did not find any systematic pattern regarding the aggregate level of non-disclosure by firm size and found positive relationship between size and disclosure compliance.

Table 3. Compliance rate by year

	Compliance Rate % 2006	Compliance Rate % 2008	Test of Difference (T-test)
Dichotomous approach	74.9	75.5	-0.3734
Partial compliance unweighted method	70.9	71.5	-0.3167

Table 4. Correlation coefficient among compliance rate and independent variables

Year 2006	Compliance Rate	Compliance Rate
	Dichotomous Approach	PC Unweight Method
	Size	
ASSETS	0.240*	0.222*
EQUITY	0.271*	0.195
	Profitability	
PROFITS	0.186	0.190
ROE	0.014	0.017
ROA	0.058	0.033
	Leverage	
LEVERAGE	-0.084	0.050
Year 2008	Compliance Rate	Compliance Rate
	Dichotomous Approach	PC Unweight Method
	Size	
ASSETS	0.122	0.143
EQUITY	0.137	0.132
	Profitability	
PROFITS	0.047	0.013
ROE	0.105	0.049
ROA	0.101	0.060
	Leverage	
LEVERAGE	-0.050	-0.006
Pooled Sample (2006-2008)	Compliance Rate	Compliance Rate
	Dichotomous Approach	PC Unweight Method
	Size	
ASSETS	0.171	0.162
EQUITY	0.184	0.135
	Profitability	
PROFITS	0.111	0.067
ROE	0.060	0.016
ROA	0.080	0.030
	Leverage	
LEVERAGE	-0.050	0.029

* Significant at 5% level

Assets: is measured by the logarithm of the total assets of firm *i* in fiscal year *t*.

EQUITY: is measured by the end of year total equity of firm i in fiscal year t.

PROFITS: is measured by net income after tax at the end of the fiscal year *t* for firm *i*.

ROE: Return on equity of company *i* for fiscal year *t*. It should be noted that that in the case where equity is negative the variable ROE is not defined.

ROA: is measured by the net income of firm *i* divided by the average of assets for firm *i* at period *t* and period *t-1*.

Leverage: Debt ratio of firm *i* in fiscal year *t*.

Profitability and Disclosure

The rank correlation coefficients between the three measures of profitability used in this study and the compliance rate measured under the "dichotomous approach", presented in Table 4, are positive but not significant at the 5% level. This holds both for 2006 and 2008 and for the pooled-sample. Similar are the results when disclosure compliance is measured under "partial compliance unweighted method". These findings provide no evidence that the level of compliance is associated with profitability. Previous research provides mixed evidence regarding the association of the two variables. Wallace and Naser (1995) found that the profitability of firm affects its compliance to disclosure requirements. On the other hand, Palmer (2008) found limited support for the hypothesis that more profitable firms disclose more information. Inchausti (1997), Dunmontier and Raffourmier (1998) and Street and Bryant (2000) do not provide evidence to support the argument that the rate of firm's compliance is associated with its profitability.

Leverage and Disclosure Compliance

No significant association is observed between leverage and compliance ratio when the latter is measured under the "dichotomous approach". This holds both for years 2006 and 2008 and for the pooled-sample. When the compliance is measured using the "partial compliance unweighted method" the results are similar. This provides no evidence that the level of compliance is associated with leverage. This result is consistent with the findings of previous research that found little evidence to support the hypothesis that there is a significant association between corporate disclosures and leverage (Abraham and Cox, 2007; Amran et al. 2009; Linsley and Shrives, 2006; Mohobbot, 2005). Oliveira et al. (2011) found that firms' leverage is important in explaining the risk related disclosure.

Ownership Structure and Disclosure Compliance

The concentrated ownership firms exhibit a higher compliance rate comparing to the diffused-ownership firms. This holds under both approaches being used in order to measure disclosure compliance. Yet this association is statistically significant only for year 2008 under the "partial compliance unweighted method" (see Table 5). A further statistical analysis being conducted by using the non-parametric Pearson chi-square test indicated that no significant association exists between the disclosure compliance and the ownership status of the sample firms. It should be noted that previous research has indicated that the widely-held firms comply better with the disclosure requirements of IFRS (Klassen, 1997; Birt et al. 2006; Soderstrom and Sun,

Table 5. Ownership structure and disclosure compliance

Dichotomous Approach			
Year	**Concentrated Ownership**	**Diffuse Ownership**	**Test of Difference (p-Values)**
2006	0.756 (obs=42)	0.730 (obs=16)	0.349
2008	0.767 (obs=43)	0.721 (obs=15)	0.107
Partial Compliance Unweighted Method			
Year	**Concentrated Ownership**	**Diffuse Ownership**	**Test of Difference (p-Values)**
2006	0.717 (obs=42)	0.687 (obs=16)	0.285
2008	0.736 (obs= 43)	0.656 (obs=15)	0.043 *

* significant at 5% level

2007). On the other hand, Mohobbot (2005), Oliveira et al. (2011) and Setyadi et al (2011) found no relation between firms' ownership structure and level of disclosure, while Abraham and Cox (2007) provide mixed evidence regarding the association between firms' disclosure compliance and their ownership structure. Kajuter (2006) and Lajili (2007) found negative association between owners' holdings and disclosure.

Auditor Type and Disclosure Compliance

The firms that employ one of the Big-4 international auditing firms exhibit a higher compliance rate comparing to the firms that appoint other auditing firms. This association is statistically significant for 2006 under both approaches being used in order to measure disclosure compliance (see Table 6). The application of the non-parametric Pearson chi-square test provided similar results. In particular, under the dichotomous approach the value of the Pearson chi-square test for the year 2006 was 10.70 (significant at the 1% level) while for the same year under the "partial compliance unweighted method" the value of the Pearson chi-square test was 6.74 (significant at the 1% level). These findings are in line with the findings of previous research. Inchausti (1997), Glaum and Street (2003) and Oliveira (2011) found positive relationship between disclosure and auditor type.

Multivariate Analysis

The dependent variable, compliance rate, was regressed against the independent variables of Size, Profitability, Leverage and dummy variables for ownership status and auditor type. Assets were chosen as a proxy for size in order to be consistent with previous studies, while profitability is measured by reference to ROE.

Table 6. Auditor type and disclosure compliance

Dichotomous Approach			
Year	**Big-4 Auditing Firms**	**Other Auditing Firms**	**Test of Difference (p-Values)**
2006	0.810 (obs=17)	0.723 (obs=41)	0.000 *
2008	0.783 (obs=16)	0.744 (obs=16)	0.169
Partial Compliance Unweighted Method			
Year	**Big-4 Auditing Firms**	**Other Auditing Firms**	**Test of Difference (p-Values)**
2006	0.772 (obs=17)	0.682 (obs=41)	0.000 *
2008	0.750 (obs= 16)	0.702 (obs=42)	0.221

* Significant at 5% level

Given the small size of the sample, the skewed distribution of the explanatory variables and therefore the possible presence of outliers that would make the analysis unreliable, a non-parametric estimation technique was used, namely quantile regression (Koenker and Hallock, 2001). This technique differs from traditional OLS because instead of minimizing the sum of squared residuals, the objective function is to minimize the mean absolute deviation (MAD). Regression results when the dependant variable is measured under the "dichotomous approach" are presented in Table7. Panels A and B report estimated coefficients and standard errors for the 2006 and 2008 samples correspondingly. The estimated coefficients and standard errors for the pooled-sample are presented in Panel C.

Regression results when the dependent variable is measured under the "partial compliance unweighted method" are presented in Table 8. Panels A and B report estimated coefficients and standard errors for the 2006 and 2008 samples correspondingly. The estimated coefficients and standard errors for the pooled-sample are presented in Panel C.

In line with the findings of the univariate analysis the profitability and the leverage of sample firms do not appear to influence their disclosure compliance. Similarly, size is not associated with the disclosure compliance, although the univariate analysis has indicated that for 2006 the larger are more likely to comply with the IFRS disclosure requirements. This result is not in line with the findings of previous research which found a significant association between firms' size and their disclosure compliance. The ownership status and the type of the external auditor appointed of the sample firms are factors are more likely to explain their compliance with the disclosure requirements provided by IFRS. In particular it appears that concentrated-ownership firms achieve higher compliance rates compared to widely-held firms. This association is statistically significant for year 2008 and for the pooled-sample under both

Table 7. Regression of size, profitability, leverage, ownership status and auditor type on disclosure compliance (dichotomous approach)

CR= C + (β1 X ASSETS) + (β2 X ROE) + (β3 X LEV) + (β4 X OWNS) + (β5 X AUDTYPE)			
Variables	**2006**	**2008**	**Pooled Sample**
Constant	0.730*	0.678*	0.657*
	(0.162)	(0.173)	(0.122)
Assets	-0.003	0.004	0.004
	(0.015)	(0.016)	(0.011)
ROE	0.006	0.006	0.041
	(0.093)	(0.105)	(0.067)
Leverage	0.009	-0.105	-0.060
	(0.096)	(0.114)	(0.073)
Ownership	0.032	0.118*	0.083*
	(0.038)	(0.044)	(0.026)
Auditor type	0.111*	0.051	0.061
	(0.049)	(0.052)	(0.036)
pseudo R^2	**0.13**	**0.16**	**0.11**

* Significant at 5% level

Standard errors in parentheses

Compliance Rate - Dichotomous Approach (%): is measured by the total compliance score for each company divided by the total number of items disclosed.

Assets: is measured by the logarithm of the total assets of firm *i* in fiscal year *t*.

ROE: Return on equity of company *i* for fiscal year *t*. It should be noted that that in the case where equity is negative the variable ROE is not defined.

Leverage: Debt ratio of firm *i* in fiscal year *t*.

Ownership: equal to 1 for concentrated ownership and 0 otherwise.

Auditor Type: equal to 1 when the auditor of the firm is a Big-4 audit company and 0 otherwise.

measures of disclosure compliance. The univariate analysis has found a significant association for year 2008 only under the "partial compliance unweighted method". These findings suggest that firms' disclosure compliance can be associated with the ownership structure. Yet the observed relationship does not support the widely accepted contention that the widely-held firms comply better with the accounting standards' disclosure requirements. In fact, it appears that closely held firms are more likely to comply with disclosure requirements. The observed relationship can be explained within the context of agency theory. The major shareholders aim to maximize firm's value and as a consequence the agency costs are low. As mentioned earlier when major shareholders aim to maximize firm's value a positive association is expected between owners' holdings and disclosure.

Table 8. Regression of size, profitability, leverage, ownership status and auditor type on disclosure compliance (Partial compliance unweighted method)

CR= C + (β1 X ASSETS) + (β2 X ROE) + (β3 X LEV) + (β4 X OWNS) + (β5 X AUDTYPE)			
Variables	**2006**	**2008**	**Pooled Sample**
Constant	0.671*	0.462*	0.474*
	(0.158)	(0.263)	(0.130)
Assets	-0.004	0.010	0.013
	(0.014)	(0.024)	(0.011)
ROE	0.044	-0.010	0.091
	(0.090)	(0.160)	(0.072)
Leverage	0.039	-0.035	-0.005
	(0.093)	(0.173)	(0.077)
Ownership	0.039	0.201*	0.0831*
	(0.037)	(0.067)	(0.031)
Auditor type	0.116*	0.072	0.054
	(0.047)	(0.078)	(0.039)
pseudo R^2	**0.15**	**0.17**	**0.11**

* Significant at 5% level

Standard errors in parentheses

Compliance Rate - PC Unweighted Method (%): is measured by the sum of the compliance scores for each standard divided by the total number of applicable standards (*R*) for each sample firm.

Assets: is measured by the logarithm of the total assets of firm *i* in fiscal year *t*.

ROE: Return on equity of company *i* for fiscal year *t*. It should be noted that that in the case where equity is negative the variable ROE is not defined.

Leverage: Debt ratio of firm *i* in fiscal year *t*.

Ownership: equal to 1 for concentrated ownership and 0 otherwise.

Auditor Type: equal to 1 when the auditor of the firm is a Big-4 audit company and 0 otherwise

With respect with the type of external auditor appointed it appears that the firms that employ one of the Big-4 international auditing firms exhibit a higher compliance rate comparing to the firms that appoint other auditing firms. This association is statistically significant for the year 2006 under both measures of disclosure compliance. These results are similar with those provided by the univariate analysis. These findings indicate that the disclosure compliance is higher in companies audited by the Big-4 auditing firms. Results regarding the auditor type are consistent with the findings of previous research. The fact that the association is significant for year 2006 suggests that the local auditing firms, and in general smaller auditing firms, might not have possessed in that year the superior knowledge and experience that the Big-4 international auditing firms possessed with respect to the application of

IFRS and the auditing of financial statements prepared according to IFRS. As a consequence the disclosure compliance of the firms audited by Big-4 international auditing firms was higher comparing to the disclosure compliance of firms being audited by local auditing firms. However, by 2008 that gap between Big-4 international auditing firms and local auditing firms regarding the expertise upon the application of IFRS might have narrowed.

With respect to the hypothesis tested within this study, it appears that the two methods employed for measuring disclosure compliance do not produce significantly different results. In fact, we found similar association between the dependent variable (disclosure compliance) and the independent variables under each method employed for measuring dependent variable. This holds for both the univariate and the multivariate analysis. As a consequence we reject the main hypothesis that the dichotomous method produces significantly different compliance scores from the partial compliance method.

5. CONCLUSION

This study examines the compliance of Greek firms to the IFRS disclosure requirements. We examine the relation between disclosure compliance and certain firms' characteristics for a sample of 58 Greek listed firms for 2006 and 2008. Disclosure compliance has been estimated under two approaches proposed in the literature, which are the "dichotomous approach" and the "partial compliance unweighted method". Prior research has indicated that these two methods can produce significantly different results. It should be noted that contrary to the findings of previous research, our results were similar under both methods employed in this study for measuring disclosure compliance.

It appears that for the sample firms the ownership structure and the type of external auditor appointed are the most important factors in explaining disclosure compliance. Contrary to the findings of previous research, we found that the closely-held firms exhibit higher compliance rate comparing to the widely held ones. Results regarding the auditor type are consistent with the findings of previous research, which indicated that firms that are being audited by one of the Big-4 international auditing firms comply better with the disclosure requirements of IFRS. On the other hand, the leverage of a firm its profitability and its size do not appear to be statistically significant variables in explaining disclosure compliance. Although firms' size appear to be positively associated with firms' disclosure compliance, other factors appear to influence to a greater extent the compliance of sample firms with the disclosure requirements of IFRS.

Measuring compliance with mandatory disclosure requirements is of interest not only because it contributes to the existing empirical literature on this topic but also because it provides some useful insight into the factors that can explain this compliance. Furthermore, given the similarities of Greek business environment with the environment prevailing in other European countries the findings of this study can be useful to researchers that examine disclosure compliance in other European countries. This study contributes to the knowledge base that accounting regulators can use to determine the extent to which Greek firms comply with the disclosure requirements of IFRS and will assist in future directions in developing mechanisms that will monitor the implementation of IFRS. In addition, by adopting both approaches proposed in the literature for measuring disclosure compliance, this study provides empirical evidence concerning the extent to which the two methods provide significantly different results.

REFERENCES

Abdullah, Evans, Fraser, & Tsalavoutas. (2015). IFRS Mandatory disclosures in Malaysia: the influence of family control and the value (ir)relevance of compliance levels. *Accounting Forum, 39*(4), 328-348.

Abdullah & Minhat. (2013). Measuring compliance with IFRS mandator y disclosure requirements: Some evidence from Malaysia. *Australian Journal of Basic and Applied Sciences, 7*(8), 163-169.

Abraham, S., & Cox, P. (2007). Analysing the determinants of narrative risk information in UK FTSE 100 annual reports. *The British Accounting Review, 39*(3), 227–248. doi:10.1016/j.bar.2007.06.002

Al Mutawaa & Hewaidy. (2010). Disclosure Level And Compliance With IFRSs: An Empirical Investigation Of Kuwaiti Companies. *International Business & Economics Research Journal, 9*(5), 33-50.

Al-Shiab, M. (2008). The effectiveness of International Financial Reporting Standards adoption on cost of equity capital: A vector error correction model. *International Journal of Business., 13*, 271–298.

Alanezi Faisal & Albuloushi. (2011). Does the existence of voluntary audit committees really affect IFRS-required disclosure? The Kuwaiti evidence. *International Journal of Disclosure and Governance, 8*(2), 148–173.

Ali, A., & Kumar, K. (1994). The magnitudes of financial statement effects and accounting choice; the case of the adoption of SFAS 87. *Journal of Accounting and Economics, 18*(1), 89–114. doi:10.1016/0165-4101(94)90020-5

Ali, J. M., Ahmed, K., & Herny, D. (2004). Disclosure compliance with national accounting standards by listed companies in South Asia. *Accounting and Business Research, 34*(3), 183–199. doi:10.1080/00014788.2004.9729963

Amran, A., Bin, A. M. R., & Hassan, B. C. H. M. (2009). Risk Reporting: An exploratory study on risk management disclosure in Malaysian annual reports. *Managerial Auditing Journal, 24*(1), 39–57. doi:10.1108/02686900910919893

Atanasovski, A. (2015). Empirical Investigation into the Determinants of Compliance with IFRS 7 Disclosure Requirements. *Acta Universitatis Danubius. Œconomica, 11*(2), 517.

Barako, D. G., Hancock, P., & Izan, H. Y. (2006). Factors influencing voluntary corporate disclosure by Kenyan companies. *Corporate Governance, 14*(2), 107–125. doi:10.1111/j.1467-8683.2006.00491.x

Bepari, M. K., Rahman, S. F., & Mollik, A. T. (2014). Firms' compliance with the disclosure requirements of IFRS for goodwill impairment testing: Effect of the global financial crisis and other firm characteristics. *Journal of Accounting & Organizational Change, 10*(1), 116–149. doi:10.1108/JAOC-02-2011-0008

Bhattacharya, U., Daouk, H., & Welker, M. (2003). The world price of earnings opacity. *The Accounting Review, 78*(3), 641–678. doi:10.2308/accr.2003.78.3.641

Birt, J. L., Bilson, C. M., Smith, T., & Whaley, R. E. (2006). Ownership, competition, and financial disclosure. *Australian Journal of Management, 31*(2), 235–263. doi:10.1177/031289620603100204

Bova & Pereira. (2012). The Determinants and Consequences of Heterogeneous IFRS Compliance Levels Following Mandatory IFRS Adoption: Evidence from a Developing Country. *Journal of International Accounting Research: Spring, 11*(1), 83-111.

Cascino & Gassen. (2015). What drives the comparability effect of mandatory IFRS adoption? *Review of Accounting Studies, 20*(1), 242–282.

Chalmers, K., & Godfrey, J. (2004). Reputation Costs: The Impetus for Voluntary Derivative Financial Instrument Reporting. *Accounting, Organizations and Society, 29*(2), 95–125. doi:10.1016/S0361-3682(02)00034-X

Cooke, T. E. (1989). Voluntary corporate disclosure by Swedish companies. *Journal of International Financial Management & Accounting*, *1*(2), 171–195. doi:10.1111/j.1467-646X.1989.tb00009.x

Demir & Bahadir. (2014). An investigation of compliance with International Financial Reporting Standards by listed companies in Turkey. *Accounting and Management Information Systems*, *13*(1), 4–34.

Dunmontier, P., & Raffourmier, B. (1998). Why firm comply voluntarily with IAS: An empirical analysis with Swiss data. *Journal of International Financial Management & Accounting*, *9*(3), 216–245. doi:10.1111/1467-646X.00038

Dye, R. A. (1985). Disclosure of Nonproprietary Information. *Journal of Accounting Research*, *23*(1), 123–145. doi:10.2307/2490910

Florou, A., & Galarniotis, A. (2007). Benchmarking Greek Corporate Governance Against Different Standards. *Corporate Governance*, *15*(5), 979–998. doi:10.1111/j.1467-8683.2007.00614.x

Fox, A., Gwen, H., Helliar, C., & Veneziani, M. (2013). The costs and benefits of IFRS implementation in the UK and Italy. *Journal of Applied Accounting Research*, *14*(1), 86–101. doi:10.1108/09675421311282568

Glaum, M., & Street, D. (2003). Compliance with the disclosure requirements of Germany's new market: IAS versus US GAAP. *Journal of International Financial Management & Accounting*, *14*(1), 64–100. doi:10.1111/1467-646X.00090

Hodgdon, C., Tondkar, R., Harless, D., & Adhikari, A. (2008). Compliance with IFRS disclosure requirements and individual analysts' forecast errors. *Journal of International Accounting, Auditing & Taxation*, *17*(1), 1–13. doi:10.1016/j.intaccaudtax.2008.01.002

Hossain, M., & Adams, M. (1995). Voluntary financial disclosure by Australian listed companies. *Australian Accounting Review*, *5*(10), 45–55. doi:10.1111/j.1835-2561.1995.tb00381.x

Iatrides, G. (2008). I Accounting disclosure and firms' financial attributes: Evidence from the UK stock market. *International Review of Financial Analysis*, *17*(2), 219–241. doi:10.1016/j.irfa.2006.05.003

Inchausti, B. G. (1997). The influence of company characteristics and accounting regulation on information disclosed by Spanish firms. *European Accounting Review*, *6*(1), 45–68. doi:10.1080/096381897336863

Jensen, M. C., & Meckling, W. H. (1976). Theory of the firm: Managerial behaviour agency costs and ownership structure. *Journal of Financial Economics, 3*(4), 305–360. doi:10.1016/0304-405X(76)90026-X

Jones, S., & Higgins, A. D. (2006). Australia's switch to international financial reporting standards: A perspective from account preparers. *Accounting and Finance, 46*(4), 629–652. doi:10.1111/j.1467-629X.2006.00186.x

Jung, W., & Kwon, Y. (1988). Disclosure when the market is unsure of information endowment of managers. *Journal of Accounting Research, 26*(1), 146–153. doi:10.2307/2491118

Kajuter, P. (2006). *Risk disclosures of listed firms in Germany: a longitudinal study.* Presented at the 10th Financial Reporting & Business Communication Conference, Cardiff Business School "Unpublished results".

Karamanis & Papadakis. (2008). *The application of IFRS in Greece.* Athens University of Economics and Business. (in Greek)

Klassen, K. J. (1997). The Impact of Inside Ownership Concentration on the Trade-Off Between Financial and Tax Reporting. *The Accounting Review, 72*, 455–474.

Koenker, R., & Hallock, K. (2001). Quantile Regression. *The Journal of Economic Perspectives, 15*(4), 143–156. doi:10.1257/jep.15.4.143

La Porta, R., Lopez-de-Silanes, F., Shleifer, A., & Vishny, W. R. (1998). Law and finance. *Journal of Political Economy, 106*(6), 1113–1155. doi:10.1086/250042

Lajili, K. (2007). *Corporate governance and risk disclosure.* Working Paper No. 2007-24, University of Ottawa, Tefler School of Management, Ottawa, ON.

Lang, M. H., & Lundholm, R. J. (1993). Cross sectional determinants of analysis rating of corporate disclosure. *Journal of Accounting Research, 31*(2), 246–271. doi:10.2307/2491273

Leuz, C., Nanda, D., & Wysocki, P. (2003). Earnings management and investor protection: An international comparison. *Journal of Financial Economics, 69*(3), 505–527. doi:10.1016/S0304-405X(03)00121-1

Leuz, C., Pfaff, D., & Hopwood, A. (2004). *The Economics and Politics of Accounting International Perspectives on Research Trends, Policy and Practice.* New York, NY: Oxford University Press.

Linsley, P. M., & Shrives, P. J. (2006). Risk reporting: A study of risk disclosures in the annual reports of UK companies. *The British Accounting Review, 38*(4), 387–404. doi:10.1016/j.bar.2006.05.002

Lopes, P., & Rodrigues, L. L. (2007). Accounting for financial instruments: An analysis of the determinants of the disclosure in the Portuguese stock exchange. *The International Journal of Accounting, 42*(1), 25–26. doi:10.1016/j.intacc.2006.12.002

Miihkinen, A. (2012). What Drives Quality of Firm Risk Disclosure?: The Impact of a National Disclosure Standard and Reporting Incentives under IFRS. *The International Journal of Accounting, 47*(4), 437–468. doi:10.1016/j.intacc.2012.10.005

Miller, G. S. (2002). Earnings performance and discretionary disclosure. *Journal of Accounting Research, 40*(1), 173–204. doi:10.1111/1475-679X.00043

Mohobbot, A. (2005). Corporate risk reporting practices in annual reports of Japanese companies. *Japanese Journal of Accounting., 16*, 113–133.

Moses, D. (1987, April). Income smoothing and incentives: Empirical test using accounting changes. *The Accounting Review*, 358–373.

Ndubizu, G., & Tsetsekos, G. (1992). Functional currency smoothing and managerial incentives: An empirical test. *The International Journal of Accounting, 27*, 27–37.

Nobes, C., & Parker, R. (2000). *Comparative International Accounting* (6th ed.). Financial Times-Prentice Hall.

Oliveira, J., Rodrigues, L. L., & Russell, C. (2011). Risk-related disclosures by non-finance companies: Portuguese practices and disclosure characteristics. *Managerial Auditing Journal, 26*(9), 817–839. doi:10.1108/02686901111171466

Owusu-Ansah, S. (2000). Noncompliance with corporate annual report disclosure requirements in Zimbabwe. *Research in Accounting in Emerging Economies., 4*, 289–305.

Palmer, P. (2008). Disclosure of the impacts of abandoning Australian equivalents of International Financial reporting Standards. *Accounting and Finance, 48*, 847–870.

Raffournier, B. (1995). The determinants of voluntary financial disclosure by Swiss listed companies. *European Accounting Review, 4*(2), 261–280. doi:10.1080/09638189500000016

Rajhi, M. (2014). International Financial Reporting Standards and Level of Compliance with Mandatory Disclosure Requirements. *International Journal of Multidisciplinary Sciences and Engineering, 5*(5), 1–6.

Rodosthenous, M. (2012). The impact of Corporate Governance on enterprises efficiency. The NASDAQ and NYSE listed Greek shipping companies. *The Southeuropean Review of Business Finance and Accounting*, *10*, 41–51.

Setyadi, A., Rusmin, R., Tower, G., & Brown, A. (2011). Measurement vs. disclosure of accounting compliance in Indonesia. International Journal of Accounting. *Auditing and Performance Evaluation.*, *7*(1/2), 94–119. doi:10.1504/IJAAPE.2011.037727

Shleifer, A., & Vishny, R. (1997). A survey of corporate governance. *The Journal of Finance*, *52*(2), 737–783. doi:10.1111/j.1540-6261.1997.tb04820.x

Soderstrom, N. S., & Sun, K. J. (2007). IFRS Adoption and Accounting Quality: A review. *European Accounting Review*, *16*(4), 675–702. doi:10.1080/09638180701706732

Street, D. L., & Bryant, S. M. (2000). Disclosure Level and Compliance with IASs: A Comparison of Companies With and Without U.S. Listings and Filings. *The International Journal of Accounting*, *35*(3), 305–329. doi:10.1016/S0020-7063(00)00060-1

Street, D. L., & Gray, S. J. (2001). *Observance of international accounting standards: Factors explaining noncompliance*. ACCA Research Report No. 74. The Association of Chartered Certified Accountants.

Sunder, S. (2007). *Adverse Effects of Accounting Uniformity on Practice, Education, and Research.* Working paper. Available at SSRN: http://ssrn.com/abstract=1028517

Sykianakis, N. (2004). Factors affecting Greek FDI in the Balkans: The case of Ice – Cream Industry. *Archives of Economic History*, *15*, 85–107.

Trueman, B. (1986). Why do managers voluntarily release earnings forecasts? *Journal of Accounting and Economics*, *8*(1), 53–72. doi:10.1016/0165-4101(86)90010-8

Tsalavoutas, I., & Evans, L. (2010). Transition to IFRS in Greece: Financial Statement Effects and Auditor Size. *Managerial Auditing Journal*, *25*(8), 814–842. doi:10.1108/02686901011069560

Tsalavoutas, I., Evans, L., & Smith, M. (2010). Comparison of two methods for measuring compliance with IFRS mandatory disclosure requirements. *Journal of Applied Accounting Research.*, *11*(3), 213–228. doi:10.1108/09675421011088143

Tzovas, C. (2006). Factors Influencing Firms' Accounting Policy Decisions When Tax Accounting And Financial Accounting Coincide. *Managerial Auditing Journal*, *21*(4), 372–386. doi:10.1108/02686900610661397

Vasilios-Christos, Sykianakis, & Christos. (2011). The perceptions of managers of Greek firms regarding the costs and benefits ensuing from the adoption of International Financial Reporting Standards in Greece. *International Journal of Economic Sciences and Applied Research, 4*(3), 59-74.

Verrachia, R. E. (1983). Discretionary disclosure. *Journal of Accounting and Economics, 5*, 179–194. doi:10.1016/0165-4101(83)90011-3

Wallace, R. S. O., & Naser, K. (1995). Firm-specific determinants of the comprehensiveness of mandatory disclosure in the corporate annual reports of firms listed on the stock exchange of Hong Kong. *Journal of Accounting and Public Policy, 14*(4), 311–368. doi:10.1016/0278-4254(95)00042-9

Watts, R., & Zimmerman, J. (1986). *Positive theory of accounting*. Englewood-Cliffs, NJ: Prentice-Hall.

Zimmerman, J. (1983). Taxes and firm size. *Journal of Accounting and Economics, 5*, 119–149. doi:10.1016/0165-4101(83)90008-3

Chapter 12
Determinant Factors of the Quality Management Commentary Reports

Alexandros E. Garefalakis
Hellenic Open University, Greece

Augustinos I. Dimitras
Hellenic Open University, Greece

Panagiotis Ballas
Technical University of Crete, Greece

ABSTRACT

The adoption of International Financial Reporting Standards (IFRS) is now accepted by all researchers in the last decade at least. At the same time, researchers show particular interest in the impact of adoption of IFRS in several areas of economic life and particularly in the banking sector. What IFRS offer is standardization in accounting principles based on which companies prepare their financial statements, which allow for comparisons of performance of companies around the globe. Investors and creditors belong to the long list of stakeholders of a business entity, who require information regarding specific companies and business sectors in order to make their decisions. Annual reports are a formal communication channel for the company to contact with its stakeholders and to report details about its performance and future progress. That is why annual reports include both quantitative and qualitative data; the former could take the form of figures, tables, and ratios, whereas the latter are expressed as management views on present situation, future prospects, risks, and proposed strategy. Our study investigates the disclosure policy that companies follow in their published statements focusing on the determinant factors of quality Management Commentary Reports.

DOI: 10.4018/978-1-5225-6114-9.ch012

1. INTRODUCTION

Building on the above, companies may decide to present details regarding the explanation of the figures presented in annual reports, their origin, details of the organization's financial position, performance and future strategy in a separate report; namely, Management Commentary Report (MCR). Such type of report is not compulsory under IFRS in all countries. Entities operating in US is compulsory to issue, whereas in EU is voluntary.

Our aim is to utilise such reports to investigate disclosure. Being more specific, we explore the type and load of information disclosed in Management Discussion and Analysis (MD&A), Management Commentary or Operating and Financial Review (OFR) reports and we proceed to a comparison between contexts where it is compulsory to issue such statements (i.e. USA and Canada) and contexts that is voluntary to do so (i.e. West and South European countries). In achieving our aim, we utilise a matched sample of the 30 biggest firms from banking sector for the years from 2002 to 2008. We intentionally excluded the period after 2008 to avoid including noise in our data and to reach to conclusions regarding disclosure that are free from the global economic crisis bias. A major finding is that entities that operate in larger capital markets may disclose more information compared to entities that operate in smaller counterparts.

Companies in their everyday operation use reports (e.g. annual reports) as a channel to communicate information about their performance to their stakeholders with investors (existing and potential), lenders and creditors being in a major target audience. Such reports include not only quantitative data in the form of figures, tables, and ratios, but also provide details regarding the structure of the company, future strategy and prospects, and challenges that the company will face in the future. That is why they operate complementary to other statements such as financial statements, cash flow statements, etc. Through an MCR top management of an entity describes its aims and objectives for the company and elaborates on the strategies in order to achieve them.

It is widely recognised that firms provide proprietary information to various stakeholders and outsiders in an effort to eliminate agency costs and obtain capital on the most favourable terms (Botosan, 1997). Disclosure will be affected by managers' assessments of the costs and benefits of disclosure (Dye, 1985; Verrecchia, 1983) and has been shown to be associated with firm attributes such as size, internationality, growth, profitability and country of origin (Archambault and Archambault, 2003; Meek et al., 1995; Clarkson et al., 1999; Khanna et al., 2004; Zarzeski, 1996). We focus on the material included in the MCR to explore whether different approaches to the regulation of narrative disclosure impact on the amount and type of information provided.

Narrative information appears to fulfil an important communication role in reports issued either voluntarily or compulsory by business entities. However, MCRs are subject to a range of company and securities law requirements. In the United States of America (USA) and Canada the Securities and Exchange Commission (SEC) has issued a series of directives and codes of practice when preparing such reports and has been active in enforcement of MD&A requirements.

The European Union (EU) supports the importance of MCRs without making them compulsory for an entity to prepare. What is worth noting though is that in UK firms are encouraged to comply with the so-called *Operating and Financial Review Statement* issued by the Accounting Standards Board (ASB). The particular report is another type of narrative reporting is applied on a voluntary basis and gives directions to companies that would find beneficial in preparing it as to what type of information to include making it useful to their stakeholders.

We measured the amount and type of disclosure provided in the MCRs as part of the annual reports prepared by 30 banks from the American continent (specifically USA and Canada) and the European continent (specifically UK, France, Germany, Spain, Italy and Netherland). All firms selected were from the Banking services sector and were selected after screening based on their size and importance to their respective countries. Disclosure was measured using a self-constructed checklist based on the Discussion Paper of Management Commentary disclosure requirements (Garefalakis et al., 2016; Garefalakis and Dimitras, 2016).

The chapter is organised as follows. The next section discusses relevant studies about firm disclosure. Section 3 proposes research hypotheses, Section 4 describes data and method and Section 5 discusses the empirical framework and estimation results. The final section provides a summary, conclusions and limitations.

2. PRIOR LITERATURE

Annual reports provide information regarding the performance of a company to various stakeholders including existing and potential investors, analysts, creditors among others (Tiexiera, 2004). Due to the abundance of information available in an annual report, they have been heavily used by researchers in the field of corporate performance and information acquisition by various stakeholderds (Abeysekera and Guthrie, 2004) mainly because it is a formal means of communication between the company and the wider community (Barlett and Chandler, 1997). Such reports include a part which depicts performance expressed in numerical form (i.e. numbers, figures, ratios) and another part which offers an analysis to these numbers in an effort to reveal the hidden picture behind them. The first part is the statutory obligation of the company and is imposed by law, whereas the second part is voluntary in nature.

In other words, companies are free to provide any information they regard as relevant so stakeholders better understand the first part as well as have a clearer idea of the company. This second voluntary part is constructed in a narrative form expressing the views of management regarding financial performance, risk management, and future strategy. It is so important that stakeholders may find it more valuable source of information compared to the rest of the annual report (Smith and Taffler, 2000). The rationale behind it is that quantity of data in a report, especially if it is quantitative in nature, does not always improve quality of information offered to the interested parties; rather, it is the necessity of qualitative data that enhances quality of information (IASB, 2006).

Previous research has shed light on the role of aesthetics (e.g. tables, figures, graphical representations, selection of colors) to the quality of annual reports prepared (Barlett and Chandler, 1997; Beattie and Jones, 2000, Courtis and Hassen, 2002). Focusing on narrative disclosure, Deloitte (2006) performed a longitudinal survey that started in 1996 and ended in 2006 and found evidence to support the increase in the length of annual reports and the increase to the risks discussed in these reports as years passed. Clatworthy and Jones (2001) investigated the readability of annual reports focusing their study to the analysis of 60 UK chairman's statements inferring that chairman's introduction is easier to read compared to the rest parts of the statement. The idea of utilizing chairman's statement had been used by Smith and Taffler (2000) too, who examined whether the discretionary narrative disclosures measure the risk of bankruptcy for a company.

Another stream of research has focused on MCRs that has focused on narratives. Various scholars in the past have focused on the investigation of narrative reports suggesting various methods with the Disclosure index being a widely used one. Botosan (1997) applied the specific method to 122 companies from the machinery industry that voluntarily disclosed information through their annual reports. The disclosures made to latter reports are widely used in particular research since they positively correlate with the amount disclosed to other reports/statements and also their importance to corporate information is commonly accepted. Jenkins Report (AICPA, 1994) set, principally, the guidelines for the selection of items included in the index, and study of the annual report was made by the Canadian Institute of Chartered Accountants (1991). The categories of information proposed were five: background information; historical results; key non-financial data; projected information; and MD&A. The index comprised 35 major items spread across these categories.

Robb et al., (2001), being in line with the proposals made in Jenkins Report, included non-financial disclosures by entities in Australia, Canada, and the USA in their work. Defining non-financial disclosures, they are qualitative information included in the annual reports, but not in the financial statements and notes.

Their disclosure scoring sheet uses categories which are focusing on the list of non-financial information (NFI) items desired by users included in the database of materials used by the Jenkins Committee. These items were grouped into six categories, three forward-looking topics and three historical topics. A total of 65 items were included. For each item, a score of 1 (no disclosure), 2 (some disclosure) or 3 (extensive disclosure) was awarded. An overall disclosure score was the goal. The specific study highlighted the various disclosure levels for the above mentioned NFI categories, taking into consideration firm size, industry classification, degree of geographic dispersion and country of domicile.

Two other methods for analyzing narrative reports are proposed in the literature; namely, the Readability and Linguistic analysis. Applying the former of these two, Jones and Shoemaker (1994) review 32 readability studies. Their purpose is to measure the cognitive difficulty of text and generally use of a readability formula such as the Flesch Index, which produces results measuring the length of certain sentences and counting syllable words. The particular analysis is performed with the use of computer software. The findings-scores taken are then contrasted to benchmarks from other studies in order to assess the degree of difficulty of the text. Although this approach offers methodological advantages in terms of objectivity and reliability, problems on the application of readability scores taken to narratives from reports may arise. The particular difficulty most of times originates from the low level of readability of the annual reports.

Following a different approach, Sydserff and Weetman (1999) applied Linguistic analysis and offered a significant methodological contribution by utilising texture index (as a counterpart to readability formulas) to the evaluation of information in the form of narratives available to company's annual reports. This new method contributed to the isolation and the highlight of a wider set of characteristics compared to readability formulas presented above. Moreover, the association with readability scores is absent with the use of texture index.

Our review of existing literature on accounting narratives has revealed two limitations. The first limitation is that numerous scholars either select specific sections of annual reports to include in their analysis or specific topics and pre-selected index items are under research. This partial methodological approach applied eliminates the validity of the results. This problem was eliminated with the approach proposed by Sydserff and Weetman (1999).

The second limitation stems from the fact that even though disclosure is a complicated and multi-faceted concept, literature has treated it as being unidimensional. Also, what literature seems to neglect is the proposal of a framework to be able to extract important elements from disclosure analysis. Hence, the debate on business reporting should flourish and scholars should proceed with the investigation of methodologies to extract information items or critical relevance. In line with the above rationale, Beattie et. al. (2001, 2004) proposed a framework to classify and describe information items, according to which information items should be nested within broader themes/categories in a hierarchical structure. Furthermore, the specific approach asserts that future research could categorize information items based on the following attributes: historical/forward-looking; financial/non-financial; and quantitative/non-quantitative (Beattie et al., 2004). For the above reasons, we believe this is the appropriate framework to be applied to our study.

3. HYPOTHESES

Capital markets, through financial institutions which act as mediators to the transactions, facilitate users of capital to meet with suppliers. Through the numerous financial instruments on which investor's trade, instead of exchange of money there is exchange of risk. Thus, it is more than clear that in order for investors to take correct decisions and proper positions in these markets, the quality of information is of outmost importance. Irrespective if it is compulsory or voluntary, the disclosure of information in various capital markets has been examined in the past and has concluded to a positive relationship between disclosures in financial statements and the size of the capital market (Adhikari and Tondkar, 1992; Doupnik and Salter, 1995). Thus, business entities that are based in countries with developed and expanded capital markets, they are more prone and willing to disclose more information in their statements compared to companies from smaller counterparts. Given the differences in size between the capital market in USA and Canada compared to the various countries in the European continent, banks from the America continent are expected to disclose more information in their financial statements compared to the ones from Europe. In addition to the above, we predict that cultural differences of not only companies'-top management but also investors' together with the differences in market size could initiate changes regarding the decision to disclose different amount and depth of information in narrative reports among countries.

As a result of the above, we could formally state the hypotheses in alternative form as follows:

H1: *There is a significant difference in amount of disclosure in MD&A reports provided by firms from the USA and Canada compared to MCR in European countries.*

Building on the discussion made in the literature review part on the mandatory or voluntary nature of disclosures, we could interlard cultural and capital market factors with Management Commentary (MC) requirements. Specifically, the stance towards implementation of MC directly relates to disclosure. As we have presented earlier, there is lack of universal regulation on disclosure. Business entities in USA should adopt mandatory requirements regarding the content of disclosure reports, whereas their counterparts from Europe adopt a voluntary approach to such disclosures. In the latter case, European countries issue only guidelines regarding the style, the type and content of such reports, which are not binding for companies to adopt and follow. For example, companies that publish their reports to the EU market are more reserved regarding the information disclosed to stakeholders compared to companies from the USA. Hence, the hypotheses can be stated formally as follows:

H2: *Firms subject to mandatory requirements (in the USA) provide significantly more disclosure in their MC reports than firms following voluntary guidelines (in the EU).*

In addition to country, market, and cultural factors, there is evidence to support that the degree of disclosure is influenced by special characteristics of firms (firm specific factors). Existing literature has identified attributes, which could significantly affect the decision of a company to disclose information or not. Representative attributes that have been employed by previous researchers are the company size, type of auditor, foreign stock exchange listing and country (or region) of origin (Archambault and Archambault, 2003; Hossain and Adams, 1995; Meek et al., 1995). Building on the rationale of the importance of context and specifically the country of origin we mentioned in the previous hypothesis, there is evidence that companies with greater involvement in international capital and product markets disclose more information (Zarzeski, 1996; Khanna et al., 2003). Hence, multinational companies that operate worldwide and offer their products and services to many different markets, are more likely to disclose more information to their statements. Also, larger companies and companies with earnings are inclined to unveil more information to various stakeholders, communicating in such a way their success and divulge future prospects and strategy (Clarkson et al., 1999; Khanna et al., 2003).

4. DATA AND METHOD

Management commentary (or equivalent) reports were extracted from the Datastream database. Foreign listing status, auditor identity and financial information were obtained from annual reports.

The authors performed analysis of management commentary reports using a checklist as a data analysis tool constructed by one of the authors (Garefalakis et al.,

2016), which includes five (5) categories and is called Management Commentary Index (Ma.Co.I).

Based on a scoring system devised by Saaty (1994) each item disclosed in the MCR was measured by considering the amount of disclosure (brief or substantial) giving a score of up to five points for each item disclosed. Scoring is 0 = no discussion, 1 = brief discussion, 2 = Moderate discussion, 3 =Strong discussion, 4 = very strong discussion, 5 = substantial discussion. The specific scoring system employed aims to rank items based on their information content. Given that there are 70 items on the checklist, the maximum possible score attainable by a firm is 350. The advantage of this scoring method is that it concludes to more robust disclosure score contrasting what the commonly used binary method produces where each item takes the score 1 if included and 0 if omitted (as in Archambault and Archambault, 2003).

Our research focused on the examination of the following regression model:

$$Total\_MC = b_0 + b_1 Auditor + b_2 RE + b_3 Size + b_4 US + u_i$$

The above contributes to the investigation of the relationship between disclosure scores (Total_MC) and independent variables, which represent the country of origin and whether narrative reports are subject to mandatory requirements. Control variables for size, RE (Return of Earnings) and the type of audit firm are included to investigate their impact on information disclosure. Running our regression, we used a sample of 30 Banking institutions (see Appendix), which operate both in the American and the European continents.

5. EMPIRICAL FRAMEWORK AND ESTIMATION RESULTS

Table 1 presents the summary statistics for Total_MC, Logsize, and RE series. Specifically, the mean of Total_MC is about 136 and the mean of Logsize and RE are 7.050 and 0.154 respectively. Also, the coefficients of skewness and kurtosis indicate that the Total_MC and Logsize series have positive asymmetric but mesokurtic[1] features. In contrast, the RE variable have negative asymmetry and leptokurtic distribution. Moreover, according to the Jarque-Bera statistics and the value of kurtosis, there are significant departures from the normality hypothesis only for the RE series.

Some diagnostic tests were performed to establish goodness of fit and appropriateness of the model. First, it was examined whether the standardized residuals and squared standardized residuals of the estimated model are free from serial correlation. The results show (Table 2) that the LB statistics for the standardized residuals and standardized squared residuals are not significant (Ljung – Box,

Table 1. Sample statistics for Total_mc, Size, and RE (return of earnings) series

Statistics	TOTAL_MC	SIZE	RE
Observations	30	30	30
Mean	136.810	7.050	0.154
Median	137.583	7.092	-0.049
Std. Dev.	20.686	1.596	5.210
Skewness	0.504	0.535	-0.412
Kurtosis	3.243	3.563	6.692
Jarque-Bera	1.344	1.825	17.887

1978). In addition, the independence of the standardized residuals is confirmed by the Durbin-Watson statistics 1.74 (Durbin and Watson, 1950). Moreover, the Breusch–Pagan test ($N^*R^2 = 2.96$ with 0.60 p-value) showed that the variance does not exhibit heteroskedasticity. Finally, with the application of the Jarque-Bera test (0.457) it was found that the normality of the residuals u_i cannot be rejected (Jarque and Bera, 1987).

Table 3 presents results of the regression. The adjusted R^2 (0.542) indicates that changes of the quality management commentary reports (Total_MC) are affected considerably by the used independent variables. Specifically, the statistically

Table 2. LB test for residuals and squared residuals from the regression estimation

Standardized Residuals				Squared Standardized Residuals			
Lags	Autocorrelation	Partial Correlation	LB(n)	Lags	Autocorrelation	Partial Correlation	LB(n)
1	0.109	0.109	0.3945	1	-0.248	-0.248	2.0376
2	-0.142	-0.156	1.0907	2	-0.181	-0.259	3.1618
3	-0.244	-0.216	3.1995	3	0.169	0.055	4.1788
4	-0.156	-0.14	4.098	4	-0.144	-0.142	4.9488
5	-0.247	-0.318	6.4411	5	0.068	0.047	5.1277
6	0.147	0.093	7.3058	6	-0.148	-0.216	5.9991
7	0.195	0.029	8.8964	7	0.149	0.134	6.9207
8	0.064	-0.066	9.0748	8	0.053	0.012	7.0429
9	-0.104	-0.1	9.5666	9	-0.209	-0.087	9.0469
10	-0.087	-0.095	9.9289	10	0.111	-0.034	9.6337

Note: LB(n) are the n-lag Ljung-Box statistics for the residual series. LB(n) follows chi-square variable with n degree of freedom; the series of residual contains 30 observations .

Table 3. Regression results

Independent Variables	Coefficients	Coefficients (Standards Errors)
US (Dummy variable whether the company is from North America or Europe)	b_1	-25.14307*
		(-6.660975)
RE (Return of earnings)	b_2	-0.961429***
		(-0.510539)
Size (Market value)	b_3	4.890492**
		(-1.833747)
Auditor (Big 4 or non big 4)	b_4	-6.012133
		(-6.49074)
N = 30 companies Adjusted $R^2 = 0.542$ F value p = 0.000		

Notes: Standards errors are shown in parentheses. *indicates statistical significance at the 1% level. **indicates statistical significance at the 5% level. ***indicates statistical significance at the 10% level.

significance of the b_1 coefficient implies that the companies from the North American continent have lower quality of management commentary reports compared to the ones from Europe. Regarding the effect of the RE, the coefficient b_2 has been found negative and statistically significant indicating that the companies with lower earnings have better narrative reports quality. Moreover, the coefficient b_3, which measures the size of the firms, is positive and statistically significant implying that the size of the firms determines, to some extent the quality of MC report. Finally, the coefficient b_4 has been found that is not statistically significant.

6. CONCLUSION

In this research, we explored the determinant factors of the quality management commentary reports. The rationale for the specific study was the various policies employed by companies regarding the disclosure policy they follow in the various statements they produce and publish. Such disclosures capture various details such as the impact on environment, society, employees, various ethical matters applicable and the management suggests strategies on how to tackle dangers regarding them and transform them into opportunities for the shape of the future strategy. Having identified gaps in the existing accounting literature, we investigated the relationship between disclosure scores (Total_MC) and independent variables, which represent the country of origin and whether narrative reports are subject to mandatory requirements.

Control variables for size, RE and the type of audit firm were included to investigate their impact on information disclosure. Our regression revealed that changes to quality management commentary reports were affected by independent variables. This means that banks from America present lower quality MCR compared to their peers from Europe. The analysis also revealed a negative relationship between RE and disclosure, which means that companies with lower RE are prone to disclose quality narrative reports. Moreover, we found a positive correlation between the size of the firm and the disclosure of information.

As a way forward, we would suggest to proceed to comparisons between sub groups in the European continent in order to identify similarities and differences in a context where disclosure is voluntary.

REFERENCES

Abeysekera, I., & Guthrie, J. (2004). Human capital reporting in a developing nation. *The British Accounting Review*, *36*(3), 251–268. doi:10.1016/j.bar.2004.03.004

Adhikari, A., & Tondkar, R. H. (1992). Environmental Factors Influencing Accounting Disclosure Requirements of Global Stock Exchanges. *Journal of International Financial Management & Accounting*, *4*(2), 75–105. doi:10.1111/j.1467-646X.1992.tb00024.x

Archambault, J., & Archambault, M. (2003). A Multinational Test of Determinants of Corporate Disclosure. *The International Journal of Accounting*, *38*(2), 173–194. doi:10.1016/S0020-7063(03)00021-9

Association of International Certified Professional Accountants. (1994). *Improving Business Reporting—A Customer Focus: Meeting the Information Needs of Investors and Creditors, Comprehensive Report of the Special Committee on Financial Reporting. The Jenkins Report*. New York: American Institute of Certified Public Accountants.

Barlett, S., & Chandler, R. (1997). The corporate report and the private shareholders: Lee and Tweedie twenty years. *The British Accounting Review*, *29*(3), 245–261. doi:10.1006/bare.1996.0044

Beattie, V., & Jones, M. (2000). Impression Management: The case of Inter-country financial graphs. *Journal of International Accounting, Auditing & Taxation*, *9*(2), 159–183. doi:10.1016/S1061-9518(00)00030-6

Beattie, V., McInnes, B., & Fearnley, S. (2001). *The Analysis of Narratives in Annual Reports: A Multidimensional Framework*. Working Paper, University of Stirling.

Beattie, V., McInnes, W., & Fearnley, S. (2004). A methodology for analysing and evaluating narratives in annual reports: A comprehensive descriptive profile and metrics for disclosure quality attributes. *Accounting Forum*, *28*(3), 205–236. doi:10.1016/j.accfor.2004.07.001

Botosan, C. (1997). Disclosure Level and the Cost of Equity Capital. *The Accounting Review*, *72*(3), 323–349.

Canadian Institute of Chartered Accountants. (1991). *Information to be included in the Annual Report to Shareholders*. Research Study.

Clarkson, P. M., Kao, J. L., & Richardson, G. D. (1999). Evidence that management discussion and analysis (MD&A) is part of a firm's overall disclosure package. *Contemporary Accounting Research*, *16*(1), 111–134. doi:10.1111/j.1911-3846.1999.tb00576.x

Clatworthy, M., & Jones, M. J. (2001). The effect of thematic structure on the variability of annual report readability. *Accounting, Auditing & Accountability Journal*, *14*(3), 311–326. doi:10.1108/09513570110399890

Courtis, J., & Hassen, S. (2002). Reading ease of bilingual annual reports. *Journal of Business Communication*, *39*(3), 394–413. doi:10.1177/002194360203900401

Deloitte. (2006). *Write to reason: Surveying OFRs and narrative reporting in annual reports*. London: Author.

Doupnik, T. S., & Salter, S. B. (1995). External environment, Culture and Accounting Practice: A Preliminary Test of A General Model of International Accounting Development. *The International Journal of Accounting*, *30*(3), 189–202.

Durbin, J., & Watson, G. S. (1950). Testing for serial correlation in least square regression. *Biometrika*, *37*, 409–428. PMID:14801065

Dye, R. (1985). Disclosure of Nonproprietary Information. *Journal of Accounting Research*, *23*(1), 123–145. doi:10.2307/2490910

Garefalakis, A., & Dimitras, A. (2016). The Contribution of Management Commentary Index (Ma.Co.I) in Annual Banking Reports (ABR) and the Chronicle of the Great Greek Crisis. *Theoretical Economics Letters*, *06*(05), 1060–1087. doi:10.4236/tel.2016.65103

Garefalakis, A., Dimitras, A., Floros, C., & Lemonakis, C. (2016). How Narrative Reporting changed the Business World: Providing a new measurement tool. *Corporate Ownership and Control*, *13*(4), 317–334. doi:10.22495/cocv13i4c2p5

Hossain, M., Perera, M. H. B., & Rahman, A. R. (1995). Voluntary Disclosure in the Annual Reports of New Zealand Companies. *Journal of International Financial Management & Accounting*, *6*(1), 69–87. doi:10.1111/j.1467-646X.1995.tb00050.x

International Accounting Standards Board. (2005). *Discussion Paper: Management Commentary*. London: Author.

International Accounting Standards Board. (2006). *Discussion Paper: Management Commentary*. London: Author.

Jarque, M., & Bera, K. (1987). A test of normality of observations and regression Residuals. *International Statistical Review*, *55*(2), 163–172. doi:10.2307/1403192

Jones, M., & Shoemaker, P. (1994). Accounting narratives: A review of empirical studies of content and readability. *The Journal ofAccounting Literature*, *13*, 142–184.

Khanna, T., Palepu, K. G., & Srinivasan, S. (2004). Disclosure Practices of Foreign Companies Interaction with U.S. Markets. *Journal of Accounting Research*, *42*(2), 475–508. doi:10.1111/j.1475-679X.2004.00146.x

Ljung, G. M., & Box, G. E. P. (1978). On a measure of lack of fit in time series models. *Biometrika*, *65*(2), 297–303. doi:10.1093/biomet/65.2.297

Meek, G. K., Roberts, C. B., & Gray, S. J. (1995). Factors Influencing Voluntary Annual Report Disclosures by U.S., U.K. and Continental European Multinational Corporations. *Journal of International Business Studies*, *26*(3), 555–572. doi:10.1057/palgrave.jibs.8490186

Robb, S. W. G., Single, L. E., & Zarzeski, M. T. (2001). Nonfinancial Disclosures Across Anglo-American Countries. *Journal of International Accounting*, *10*(1), 71–83.

Saaty, T. L. (1994). How to make a decision: The analytic hierarchy process. *Interfaces*, *24*(6), 19–43. doi:10.1287/inte.24.6.19

Smith, M., & Taffler, R. (2000). The chairpersons' statement: A content analysis of discretionary narrative disclosures. *Accounting, Auditing & Accountability Journal*, *13*(5), 624–646. doi:10.1108/09513570010353738

Sydserff, R., & Weetman, P. (1999). A texture index for evaluating accounting narratives: An alternative to readability formulas. *Accounting, Auditing & Accountability Journal*, *12*(4), 459–488. doi:10.1108/09513579910283503

Teixeira, A. (2004). Management Commentary. *Chartered Accounts Journal of New Zealand*, *83*(6), 17–20.

Verrecchia, R. E. (1983). Discretionary Disclosure. *Journal of Accounting and Economics*, *5*, 179–194. doi:10.1016/0165-4101(83)90011-3

Zarzeski, M. T. (1996). Spontaneous Harmonization Effects of Culture and Market Forces on Accounting Disclosure Practices. *Accounting Horizons*, *10*(1), 18–37.

APPENDIX

Table 4. Sample of banking institutions

a/a	Country	Bank name	Region
1		JPMorgan Chase & Co.	US
2		HSBC Holdings PLC	WE
3		BNP Paribas	WE
4		Bank of America	US
5		Wells Fargo & Co.	US
6		Crédit Agricole	WE
7		Citigroup Inc.	US
8		Deutsche Bank	WE
9		Barclays PLC	WE
10		Société Générale	WE
11		Banco Santander	SE
12		Groupe BPCE	WE
13		Lloyds Banking Group	WE
14		Royal Bank of Scotland Group	WE
15		Toronto-Dominion Bank	CAN
16		Royal Bank of Canada	CAN
17		ING Group	WE
18		UniCredit	SE
19		Goldman Sachs	US
20		Morgan Stanley	US
21		Crédit Mutuel	WE
22		Banco Bilbao Vizcaya Argentaria	SE
23		Intesa Sanpaolo	SE
24		Rabobank	WE
25		Scotiabank	CAN
26		Standard Chartered	WE
27		DZ Bank	WE
28		Commerzbank	WE
29		U.S. Bancorp	US
30		Cassa Depositi e Prestiti	SE

[1] The value of kurtosis for normal distribution is three.

Compilation of References

Abdullah & Minhat. (2013). Measuring compliance with IFRS mandatory disclosure requirements: Some evidence from Malaysia. *Australian Journal of Basic and Applied Sciences, 7*(8), 163-169.

Abdullah, Evans, Fraser, & Tsalavoutas. (2015). IFRS Mandatory disclosures in Malaysia: the influence of family control and the value (ir)relevance of compliance levels. *Accounting Forum, 39*(4), 328-348.

Abdulrahim, S. (2011). *Nigerian Stock Returns and Macroeconomic variables: Evidence from the APT Model.* Retrieved 28/02/2016 from http://i-rep.emu.edu.tr:8080/jspui/bitstream/11129/186/1/Saliha.pdf

Abeysekera, I., & Guthrie, J. (2004). Human capital reporting in a developing nation. *The British Accounting Review*, *36*(3), 251–268. doi:10.1016/j.bar.2004.03.004

Abor, J. (2005). The effect of capital structure on profitability: An empirical analysis of listed firms in Ghana. *The Journal of Risk Finance*, *6*(5), 438–445. doi:10.1108/15265940510633505

Abraham, S., & Cox, P. (2007). Analysing the determinants of narrative risk information in UK FTSE 100 annual reports. *The British Accounting Review*, *39*(3), 227–248. doi:10.1016/j.bar.2007.06.002

Acikalin, S., Aktas, R., & Unal, S. (2008). Relationships between stock markets and macroeconomic variables: An empirical analysis of the Istanbul Stock Exchange. *Investment Management and Financial Innovations*, *5*(1), 8–16.

Adam, C., & Bevan, D. (2005). Fiscal deficits and growth in developing countries. *Journal of Public Economics*, *89*(4), 571–597. doi:10.1016/j.jpubeco.2004.02.006

Adhikari, A., & Tondkar, R. H. (1992). Environmental Factors Influencing Accounting Disclosure Requirements of Global Stock Exchanges. *Journal of International Financial Management & Accounting*, *4*(2), 75–105. doi:10.1111/j.1467-646X.1992.tb00024.x

Adıgüzel, H. (2012). *The effect of internal corporate governance structure to the earnings management practice in Turkey* (Ph.D. Thesis). Marmara University Institute of Social Sciences.

Afonso, A., & González-Alegre, J. (2008). *Economic growth and budgetary components: A panel assessment for the EU*. ECB Working Paper 848.

Ağca, Ş., & Celasun, O. (2012). Sovereign debt and corporate borrowing costs in emerging markets. *Journal of International Economics*, *88*(1), 198–208. doi:10.1016/j.jinteco.2012.02.009

Ahmed, S., & Zlate, A. (2014). Capital flows to emerging market economies: A brave new world? *Journal of International Money and Finance*, *48*, 221–248. doi:10.1016/j.jimonfin.2014.05.015

Akbar, S., Rehman, S. U., & Ormrod, P. (2013). The impact of recent financial shocks on the financing and investment policies of UK private firms. *International Review of Financial Analysis*, *26*, 59–70. doi:10.1016/j.irfa.2012.05.004

Akben-Selcuk, E. (2016). Factors affecting firm competitiveness: Evidence from an emerging market. *International Journal of Financial Studies*, *4*(2), 9. doi:10.3390/ijfs4020009

Akintoye, I. R. (2008). Sensitivity of Performance to Capital Structure. *European Journal of Soil Science*, *7*, 1.

Al Mutawaa & Hewaidy. (2010). Disclosure Level And Compliance With IFRSs: An Empirical Investigation Of Kuwaiti Companies. *International Business & Economics Research Journal*, *9*(5), 33-50.

Alanezi Faisal & Albuloushi. (2011). Does the existence of voluntary audit committees really affect IFRS-required disclosure? The Kuwaiti evidence. *International Journal of Disclosure and Governance*, *8*(2), 148–173.

Alesina, A., Campante, F. R., & Tabellini, G. (2008). Why Is Fiscal Policy Often Procyclical? *Journal of the European Economic Association*, *6*(5), 1006–1036. doi:10.1162/JEEA.2008.6.5.1006

Alesina, A., de Broeck, M., Prati, A., & Tabellini, G. (1992). Default Risk on Government Debt in OECD Countries. *Economic Policy*, *15*(15), 427–463. doi:10.2307/1344548

Ali, A., & Kumar, K. (1994). The magnitudes of financial statement effects and accounting choice; the case of the adoption of SFAS 87. *Journal of Accounting and Economics*, *18*(1), 89–114. doi:10.1016/0165-4101(94)90020-5

Ali, J. M., Ahmed, K., & Herny, D. (2004). Disclosure compliance with national accounting standards by listed companies in South Asia. *Accounting and Business Research*, *34*(3), 183–199. doi:10.1080/00014788.2004.9729963

Allen, F., & Gale, D. (2000). *Comparing Financial Systems*. Cambridge, MA: MIT Press.

Al-Shiab, M. (2008). The effectiveness of International Financial Reporting Standards adoption on cost of equity capital: A vector error correction model. *International Journal of Business.*, *13*, 271–298.

Amir, E., Kirschenheiter, M., & Willard, K. (1997). The Valuation of Deferred Taxes. *Contemporary Accounting Research*, *14*(4), 597–622. doi:10.1111/j.1911-3846.1997.tb00543.x

Amir, E., & Sougiannis, T. (1999). Analysts' Interpretation and Investors' Valuation of Tax Carryforwards. *Contemporary Accounting Research*, *16*(1), 1–33. doi:10.1111/j.1911-3846.1999.tb00572.x

Amran, A., Bin, A. M. R., & Hassan, B. C. H. M. (2009). Risk Reporting: An exploratory study on risk management disclosure in Malaysian annual reports. *Managerial Auditing Journal*, *24*(1), 39–57. doi:10.1108/02686900910919893

Angelelli, E., Mansini, R., & Speranza, M. G. (2008). A comparison of MAD and CVaR models with real features. *Journal of Banking & Finance*, *32*(7), 1188–1197. doi:10.1016/j.jbankfin.2006.07.015

Ang, J. B., & McKibbin, W. J. (2007). Financial liberalization, financial sector development and growth: Evidence from Malaysia. *Journal of Development Economics*, *84*(1), 215–233. doi:10.1016/j.jdeveco.2006.11.006

Anwar, S., & Sun, S. (2011). Financial development, foreign investment and economic growth in Malaysia. *Journal of Asian Economics*, *22*(4), 335–342. doi:10.1016/j.asieco.2011.04.001

Arcand, J. L., Berkes, E., & Panizza, U. (2015). Too Much Finance? *Journal of Economic Growth*, *20*(2), 105–148. doi:10.100710887-015-9115-2

Arcand, J., Berkes, E., & Panizza, U. (2012). *Too much finance?* International Monetary Fund, Research Department.

Archambault, J., & Archambault, M. (2003). A Multinational Test of Determinants of Corporate Disclosure. *The International Journal of Accounting*, *38*(2), 173–194. doi:10.1016/S0020-7063(03)00021-9

Arellano, M., & Bond, S. (1991). Some tests of specification for panel data: Monte Carlo evidence and an application to employment equations. *The Review of Economic Studies*, *58*(2), 277–297. doi:10.2307/2297968

Arellano, M., & Bover, O. (1995). Another look at the instrumental-variable estimation of error-components models. *Journal of Econometrics*, *68*(1), 29–52. doi:10.1016/0304-4076(94)01642-D

Arteta, C., & Hale, G. (2008). Sovereign debt crises and credit to the private sector. *Journal of International Economics*, *74*(1), 53–69. doi:10.1016/j.jinteco.2007.05.008

Artzner, P., Delbaen, F., Eber, J.-M., & Heath, D. (1999). Coherent Measures of Risk. *Mathematical Finance*, *9*(3), 203–228. doi:10.1111/1467-9965.00068

Association of International Certified Professional Accountants. (1994). *Improving Business Reporting—A Customer Focus: Meeting the Information Needs of Investors and Creditors, Comprehensive Report of the Special Committee on Financial Reporting. The Jenkins Report.* New York: American Institute of Certified Public Accountants.

Atanasovski, A. (2015). Empirical Investigation into the Determinants of Compliance with IFRS 7 Disclosure Requirements. *Acta Universitatis Danubius. Œconomica*, *11*(2), 517.

Atik, A. (2009). Detecting income-smoothing behaviors of Turkish listed companies through empirical tests using discretionary accounting changes. *Critical Perspectives on Accounting*, *20*(5), 591–613. doi:10.1016/j.cpa.2008.01.003

Atik, A., & Ismail, T. H. (2011). Ethical perceptions on earnings manipulation in Turkey: An exploration of differences in preparers' and users' perspectives. *Research Journal of Finance and Accounting*, *2*(3), 169–186.

Attari, M., & Safdar, L. (2013). The Relationship between Macroeconomic Volatility and the Stock Market Volatility: Empirical Evidence from Pakistan. *Pakistan Journal of Commerce and Social Sciences*, *7*(2), 309–320.

Ayarlıoğlu, M. A. (2007). *Kar Yönetimi Uygulamaları ve İstanbul Menkul Kıymetler Borsası'nda Test Edilmesi* (Ph.D. Thesis). Hacettepe University Institute of Social Sciences.

Ayele, G. A. (2012). *Factors Affecting profitability of insurance companies in Ethiopia: Panel evidence*. Addis Ababa University.

Ayers, B. C. (1998). Deferred tax accounting under SFAS No. 109: An empirical investigation of its incremental value-relevance relative to APB No. 11. *The Accounting Review*, 195–212.

Baek, I. M. (2006). Portfolio investment flows to Asia and Latin America: Pull, push or market sentiment? *Journal of Asian Economics*, *17*(2), 363–373. doi:10.1016/j.asieco.2006.02.007

Bagehot, W. (1873). *Lombard Street* (1962 ed.). Homewood, IL: Richard D. Irwin.

Baker, M., & Wurgler, J. (2007). Investors Sentiment in the Stock Market. *The Journal of Economic Perspectives*, *21*(2), 129–151. doi:10.1257/jep.21.2.129

Baldacci, E., Hillman, A., & Kojo, N. (2004). Growth, governance and fiscal-policy transmission channels in low-income countries. *European Journal of Political Economy*, *20*(3), 517–549. doi:10.1016/j.ejpoleco.2003.12.002

Baldwin, R. E., & Forslid, R. (1998). Trade and growth Any unfinished business? *European Economic Review*, *42*(3-5), 695–703. doi:10.1016/S0014-2921(98)00010-5

Ballestero, E., Bravo, M., Perez-Gladish, B., Arenas-Parra, M., & Pia-Santamaria, D. (2012). Socially responsible investment: A multicriteria approach to portfolio selection combining ethical and financial objectives. *European Journal of Operational Research*, *216*(2), 487–494. doi:10.1016/j.ejor.2011.07.011

Baltagi, B. H. (2001). *Econometric analysis of panel data* (2nd ed.). Chichester, UK: John Wiley & Sons.

Baltagi, B. H., Demetriades, P. O., & Law, S. H. (2009). Financial development and openness: Evidence from panel data. *Journal of Development Economics*, *89*(2), 285–296. doi:10.1016/j.jdeveco.2008.06.006

Barako, D. G., Hancock, P., & Izan, H. Y. (2006). Factors influencing voluntary corporate disclosure by Kenyan companies. *Corporate Governance, 14*(2), 107–125. doi:10.1111/j.1467-8683.2006.00491.x

Barbiero, F., Brutscher, P.-B., Kolev, A., Popov, M., & Wolski, M. (2016). *Misallocation of investment in Europe: Debt overhang, credit market distress, or weak demand?* European Investment Bank.

Barlett, S., & Chandler, R. (1997). The corporate report and the private shareholders: Lee and Tweedie twenty years. *The British Accounting Review, 29*(3), 245–261. doi:10.1006/bare.1996.0044

Barnea, A., Ronen, J., & Sadan, S. (1975). The implementation of accounting objectives: An application to extraordinary Items. *The Accounting Review, 50*, 58–68.

Barro, R. J. (1991). Economic growth in a cross section of countries. *The Quarterly Journal of Economics, 106*(2), 407–443. doi:10.2307/2937943

Barro, R. J., & Redlick, C. J. (2011). Macroeconomic effects from government purchases and Taxes. *The Quarterly Journal of Economics, 126*(1), 51–102. doi:10.1093/qje/qjq002

Bartov, E., Gul, F. A., & Tsui, J. S. L. (2001). Discretionary-accruals models and audit qualifications. *Journal of Accounting and Economics, 30*(3), 421–452. doi:10.1016/S0165-4101(01)00015-5

Bauman, C. C., & Bauman, M. P. (2002). The deferred tax asset valuation allowance and earnings quality. *Review of Accounting and Finance, 1*(1), 72–87. doi:10.1108/eb026980

Bauman, C. C., Bauman, M. P., & Halsey, R. F. (2001). Do firms use the deferred tax asset valuation allowance to manage earnings? *The Journal of the American Taxation Association, 23*(s-1), 27–48. doi:10.2308/jata.2001.23.s-1.27

Bauman, M. P., & Das, S. (2004). Stock market valuation of deferred tax assets: Evidence from internet firms. *Journal of Business Finance & Accounting, 31*(9-10), 1223–1260. doi:10.1111/j.0306-686X.2004.00573.x

Baxter, P., & Cotter, J. (2009). Audit committees and earnings quality'. *Accounting and Finance, 49*(2), 267–290. doi:10.1111/j.1467-629X.2008.00290.x

Baysinger, B. D., Kosnik, R. D., & Turk, T. A. (1991). Effects of board and ownership structure on corporate R&D strategy. *Academy of Management Journal, 34*(1), 205–214. doi:10.2307/256308

Beattie, V., McInnes, B., & Fearnley, S. (2001). *The Analysis of Narratives in Annual Reports: A Multidimensional Framework.* Working Paper, University of Stirling.

Beattie, V., & Jones, M. (2000). Impression Management: The case of Inter-country financial graphs. *Journal of International Accounting, Auditing & Taxation, 9*(2), 159–183. doi:10.1016/S1061-9518(00)00030-6

Beattie, V., McInnes, W., & Fearnley, S. (2004). A methodology for analysing and evaluating narratives in annual reports: A comprehensive descriptive profile and metrics for disclosure quality attributes. *Accounting Forum*, *28*(3), 205–236. doi:10.1016/j.accfor.2004.07.001

Beck, N., & Katz, J. N. (1995). What to Do (and Not to Do) With Time-series Cross-section Data. *The American Political Science Review*, *89*(3), 634–647. doi:10.2307/2082979

Beck, T., Buyukkarabacak, B., Rioja, F. K., & Valev, N. T. (2012). Who Gets the Credit? And Does It Matter? Household vs. Firm Lending across Countries. *The B.E. Journal of Macroeconomics*, *12*(1), 1–46. doi:10.1515/1935-1690.2262

Beck, T., Degryse, H., & Kneer, C. (2014). Is more finance better? Disentangling intermediation and size effects of financial systems. *Journal of Financial Stability*, *10*, 50–64. doi:10.1016/j.jfs.2013.03.005

Beck, T., & Levine, R. (2004). Stock markets, banks, and growth: Panel evidence. *Journal of Banking & Finance*, *28*(3), 423–442. doi:10.1016/S0378-4266(02)00408-9

Behn, B. K., Eaton, T. V., & Williams, J. R. (1998). The determinants of the deferred tax allowance account under SFAS No. 109. *Accounting Horizons*, *12*(1), 63–78.

Beidleman, C. R. (1973). Income smoothing: The role of management. *The Accounting Review*, *48*, 653–667.

Bekaert, G., & Harvey, C. R. (1997). *Foreign speculators and emerging equity markets*. The Davidson Institute Working Paper Series, Working Paper Number 79.

Bekaert, G., Harvey, C. R., & Lundblad, C. (2002). *Growth volatility and equity market liberalization?* Unpublished working paper. Columbia, Duke and Indiana Universities.

Bekaert, G., & Harvey, C. R. (2000). Foreign speculators and emerging equity markets. *The Journal of Finance*, *55*(2), 565–613. doi:10.1111/0022-1082.00220

Bellman, R. (2013). *Dynamic programming*. Courier Corporation.

Bencivenga, V. R., & Smith, B. D. (1991). Financial intermediation and endogenous growth. *The Review of Economic Studies*, *58*(2), 195–209. doi:10.2307/2297964

Bencivenga, V. R., Smith, B. D., & Starr, R. M. (1995). Transaction costs, technological choice, and endogenous growth. *Journal of Economic Theory*, *67*(1), 53–117. doi:10.1006/jeth.1995.1069

Benito, A., & Hernando, I. (2007). Firm behavior and financial pressure: Evidence from Spanish Panel Data. *Bulletin of Economic Research*, *59*(4), 283–311. doi:10.1111/j.0307-3378.2007.00266.x

Bepari, M. K., Rahman, S. F., & Mollik, A. T. (2014). Firms' compliance with the disclosure requirements of IFRS for goodwill impairment testing: Effect of the global financial crisis and other firm characteristics. *Journal of Accounting & Organizational Change*, *10*(1), 116–149. doi:10.1108/JAOC-02-2011-0008

Bhattacharya, U., Daouk, H., & Welker, M. (2003). The world price of earnings opacity. *The Accounting Review*, *78*(3), 641–678. doi:10.2308/accr.2003.78.3.641

Bhide, A. (1993). The hidden costs of stock market liquidity. *Journal of Financial Economics*, *34*(1), 1–51. doi:10.1016/0304-405X(93)90039-E

Bildirici, M. E., Aykaç Alp, E., Ersin, Ö. Ö., & Bozoklu, Ü. (2010). *İktisatta kullanılan doğrusal olmayan zaman serisi yöntemleri*. Türkmen Kitabevi.

Birt, J. L., Bilson, C. M., Smith, T., & Whaley, R. E. (2006). Ownership, competition, and financial disclosure. *Australian Journal of Management*, *31*(2), 235–263. doi:10.1177/031289620603100204

Bittencourt, M. (2012). Financial development and economic growth in Latin America: Is Schumpeter right? *Journal of Policy Modeling*, *34*(3), 341–355. doi:10.1016/j.jpolmod.2012.01.012

Blanchard, J. O., & Fischer, S. (1989). *Lectures in Macroeconomics*. MIT Press.

Blundell, R., & Bond, S. (1998). Initial conditions and moment restrictions in dynamic panel data models. *Journal of Econometrics*, *87*(1), 115–143. doi:10.1016/S0304-4076(98)00009-8

Bond, S. R., Hoeffler, A., & Temple, J. (2001). *GMM estimation of empirical growth models*. CEPR Discussion Paper No. 3048. Centre for Economic Policy Research, London, UK.

Bonini, S., Capizzi, V., Cipollini, A., & Erbetta, F. (2007). *The Effect of Analysts' Forecasts on Stock Market Returns: A Composite Multifactor Approach*. 10.2139/ssrn.990047

Bordo, M. D., & Rousseau, P. L. (2012). Historical evidence on the finance-trade-growth nexus. *Journal of Banking & Finance*, *36*(4), 1236–1243. doi:10.1016/j.jbankfin.2011.11.012

Borensztein, E., Cowan, K., & Valenzuela, P. (2007). *Sovereign Ceilings Lite? The Impact of Sovereign Ratings on Corporate Ratings in Emerging Market Economies*. IMF Working Paper No. 07/75.

Botosan, C. (1997). Disclosure Level and the Cost of Equity Capital. *The Accounting Review*, *72*(3), 323–349.

Bova & Pereira. (2012). The Determinants and Consequences of Heterogeneous IFRS Compliance Levels Following Mandatory IFRS Adoption: Evidence from a Developing Country. *Journal of International Accounting Research: Spring*, *11*(1), 83-111.

Boyd, J. H., & Prescott, E. C. (1986). Financial intermediary-coalitions. *Journal of Economic Theory*, *38*(2), 211–232. doi:10.1016/0022-0531(86)90115-8

Boyd, J., Hu, J., & Jagannathan, R. (2005). The stock Market's Reaction to Unemployment News: Why Bad News is usually Good for Stocks. *The Journal of Finance*, *60*(2), 649–672. doi:10.1111/j.1540-6261.2005.00742.x

Brahmasrene, T., & Jiranyakul, K. (2007). Cointegration and Causality between Stock Index and Macroeconomic Variables in an Emerging Market. *Academy of Accounting and Financial Studies Journal*, *11*(3), 17–29.

Brailsford, T., & Hooper, V. (2001). Selecting macroeconomic variables as explanatory factors of emerging stock market returns. *Pacific-Basin Finance Journal*, *9*(4), 401–426. doi:10.1016/S0927-538X(01)00020-8

Breusch, T. S., & Pagan, A. R. (1979). A simple test for heteroscedasticity and randon coefficient variation. *Econometrica*, *47*(5), 1287–1294. doi:10.2307/1911963

Brooks, R., Edison, H., Kumar, M. S., & Slok, T. (2004). Exchange rates and capital flows. *European Financial Management*, *10*(3), 511–533. doi:10.1111/j.1354-7798.2004.00261.x

Brown, G. W., & Cliff, M. T. (2004). Investor Sentiment and the Near-term Stock Market. *Journal of Empirical Finance*, *11*(1), 1–27. doi:10.1016/j.jempfin.2002.12.001

Brown, G. W., & Cliff, M. T. (2005). Investor Sentiment and Asset Valuation. *The Journal of Business*, *78*(2), 405–439. doi:10.1086/427633

Bukowski, S. (2011). Economic and Monetary Union - Current Fiscal Disturbances and the Future. *International Advances in Economic Research*, *17*(3), 274–287. doi:10.100711294-011-9310-7

Burgstahler, D., Elliott, W. B., & Hanlon, M. (2002). *How firms avoid losses: Evidence of use of the net deferred tax asset account.* Working Paper, University of Washington.

Burja, C. (2011). Factors influencing the companies' profitability. *Annales Universitatis Apulensis Series Oeconomica*, *13*(2), 215–224.

Bushee, B. J. (1997). *Institutional investors, longterm investment and earnings management* (Ph.D. Thesis). University of Michigan.

Bushee, B. J. (1998). The influence of institutional investors on myopic R&D investment behavior. *The Accounting Review*, *73*(3), 305–333.

Buyuksalvarci, A. (2010). The Effects of Macroeconomics Variables on Stock Returns: Evidence from Turkey. *European Journal of Soil Science*, *14*(3), 70–83.

Buyya, R., Venugopal, S., Broberg, J., & Brandic, I. (2009). Cloud computing and emerging IT platforms: Vision, hype, and reality for delivering computing as the 5th utility. *Future Generation Computer Systems*, *25*(18), 599–616. doi:10.1016/j.future.2008.12.001

Calvo, G. A., & Reinhart, C. M. (2002). Fear of floating. *The Quarterly Journal of Economics*, *117*(2), 379–408. doi:10.1162/003355302753650274

Campbell, J. Y., & Mankiw, N. G. (1987). Are output fluctuations transitory? *The Quarterly Journal of Economics*, *102*(4), 857–880. doi:10.2307/1884285

Campos, N. F., Karanasos, M. G., & Tan, B. (2012). Two to tangle: Financial development, political instability and economic growth in Argentina. *Journal of Banking & Finance*, *36*(1), 290–304. doi:10.1016/j.jbankfin.2011.07.011

Canadian Institute of Chartered Accountants. (1991). *Information to be included in the Annual Report to Shareholders*. Research Study.

Caporale, G. M., Ali, F. M., Spagnolo, F., & Spagnolo, N. (2017). International portfolio flows and exchange rate volatility in emerging Asian markets. *Journal of International Money and Finance*, *76*, 1–15. doi:10.1016/j.jimonfin.2017.03.002

Cartlidge, J., & Clamp, P. (2014). Correcting a financial brokerage model for cloud computing: Closing the window of opportunity for commercialisation. *Journal of Cloud Computing*, *3*(1), 2. doi:10.1186/2192-113X-3-2

Cascino & Gassen. (2015). What drives the comparability effect of mandatory IFRS adoption? *Review of Accounting Studies, 20*(1), 242–282.

Cecchetti, G., & Kharroubi, E. (2012). *Reassessing the impact of finance on growth*. BIS Working Paper No. 381. Bank for International Settlements.

Celasun, O., & Agsa, S. (2009). *How Does Public External Debt Affect Corporate Borrowing Costs In Emerging Markets?* IMF Working Paper.

Chaban, M. (2009). Commodity currencies and equity flows. *Journal of International Money and Finance*, *28*(5), 836–852. doi:10.1016/j.jimonfin.2008.08.004

Chalikias, M. S. (2013a). Research of personnel selection methods in the Greek private bank sector. *African Journal of Business Management*, *7*(26), 2570–2575.

Chalikias, M. S. (2013b). Citizens' views in Southern Greece PART I: The forests' threats. *Journal of Environmental Protection and Ecology*, *14*(2), 509–516.

Chalikias, M.S., & Kolovos, K.G. (2013). Citizens' views in Southern Greece PART II: The contribution of forests to quality of life. *Journal of Environmental Protection and Ecology*, *14*(2), 629–637.

Chalmers, K., & Godfrey, J. (2004). Reputation Costs: The Impetus for Voluntary Derivative Financial Instrument Reporting. *Accounting, Organizations and Society*, *29*(2), 95–125. doi:10.1016/S0361-3682(02)00034-X

Chaney, P. K., & Lewis, C. M. (1995). Earnings management and firm valuation under asymmetric information. *Journal of Corporate Finance*, *1*(3-4), 319–345. doi:10.1016/0929-1199(94)00008-I

Chao, C. L., Kelsey, R. L., Horng, S. M., & Chiu, C. Y. (2004). Evidence of earnings management from the measurement of the deferred tax allowance account. *The Engineering Economist*, *49*(1), 63–93. doi:10.1080/00137910490432683

Charitou, S., Elfani, M., & Lois, P. (2010). The Effect of Working Capital Management on Firm's Profitability: Empirical Evidence From An Emerging Markets. *Journal of Business & Economics Research*, *8*(12), 63–68. doi:10.19030/jber.v8i12.782

Checherita, C., & Rother, P. (2010). *The impact of high and growing government debt on economic growth an empirical investigation for the euro area*. ECB Working Paper Series No 1237.

Cheng, C. S. A., & Reitenga, A. (2009). Characteristics of institutional investors and discretionary accruals. *International Journal of Accounting and Information Management*, *17*(1), 5–26. doi:10.1108/18347640910967717

Chen, N.-F., Roll, R., & Ross, S. A. (1986). Economic Forces and the Stock Market. *The Journal of Business*, *59*(3), 383–403. doi:10.1086/296344

Christensen, T. E., Paik, G. H., & Stice, E. K. (2008). Creating a bigger bath using the deferred tax valuation allowance. *Journal of Business Finance & Accounting*, *35*(5-6), 601–625. doi:10.1111/j.1468-5957.2008.02092.x

Christopoulos, A., Dokas, I., & Matzaris, D. (2013). The estimation of corporate liquidity management using artificial neural networks. *International Journal of Financial Engineering and Risk Management*, *1*(2), 193–210. doi:10.1504/IJFERM.2013.055849

Chtourou, S. M., Bedard, J., & Courteau, L. (2001). *Corporate governance and earnings management*. Retrieved from http://ssrn.com/abstract=275053

Chung, R., Firth, M., & Kim, J.-B. (2002). Institutional monitoring and opportunistic earnings management. *Journal of Corporate Finance*, *8*(1), 29–48. doi:10.1016/S0929-1199(01)00039-6

Chytis, E., Koumanakos, E., & Siriopoulos, C. (2013). Deferred Tax Positions under the prism of financial crisis and the effects of a corporate tax reform. *12th Annual Conference of the Hellenic Finance and Accounting Association (HFAA), organized by the Department of Accounting and Finance of the University of Macedonia.*

Clamp, P., & Cartlidge, J. (2013). Pricing the cloud: an adaptive brokerage for cloud computing. In *5th International conference on advances in system simulation (SIMUL-2013)*. IARIA XPS Press.

Clarkson, P. M., Kao, J. L., & Richardson, G. D. (1999). Evidence that management discussion and analysis (MD&A) is part of a firm's overall disclosure package. *Contemporary Accounting Research*, *16*(1), 111–134. doi:10.1111/j.1911-3846.1999.tb00576.x

Clatworthy, M., & Jones, M. J. (2001). The effect of thematic structure on the variability of annual report readability. *Accounting, Auditing & Accountability Journal*, *14*(3), 311–326. doi:10.1108/09513570110399890

Cole, R. A., Moshirian, F., & Wu, Q. (2008). Bank stock returns and economic growth. *Journal of Banking & Finance*, *32*(6), 995–1007. doi:10.1016/j.jbankfin.2007.07.006

Cooke, T. E. (1989). Voluntary corporate disclosure by Swedish companies. *Journal of International Financial Management & Accounting*, *1*(2), 171–195. doi:10.1111/j.1467-646X.1989.tb00009.x

Cornett, M. M., Marcus, A. J., & Tehranian, H. (2008). Corporate governance and pay-for-performance: The impact of earnings management. *Journal of Financial Economics*, *87*, 357–373. doi:.jfineco.2007.03.00310.1016/j

Cornett, M. M., Marcus, A. J., Saunders, A., & Tehranian, H. (2007). The impact of institutional ownership on corporate operating performance. *Journal of Banking & Finance*, *31*(6), 1771–1794. doi:10.1016/j.jbankfin.2006.08.006

Courtis, J., & Hassen, S. (2002). Reading ease of bilingual annual reports. *Journal of Business Communication*, *39*(3), 394–413. doi:10.1177/002194360203900401

Çulha, A. A. (2006). A Structural VAR Analysis of the Determinants of Capital Flows into Turkey. *Central Bank Review*, *2*, 11–35.

Daskalakis, N., & Psillaki, M. (2008). Do country or firm factors explain capital structure? Evidence from SMEs in France and Greece. *Applied Financial Economics*, *18*(2), 87–97. doi:10.1080/09603100601018864

David, P., & Kochhar, R. (1996). Barriers to effective governance by institutional investors: Implications for theory and practice. *European Management Journal*, *14*(5), 457–466. doi:10.1016/0263-2373(96)00039-4

Davies, R. B. (1987). Hypothesis Testing when a Nuisance Parameter is Present Only Under the Alternatives. *Biometrika Trust*, *74*(1), 33–43.

De Gregorio, J. (1993). Inflation, taxation and long-run growth. *Journal of Monetary Economics*, *31*(3), 271–298. doi:10.1016/0304-3932(93)90049-L

De Gregorio, J., & Guidotti, P. (1995). Financial development and economic growth. *World Development*, *23*(3), 433–448. doi:10.1016/0305-750X(94)00132-I

De Long, J., Shleifer, A., Summers, L., & Waldmann, R. (1989). The size and incidence of the losses from noise trading. *The Journal of Finance*, *44*(3), 681–696. doi:10.1111/j.1540-6261.1989.tb04385.x

Dechow, P. M. (1994). Accounting Earnings and Cash Flows as Measures of Firm Performance: The Role of Accounting Accruals. *Journal of Accounting and Economics*, *18*(1), 3–42. doi:10.1016/0165-4101(94)90016-7

Dechow, P. M., & Dichev, I. D. (2002). The quality of accruals and earnings: The role of accrual estimation errors. *The Accounting Review*, *77*(s1), 35–59. doi:10.2308/accr.2002.77.s-1.35

Dechow, P. M., Ge, W., & Schrand, C. (2010). Understanding earning quality: A review of the proxies, their determinants and their Consequences. *Journal of Accounting and Economics*, *50*(2-3), 344–401. doi:10.1016/j.jacceco.2010.09.001

Dechow, P. M., Sloan, R. G., & Sweeney, A. P. (1995). Detecting earnings management. *The Accounting Review*, *70*(2), 193–225.

Dechow, P. M., Sloan, R. G., & Sweeney, A. P. (1996). Causes and consequences of earnings manipulations: An analysis of firms subject to enforcement actions by the SEC. *Contemporary Accounting Research*, *13*(1), 1–36. doi:10.1111/j.1911-3846.1996.tb00489.x

Dechow, P., Kothari, S., & Watts, R. (1998). The relation between earnings and cash flows. *Journal of Accounting and Economics*, *25*, 133–168. doi:10.1016/S0165-4101(98)00020-2

DeFond, M. L., & Jiambalvo, J. (1994). Debt covenant violation and manipulation of accruals. *Journal of Accounting and Economics*, *17*(1-2), 145–176. doi:10.1016/0165-4101(94)90008-6

Deidda, L., & Fattouh, B. (2002). Non-linearity between finance and growth. *Economics Letters*, *74*(3), 339–345. doi:10.1016/S0165-1765(01)00571-7

Deloitte. (2006). *Write to reason: Surveying OFRs and narrative reporting in annual reports.* London: Author.

Deloof, M. (2003). Does Working Capital Management Affect Profitability of Belgian Firm? *Journal of Business and Accounting*, *30*(3-4), 573–587. doi:10.1111/1468-5957.00008

DeMiguel, V., Garlappi, L., & Uppal, R. (2009). Optimal Versus Naive Diversification: How Inefficient is the 1/ N Portfolio Strategy? *Review of Financial Studies*, *22*(5), 1915–1953. doi:10.1093/rfs/hhm075

Demir & Bahadir. (2014). An investigation of compliance with International Financial Reporting Standards by listed companies in Turkey. *Accounting and Management Information Systems*, *13*(1), 4–34.

Devereux, M., & Smith, G. (1994). International risk sharing and economic growth. *International Economic Review*, *35*(3), 535–550. doi:10.2307/2527072

Dhawan, R. (2001). Firm size and productivity differential: Theory and evidence from a panel of US firms. *Journal of Economic Behavior & Organization*, *44*(3), 269–293. doi:10.1016/S0167-2681(00)00139-6

Dichev, I. D., & Skinner, D. J. (2002). Largesample evidence on the debt covenant hypothesis. *Journal of Accounting Research*, *40*(4), 1091–1123. doi:10.1111/1475-679X.00083

Ding, S., & Knight, J. (2009). Can the augmented Solow model explain China's remarkable economic growth? A cross-country panel data analysis. *Journal of Comparative Economics*, *37*(3), 432–452. doi:10.1016/j.jce.2009.04.006

Dockery, E., & Kavussanos, M. G. (1996). Testing the Efficient Market Hypothesis Using Panel Data, with Application to the Athens Stock Market. *Applied Economics Letters*, *3*(2), 121–123. doi:10.1080/135048596356834

Dogan, M. (2013). Does Firm Size Affect the Firm Profitability? Evidence from Turkey. *Research Journal of Finance and Accounting*, *4*, 53–59.

Dong, H., & Su, T. (2010). The relationship between working capital management and profitability: A Vietnam case. *International Research Journal of Finance and Economics*, *49*, 62–71.

Doupnik, T. S., & Salter, S. B. (1995). External environment, Culture and Accounting Practice: A Preliminary Test of A General Model of International Accounting Development. *The International Journal of Accounting*, *30*(3), 189–202.

Dritsaki, C., & Dritsaki-Bargiota, M. (2005). The Causal Relationship between Stock, Credit Market and Economic Development: An Empirical Evidence for Greece. *Economic Change and Restructuring*, *38*(1), 113–127. doi:10.100710644-005-4525-3

Duggal, R., & Millar, J. A. (1999). Institutional ownership and firm performance: The case of bidder returns. *Journal of Corporate Finance*, *5*(2), 103–117. doi:10.1016/S0929-1199(98)00018-2

Duman, H. (2010). *Kamunun Aydınlatılması İlkesi Kapsamında Kazanç Yönetimi Uygulamalarının Finansal Raporlama Kalitesi ve Şirket Performansı Üzerine Etkisi: İMKB'de Bir Uygulama* (Ph.D. Thesis). Selçuk University Institute of Social Sciences.

Dunmontier, P., & Raffourmier, B. (1998). Why firm comply voluntarily with IAS: An empirical analysis with Swiss data. *Journal of International Financial Management & Accounting*, *9*(3), 216–245. doi:10.1111/1467-646X.00038

Durbin, J., & Watson, G. S. (1950). Testing for serial correlation in least square regression. *Biometrika*, *37*, 409–428. PMID:14801065

Dye, R. A. (1985). Disclosure of Nonproprietary Information. *Journal of Accounting Research*, *23*(1), 123–145. doi:10.2307/2490910

Easterly, W., Islam, R., & Stiglitz, J. E. (2000). *Explaining growth volatility*. The World Bank.

Easterly, W., & Levine, R. (2001). What have we learned from a decade of empirical research on growth? It's not factor accumulation: Stylized facts and growth models. *The World Bank Economic Review*, *15*(2), 177–219. doi:10.1093/wber/15.2.177

Easterly, W., & Rebelo, S. (1993). Fiscal policy and economic growth: An empirical investigation. *Journal of Monetary Economics*, *32*(3), 417–458. doi:10.1016/0304-3932(93)90025-B

Ebrahim, A. M. (2004). *The effectiveness of corporate governance, institutional ownership, and audit quality as monitoring devices of earnings management* (Ph.D. Thesis). Graduate School Newark, State University of New Jersey.

ECB. (2017). *The use of cash by households in the euro area*. Retrieved from https://www.ecb.europa.eu/pub/pdf/scpops/ecb.op201.en.pdf

EFRAG. (2013). *EFRAG and the FRC issue the Feedback Statement on the Discussion Paper Improving the Financial Reporting of Income Tax*. Retrieved from http://www.efrag.org/Front/n1-1102/EFRAG-and-the-FRC-issue-the-Feedback-Statement-on-the-Discussion-Paper--Improving-the-Financial-Reporting-of-Income-Tax.aspx

Eljelly, A. (2004). Liquidity-Profitability Tradeoff: An empirical Investigation in an Emerging Market. *International Journal of Commerce and Management*, *14*(2), 48–61. doi:10.1108/10569210480000179

Elton, E. J., Gruber, M. J., & Busse, A. (1998). Do Investors Care about Sentiment? *The Journal of Business*, *71*(4), 477–500. doi:10.1086/209754

Eng, L. L. (1995). *The implications of managerial incentives and institutional ownership for firms' research and development (R&D) investments* (Ph.D. Thesis). University of Michigan.

Eriotis, N., Vasiliou, D., & Ventoura-Neokosmidi, Z. (2007). How firm characteristics affect capital structure: An empirical study. *Managerial Finance*, *33*(5), 321–331. doi:10.1108/03074350710739605

Eugene, F. (1981). Stock returns, Real Activity, Inflation and Money. *The American Economic Review*, *71*(4), 545–565.

Evsey, D. (1946). Capital Expansion, Rate of Growth and Employment. *Econometrica*, *14*(2), 137–147. doi:10.2307/1905364

Fabozzi, F. J., Huang, D., & Zhou, G. (2010). Robust portfolios: Contributions from operations research and finance. *Annals of Operations Research*, *176*(1), 191–220. doi:10.100710479-009-0515-6

Fabozzi, F., Neave, E., & Zhou, G. (2012). *Financial Economics*. John Wiley & Sons.

Fama, E. (1990). Stock returns, Expected Returns and Real Activity. *The Journal of Finance*, *45*(4), 1089–1108. doi:10.1111/j.1540-6261.1990.tb02428.x

Fama, E., & French, K. (1989). Business Conditions and Expected Returns on Stocks and Bonds. *Journal of Financial Economics*, *25*(1), 23–49. doi:10.1016/0304-405X(89)90095-0

Fara, M., & Supartika, N. (2016). Factors affecting profitability of small medium enterprises (SMEs) firm listed in Indonesia Stock Exchange. *Journal of Economics, Business and Management*, *4*(2), 132-137.

Fathi, S., Sameti, M., Nouri, B., & Esfahani, S. (2012). Examining the Effect of Selective Macroeconomic Variables on The Stock Exchange's Depth and Breadth (Case Study: Tehran Stock Exchange). *International Journal of Economics and Finance*, *4*(3), 97–104. doi:10.5539/ijef.v4n3p97

Federer, P. (1993). The impact of uncertainty on aggregate investment spending. *Journal of Money, Credit and Banking*, *25*(1), 30–45. doi:10.2307/2077818

Felipe, A., Sanchez, D., Felipe, A., Sanchez, D., & Diaz-sanchez, F. (2016). Cloud brokering: New value-added services and pricing models TELECOM ParisTech Spécialité "Informatique et Réseaux" Cloud brokering. *Nouveaux services de valeur ajoutée et politique de prix.*

Fischer, S. (1993). The role of macroeconomic factors in growth. *Journal of Monetary Economics*, *32*(3), 485–512. doi:10.1016/0304-3932(93)90027-D

Flannery, M., & Protopapadakis, A. (2002). Macroeconomic factors do influence Aggregate Stock Returns. *Review of Financial Studies*, *15*(3), 751–782. doi:10.1093/rfs/15.3.751

Florou, A., & Galarniotis, A. (2007). Benchmarking Greek Corporate Governance Against Different Standards. *Corporate Governance*, *15*(5), 979–998. doi:10.1111/j.1467-8683.2007.00614.x

Fox, A., Gwen, H., Helliar, C., & Veneziani, M. (2013). The costs and benefits of IFRS implementation in the UK and Italy. *Journal of Applied Accounting Research*, *14*(1), 86–101. doi:10.1108/09675421311282568

Frank, M. M., & Rego, S. O. (2006). Do managers use the valuation allowance account to manage earnings around certain earnings targets? *The Journal of the American Taxation Association*, *28*(1), 43–65. doi:10.2308/jata.2006.28.1.43

Franses, P. H. H. & Dijk, D. (2000). *Nonlinear Time Series Models in Empirical Finance*. Cambridge University Press.

Friedman, M. (1957). *A Theory of the Consumption Function*. Princeton University Press.

Fry, M. J. (1997). In favour of financial liberalization. *Economic Journal (London)*, *107*(442), 754–770. doi:10.1111/j.1468-0297.1997.tb00041.x

G4S. (2016). *Update G4S Cash Report Europe 2016*. Retrieved from https://www.thefutureofcash.com/userfiles/files/the-future-of-cash-2016a.pdf

Gan, Lee, Yong, & Zhang. (2006). Macroeconomic Variables and Stock Market Interactions: New Zealand Evidence. *Investment Management and Financial Innovations*, *3*(4), 89–101.

Garbellini, N., Marelli, E., & Wirkierman, A. L. (2014). Domestic demand and global production in the Eurozone: A multi-regional input-output assessment of the global crisis. *International Review of Applied Economics*, *28*(3), 336–364. doi:10.1080/02692171.2013.872086

Garefalakis, A., & Dimitras, A. (2016). The Contribution of Management Commentary Index (Ma.Co.I) in Annual Banking Reports (ABR) and the Chronicle of the Great Greek Crisis. *Theoretical Economics Letters*, *06*(05), 1060–1087. doi:10.4236/tel.2016.65103

Garefalakis, A., Dimitras, A., Floros, C., & Lemonakis, C. (2016). How Narrative Reporting changed the Business World: Providing a new measurement tool. *Corporate Ownership and Control*, *13*(4), 317–334. doi:10.22495/cocv13i4c2p5

Gebauer, S., Setzer, R., & Westphal, A. (2017). *Corporate debt and investment: a firm level analysis for stressed euro area countries*. Working paper Series, No 2101, European Central Bank.

Georgantopoulos, A., & Tsamis, A. (2011). The Triangular Causal Links between Economic Development, FDI and Exports: Evidence from Turkey. *Middle Eastern Finance and Economics*, *15*, 66–75.

Georgantopoulos, A., Tsamis, A., & Agoraki, M. (2015). The Euro-adoption effect and the bank, market, and growth nexus: New evidence from EU panels. *Journal of Economic Asymmetries*, *12*(1), 41–51. doi:10.1016/j.jeca.2015.01.002

Georgiadis, G., & Grab, J. (2015). *Global Financial Market Impact of the Announcement of the ECB's Extended Asset Purchase Programme*. Federal Reserve Bank of Dallas Globalization and Monetary Policy Institute. Working Paper No. 232

Geske, R., & Roll, R. (1983). The Fiscal and Monetary Linkage Between Stock Returns and Inflation. *The Journal of Finance*, *38*(1), 1–33. doi:10.1111/j.1540-6261.1983.tb03623.x

Ghazani, M., & Araghi, M. (2014). Evaluation of the adaptive market hypothesis as an evolutionary perspective on market efficiency: Evidence from the Tehran stock exchange. *Research in International Business and Finance*, *32*, 50–59. doi:10.1016/j.ribaf.2014.03.002

Ghosh, S., & Herwadkar, S. (2009). Foreign Portfolio Flows and their Impact on Financial Markets in India. *Reserve Bank of India Occasional Papers*, *30*(3), 51-72.

Gikas, G., Hyz, A., & Tagkas, P. (2013). The Experience of Greece from its participation in the Eurozone. *Management Insight. The Journal of Incisive Analysers, 9*(1).

Gill, A., Biger, N., & Mathur, N. (2010). The relationship between working capital management and profitability: Evidence from the United States. *Business and Economic Journal*, 1-9.

Gilli, M., & Schumann, E. (2011). Optimal enough? *Journal of Heuristics*, *17*(4), 373–387. doi:10.100710732-010-9138-y

Giovanis, E. (2010). *Application of Capital Asset Pricing (CAPM) and Arbitrage Pricing Theory (APT) Models in Athens Exchange Stock Market*. GRIN Verlag.

Giovanis, E., & Ozdamar, O. (2014). *Determinants of Profitability: Evidence from US Firms*. Facoltà di Economia, Università degli Studi di Verona.

Gitman, L. J., & Zutter, C. J. (2012). *Principles ofManagerial Finance* (13th ed.). Addison Wesley.

Glaum, M., & Street, D. (2003). Compliance with the disclosure requirements of Germany's new market: IAS versus US GAAP. *Journal of International Financial Management & Accounting*, *14*(1), 64–100. doi:10.1111/1467-646X.00090

Goddard, J., Tavakoli, M., & Wilson, J. O. S. (2005). Determinants of profitability in European manufacturing and services: Evidence from a dynamic panel model. *Applied Financial Economics*, *15*(18), 1269–1282. doi:10.1080/09603100500387139

Godfrey, J., Hodgson, A., Tarca, A., Hamilton, J., & Holmes, S. (2010). Accounting theory (7th ed.). John Wiley & Sons Australia, Ltd.

Goulas, E., & Zervoyianni, A. (2013). Growth, deficits and uncertainty: Theoretical aspects and empirical evidence from a panel of 27 countries. *The Quarterly Review of Economics and Finance*, *53*(4), 380–392. doi:10.1016/j.qref.2013.07.005

Granger, C. W. J. (1969). Investigating causal relations by econometric models and cross – spectral methods. *Econometrica*, *37*(3), 424–438. doi:10.2307/1912791

Graves, S. B. (1988). Institutional ownership and corporate R&D in the computer industry. *Academy of Management Journal*, *31*(2), 417–428. doi:10.2307/256557

Griliches, Z., & Hausman, J. A. (1986). Errors in variables in panel data. *Journal of Econometrics*, *31*(1), 93–118. doi:10.1016/0304-4076(86)90058-8

Grossman, G. M., & Helpman, E. (1992). *Innovation and growth: Technological competition in the global economy*. Boston: MIT Press.

Guidolin, M. (n.d.). *Modelling, Estimating and Forecasting Financial Data under Regime (Markov) Switching*. Lecture 7. Department of Finance. Bocconi University. Retrieved from http://didattica.unibocconi.it/mypage/dwload.php?nomefile=Lecture_7_-_Markov_Switching_Models20130520235704.pdf, 30.03.2016.

Gupta, S., Clements, B., Baldacci, E., & Mulas-Granados, C. (2005). Fiscal policy, expenditure composition and growth in low-income countries. *Journal of International Money and Finance*, *24*(3), 441–463. doi:10.1016/j.jimonfin.2005.01.004

Gurbuz, A. O., Aybars, A., & Kutlu, O. (2010). Corporate governance and financial performance with a perspective on institutional ownership: Empirical evidence from Turkey. *Journal of Applied Managerial Accounting Research*, *8*, 21–38.

Hamilton, J. D. (1989). A New Approach to the Economic Analysis of Nonstationary Time Series and the Business Cycle. *Econometrica*, *57*(2), 357–384. doi:10.2307/1912559

Hansen, G. A. (1999). *Bias and estimation error in discretionary accrual models*. Working Paper, Penn State University. Retrieved from http://ssrn.com/abstract=192748

Hansen, G. S., & Hill, C. W. L. (1991). Are institutional investors myophic? A time-series study of four technology-driven industries. *Strategic Management Journal*, *12*(1), 1–16. doi:10.1002mj.4250120102

Hasan, E. (2010). *Behavioral approach to Arbitrage Pricing Theory*. Retrieved 17/02/2016 from http://mpra.ub.uni-muenchen.de/26343/1/MPRA_paper_26343.pdf

Hasan, I., Wachtel, P., & Zhou, M. (2009). Institutional development, financial deepening, and economic growth: Evidence from China. *Journal of Banking & Finance*, *33*(1), 157–170. doi:10.1016/j.jbankfin.2007.11.016

Hassan, Q. F. (2011). Demystifying Cloud Security. *Crosstalk*, 6–21. Retrieved from http://www.crosstalkonline.org/storage/issue-archives/2011/201101/201101-Hassan.pdf

Hayajneh, O. S., & Yassine, F. L. A. (2011). The impact of Working Capital Efficiency on Profitability – an Empirical Analysis on Jordanian Manufacturing Firms. *International Research Journal of Finance and Economics*, *66*, 67–76.

Herbohn, K., Tutticci, I., & Khor, P. S. (2010). Changes in Unrecognised Deferred Tax Accruals from Carry-Forward Losses: Earnings Management or Signalling? *Journal of Business Finance & Accounting*, *37*(7-8), 763–791. doi:10.1111/j.1468-5957.2010.02207.x

Hill, C. W. L., & Hansen, G. S. (1989). Institutional holdings and corporate R&D intensity in research intensive industries. Academy of Management Best Papers Proceedings, 17-21.

Hodgdon, C., Tondkar, R., Harless, D., & Adhikari, A. (2008). Compliance with IFRS disclosure requirements and individual analysts' forecast errors. *Journal of International Accounting, Auditing & Taxation*, *17*(1), 1–13. doi:10.1016/j.intaccaudtax.2008.01.002

Holthausen, R. W. (1990). Accounting method choice: Opportunistic behavior, efficient contracting, and information perspectives. *Journal of Accounting and Economics*, *12*(1-3), 207–218. doi:10.1016/0165-4101(90)90047-8

Holthausen, R. W., & Leftwich, R. W. (1983). the economic consequences of accounting choice implications of costly contracting and monitoring. *Journal of Accounting and Economics*, *5*(2), 77–119. doi:10.1016/0165-4101(83)90007-1

Hossain, M., & Adams, M. (1995). Voluntary financial disclosure by Australian listed companies. *Australian Accounting Review*, *5*(10), 45–55. doi:10.1111/j.1835-2561.1995.tb00381.x

Hossain, M., Perera, M. H. B., & Rahman, A. R. (1995). Voluntary Disclosure in the Annual Reports of New Zealand Companies. *Journal of International Financial Management & Accounting*, *6*(l), 69–87. doi:10.1111/j.1467-646X.1995.tb00050.x

Hribar, P., & Collins, D. W. (2002). Errors in estimating accruals: Implications for empirical research. *Journal of Accounting Research*, *40*(1), 105–134. doi:10.1111/1475-679X.00041

Hsu, G. C.-M., & Koh, P.-S. (2005). Does the presence of institutional investors influence accruals management? Evidence from Australia. *Corporate Governance*, *13*(6), 809–823. doi:10.1111/j.1467-8683.2005.00472.x

Hur, J., Raj, M., & Riyanto, E. Y. (2006). Finance and trade: A cross-country empirical analysis on the impact of financial development and asset tangibility on international trade. *World Development*, *34*(10), 1728–1741. doi:10.1016/j.worlddev.2006.02.003

Hussin, M., Muhammad, F., Awang, S., Marwan, N., & Razak, A. (2013). The Impact of Oil Price Shocks on Islamic Financial Market in Malaysia. *Journal of Islamic Economics, Banking and Finance*, *9*(3), 53–68. doi:10.12816/0001611

Hyz, A., & Gikas, G. (2016). CAMELS and Greek banking sector performance during the crisis. An analysis and review of the evidence. *Acta Universitatis Lodziensis. Folia Oeconomica, 5*(316).

Hyz, A., Kalandonis, P., & Stavroulakis, D. (2017). Management of working capital - The Achilles heel of small and medium enterprises (SMEs). The case of Greece. *Central European Review of Economics and Finance, 2017*(2).

IASB. (2014). *IAS 12 Income Taxes: Recognition of Deferred Tax Assets for Unrealised Losses.* Retrieved from http://www.ifrs.org/Current-Projects/IASB-Projects/Pages/IASB-Work-Plan.aspx

IASB/FASB. (2006). *A Roadmap for Convergence between IFRSs and US GAAP-2006-2008-Memorandum of Understanding between the FASB and the IASB*. Retrieved from http://www.ifrs.org/Use-around-the-world/Global-convergence/Convergence-with-US-GAAP/Documents/MoU.pdf

Iatrides, G. (2008). I Accounting disclosure and firms' financial attributes: Evidence from the UK stock market. *International Review of Financial Analysis, 17*(2), 219–241. doi:10.1016/j.irfa.2006.05.003

IFRS. (n.d.). *IAS 12 Income Taxes*. Retrieved from http://www.ifrs.org/Current-Projects/IASB-Projects/Income-Taxes/Pages/Income-taxes-research-project.aspx

IME GSEVEE. (2016). *Economic Climate Trends*. Retrieved from http://www.imegsevee.gr/pressrelease/1085-ime-gsevee-survey-february-2016--biannual-representation-of-economic-climate-in-small-enterprises-

Inchausti, B. G. (1997). The influence of company characteristics and accounting regulation on information disclosed by Spanish firms. *European Accounting Review, 6*(1), 45–68. doi:10.1080/096381897336863

International Accounting Standards Board. (2005). *Discussion Paper: Management Commentary*. London: Author.

International Accounting Standards Board. (2006). *Discussion Paper: Management Commentary*. London: Author.

International Monetary Fund. (2017). *World Economic Outlook Update*. Retrieved from http://www.imf.org/en/Publications/WEO/Issues/2017/07/07/world-economic-outlook-update-july-2017

IOBE (Foundation for Economic & Industrial Research). (2015). *Digital payments and tax revenues in Greece*. Retrieved from http://iobe.gr/docs/research/en/RES_05_F_21102015_REP_EN.pdf

Iturriaga, S., Nesmachnow, S., & Dorronsoro, B. (2017). Optimizing the Profit and QoS of Virtual Brokers in the Cloud. In Cloud Computing (pp. 277-300). Springer International Publishing. doi:10.1007/978-3-319-54645-2_11

Jandik, T., & Makhija, A. K. (2005). Debt, Debt Structure and Corporate Performance after Unsuccessful Takeovers: Evidence from Targets that Remain Independent. *Journal of Corporate Finance, 11*(5), 882–914. doi:10.1016/j.jcorpfin.2004.04.002

Jarque, M., & Bera, K. (1987). A test of normality of observations and regression Residuals. *International Statistical Review, 55*(2), 163–172. doi:10.2307/1403192

Jensen, M. C., & Meckling, W. H. (1976). Theory of the firm: Managerial behaviour agency costs and ownership structure. *Journal of Financial Economics, 3*(4), 305–360. doi:10.1016/0304-405X(76)90026-X

Johansen, S. (1988). Statistical Analysis of Cointegration Vectors. *Journal of Economic Dynamics & Control, 12*(2–3), 231–254. doi:10.1016/0165-1889(88)90041-3

Johansen, S. (1991). Estimation and Hypothesis Testing of Cointegration Vectors in Gaussian Vector Autoregressive Models. *Econometrica*, *59*(6), 1551–1580. doi:10.2307/2938278

John, C., Jonathan, I., & Ross, S. A. (1985). An intertemporal general equilibrium model of asset prices. *Econometrica*, *53*(2), 363–384. doi:10.2307/1911241

Jones, J. J. (1991). Earnings management during import relief investigations. *Journal of Accounting Research*, *29*(2), 193–228. doi:10.2307/2491047

Jones, M., & Shoemaker, P. (1994). Accounting narratives: A review of empirical studies of content and readability. *The Journal of Accounting Literature*, *13*, 142–184.

Jones, S., & Higgins, A. D. (2006). Australia's switch to international financial reporting standards: A perspective from account preparers. *Accounting and Finance*, *46*(4), 629–652. doi:10.1111/j.1467-629X.2006.00186.x

Jorion, P. (2006). *Value at risk : The new benchmark for managing financial risk*. McGraw-Hill.

Jung, W., & Kwon, Y. (1988). Disclosure when the market is unsure of information endowment of managers. *Journal of Accounting Research*, *26*(1), 146–153. doi:10.2307/2491118

Kajuter, P. (2006). *Risk disclosures of listed firms in Germany: a longitudinal study*. Presented at the 10th Financial Reporting & Business Communication Conference, Cardiff Business School "Unpublished results".

Kalemli-¨Ozcan, S., Laeven, L., & Moreno, D. (2015a). *Debt Overhang, Rollover Risk and Investment in Europe*. ECB and University of Maryland.

Kaminsky, G. L., & Reinhart, C. M. (1999). The twin crises: The causes of banking and balance-of-payments problems. *The American Economic Review*, *89*(3), 473–500. doi:10.1257/aer.89.3.473

Kao, C., & Steuer, R. E. (2016). Value of information in portfolio selection, with a Taiwan stock market application illustration. *European Journal of Operational Research*, *253*(2), 418–427. doi:10.1016/j.ejor.2016.02.011

Karaduman, H. A., Akbas, H. E., Ozsozgun, A., & Ducer, S. (2010). Effects of Working Capital management on profitability: The Case for selected companies in the Istanbul Stock Exchange (2005-2008). *International Journal of Economics and Finance Studies*, *2*, 47–54.

Karaibrahimoğlu, Y. (2010). *The role of corporate governance on earnings management: Quarterly evidence from Turkey* (Ph.D. Thesis). İzmir University of Economics.

Karamanis & Papadakis. (2008). *The application of IFRS in Greece*. Athens University of Economics and Business. (in Greek)

Karamanis, K., & Hyz, A. (2014). Flexible working and Unemployment in Greece: An Analysis and Review of the Evidence. *International Journal of Academic Research in Business and Social Sciences, 4*(10).

Katsampoxakis, I., Basdekis, H., & Anathreptakis, K. (2015). How firm and market characteristics affect profitability: An empirical study. *International Journal of Corporate Finance and Accounting*, *2*(1), 67–83. doi:10.4018/IJCFA.2015010104

Kennet, M., Drosos, D., & Tsotsolas, N. (2013). Special Issue: The Greek Crisis: Some Environmental and Economic initiatives and the first steps towards implementing Green Economics. *International Journal of Green Economics*, *7*(4), 315–319.

Keynes, J. M. (1936). *The general theory of employment, interest, and money*. London: Macmillan.

Khanna, T., Palepu, K. G., & Srinivasan, S. (2004). Disclosure Practices of Foreign Companies Interaction with U.S. Markets. *Journal of Accounting Research*, *42*(2), 475–508. doi:10.1111/j.1475-679X.2004.00146.x

Kimani, D., & Mutuku, C. (2013). Inflation Dynamics on the Overall Stock Market Performance: The Case of Nairobi Securities Exchange in Kenya. *Economics and Finance Review, 2*(11), 1 – 11.

Kim, H., Heshmati, A., & Aoun, D. (2005). Dynamics of Capital Structure: The Case of Korean Listed Manufacturing Companies. *Asian Economic Journal*, 275–302.

King, R. G., & Levine, R. (1993a). Finance and growth: Schumpeter might be right. *The Quarterly Journal of Economics*, *108*(3), 717–737. doi:10.2307/2118406

King, R. G., & Levine, R. (1993b). Finance, entrepreneurship, and growth. *Journal of Monetary Economics*, *32*(3), 513–542. doi:10.1016/0304-3932(93)90028-E

Klassen, K. J. (1997). The Impact of Inside Ownership Concentration on the Trade-Off Between Financial and Tax Reporting. *The Accounting Review*, *72*, 455–474.

Knowles, J., & Corne, D. (2002). On metrics for comparing nondominated sets. *Proceedings of the 2002 Congress on Evolutionary Computation, CEC 2002*, 711–716.

Koch, C. (2009). *The Arbitrage Pricing Theory as an Approach to Capital Asset Valuation.* GRIN Verlag.

Koenker, R., & Hallock, K. (2001). Quantile Regression. *The Journal of Economic Perspectives*, *15*(4), 143–156. doi:10.1257/jep.15.4.143

Kohlscheen, E., & O'Connell, S. A. (2008). *Trade Credit and Sovereign Debt.* Department of Economics, University of Warwick.

Koh, P.-S. (2003). On the association between institutional ownership and aggressive corporate earnings management in Australia. *The British Accounting Review*, *35*(2), 105–128. doi:10.1016/S0890-8389(03)00014-3

Koh, P.-S. (2007). Institutional investor type, earnings management and benchmark beaters. *Journal of Accounting and Public Policy*, *26*(3), 267–299. doi:10.1016/j.jaccpubpol.2006.10.001

Kolm, P. N., Tutuncu, R., & Fabozzi, F. J. (2014). 60 Years of portfolio optimization: Practical challenges and current trends. *European Journal of Operational Research*, *234*(2), 356–371. doi:10.1016/j.ejor.2013.10.060

Konno, H., & Yamazaki, H. (1991). Mean-Absolute Deviation portfolio optimization model and its applications to Tokyo Stock Market. *Management Science*, *37*(5), 519–531. doi:10.1287/mnsc.37.5.519

Kothari, S. P., Leone, A. J., & Wasley, C. E. (2005). Performance matched discretionary accrual measures. *Journal of Accounting and Economics*, *39*(1), 163–197. doi:10.1016/j.jacceco.2004.11.002

KPMG. (2017). *Greece – New Law Amends Income Tax System*. Retrieved from https://home.kpmg.com/xx/en/home/insights/2017/04/flash-alert-2017-073.html

Krishnamurthy, A., & Vissing-Jorgensen, A. (2010). *The Aggregate Demand for Treasury Debt*. Working paper. Northwestern University.

Krokhmal, P., Palmquist, J., & Uryasev, S. (2001). Portfolio optimization with Conditional Value-At-Risk objective and constraints. *The Journal of Risk*, *4*(2), 1–36. doi:10.21314/JOR.2002.057

Krolzig, H. M. (2000). *Predicting Markov-switching vector autoregressive processes*. Oxford University Working Paper 2000W31.

Krolzig, H. M. (1998). *Markov Switching Vector Autoregressions: Modelling, Statistical Inference, and Application to Business Cycle Analysis*. Berlin: Springer-Verlag.

Kumar, K. R., & Visvanathan, G. (2003). The information content of the deferred tax valuation allowance. *The Accounting Review*, *78*(2), 471–490. doi:10.2308/accr.2003.78.2.471

Kumar, R. (2013). The Effect of Macroeconomic Factors on Indian Stock Market Performance: A Factor Analysis Approach. *IOSR Journal of Economics and Finance*, *1*(3), 14–21. doi:10.9790/5933-0131421

La Porta, R., Lopez-de-Silanes, F., Shleifer, A., & Vishny, W. R. (1998). Law and finance. *Journal of Political Economy*, *106*(6), 1113–1155. doi:10.1086/250042

Lajili, K. (2007). *Corporate governance and risk disclosure*. Working Paper No. 2007-24, University of Ottawa, Tefler School of Management, Ottawa, ON.

Lalou, P., Chalikias, M., Skordoulis, M., Papadopoulos, P., & Fatouros, S. (2016). A Probabilistic Evaluation of sales expansion. *5th International Symposium and 27th National Conference on Operation Research*, 109-112.

Lang, M. H., & Lundholm, R. J. (1993). Cross sectional determinants of analysis rating of corporate disclosure. *Journal of Accounting Research*, *31*(2), 246–271. doi:10.2307/2491273

Law, S. H., & Singh, N. (2014). Does too much finance harm economic growth? *Journal of Banking & Finance*, *41*, 36–44. doi:10.1016/j.jbankfin.2013.12.020

Lazaridis, I., & Tryfonidis, D. (2006). Relationship Between Working Capital Management and Profitability of Listed Companies in Athens Stock Exchange. *Journal of Financial Management and Analysis*, *19*, 1.

Lee, B.-S. (1992). Causal Relations among Stock Returns, Interest Rates, Real Activity and Inflation. *The Journal of Finance*, *47*(4), 1591–1603. doi:10.1111/j.1540-6261.1992.tb04673.x

Lee, C., & Lee, J. (2009). Energy prices, multiple structural breaks, and efficient market hypothesis. *Applied Energy*, *86*(4), 466–479. doi:10.1016/j.apenergy.2008.10.006

Lee, C., Lee, J., & Lee, C. (2010). Stock prices and the efficient market hypothesis: Evidence from a panel stationary test with structural breaks. *Japan and the World Economy*, *22*(1), 49–58. doi:10.1016/j.japwor.2009.04.002

Lee, C., Shleifer, A., & Thaler, R. (1991). Investor Sentiment and the Closed-end Fund Puzzle. *The Journal of Finance*, *46*(1), 75–109. doi:10.1111/j.1540-6261.1991.tb03746.x

Lemmon, M., & Portniaguina, E. (2006). Consumer Confidence and Asset Prices: Some Empirical Evidence. *Review of Financial Studies*, *19*(4), 1499–1529. doi:10.1093/rfs/hhj038

Leuz, C., Nanda, D., & Wysocki, P. D. (2003). Earnings management and investor protection: An international comparison. *Journal of Financial Economics*, *69*(3), 505–527. doi:10.1016/S0304-405X(03)00121-1

Leuz, C., Pfaff, D., & Hopwood, A. (2004). *The Economics and Politics of Accounting International Perspectives on Research Trends, Policy and Practice*. New York, NY: Oxford University Press.

Leventides, J., & Kollias, I. (2014). Optimal Control Indicators for the Assessment of the Influence of Government Policy to Business Cycle Shocks. *Journal of Dynamics and Games*, 79 – 104.

Levine, R., Loayza, N., & Beck, T. (2000). Financial intermediation and growth: Causality and causes. *Journal of Monetary Economics*, *46*(1), 31–77. doi:10.1016/S0304-3932(00)00017-9

Levine, R., & Renelt, D. (1992). A sensitivity analysis of cross-country growth regressions. *The American Economic Review*, *82*, 942–963.

Levine, R., & Zervos, S. (1998). Stock markets, banks and economic growth. *The American Economic Review*, *88*, 537–558.

Liargovas, P., & Skandalis, K. (2010). Factors affecting firm competitiveness: The case of Greek industry. *European Industrial Journal*, *2*, 184–197.

Li, M. Y. L., & Hwang, N. C. R. (2011). "Effects of Firm size, Financial Leverage and R&D Expenditures on Firm Earnings: An Analysis Using Quintile Regression Approach", A Journal of Accounting. *Finance and Business Studies*, *47*(2), 182–204.

Lim, A. E. B., Shanthikumar, J. G., & Vahn, G.-Y. (2011). Conditional value-at-risk in portfolio optimization: Coherent but fragile. *Operations Research Letters*, *39*(3), 163–171. doi:10.1016/j.orl.2011.03.004

Lin, T., Hutchinson, M., & Percy, M. (2009). The role of audit committee and institutional investors in constraining earnings management: Evidence from Chinese firms listed in Hong Kong. *Proceedings of Accounting & Finance Association of Australia & New Zealand Annual Conference,* 1-40.

Lin, L., & Manowan, P. (2012). Institutional ownership composition and earnings management. *Review of Pacific Basin Financial Markets and Policies, 15*(4), 1250022. doi:10.1142/S0219091512500221

Linsley, P. M., & Shrives, P. J. (2006). Risk reporting: A study of risk disclosures in the annual reports of UK companies. *The British Accounting Review, 38*(4), 387–404. doi:10.1016/j.bar.2006.05.002

Liu, A. Z. (2005). *The role of financial analysts and institutional investors in the numbers game.* Retrieved from http://ssrn.com/abstract=705385

Ljung, G. M., & Box, G. E. P. (1978). On a measure of lack of fit in time series models. *Biometrika, 65*(2), 297–303. doi:10.1093/biomet/65.2.297

Loayza, N. V., & Ranciere, R. (2006). Financial development, financial fragility and growth. *Journal of Money, Credit and Banking, 38*(4), 1051–1076. doi:10.1353/mcb.2006.0060

Lopes, P., & Rodrigues, L. L. (2007). Accounting for financial instruments: An analysis of the determinants of the disclosure in the Portuguese stock exchange. *The International Journal of Accounting, 42*(1), 25–26. doi:10.1016/j.intacc.2006.12.002

MacKinnon, J. (1996). Numerical Distribution Function for Unit Root and Cointegration Tests. *Journal of Applied Econometrics, 11*(6), 601–618. doi:

Mahanov, V., & Hudson, R. (2014). A note on the relationship between market efficiency and adaptability – New evidence from artificial stock markets. *Expert Systems with Applications, 41*(16), 7436–7454. doi:10.1016/j.eswa.2014.06.004

Majumdar, S. K., & Nagarajan, A. (1997). The impact of changing stock ownership patterns in the United States: Theoretical implications and some evidence. *Revue d'Economie Industrielle, 82*(1), 39–54. doi:10.3406/rei.1997.1686

Malliaris & Urrutia. (2005). How big is the random walk in macroeconomic time series: Variance ratio tests. *Economic Uncertainty, Instabilities And Asset Bubbles*, 9 – 12.

Mansini, R., Ogryczak, W., & Speranza, M. G. (2003). LP Solvable Models for Portfolio Optimization: A Classification and Computational Comparison. *IMA Journal of Management Mathematics, 14*(3), 187–220. doi:10.1093/imaman/14.3.187

Mansini, R., Ogryczak, W., & Speranza, M. G. (2014). Twenty years of linear programming based portfolio optimization. *European Journal of Operational Research, 234*(2), 518–535. doi:10.1016/j.ejor.2013.08.035

Marinescu, D. C. (2012). Cloud Computing. *Theory into Practice*, 1–403. PMID:22333270

Markowitz, H. (1952). Portfolio Selection. *The Journal of Finance*, *7*(1), 77–91.

Martinez, J. V., & Sandleris, G. (2008). *Is It Punishment? Sovereign Defaults and the Decline in Trade*. Universidad Torcuato Di Tella, Working Paper.

Martinez-Carrascal, C., & Herrando, A. (2008). *The impact of financial position on investment: An analysis for non-financial corporations in the Euro Area*. ECB Working Paper Series, 943.

Mashayekhy, L., Nejad, M. M., & Grosu, D. (2014, October). A two-sided market mechanism for trading big data computing commodities. In *Big Data (Big Data), 2014 IEEE International Conference on* (pp. 153-158). IEEE. 10.1109/BigData.2014.7004225

Mathuva, D. M. (2010). The influence of working capital management components on corporate profitability: A survey on Kenyan listed firms. *Research Journal of Business Management*, *4*(1), 1–11. doi:10.3923/rjbm.2010.1.11

McConnell, J. J., & Servaes, H. (1995). Equity ownership and the two faces of debt. *Journal of Financial Economics*, *39*(1), 131–157. doi:10.1016/0304-405X(95)00824-X

McInnis, J. (2010). Earnings smoothness, average returns, and implied cost of equity capital. *The Accounting Review*, *85*(1), 315–341. doi:10.2308/accr.2010.85.1.315

McNichols, M. F. (2000). Research design issues in earnings management studies. *Journal of Accounting and Public Policy*, *19*(4-5), 313–345. doi:10.1016/S0278-4254(00)00018-1

Meek, G. K., Roberts, C. B., & Gray, S. J. (1995). Factors Influencing Voluntary Annual Report Disclosures by U.S., U.K. and Continental European Multinational Corporations. *Journal of International Business Studies*, *26*(3), 555–572. doi:10.1057/palgrave.jibs.8490186

Mell, P., & Grance, T. (2011). The NIST definition of cloud computing. *NIST Special Publication*, *145*, 7. doi:10.1136/emj.2010.096966

Merton, R. C. (1973). An intertemporal capital asset pricing model. *Econometrica*, *41*(5), 867–887. doi:10.2307/1913811

Metaxiotis, K., & Liagkouras, K. (2012). Multiobjective Evolutionary Algorithms for Portfolio Management: A comprehensive literature review. *Expert Systems with Applications*, *39*(14), 11685–11698. doi:10.1016/j.eswa.2012.04.053

Miihkinen, A. (2012). What Drives Quality of Firm Risk Disclosure?: The Impact of a National Disclosure Standard and Reporting Incentives under IFRS. *The International Journal of Accounting*, *47*(4), 437–468. doi:10.1016/j.intacc.2012.10.005

Miller, G. S. (2002). Earnings performance and discretionary disclosure. *Journal of Accounting Research*, *40*(1), 173–204. doi:10.1111/1475-679X.00043

Miller, G. S., & Skinner, D. J. (1998). Determinants of the valuation allowance for deferred tax assets under SFAS No. 109. *The Accounting Review*, 213–233.

Miller, S., & Russek, F. (1997). Fiscal structures and economic growth. *Economic Inquiry, 35*(3), 603–613. doi:10.1111/j.1465-7295.1997.tb02036.x

Mishra, P., Moriyama, K., N'diaye, P. M. B. P., & Nguyen, L. (2014). *Impact of Fed Tapering Announcements on Emerging Markets*. IMF Working Paper. WP/14/109.

Mitani, H. (2010). *Additional evidence on earnings management and corporate governance.* Financial Research and Training Center Discussion Paper Series. DP 2009-7.

Mitra, S. (2002). *The impact of institutional stock ownership on a firm's earnings management practice: An empirical investigation* (Ph.D. Thesis). Louisiana State University and Agricultural and Mechanical College.

Mitra, S., & Cready, W. M. (2005). Institutional ownership, accrual management, and information environment. *Journal of Accounting, Auditing & Finance, 20*(3), 257–286. doi:10.1177/0148558X0502000304

Modigliani, F., & Brumberg, R. (1954). Utility Analysis and the Consumption Function: an interpretation of cross-section data. In K. K. Kurihara (Ed.), *Post-Keynesian Economics*. New Brunswick, NJ: Rutgers University Press.

Modigliani, F., & Miller, M. H. (1958). The cost of capital, corporate finance and the theory of investment. *The American Economic Review, 48*(3), 261–297.

Modigliani, F., & Miller, M. H. (1963). Corporate Income Taxes and Cost of Capital: A correction. *The American Economic Review, 53*(3), 433–443.

Mohobbot, A. (2005). Corporate risk reporting practices in annual reports of Japanese companies. *Japanese Journal of Accounting., 16*, 113–133.

Morgese-Borys, M., Polgàr, K., & Zlate, A. (2008). *Real convergence and determinants of growth in the EURO candidate and potential candidate countries: A panel data approach, ECB occasional Paper No. 86*. European Central Bank.

Moses, D. (1987, April). Income smoothing and incentives: Empirical test using accounting changes. *The Accounting Review*, 358–373.

Mundell, R. (1965). Growth, stability and inflationary finance. *Journal of Political Economy, 73*(2), 97–109. doi:10.1086/258999

Myers, J., Myers, L., & Skinner, D. (2007). Earnings momentum and earnings management. *Journal of Accounting, Auditing & Finance, 22*(2), 249–284. doi:10.1177/0148558X0702200211

Narayan, K. P., Mishra, S., & Narayan, S. (2011). Do market capitalisation and stocks traded converge? New global evidence. *Journal of Banking & Finance, 35*(10), 2771–2781. doi:10.1016/j.jbankfin.2011.03.010

Narayan, K. P., & Narayan, S. (2013). The short-run relationship between the financial system and economic growth: New evidence from regional panels. *International Review of Financial Analysis*, *29*, 70–78. doi:10.1016/j.irfa.2013.03.012

Narware, P. C. (2010). Working Capital Management: The Effect of Market Valuation and Profitability in Malaysia. *International Journal of Business and Management*, *5*, 11.

Nazir, M. S., & Afza, T. (2009). Impact of aggressive working capital management policy in firms profitability. *The IUP Journal of Applied Finance*, *15*(8), 19–30.

Ndubizu, G., & Tsetsekos, G. (1992). Functional currency smoothing and managerial incentives: An empirical test. *The International Journal of Accounting*, *27*, 27–37.

Neal, R., & Wheatley, S. M. (1998). Do Measures of Investor Sentiment Predict Returns? *Journal of Financial and Quantitative Analysis*, *333*(4), 523–547. doi:10.2307/2331130

Nesmachnow, S., Iturriaga, S., Dorronsoro, B., El-Ghazali, T., & Bouvry, P. (2013). List scheduling heuristics for virtual machine mapping in cloud systems. *VI Latin American Symposium on High Performance Computing (HPCLatam)*, 37-48.

Nesmachnow, S., Iturriaga, S., & Dorronsoro, B.IEEE. (2015). Efficient heuristics for profit optimization of virtual cloud brokers. *IEEE Computational Intelligence Magazine*, *10*(1), 33–43. doi:10.1109/MCI.2014.2369893

Niarchos, N. A., & Alexakis, C. A. (2000). The Predictive Power of Macroeconomic Variables on Stock Market Returns: The Case of the Athens Stock Exchange. *SPOUDAI*, *50*(1/2), 74–86.

Niarchos, N., & Alexakis, C. (1998). Stock market prices, 'causality' and efficiency: Evidence from the Athens stock exchange. *Applied Financial Economics*, *8*(2), 167–174.

Nieuwerburgh, S. V., Buelens, F., & Cuyvers, L. (2006). Stock market development and economic growth in Belgium. *Explorations in Economic History*, *43*(1), 13–38. doi:10.1016/j.eeh.2005.06.002

Nobes, C., & Parker, R. (2000). *Comparative International Accounting* (6th ed.). Financial Times-Prentice Hall.

Nopphon, T. (2011). Macroeconomic Factors of Emerging Stock Market: The Evidence from Thailand. *International Journal of Financial Research*, *3*(2), 105–114.

Obstfeld, M. (1994). Risk taking, global diversification, and growth. *The American Economic Review*, 1310–1329.

Oliveira, J., Rodrigues, L. L., & Russell, C. (2011). Risk-related disclosures by non-finance companies: Portuguese practices and disclosure characteristics. *Managerial Auditing Journal*, *26*(9), 817–839. doi:10.1108/02686901111171466

Onyeisi, O. S., Odo, I. S., & Anoke, C. I. (2016). Foreign Portfolio Investment and Stock Market Growth in Nigeria. *Developing Country Studies*, *6*(11), 64–76.

Owen, A. L., & Temesvary, J. (2014). Heterogeneity in the growth and finance relationship: How does the impact of bank finance vary by country and type of lending? *International Review of Economics & Finance*, *31*, 275–288. doi:10.1016/j.iref.2014.02.007

Owusu-Ansah, S. (2000). Noncompliance with corporate annual report disclosure requirements in Zimbabwe. *Research in Accounting in Emerging Economies.*, *4*, 289–305.

Øystein, G., & Frode, S. (1999). Causal relations among stock returns and macroeconomic variables in a small, open economy. *Journal of International Financial Markets, Institutions and Money*, *9*(1), 61–74. doi:10.1016/S1042-4431(98)00036-5

Ozcan, A. (2012). The Relationship Between Macroeconomic Variables and ISE Industry Index. *International Journal of Economics and Financial Issues*, *2*(2), 184–189.

Padachi, K. (2006). Trends in Working Capital Management and its Impact on Firm's Performance: An Analysis of Mauritian Small Manufacturing Firms. *International Review of Business Research Papers*, *2*, 45–58.

Palan, S. (2007). *The efficient market hypothesis and its validity in today's markets*. GRIN Verlag.

Palmer, P. (2008). Disclosure of the impacts of abandoning Australian equivalents of International Financial reporting Standards. *Accounting and Finance*, *48*, 847–870.

Pal, R., & Ferrando, A. (2010). Financing constraints and firms cash policy in the euro area. *European Journal of Finance*, *16*(2), 153–171. doi:10.1080/13518470903075748

Pennachi, G. (2007). *Theory of Asset Pricing*. Prentice Hall.

Pervan, M., & Visic, J. (2012). Influence of firm size on its business success. *Croatian Operational Research Review*, *3*, 213–223.

Pesaran, H., & Smith, R. (1995). Estimating long-run relationships from dynamic heterogeneous panels. *Journal of Econometrics*, *68*(1), 79–113. doi:10.1016/0304-4076(94)01644-F

Pindyck, R., & Solimano, A. (1993). Economic instability and aggregate investment. *NBER Macroeconomics Annual*, *8*, 259–303. doi:10.1086/654223

Poon, S. H., & Taylor, S. J. (1992). Stock returns and volatility: An empirical study of the UK stock market. *Journal of Banking & Finance*, *16*(1), 37–59. doi:10.1016/0378-4266(92)90077-D

Porter, M. E. (1992). Capital disadvantage: America's failing capital investment system. *Harvard Business Review*, 65–82. PMID:10121317

Powell, W. B. (2007). *Approximate Dynamic Programming: Solving the curses of dimensionality* (Vol. 703). Wiley-Interscience. doi:10.1002/9780470182963

Prawitt, D. F., Jason, L. S., & Wood, D. A. (2009). Internal audit quality and earnings management. *The Accounting Review*, *84*(4), 1255–1280. doi:10.2308/accr.2009.84.4.1255

Qiu, M., & La, B. (2010). Firm Characteristics as Determinants of Capital Structures in Australia. *International Journal of the Economics of Business*, *17*(3), 277–287. doi:10.1080/13571516.2010.513810

Raffournier, B. (1995). The determinants of voluntary financial disclosure by Swiss listed companies. *European Accounting Review*, *4*(2), 261–280. doi:10.1080/09638189500000016

Raheman, A., Afza, T., Qayyum, A., & Bodla, M.A. (2010). Working Capital Management and Corporate Performance of Manufacturing Sector in Pakistan. *International Research Journal of Finance and Economics,* (47).

Rajgopal, S., & Venkatachalam, M. (1997). *The role of institutional investors in corporate governance: An empirical investigation.* Research Paper, 1436.

Rajgopal, S., Venkatachalam, M., & Jiambalvo, J. (1999). *Is institutional ownership associated with earnings management and the extent to which stock prices reflect future earnings?* SSRN Working Paper Series.

Rajhi, M. (2014). International Financial Reporting Standards and Level of Compliance with Mandatory Disclosure Requirements. *International Journal of Multidisciplinary Sciences and Engineering, 5*(5), 1–6.

Ramasamy, B. (2005). Firm size, ownership and performance in the Malaysian palm oil industry. *Asian Academy of Management Journal of Accounting and Finance*, *1*, 81–104.

Rayan, K. (2008). *Financial leverage and firm value*. Gordon Institute of Business Science, University of Protoria.

Richardson, S. A., Sloan, R. G., Soliman, M. T., & Tuna, A. I. (2001). *Information in Accruals About the Quality of Earnings*. SSRN.

Rjoub, H., Tursoy, T., & Gunsel, N. (2009). The effects of macroeconomic factors on stock returns: Istanbul Stock Market. *Studies in Economics and Finance*, *26*(1), 36–45. doi:10.1108/10867370910946315

Robb, S. W. G., Single, L. E., & Zarzeski, M. T. (2001). Nonfinancial Disclosures Across Anglo-American Countries. *Journal of International Accounting*, *10*(1), 71–83.

Robert, G. (2008). Effect of Macroeconomic Variables on Stock Market Returns For Four Emerging Economies: Brazil, Russia, India, And China. *International Business & Economics Research Journal*, *7*(3), 42–56.

Robert, S. (1956). A Contribution to the Theory of Economic Growth. *The Quarterly Journal of Economics*, *70*(1), 65–94. doi:10.2307/1884513

Rockafellar, R. T., & Uryasev, S. (2002). Conditional value-at-risk for general loss distributions. *Journal of Banking & Finance*, *26*(7), 1443–1471. doi:10.1016/S0378-4266(02)00271-6

Rodosthenous, M. (2012). The impact of Corporate Governance on enterprises efficiency. The NASDAQ and NYSE listed Greek shipping companies. *The Southeuropean Review of Business Finance and Accounting*, *10*, 41–51.

Rogers, O., & Cliff, D. (2012). A financial brokerage model for cloud computing. Journal of Cloud Computing: Advances. *Systems and Applications*, *1*(1), 2.

Roll, R. (1977). A Critique of the Asset Pricing Theory's Tests. *Journal of Financial Economics*, *4*(2), 129–176. doi:10.1016/0304-405X(77)90009-5

Romero-Avila, D., & Strauch, R. (2008). Public finances and long-term growth in Europe: Evidence from a panel data analysis. *European Journal of Political Economy*, *24*(1), 172–191. doi:10.1016/j.ejpoleco.2007.06.008

Roodman, D. (2006a). *How to Do xtabond2: An Introduction to Difference and System GMM in Stata*. Center for Global Development, Working Paper Number 103.

Roodman, D. (2006b). *A Note on the Theme of Too Many Instruments*. Center for Global Development, Working Paper Number 125.

Rose, A. K. (2005). One Reason Countries Pay Their Debts: Renegotiation and International Trade. *Journal of Development Economics*, *77*(1), 189–206. doi:10.1016/j.jdeveco.2004.03.006

Ross, S. A. (1976). The arbitrage theory of capital asset pricing. *Journal of Economic Theory*, *13*(3), 341–360. doi:10.1016/0022-0531(76)90046-6

Roy, H. (1939). An essay in Dynamic Theory. *Economic Journal (London)*, *49*(193), 14–33. doi:10.2307/2225181

Rujiravanich, N. (2013). Impacts of Foreign Portfolio Investment Flows on Stock Prices and Exchange Rate *in* Thailand after Asian Financial Crisis. *Economics and Public Policy*, *4*(8), 1–20.

Russell, D., & MacKinnon, J. G. (1993). *Estimation and Inference in Econometrics*. Oxford University Press.

Saaty, T. L. (1994). How to make a decision: The analytic hierarchy process. *Interfaces*, *24*(6), 19–43. doi:10.1287/inte.24.6.19

Saha, G., & Pasumarthy, R. (2015, September). Maximizing profit of cloud brokers under quantized billing cycles: a dynamic pricing strategy based on ski-rental problem. In *Communication, Control, and Computing (Allerton), 2015 53rd Annual Allerton Conference on* (pp. 1000-1007). IEEE. 10.1109/ALLERTON.2015.7447117

Salman, A. K., & Yazdanfar, D. (2012). Profitability in Swedish SME firms: A quantile regression approach. *International Business Research*, *5*(8), 94–106. doi:10.5539/ibr.v5n8p94

Samargandi, N., Firdmuc, J., & Ghosh, S. (2015). Is the Relationship between Financial Development and Economic Growth Monotonic? Evidence from a Sample of Middle-Income Countries. *World Development*, *68*, 66–81. doi:10.1016/j.worlddev.2014.11.010

Samitas, A. (2004). Testing the Efficient Market Hypothesis in The Greek Secondary Capital Market. *Zegreb International Review of Economics and Business*, *7*(1), 23–38.

Samitas, A., & Polyzos, S. (2016). Freeing Greece from capital controls: Were the restrictions enforced in time? *Research in International Business and Finance*, *37*, 196–213. doi:10.1016/j.ribaf.2015.11.005

Sangara, İ. (2016). External shocks and exchange rate regimes in Southeast Asia: A DSGE analysis. *Economic Modelling*, *58*, 365–382. doi:10.1016/j.econmod.2016.06.004

Schmeling, M. (2009). Investor Sentiment and Stock Returns: Some International Evidence. *Journal of Empirical Finance*, *16*(3), 394–408. doi:10.1016/j.jempfin.2009.01.002

Schrand, C. M., & Wong, M. H. (2003). Earnings management using the valuation allowance for deferred tax assets under SFAS no. 109. *Contemporary Accounting Research*, *20*(3), 579–611. doi:10.1506/480D-098U-607R-5D9W

Schumpeter, J. (1911). *Theorie der Wirtschaftlichen Entwicklung Leipzig*. Duncker and Humblot.

Schumpeter, J. A. (1934). *The theory of economic development*. Cambridge, MA: Harvard University Press.

Schwert, W. (1990). Stock Returns and Real Activity: A Century of Evidence. *The Journal of Finance*, *45*(4), 1237–1257. doi:10.1111/j.1540-6261.1990.tb02434.x

Scott, W. R. (2011). *Financial accounting theory* (6th ed.). Pearson Prentice Hall.

Sean Marston, Z. L. (2011). Cloud computing — The business perspective. *Elsevier BV.*, *51*(1), 176–189.

Sethi, N. (2012). Inflows and Their Macroeconomics Impact in India a VAR Analysis. *The Romanian Economic Journal*, *46*, 93–142.

Setyadi, A., Rusmin, R., Tower, G., & Brown, A. (2011). Measurement vs. disclosure of accounting compliance in Indonesia. International Journal of Accounting. *Auditing and Performance Evaluation.*, *7*(1/2), 94–119. doi:10.1504/IJAAPE.2011.037727

Sewell, M. (2007). *Behavioural Finance*. University of Cambridge.

Shahbaz, M. (2012). Does trade openness affect long run growth? Cointegration, causality and forecast error variance decomposition tests for Pakistan. *Economic Modelling*, *29*(6), 2325–2339. doi:10.1016/j.econmod.2012.07.015

Shen, C. H., & Lee, C. C. (2006). Same financial development yet different economic growth — Why? *Journal of Money, Credit and Banking*, *38*(7), 1907–1944. doi:10.1353/mcb.2006.0095

Shleifer, A., & Vishny, R. (1997). A survey of corporate governance. *The Journal of Finance*, *52*(2), 737–783. doi:10.1111/j.1540-6261.1997.tb04820.x

Singh, A. (1997). Financial liberalisation, stockmarkets and economic development. *Economic Journal (London), 107*(442), 771–782. doi:10.1111/j.1468-0297.1997.tb00042.x

Singh, J. P., & Pandey, S. (2008). Impact of working Capital Management in the Profitability of Hindalco Industries Limited. *Icfai University Journal of Financial Economics, 6*(4), 62–69.

Skiadas, C. (2009). *Asset Pricing Theory*. Princeton University Press.

Skordoulis, M., Chalikias, M., & Koniordos, M. (2014). Students' satisfaction through DREEM and LOT-R. In *Communications in Computer and Information Science. 466: Knowledge-Based Software Engineering: Proceedings of 11th Joint Conference on Knowledge-Based software Engineering*. Springer International Publishing.

Sloan, R. (1996). Do stock prices fully reflect information in accruals and cash flows about future earnings? *The Accounting Review, 71*, 289–315.

Smith, C., & Watts, R. (1992). The investment opportunity set and corporate financing, dividend, and compensation policies. *Journal of Financial Economics, 32*(3), 263–292. doi: X (92)90029-W10.1016/0304405

Smith, C. W., & Stulz, R. M. (1985). The determinants of firms' hedging policies. *Journal of Financial and Quantitative Analysis, 20*(4), 391–405. doi:10.2307/2330757

Smith, M., & Taffler, R. (2000). The chairpersons' statement: A content analysis of discretionary narrative disclosures. *Accounting, Auditing & Accountability Journal, 13*(5), 624–646. doi:10.1108/09513570010353738

Soderstrom, N. S., & Sun, K. J. (2007). IFRS Adoption and Accounting Quality: A review. *European Accounting Review, 16*(4), 675–702. doi:10.1080/09638180701706732

Solow, R. (1957). Technical change and the aggregate production function. *The Review of Economics and Statistics*, 70–92.

Spyridis, T., Sevic, Z., & Theriou, N. (2012). Macroeconomic vs Statistical APT in the Athens Stock Exchange. *International Journal Of Business, 17*(1), 39–64.

Srinivasan, R., Lilien, G. L., & Shridhar, S. (2011). Should Firms Spend More on Research and Development and Advertising During Recessions? *Journal of Marketing, 75*(3), 49–65. doi:10.1509/jmkg.75.3.49

Statista. (n.d.). *Banks and Financial Services*. Retrieved from https://www.statista.com/markets/414/topic/459/banks-financial-services/

Stengos, T., & Panas, E. (1992). Testing the efficiency of the ASE: Some results from the banking sector. *Empirical Economics, 17*, 239–252. doi:10.1007/BF01206285

Steuer, R. E. (1986). *Multiple Criteria Optimization: Theory, Computation and Application*. New York: John Wiley and Sons.

Steuer, R. E., & Choo, E. U. (1983). An interactive weighted Tchebycheff procedure for multiple objective programming. *Mathematical Programming*, *26*(3), 326–344.

Stierwald, A. (2009). *Determinants of firm profitability-The effect of productivity and its persistence*. Melbourne Institute of Applied Economic and Social Research, The University of Melbourne.

Stiglitz, J. E. (1985). Credit markets and the control of capital. *Journal of Money, Credit and Banking*, *17*(2), 133–152. doi:10.2307/1992329

Stock, J. H., & Watson, M. W. (1986). Does GNP have a unit root? *Economics Letters*, *22*(2-3), 147–151. doi:10.1016/0165-1765(86)90222-3

Stockman, A. C. (1981). Anticipated inflation and the capital stock in a cash-in-advance economy. *Journal of Monetary Economics*, *8*(3), 387–393. doi:10.1016/0304-3932(81)90018-0

Street, D. L., & Gray, S. J. (2001). *Observance of international accounting standards: Factors explaining noncompliance*. ACCA Research Report No. 74. The Association of Chartered Certified Accountants.

Street, D. L., & Bryant, S. M. (2000). Disclosure Level and Compliance with IASs: A Comparison of Companies With and Without U.S. Listings and Filings. *The International Journal of Accounting*, *35*(3), 305–329. doi:10.1016/S0020-7063(00)00060-1

Sunder, S. (2007). *Adverse Effects of Accounting Uniformity on Practice, Education, and Research.* Working paper. Available at SSRN: http://ssrn.com/abstract=1028517

Sydserff, R., & Weetman, P. (1999). A texture index for evaluating accounting narratives: An alternative to readability formulas. *Accounting, Auditing & Accountability Journal*, *12*(4), 459–488. doi:10.1108/09513579910283503

Sykianakis, N. (2004). Factors affecting Greek FDI in the Balkans: The case of Ice – Cream Industry. *Archives of Economic History*, *15*, 85–107.

Szegö, G. (2002). Measures of risk. *Journal of Banking & Finance*, *26*(7), 1253–1272. doi:10.1016/S0378-4266(02)00262-5

Tailab, M. M. (2014). Analyzing Factors Effecting Profitability of Non-Financial U.S. Firms. *Research Journal of Finance and Accounting*, *5*, 17–26.

Talangi, A. (2004). Modern Finance Versus Behavioral Finance. *Quarterly Journal of Financial Research*, 3-25.

Talvi, E., & Vegh, C. (2005). Tax Base Variability and Procyclical Fiscal Policy in Developing Countries. *Journal of Development Economics*, *78*(1), 156–190. doi:10.1016/j.jdeveco.2004.07.002

Tamai, T. (2014). Public capital, deficit financing, and economic growth in a stochastic economy. *Journal of Macroeconomics*, *42*, 14–26. doi:10.1016/j.jmacro.2014.06.006

Tambouratzis, T., Souliou, D., Chalikias M., & Gregoriades, A. (2010). Combining probabilistic neural networks and decision trees for maximally accurate and efficient accident prediction. *Proceedings of the IEEE International Joint Conference on Neural Network*, 1-8.

Tambouratzis, T., Souliou, D., Chalikias, M., & Gregoriades, A. (2014). Maximising accuracy and efficiency of traffic accident prediction by combining information mining with computational intelligence approaches and decision trees. *Journal of Artificial Intelligence and Soft Computing Research*, *4*(1), 31–42.

Taylor, M. A., & Wilson, F. L. J. (2011). International trade and finance: Complementaries in the United Kingdom 1870–1913 and the United States 1920–1930. *Journal of International Money and Finance*, *30*(1), 268–288. doi:10.1016/j.jimonfin.2010.10.002

Teixeira, A. (2004). Management Commentary. *Chartered Accounts Journal of New Zealand*, *83*(6), 17–20.

Teles, K., & Mussolini, C. (2014). Public debt and the limits of fiscal policy to increase economic growth. *European Economic Review*, *66*, 1–15. doi:10.1016/j.euroecorev.2013.11.003

Teruel, P. L., & Solano, P. M. (2007). Effects of working capital management on SME profitability. *International Journal of Management Finance*, *3*(2), 164–177.

Theophano, P., & Sunil, P. (2006). Economic variables and stock market returns: Evidence from the Athens stock exchange. *Applied Financial Economics*, *16*(3), 993–1005.

Timmermann, A., & Granger, C. (2004). Efficient market hypothesis and forecasting. *International Journal of Forecasting*, *20*(1), 15–27. doi:10.1016/S0169-2070(03)00012-8

Tobin, J. (1965). Money and economic growth. *Econometrica*, *33*(4), 671–684. doi:10.2307/1910352

Tornell, A., & Lane, P. (1999). The Voracity Effect. *The American Economic Review*, *89*(1), 22–46. doi:10.1257/aer.89.1.22

Trevor, S. (1956). Economic Growth and Capital Accumulation. *The Economic Record*, *32*(2), 334–361. doi:10.1111/j.1475-4932.1956.tb00434.x

Trueman, B. (1986). Why do managers voluntarily release earnings forecasts? *Journal of Accounting and Economics*, *8*(1), 53–72. doi:10.1016/0165-4101(86)90010-8

Trueman, B., & Titman, S. (1988). An explanation for accounting income smoothing. *Journal of Accounting Research*, *26*, 127–139. doi:10.2307/2491184

Tsalavoutas, I., & Evans, L. (2010). Transition to IFRS in Greece: Financial Statement Effects and Auditor Size. *Managerial Auditing Journal*, *25*(8), 814–842. doi:10.1108/02686901011069560

Tsalavoutas, I., Evans, L., & Smith, M. (2010). Comparison of two methods for measuring compliance with IFRS mandatory disclosure requirements. *Journal of Applied Accounting Research.*, *11*(3), 213–228. doi:10.1108/09675421011088143

Tzovas, C. (2006). Factors Influencing Firms' Accounting Policy Decisions When Tax Accounting And Financial Accounting Coincide. *Managerial Auditing Journal*, *21*(4), 372–386. doi:10.1108/02686900610661397

Urquhart, A., & Hudson, R. (2013). Efficient or adaptive markets? Evidence from major stock markets using very long run historic data. *International Review of Financial Analysis*, *28*, 130–142. doi:10.1016/j.irfa.2013.03.005

Vasilios-Christos, Sykianakis, & Christos. (2011). The perceptions of managers of Greek firms regarding the costs and benefits ensuing from the adoption of International Financial Reporting Standards in Greece. *International Journal of Economic Sciences and Applied Research, 4*(3), 59-74.

Verma, S. (2013). Profitability of commercial banks after the reforms: A study of selected banks in India. *International Journal of Research in Finance and Marketing*, *3*, 2.

Vermeulen, P. (2002). Business fixed investment: Evidence of a financial accelerator in Europe. *Oxford Bulletin of Economics and Statistics*, *64*(3), 217–235. doi:10.1111/1468-0084.00020

Verrachia, R. E. (1983). Discretionary disclosure. *Journal of Accounting and Economics*, *5*, 179–194. doi:10.1016/0165-4101(83)90011-3

Vijayakumar, A. (2011). An empirical study of firm structure and profitability relationship: The case Of Indian automobile firms. *International Journal of Research in Commerce and Management*, *1*(2), 100–108.

Vijayakumar, A. (2011). The determinant of profitability: An empirical investigation using Indian automobile industry. *International Journal of Research in Commerce and Management*, *2*(1), 58–64.

Visvanathan, G. (1998). Deferred tax valuation allowances and earnings management. *Journal of Financial Statement Analysis*, *3*, 6–15.

Wahal, S., & McConnell, J. J. (2000). Do institutional investors exacerbate managerial myopia? *Journal of Corporate Finance*, *6*(3), 307–329. doi:10.1016/S0929-1199(00)00005-5

Wald, J. K. (1999). How Firm Characteristics Affect Capital Structure: An International Comparison. *Journal of Financial Research*, *22*(2), 161–187. doi:10.1111/j.1475-6803.1999.tb00721.x

Wallace, R. S. O., & Naser, K. (1995). Firm-specific determinants of the comprehensiveness of mandatory disclosure in the corporate annual reports of firms listed on the stock exchange of Hong Kong. *Journal of Accounting and Public Policy, 14*(4), 311–368. doi:10.1016/0278-4254(95)00042-9

Wang, W., Niu, D., Li, B., & Liang, B. (2013, July). Dynamic cloud resource reservation via cloud brokerage. *Distributed Computing Systems (ICDCS), 2013 IEEE 33rd International Conference on*, 400-409. 10.1109/ICDCS.2013.20

Waqas, Y., Hashmi, S. H., & Nazır, M. I. (2015). Macroeconomic factors and foreign portfolio investment volatility: A case of South Asian countries. *Future Business Journal, 1*(1-2), 65–74. doi:10.1016/j.fbj.2015.11.002

Watts, R., & Zimmerman, J. (1986). *Positive theory of accounting*. Englewood-Cliffs, NJ: Prentice-Hall.

White, H. (1980). A Heteroskedasticity-Consistent Covariance Matrix and a Direct Test for Heteroskedasticity. *Econometrica, 48*(4), 817–838. doi:10.2307/1912934

Wooldridge, J. (2002). *Econometric analysis of cross section and panel data.* The MIT Press.

Wu, F., Zhang, L., & Huberman, B. A. (2008). Truth-telling reservations. *Algorithmica, 52*(1), 65–79. doi:10.100700453-007-9107-5

Xidonas, P., Mavrotas, G., Krintas, T., Psarras, J., & Zopounidis, C. (2012). *Multicriteria Portfolio Management*. New York: Springer. doi:10.1007/978-1-4614-3670-6

Xie, H. (2001). The mispricing of abnormal accruals. *Accounting Review, 76*(3), 357-373. Doi: . 2001.76.3.35710.2308/accr

Yahyazadehfar, M., & Babaie, A. (2012). Macroeconomic Variables and Stock Price: New Evidence from Iran. *Middle East Journal of Scientific Research, 11*(4), 408–415.

Yanikkaya, H. (2003). Trade openness and economic growth: A cross-country empirical investigation. *Journal of Development Economics, 72*(1), 57–89. doi:10.1016/S0304-3878(03)00068-3

Yazdanfar, D. (2013). Profitability determinants among micro firms: Evidence from Swedish data. *The International Journal of Managerial Finance, 9*(2), 150–160. doi:10.1108/17439131311307565

Yıldız, A. (2012). Yabancı Portföy Yatırımlarını Etkileyen Faktörlerin Belirlenmesi. *Atatürk Üniversitesi İktisadi ve İdari Bilimler Dergisi, 26*(1), 23–37.

Zarzeski, M. T. (1996). Spontaneous Harmonization Effects of Culture and Market Forces on Accounting Disclosure Practices. *Accounting Horizons, 10*(1), 18–37.

Zeitun, R., Temimi, A., & Mimouni, K. (2017). Do financial crises alter the dynamics of corporate capital structure? Evidence from GCC countries. *The Quarterly Review of Economics and Finance*, *63*, 21–33. doi:10.1016/j.qref.2016.05.004

Zeng, T. (2003). The valuation of loss carryforwards. *Canadian Journal of Administrative Sciences/Revue Canadienne des Sciences de l' Administration, 20*(2), 166-176.

Zhang, J., Wang, L., & Wang, S. (2012). Financial development and economic growth: Recent evidence from China. *Journal of Comparative Economics*, *40*(3), 393–412. doi:10.1016/j.jce.2012.01.001

Zhu, B. (2012). The Effects of Macroeconomic Factors on Stock Return of Energy Sector in Shanghai Stock Market. *International Journal of Scientific and Research Publications*, *2*(11), 1–4.

Zimmerman, J. (1983). Taxes and firm size. *Journal of Accounting and Economics*, *5*, 119–149. doi:10.1016/0165-4101(83)90008-3

Δημητροπούλου, Δ., Κοτσομανώλη-Φιλιππάκη, Α., Χαραμπάκης, Ε., & Αγγέλης, Γ. (2014). Η Χρηματοδότηση των Ελληνικών Επιχειρήσεων προ και κατά τη διάρκεια της Κρίσης, Οικονομικά Δελτία, Τεύχος 39, Τράπεζα της Ελλάδος

Index

M

O

P

S

T

www.ingramcontent.com/pod-product-compliance
Lightning Source LLC
LaVergne TN
LVHW080600300926
849162LV00005B/1010